Strategic
Database
Marketing

For our grandchildren:
Sarah, Jonathan, and Joshua; Kelly and Jackie; Elliot and Eliza;
Rebecca and Rachael
Helenita and I are very proud of you.

Also by Arthur Middleton Hughes

The American Economy
    Norvec Publishing Company, 1968

Don't Blame Little Arthur; Blame the Damned Fool Who Entrusted
    Him with the Eggs
    Database Marketing Institute, 1998

The Complete Database Marketer
    McGraw-Hill Publishing Company, Inc., 1991

The Complete Database Marketer, 2nd ed.
    McGraw-Hill Publishing Company, Inc., 1996

Strategic Database Marketing
    McGraw-Hill Publishing Company, Inc., 1994

Strategic Database Marketing

The Masterplan for Starting and Managing a
Profitable, Custom-Based Marketing Program

Arthur Middleton Hughes

Second Edition

McGraw-Hill
New York San Francisco Washington, D.C. Auckland Bogotá
Caracas Lisbon London Madrid Mexico City Milan
Montreal New Delhi San Juan Singapore
Sydney Tokyo Toronto

Library of Congress Cataloging-in-Publication Data

Hughes, Arthur Middleton

   Strategic database marketing : the masterplan for starting and managing a profitable, custom-based marketing program/by Arthur Middleton Hughes—2nd ed.

     p. cm.

  ISBN 0-07-135182-5

  1. Database marketing—Planning. I. Title: Strategic data base marketing. II. Title

HG5415.126.H843 2000

658.8'4—dc21   99-059679

McGraw-Hill

A Division of The McGraw·Hill Companies

6 7 8 9 0 DOC   / DOC 0 9 8 7 6 5 4 3

ISBN 0-07-135182-5

The sponsoring editor for this book was Kelli Christiansen, the editing supervisor was Paul R. Sobel, and the production supervisor was Modestine Cameron. It was set in Baskerville by Inkwell Publishing Services.

Printed and bound by R. R. Donnelley & Sons Company.

McGraw-Hill books are available at special quantity discounts to use as premiums and sales promotions, or for use in corporate training programs. For more information, please write to the Director of Special Sales, McGraw-Hill, Professional Publishing, 2 Penn Plaza, New York, NY 10121-2298. Or contact your local bookstore.

This book is printed on recycled, acid-free paper containing a minimum of 50% recycled de-inked fiber.

Contents

Preface   vi

Part 1   Database Marketing and the Web
Introduction   3
1. Strategic Database Marketing and the Web: An Overview   17
2. "The Vision Thing"   29

Part 2   Strategy Development
3. Lifetime Value—The Criterion of Strategy   57
4. Designing a Successful Customer Strategy   85
5. Building Profits with Recency, Frequency, and Monetary
   Analysis   105
6. Communicating with Customers   137
7. Building Customer Loyalty   162
8. Using Customer Profiles in Marketing Strategy   183
9. Strategy Verification: Testing and Control Groups   213
10. Finding Customers through the Web   229

Part 3   Profiting by Experience
11. Retailing and Packaged Goods   249
12. Building Retention and Loyalty in Business Customers   281
13. Financial Services   309
14. Why Databases Fail   335
15. Database Types That Succeed   366
16. Choosing Business Partners   381
17. Database Marketing and the Internal Struggle for Power   397
    A Farewell to the Reader   423

Appendix A: How to Keep Up with Database Marketing and
Commerce on the Web   425
Appendix B: Answers to Executive Quizzes   429
Appendix C: Glossary   431

Index   436

Preface

Since my last marketing book came out in 1996, the web has become a marketing reality. It is growing faster than anyone thought possible, and altering the way we are going to deal with customers.

As you will read in these pages, it is clear that the web is fundamentally changing database marketing, customer service, tech support, and business-to-business marketing. Distributors and wholesalers are endangered species. Just about everything that we learned about targeting in direct marketing does not apply to or work on the web. We are having to learn a whole new way of reaching and building relationships with our customers.

These are great times to be alive. They are exciting. Americans have produced the most wonderful wealth-creation system that the world has ever known. Why are we so affluent and prosperous today? There are lots of very valid answers: freedom to work, to start businesses, to innovate, and to invest. Peace through strength, world trade, low taxes, and comparatively low regulation. In all of the reasons, a great deal of the credit has to go to our system and creativity in marketing. You can't manufacture 10 million computers unless you can first sell 10 million computers. We have learned how to do this. We have learned how to listen to the customer and please the customer. In America, the customer is king.

My wife, Helena, and I realized this when we traveled to Germany (reported later in these pages). We discovered that in Germany all stores were closed *by law* on Sundays and holidays. All stores were closed by law at 6:30 every night. Why, for heavens sake? For the workers! German stores are run not to serve the customers, but to provide employment for the workers in the stores. Just a little thing like that brings home to any American the significance of the marketing system we have created here, devoted to serving the customer. It is fabulous.

This book should tell you a lot of things that most marketers don't yet know about marketing and the web. Most marketers don't yet know how to compute customer lifetime value and RFM, or how to use them in planning and executing their marketing strategy. Most don't know how to use tests and controls properly. Most don't know how to get noticed on the web or why they should use an extranet to give their customers intimate access to their company's inside information. You will learn all these things in sufficient detail so that you can apply them to your business.

In building databases and creating web sites, many mistakes have been made. In a few cases, millions of dollars have been wasted on projects that did not survive. A number of projects touted as new trends by industry leaders sank like stones within months after the accolades. The reasons for these failures are many, but they center on one central fault: the inability of marketers to develop a logical, practical, and winning strategy for their programs that is customer-centric.

Building a database or a web site is not difficult. Making money with a database or a web site is the real challenge. Keeping it going, building relationships with customers, reducing attrition, and increasing sales over a multiyear period have proved to be very difficult for some, while others have mastered the art.

Clearly, as an industry, we need to look closely at the available data, study those who have succeeded and those who have failed, and from this research, come up with some sound principles that can guide strategy development onto safer ground in the future. That is the purpose of *Strategic Database Marketing*.

Paul Wang and I have taught the basic principles in this book in two-day seminars to 1,500 marketers over a six-year period. We have learned a tremendous amount from these participants, who have furnished us with scores of case studies reported in these pages. What you will be reading here, therefore, are not just my ideas, but also a distillation of ideas from a number of practicing web and database marketers. There are many profitable strategies reported here that really work.

For those who have no idea what database marketing is, *The Complete Database Marketer* (McGraw-Hill, 1996) is the best book to read. For those who already know something about database marketing and the web, but want to know how to turn them into profit centers, this is the book. It is your next step up.

This book is designed to give marketers some practical, workable theoretical underpinnings of the marketing strategies needed to create successful and profitable customer relationships. The concentration is not on the mechanics of web site or database construction. The focus is on the theories behind customer centricity, which will tell you whether an idea will work *before millions have been spent.*

Database marketing and the web are great fun. They are exciting. They are challenging. Done correctly, marketing using these vehicles holds the promise of making customers happy and loyal, and companies profitable. They will make America a more satisfying place to live in the new millennium.

Acknowledgments

The ideas that you will read in this book have occurred to me as a result of stimulating contact with the many master database and Internet marketers quoted in these pages. I particularly want to acknowledge a debt of gratitude to several who helped me in special ways:

Paul Wang, Associate Professor of Marketing, Northwestern University. Paul and I gave 30 two-day seminars together to more than 1,500 database marketers over a five-year period. Paul, more than anyone except Helena, is responsible for my success in this field.

Frederick Reichheld, author of *The Loyalty Effect*. This amazing book, filled with wonderful ideas, has been an inspiration to me. This powerful book led me to revise many of my database marketing principles.

Brian Woolf, President of the Retail Strategy Center and author of *Customer Specific Marketing*. Brian understands supermarket marketing better than anyone in America. His helpful comments on the first edition of this book were largely responsible for its success.

George Garrick, President of the Flycast Network, a leading web advertising firm. George was the first person to open my eyes to the fact that the web is the greatest database marketing medium ever invented.

Bob James, former Marketing Manager of the Centura Bank. Bob was the first to teach me the science of bank profitability analysis. He is an excellent marketer and a good teacher.

Randall Grossman, Senior Vice President of Bank One in Columbus, Ohio, formerly with Fleet Bank. He pioneered in linking profitability analysis with lifetime value and potential lifetime value to create a superbank customer marketing system.

Bruce Clarkson, General Manager of Relationship Marketing, Sears Canada. Bruce is one of those people who can see the forest when he is walking through the trees. He explained Sears Canada marketing reorganization in a way that universalizes the general principles involved.

Bob McKim and **Evelyn Schlaphoff**, who started an award-winning full service customer management and Internet marketing firm in Los Angeles: M\S Database Marketing(*www.msdbm.com*). For nine years their firm grew rapidly by successfully providing their clients with the advanced techniques outlined in this book. After admiring their happy partnership for several years, I joined them as VP for Strategic Planning in March 2000, and have lived happily ever since.

Arthur Middleton Hughes
Arlington, Virginia

Database Marketing
and the Web

Introduction

"I've got it!" David announced excitedly. "I have found the connection you were looking for!"

"What'd' you find? Lemme have it!" Sheriff Knowles responded.

"In 1991, DiLutto bought a restaurant in Rochester. He turned right around and sold it a week later to Davenport. He lost $390,000 on the deal. Why would he do that? I can't figure it out, but it does tie DiLutto to Davenport."

"You don't know how helpful this has been to our department," said Knowles. "Can you send me the details?"

"No problem. You will have them in five minutes."

David Foulke put down the phone. No money in this call, of course, but it doesn't hurt to have the sheriff's office owing him one. He might need a favor from them some day.

David runs a company that we will call Foulke Surveys, the largest surveying firm in southern Minnesota. He hung out his shingle ten years ago. When he started, his customers sent in their job orders by fax. By giving superfast service, David managed to sign up half of the title companies and banks from the Twin Cities on down.

To build his business in the beginning, David sent flowers to the receptionists at each of the banks and title companies that he visited. None of his competitors did that. Was it worth it? He should have set up a control group of receptionists who did not get flowers to prove that the flowers were helping to maintain the business. But at that point, he hadn't read this book. David was doing instinctive database marketing.

As business grew, he added surveyors and draftsmen. Much of the early work was done by hand. David soon began to use electronics. He was one of the first in the area to use AutoCAD to do his survey drawings. For a couple of years the crews came in every morning to pick up their assignments for the day. Soon, he equipped all his crew chiefs with fax machines so they could get their assignments and send in their reports by fax. This saved more than an hour and a half per day per worker in driving time alone. But it did result in a lot of paperwork in the office, transferring the fax data to the computer.

Then, two years later, e-mail came along. David set things up so his crew chiefs got their instructions and sent in their work electronically. This was a great saving since most of their work could be translated directly to the AutoCAD without a lot of retyping. His customers still used the fax for communications, though, which had to be scanned or retyped into e-mail.

A Prospect Database

To get more business, David built a customer and prospect database of every bank and title company in Minnesota. He computed the lifetime value of each customer, based on the business he got from them. Then he figured out the lifetime value of the banks and title firms that did not use his services, based on their size and the amount of mortgage work that they handled. He ranked them into five groups, from Gold down to worthless. Once he knew who the best customers and prospects were, he developed strategies to retain and acquire the best. Not only was his customer base growing, but his profits were growing as well.

David added caller ID to his telephone service, and linked it to the database. When anyone calls today, the software goes to the database and brings the caller's entire purchase history up on the screen, so David's staff can talk to them like old friends. "Did you ever sell that lot up in Red Lake?" does wonders for relationships. With this kind of folksiness, customers keep coming back.

Forget the Losers

After grouping his customers into five categories based on lifetime value, David noticed something very interesting. While some of his customers were relationship buyers, others seemed mainly motivated by price. They would ask him to shave the prices on his surveying jobs, implying that they could get better prices elsewhere. Looking at the past history of these transaction buyers, built up in his database, he noticed that they were seldom profitable. They tended to shop around, going to his competitors for some jobs and coming to Foulke Surveys for others. These were not loyal people! Understanding this situation helped him to direct his customer relationship management strategy. He decided to provide superservices for the profitable loyalists, and not to spend money and effort trying to retain the losers.

Looking at the database records of these disloyal customers, David began to see a trend. Disloyal customers came to him from yellow page ads. Loyal customers were usually referred by other customers. One winter during a lull in business, he announced a 90-day temporary price reduction. The announcement brought in several new customers. They disappeared as soon as the prices went back up. Analysis of these disloyal customers led him to revise his acquisition strategy. He never offered a discount again. He concentrated on referrals, not on unknown people.

He also started keeping track of lost customers on his database, calling them periodically to find out why they had left. The results were very interesting. Leaving the disloyal customers aside, he found few who left because of price or because of dissatisfaction with the product. Most of those who left did so because of the way that someone on the Foulke Surveys staff had treated them. He discovered that staff training in handling customers was vital to the success of his business.

Then Dave decided to set up his own web site. At first he proudly displayed the Foulke Surveys brochure, waving it out there for everyone to see. He put *www.FoulkeSurveys.com* on his stationery and ads. There wasn't much money invested in it. One bank in Duluth stumbled on the web site and gave him a few jobs. That paid for the site that year. But it was the start of something big!

Building a Property Transfer Database

A couple of years before he created his web site, David created something really new. He converted the relevant courthouse records to disk. Any of his workers, while they were in the office, could look up any past transaction going back 14 years. It saved a lot of time. Before that,

Dave's workers had to travel constantly to the courthouses to research their jobs. Now, they had most of what they needed right there in the office. Then along came the Internet.

Dave took the records he had on disk and put them on the web. He created an intranet for his workers on his web site. By putting in a password, they could access the computer data, looking up property transfers and survey reports themselves, without bothering the office staff. He saved time and cut back on his office payroll. To get a laptop for each of his field crews, Dave contacted Dell.com. Dell built a Premier Page just for Foulke Surveys. Dave's workers could see what was available, design their own computer, and order what they needed. To keep the costs in bounds, David had Dell run the orders by Tracy, Dave's wife, so she could approve them before they were billed and shipped.

The intranet proved to be so useful that Dave hired Dudley, an intern, to convert the county land records to electronic form. Dudley spent a year with his laptop in the county record offices punching away. At the end of the year, David had the remaining land transfers that were not already on his system. Dave's workers now had the background on any property in the area that had changed hands in the past 30 years!

The Internet also enabled David to save a fortune on surveying equipment (see Figure I-1). A modern electronic surveying rig can cost more than $20,000. But outside of a surveyor, who would want it? David found that the web was an ideal place to find such obscure items. He was able to find a couple of top-quality rigs in Texas for less than half their retail cost. This would have been impossible to find without the web.

Last year, Dave took a giant step. He created an *extranet* for all his customers: banks and title companies in Minnesota. Each had its own page on Dave's web site, accessed by a password. Each one could enter its orders for jobs, and see the status of all job orders placed. Customers could also do their own research, looking at property transfers.

Using his database, Dave wrote to all his customers, inviting them to use the web site, giving them their own individual passwords. He followed up with phone calls, explaining the free service. He ran seminars for his customers to teach them how to use the web site. Many were enthusiastic. Others kept on using their faxes. Banks and title companies are not the greatest early adopters in the world. One by one, though, they gradually shifted over to the new system.

Soon the word got around to the rest of the banks and title companies in Minnesota. How could they get their own password to access all that valuable information? This was a problem. Why should he give the

Figure I-1. Finding surveying equipment.

data to companies who gave their work to his competitors? He tried an experiment. He offered to create an extranet for any bank or title company in Minnesota that would give him one surveying job. The password would be valid for three months, after which it would expire if the company did not send him another job.

He needn't have worried. Just about everyone took him up on the offer. Within a year, his business had increased by 50 percent. He was frantically hiring additional staff. Not only that, the news about his web site got to the big Chicago banks and title companies. He was soon getting almost 10 percent of his surveying work from Chicago. His out-of-state work was his fastest-growing category.

Now, the problem was, how to get noticed more widely? David paid a listing service to have his site listed on all the big web search engines. Then he made a bold move: He experimented with banner ads on a couple of financial web sites in the Midwest. Bingo! He began to get surveying work from all over the region.

Call Me

Finally, Tracy put a "call-me" button on the web site. That did it! Customers and prospects from all over the Midwest were talking to Tracy every day on voice-over-IP (VoIP). "Do you know of property in Minnesota that could be developed for light business?" "What would it cost for you to survey a large tract of land and count the trees for a federal census?" "Can you do an environmental study that will meet federal standards?" Even Sheriff Knowles used the call-me button. "The guys in the county record office here were so impressed with the data you gave me that they want to know what you would charge to put all their property records on a county web site. Could you do something like that?"

Books about Minnesota

With the expansion of the Foulke Surveys web site into a Minnesota information resource, Tracy got the idea of including books about surveying and books about Minnesota. She became an Amazon.com business partner. Every couple of weeks, she went to bookstores in Minneapolis and Rochester to see the latest books of interest to Minnesotans. Then she looked them up on Amazon and clicked them onto the Foulke Surveys web site. Every time customers click on a book they want from Tracy's display on the web, they are automatically connected to Amazon.com, where they enter their order. Foulke Surveys gets about $1 per book ordered. Tracy is earning a small amount per quarter from this service. It is not a lot of money, but it gives people a reason for coming back to the web site. And they do, by the thousands. Tracy started adding articles by Minnesota writers about life in Minnesota. The articles cost her nothing. The writers were delighted to write for a larger audience.

Soon Tracy added "cookies" to the web site. By creating a cookie every time someone visited the site, and looking for that cookie on each visitor's computer when he or she logged on, Tracy was able to say "Welcome back Arthur!" when visitors returned to the site. Was this important to the success of the site? You tell me. The cookies are important in another way. When a customer clicks the call-me button, Tracy, or whoever is answering the phone, knows who is calling because of the cookie. She has the customer's whole database record in front of her while she and the customer are talking on the phone. Tracy can talk to customers like old friends even though they may never have talked to her before.

With the popularity of the site, Tracy began to get calls from banks in the area. Would she be willing to accept banner ads for mortgages and home equity loans? Why not? She joined the Minnesota Webmasters Association and now has five or six banners earning $20 per thousand impressions (see Figure I-2). She won't get rich from this, but every little bit helps.

David and Tracy's experience is typical of what the Internet has been doing to change business in America. David and Tracy started in the surveying business. David began as a surveyor, and he still is. But what kind of business are they in now? Because of database marketing and the Internet, we are on to something very big, and no one knows where it is going.

The Internet has affected the Foulke family in more ways than their business. Dave and Tracy's two kids, Elliot and Eliza, use the web every day to talk to their buddies from school, when they are not playing games on their PCs. They are growing up on the web. It will be natural for them to use the web for commerce when they are older. In the meantime, Tracy has been doing a lot of shopping on her own.

Birthdays

Tracy has more than 20 birthday and Christmas presents to buy, wrap, and dispatch to parents, grandparents, brothers, sisters, nieces, nephews, neighbors, and friends, not counting David, Elliot, and Eliza.

More than a year ago, bowled over with work in the office, Tracy responded to a direct-mail invitation from LakeWoodsStores.com. Using the store's call-me button, she spoke with Kelly, a personal gift counselor there. Kelly guided Tracy through collecting the information on the names, addresses, sexes, and ages of all the friends and relatives who Tracy was responsible for. Tracy also entered data on her relatives'

Figure I-2. Minnesota Webmasters Association.

lifestyles and interests. All this information was tucked away into Tracy's record in LakeWoodsStores.com's customer database.

Since that time, every month, Tracy gets an e-mail message from Kelly reminding her of the upcoming birthdays. Included is Kelly's list of suggested gifts for each person. If Tracy does nothing, the presents and birthday cards are gift wrapped and delivered by UPS to each recipient, along with a gift card "signed" by Tracy and David, and charged to her credit card. She can cancel any gift by clicking the e-mail. Or she can click the call-me button and call Kelly, and change the addresses, recipients, or gifts.

The service is all made possible by LakeWoodsStores.com's customer marketing database. Through this database, Kelly handles 5,000 different clients similar to Tracy. Kelly and two other gift counselors at LakeWoodsStores.com together generate more than $10 million in sales a year. The database, of course, does all the thinking and heavy lifting. Using the information furnished by Tracy, as well as inventory reports from the merchandise department, and backed up by creative ideas from the marketing department, the database automatically generates a suggested gift for everyone on Tracy's list. The software uses profiles developed for Tracy's recipients, Kelly's ideas, and the database that records what the recipients received from Tracy last year.

How useful is this service to Tracy? "I couldn't function without it," she replied recently. How important is this service to LakeWoodsStores.com? "Our business has really taken off since we set up the new system," explained the marketing manager. Not only has the service paid for itself in the items purchased, but LakeWoodsStores.com has been able to trace the activities of all the gift list members. The company's retention rate is 8 percent higher, and its annual purchases are larger than the average retail customer at Lake Woods Stores. Finally, every year 7 percent of all gift list members refer new people to the stores who become regular customers.

Vacation Planning

David and Tracy love to go snow skiing, water skiing, and camping with the kids. Where to go? The web now has details of thousands of sites. Tracy makes reservations on the web. The camping places collect Tracy's e-mail and home address when she camps there. She hears from them about special rates and vacation packages. She and David, plus the surveying company, have credit cards that give them Northwest Airlines miles. Last year they accumulated enough miles so that David and Tracy and the kids went to St. Lucia for a vacation.

David and Tracy are examples of where database marketing has taken us in the past few years. At first companies began collecting data on their customers and learning about their preferences and lifestyles so that they could make relevant offers to them. It worked. Companies began to compute customer lifetime value and use the numbers to measure their success in various marketing strategies. Database marketing became known by some as *customer relationship management* in the late 1990s, to emphasize the fact that successful database marketing looks at the transactions from the customer's point of view rather than the company's.

Then along came the Internet. Even today, no one knows where the Internet will lead us, but it has already had a profound impact on marketing strategy. It certainly will affect the channel—the wholesalers, distributors, retailers, and agents who traditionally have stocked, distributed, and sold the goods and services. The Internet has changed the channel in so many ways that no one can count them. Just about every business today has a web site. Once you have a web site, you will soon realize, as David and Tracy did, that it couldn't survive as an electronic brochure. The web site must become dynamic and interactive. Customers will want to use the web site to get information, to enter information, to register for products and services. Behind every web site, there is a database that keeps track of the customers, welcomes them back, keeps track of their preferences and purchasing habits, and enables the supplier to understand his or her customers so as to give them better service.

Where We Have Been

No one can read the foregoing without realizing how rapidly our lives have changed in the past decade. At the beginning of the decade, surveying work was done by hand with a rod and a transit. Today we have complex electronic instruments, AutoCAD drawings, customer databases, fax, e-mail, and finally the web site. Business is different. The home is different. Marketing is different. In this book, we are going to examine these differences to see where we will have to go to catch up with advancing technology.

This is a book about marketing strategy. It explains how companies in the new millennium are adapting their marketing approach to the new customers, new products, new delivery methods, and new information processing techniques.

- *Technology* is moving faster and faster. No one today can keep track of where it is going, or even where it is today. Product development, computers, software, the Internet, and call centers are becoming so advanced that it is possible to say, "If you can imagine it, it probably already exists."

- *Affluent consumers* are firmly in charge of the free-market system. They are asking for new services and products, and entrepreneurs are listening. The race is on to find out what consumers want, and to give it to them.

- *Marketing* is changing with the customer. Providers of services are realizing that they must run very fast—they must provide new products and services and new ways of delivering their products, or they will soon be swept aside.

What Customers Want

What has been happening to David and Tracy is that their customers are beginning to dominate their business lives. Instead of making one product and trying to sell it, David and Tracy are discovering what their customers want, and selling them that. It is customer-based marketing. But it is really more than that. What customers want today can be summed up in a few general concepts:

- *Recognition.* Customers want to be recognized as individuals, with individual desires and preferences. They like being called by name.

- *Service.* They want thoughtful service provided by knowledgeable people who have access to the database, and therefore know the customers they are talking to.

- *Convenience.* People are very busy. They don't have time to drive a couple of miles to do business. They want to do business from where they are with people who remember their names, addresses, credit card numbers, and purchase history.

- *Helpfulness.* Anything that you can do to make customers' lives simpler is appreciated. Merchants have to think, every day, "How can I be more helpful to my customers?" Only those who come up with good answers will survive.

- *Information.* Customers are more computer literate today than ever before. They use the Internet. Technical information is as important to many of them as the product itself.

- *Identification.* People like to identify themselves with their products (like their cars) and their suppliers (like their country clubs and con-dominiums). Companies can build on that need for identification by providing customers with a warm, friendly, helpful institution to identify with.

The Importance of Price

Many company managements think that price is the most important factor in the sale of a product or service. They argue that when the products are on sale, more people buy from them. When the competitor's products are on sale, fewer people buy from them. Doesn't that prove that price is central to profits? Not at all. As David and Tracy found out, there are two kinds of customers: transaction buyers and relationship buyers. Transaction buyers are interested in price. They have no loyalty. They will leave you for a penny's difference. Relationship buyers are looking for a reliable supplier with friendly, helpful employees. They will stick with you even when the competition is on sale.

The reason for the gain in customers when products are on sale is that the transaction buyers are moving from company to company to take advantage of the sales. The relationship buyers are staying right where they were. Here is a big secret: You can't make much money from transaction buyers. The money is in the relationship buyers. You should design your customer contacts to maximize the services and attention to the relationship buyers, and ignore the transaction buyers. Through customer relationship management we will identify our most profitable customers, and build lasting relationships with them, increasing their retention rates, spending rates, and referral rates.

What can we do with our database and our web site? We can:

- *Change* our acquisition methods to attempt to recruit loyal customers.

- *Provide* knowledgeable customer service.

- *Fashion* products and services tailored to individual preferences,

- *Lay out* individualized targeted marketing programs.

- *Open up* our company to customers, letting them rummage through our warehouse, check out our technical specifications, and place their orders themselves.

- *Conduct* one-on-one dialogs with each customer.

- *Enlist* loyal customers in referral programs to attract more customers.

- *Classify* customers by interests and profitability so as to lavish special attention on those who are most likely to build the bottom line.

- *Recognize* customers by name when they enter the web site, or call us on the phone. Make them feel like old friends.

- *Devise* effective marketing programs for new prospects.

And much, much more.

During the last 30 years companies have become so huge that they have lost the ability to touch their customers and learn their views. They need a way to accumulate and manipulate and extract knowledge from the data on thousands or millions of customers. In a small store, the owner can find out these things very directly by talking to customers on a daily basis. If they don't like some product or service, the owner will quickly sense this. If they want something that the owner does not have, this can be easily learned. These store owners were able to accumulate and manipulate information about their customers intuitively in their heads. Database marketing and the web today provide that same result through computer technology.

Database marketing and Internet commerce are primarily aimed at making customers happy and loyal. Database marketing is built on the theory that if—in addition to providing a quality product at a reasonable price—you can find a way to provide recognition, personal service, attention, helpfulness, and information to your customers, you will build a bond of loyalty that will keep them coming back for a lifetime. Database marketing, therefore, is a way of providing service that is focused on the customer, not on the product.

Modern computer technology is used to create a relational database that stores a great deal of information on each household (or company, in the case of a business-to-business product). Not only are the name and address retained, but also:

- E-mail address, plus the cookies that keep track of web visits
- Complete purchase history
- Customer service calls, complaints, returns, inquiries
- Outgoing marketing promotions, and responses
- Results of customer surveys
- Household (or business) demographics: income, age, children, home value and type, etc.

Through database marketing, it is now possible to determine the profitability of every customer in the database. Presented in this book is a fairly universal way of calculating lifetime value that has become standard practice in most modern database marketing situations. Using this method, you can test new strategies in marketing before you commit serious money.

Where We Are Going

Although database marketing was invented in the late 1970s, it did not take hold immediately. It only began to take root actively in major American corporations in the late 1980s, as a result of decreasing costs of computer storage and retrieval.

There is one factor that is often missing from database marketing as it is being practiced today. That factor is *strategy*. We have learned how to build customer databases, how to store information, and how to retrieve it at will. What most companies have not yet learned is how to make money with a database. That is the main objective of this book, *Strategic Database Marketing*. In these pages we will show the techniques whereby many companies have successfully built profitable relationships with their customers. We will explain exactly how to compute customer lifetime value, and how to use it to evaluate strategies before thousands or millions of dollars are wasted on them.

A Sense of Balance

There is something else that is needed, which this book provides. That is a *sense of balance*. Database marketing is not helpful for every product and service. Who wants to get letters from the people that make our paper clips? To visit their web site? To build a relationship with them? Life is too short. We don't have time to build up a relationship with the producers of many of the thousands of products that we use every day. There are some products where database marketing will not work and should not be attempted. In these pages you will find many examples of failure, as well as methods of determining in advance whether your great strategy will succeed or fail. This book, therefore, concentrates on the strategy that underlies database marketing.

Customer relationship management is here. It is being widely adopted. Your company is already making moves in this direction—one important step has been the acquisition of this book. Your next step must be the development of a marketing strategy, that makes profitable use of your database. No one will serve this to you on a silver platter. You must think it up yourself. This book, however, should provide you with some ideas.

Conclusion

Database marketing and the World Wide Web are not just ways to increase profits by reducing costs and selling more products and services, although those things are, and must be, the primary results. Rather, database marketing and the web are tools that provide management with customer information. That information is used in various ways to increase customer retention and increase customer acquisition rates—the essence of business strategy. The database combined with the web provides both the raw information you need and a measurement device essential for evaluating your strategy.

Looked at from the customer's point of view, database marketing and the web are ways of making customers happy—of providing them with recognition, service, friendship, and information for which, in return, they will reward you with loyalty, retention, and increased sales. Genuine customer satisfaction is the goal and hallmark of satisfactory database marketing. If you are doing things right, your customers will be *glad* that you have a database and that you have included them on it. They will want to log onto your web site. They will appreciate the things that you do for them. If you can develop and carry out strategies that bring this situation about, you are a master marketer. You will keep your customers for life, and be happy in your work. You will have made the world a better place to live in.

1

Strategic Database Marketing and the Web: An Overview

On average, US companies lose 50 percent of their customers in five years. How many leads must you pursue to get an order from a new customer? How long will it be before the profits from additional orders pay back the cost of acquiring that new customer? In some industries, recouping the cost of acquiring a new customer takes years. It's no surprise that firms that keep valuable customers are more profitable than those with little repeat business.

Electronic commerce lets you build cost-effective, loyalty-enhancing relationships with your most profitable customers. When you make it easier for them to do business with you, you "lock them in" to a level of convenience and a set of habits that's hard for competitors to beat. Customers who do business with you electronically are also more likely to up sell themselves into higher-profit-margin products and services as both Dell Computer and Wells Fargo can attest.

The best way to measure the results of your electronic commerce initiatives will be to base your return on investment on increased customer loyalty at a lower cost to serve.

PATRICIA SEYBOL

Customers.com

Somewhere in the middle 1980s some marketers discovered that customer retention was more profitable than customer acquisition. It always was, of course, but most companies were not organized to do anything about it. In his lectures, Paul Wang, a great expert on database marketing, illustrates the point by saying that:

- $100 spent on acquisition brings in about $50 in profits—in other words, it does not pay for itself.
- $100 spent on retention brings in about $150 in profits.

Numbers similar to these have been replicated in study after study in many industries. Most marketers today are aware of the significant profits involved in retention programs. Despite this recognition, most companies are still spending about 90 percent of their marketing budgets on acquisition and only about 10 percent on retention. This situation, and what to do about it, is a central theme of this book.

Why is most of the money spent on acquisition? There are a number of very valid reasons.

- *Acquisition is easier to measure than retention.* You can count the number of new customers that you acquire. It is not as easy to count the number of customers that you have hung onto through your retention programs. The critics will always say, "They would have kept on buying anyway. You just wasted your money and resources being nice to them."

- *Acquisition is easier to carry out than retention.* With acquisition, we use mass marketing and other impersonal means to bombard prospects with offers. We don't have to know very much about these prospects. If one method does not work well (the return on investment is low), we shift to another method until we get one that works. Retention, on the other hand, is more difficult. Here, we are dealing with our existing customers, people whom we have sold something to and whom we (theoretically) know. If we want to retain them, we must recognize them as individuals and show them that we remember and appreciate their business. This is much more difficult than sending promotions to prospects.

- *Acquisition involves product managers. Retention needs segment managers.* For acquisition, you put someone in charge of selling a new line of tractors, or credit cards, or computers, and you provide bonuses and incentives for success. The process is easy to measure and understand. For retention, you should create customer segment managers whose job it is to reduce attrition and to build loyalty and sales to customers in their segments. Once you have segment managers, you can't really abolish the product managers, however. Retention involves creating a new layer of managers whose responsibilities and success measures are not obvious.

■ *Retention involves maintaining a database.* You must create a database to keep track of your customers: who they are, what they have bought, what their preferences are, etc. You need this so that you can engage in meaningful dialog with customers. You need the database to provide recognition, create segments, and provide rewards. The process is expensive and complex. It costs money that has to come out of some budget somewhere. Many companies find it difficult to justify these expenses.

■ *To measure retention, you must have test and control groups.* To deal with the "They would have bought anyway" argument, you must set aside customer control groups who do not get the inducements that you shower on the customers whom you are trying to retain. If you do it right, you will lose a lower percentage of the customers in the test group than you do in your control group. This is excellent database marketing, but it is difficult to carry out in practice, and difficult to sell management on the idea of setting up control groups.

Becoming Customer-Centric

The core idea behind strategic database marketing and the web is that the behavior of customers can be changed by things that you can do. By recognition, relationships, and rewards, you can get customers to be more loyal. The graphs and case studies in this book show that long-term loyal customers:

■ Buy more often and spend more on each purchase
■ Have higher retention and referral rates
■ Are less costly to serve

Customers respond to friendship and recognition. They like to be greeted using their names. They like to be thanked. They like to build relationships with your sales and service personnel. The old corner grocers used to provide this friendly contact automatically. It is more difficult with the large numbers of customers that most firms have today. How can you possibly recognize and build a relationship with tens of thousands of customers? And even if you have a large number of customer contact personnel, they cannot possibly know more than a small fraction of the customers.

Database and the Web to the Rescue

The answer, of course, is a database aided by personal contact over the web. Companies today are building user-friendly customer databases, loaded with actionable personal information, that permit customer contact personnel to recognize and quickly establish rapport with all customers, even though they personally have never met them or talked with them before:

"L.L. Bean. May I help you?"
"Oh, hello. This is Norah Webster."
"Mrs. Webster. Glad to hear from you again. How did your granddaughter like the sweater you sent her last October?"

Wow! How could that be possible? Well, for one thing, L.L. Bean has caller ID on its telephone system. Its customer service rep knew that it was Norah Webster before she even answered the phone. Norah's entire database record was put on the screen electronically before the rep said the first word. What does this do for relationships between Mrs. Webster and L.L. Bean? What would it be worth to your company to be able to hold conversations like this? This is strategic database marketing. This is how you build customer loyalty.

The same thing is happening on the web. Using web page cookies, companies are able to keep track of customers that come back a second time, saying "Welcome back, Arthur" whenever they click on the site. Using their customer databases created from prior visits and purchases, companies are able to replicate the friendship and relationships of the old corner grocers on the web as well as on the phone.

Avoiding Discounts

Discounts don't build loyalty. They destroy relationships. Once you give a customer a discount, you send a number of messages:

- Our regular product is overpriced. If you pay full price, you are being ripped off.

- You focus the customer on the price of your product, not on the value of your product.

- You encourage your customers to shop around. Discounts can be copied by the competition. Solid relationships are hard to copy.

One of the key reasons for database marketing and creating personalized web sites is to avoid having to give discounts. The loyalty created by the relationships insulates your customers from the blandishments of the competition.

Transaction Buyers and Relationship Buyers

As noted earlier, there are really two different types of customers. Transaction buyers are only interested in price. They will drop you tomorrow if they get a lower offer from a competitor. They have absolutely no loyalty. Relationship buyers, on the other hand, are looking for a company that has good products and friendly employees. They want to get smoothed in with your bank, or insurance company, or retail store. They like it when you greet them by name and when you do favors for them. Once they have built up a relationship with you, they won't leave when they get competitive offers in the mail or over the phone. They think that it is too expensive and emotionally draining to shop around every time they want to buy something.

You can ruin good transaction buyers by offering them discounts. If your next-door neighbor jump-started your car for you when your battery was low, you might give him a cup of coffee. Would you offer him cash? It would change the whole relationship.

You can attract transaction buyers by your acquisition methods. An offer promising "2.9 percent Introductory APR" will attract credit card transaction buyers who will leave you as soon as your rates go back up to 18.9 percent. "Earn American Airlines miles with each purchase" is more likely to attract relationship buyers who will stay with you for a longer period of time. You can fool yourself, and your management, by body counts. The "2.9 percent" offer may generate more response than the "miles" offer. But customers who leave you in six months are seldom profitable. Your goal should be to create a profitable loyal customer base, not to run award-winning acquisition programs.

How the Web Changes Things

Just when most people thought that they understood database market-ing, the Internet came along. Nothing has been the same since. The World Wide Web has such potential for commerce that no one today can even guess where it is going. But it has already changed almost everything.

In the first place, the web gives us an opportunity to invite customers into the interior of our company. In the 1980s all companies learned that they had to have a toll-free number so that customers could con-tact them. It was new and expensive. Eventually, call centers developed sophisticated software so that their employees could answer a cus-tomer's difficult technical questions by reading the answers off a screen. "What is the part number for the plastic gasket on my 1984 Hotpoint Refrigerator door?" The GE Answer Center can tell you over the phone, and ship a new gasket to you, taking your credit card num-ber. This is excellent database marketing. The GE Answer Center does-n't make much money shipping out obsolete gaskets. What it is doing is building customer loyalty. GE stands behind its appliances and sup-ports its customers. This is how database marketing builds loyalty and sells products.

With the web, this is already changing. By the time you read this book, many companies will have a web site where you can look up your 1984 refrigerator yourself, find the part number of the gasket, and place the order yourself at 12:30 on Saturday night, or whenever you want to do it. What is the difference? With the present system, GE at its Answer Center is paying for the toll-free call. It is paying a good salary to an employee to talk to you, to operate a computer, and to read information off the screen to you. The web has eliminated the phone charge and the cost of the employee. Savings to GE? Hundreds of millions of dollars per year. Advantage to you as a GE customer? Easy access to information whenever you need it. When Sears Canada put its big catalog on the web, it found that 97 percent of the customers ordering products from the web site had the paper catalog in front of them. Each page of the catalog had the toll-free number on it. Customers preferred to use the web rather than talk to a live operator. This is how the web is changing things.

One word of caution: The web is where it is at. The web is the future of marketing. If you are not in control of the design and operation of your company's web site, you must fight very hard to get control, or you will be swept aside in the very near future. Don't let it be the province of some "technical" arm of your company. It is a marketing technique.

Getting the Right Customers

Frederick Reichheld in his wonderful book, *The Loyalty Effect* (see Appendix A), pointed out that some customers are loyal and some are not. He described a customer "loyalty coefficient." His ideas suggest that, rather than starting by spending money trying to change customers' behaviors, we should try to attract the right kind of customer to begin with. Analysis of customers who defect in many companies shows that loyalty and disloyalty can be predicted early in a customer's career. Disloyal customers, for example, for some products and services in some industries may be found to be:

- Transient individuals
- Young people, rather than older people
- Single people, rather than married people
- Renters, rather than home owners
- People who respond to low-ball discount offers
- People who respond to temporary sales

Your customer retention programs will be much more successful if you begin with potentially loyal customers in the first place. The way to begin is to build a database, retaining in it both the records of loyal customers and the records of those who have left you for any reason. Careful analysis of the loyalists and the defectors can lead you to develop rules for acquisition that may, in some cases, be more powerful in terms of profits than retention programs aimed at existing customers.

Creating Customer Segments

Central to strategic database marketing is the creation of customer segments. The typical segment system looks like the diagram shown in Figure 1-1.

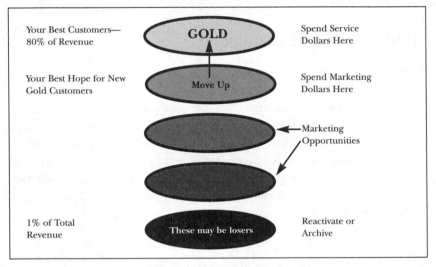

Your Best Customers—
80% of Revenue

GOLD

Spend Service
Dollars Here

Your Best Hope for New
Gold Customers

Move Up

Spend Marketing
Dollars Here

Marketing
Opportunities

1% of Total
Revenue

These may be losers

Reactivate or
Archive

Figure 1-1. Segmenting customers by lifetime value.

We will be using this diagram throughout the book. These segments don't have to be of equal size. Typically the Gold customers at the top are a small percentage, such as 5 percent, of the customer base. The losers at the bottom may represent more than half of all customers. The point in such a segmentation scheme is to direct your marketing dollars where they will do the most good.

Many companies have discovered that they cannot profitably market to their Gold customers. These are their best customers, who are placing their entire category spending with your firm. They represent 80 percent of your revenue or profits. You don't necessarily market to them. Instead, build profitable relationships with them. Provide special services to them. The ones you should be marketing to are the second, third, and fourth segments. Work to get them to migrate up to Gold status. Provide recognition, relationship, and rewards.

Don't waste your retention dollars on the losers at the bottom. These customers typically are not only not profitable; they represent a loss of profits. They should have their products and services repriced, or they should be dropped, if you can do it gracefully without adverse PR.

Building a database and a web site and identifying customer segments are elements that make up the key first step in strategic database marketing. Developing separate marketing programs for each segment is what it is all about. This is an area in which database marketing really can affect the bottom line.

Selling the Database and the Web Site to Management

There are a lot of people who have not yet read this book. This group probably includes the senior management of your company. Most of them have come up the hard way, selling products and services without a database or a web site. They don't know why a database or an extranet is necessary. How can you prove it to them?

Your first step, as soon as you have built a database, is to determine the lifetime value of your customers. You will learn:

- The retention rate
- The referral rate
- The spending rate
- How costs go down with loyal customers
- How to create customer segments
- How the lifetime value varies by segment
- How to identify Gold customers and develop strategies to keep them loyal
- How to identify worthless customers who are losing your company money
- How to modify customer behavior with recognition, relationships, and rewards, and to determine the return on investment for your efforts

You will need to educate management to understand these things. Once you have done this, you must develop an action plan designed to change customer behavior to improve customer lifetime value. Then you demonstrate, in a lifetime value spreadsheet, how your strategic database marketing programs will increase company profits.

Benefits to the Customer

In any free-market transaction, both parties always make a profit—both the buyer and the seller—because they receive something that they value more than what they give up. To assure that there are lots of transactions (sales), therefore, a marketer needs to be sure that potential customers are making what they consider to be a profit.

In today's world, profit for the customer is not necessarily measured in dollars. For most of today's busy customers, time—even leisure time—has a high value. In many cases, they value convenience and timesaving delivery processes more than a lower price. Today's customers place a high value on:

- *Recognition*. This means knowing and using their name—distinguishing their individuality and significance as a customer.

- *Service*. Most products from most companies work well. The prices are similar. What can set you apart from the others is the service you provide.

- *Helpfulness*. What distinguishes service from excellent service is helpfulness. Nordstrom finds ways to be helpful. Now that you have a database, you can invent ways of being helpful as well. The payoff is customer loyalty.

- *Information*. This is the commodity in the shortest supply today. We used to remedy this with excellent customer service. Now the web provides the most cost-effective method for giving customers information.

- *Convenience*. To survive, you need to rethink your delivery system from the customer's point of view. How can you make it easy for customers to reach you and to get your products and services? How can you use the web to make things more convenient?

■ *Inclusion.* If you give customers their own personal web page with a PIN for your web site, you will "let them behind the counter" of your company. They will feel that they belong there. They can rummage around in your warehouse, look up their accounts, and behave as if they were employees. They will love it, and stay with you for life.

Why Databases Fail

It is not all beer and skittles in the database marketing and Internet world. There have been some notable failures, involving hundreds of millions of dollars, plus hundreds of smaller database and web site projects that have not panned out as planned.

This book provides many case studies in a variety of fields, both business to consumer and business to business, which document the successes and the failures. More important, there is an analysis of why databases fail, and what you, as a marketer, can do to avoid failure in your work.

Failures come from both faulty planning and faulty execution. Planning success comes from creative strategy development based on sharp-pencil lifetime value calculation.

The Emergence of an Industry

Database marketing came about when marketers realized that they could use the power of modern computer technology to begin one-on-one dialogs with thousands of customers, to learn what they want and supply them with individualized products and services that meet their needs. This process has been tremendously advanced by the advent of the Internet.

Based on the idea that *it is easier and more profitable to keep the customers you already have than to beat the bushes for new ones,* the concept worked. Many of those who tried it found by spending a little money to build a database, create customer correspondence, take surveys, offer toll-free-number customer and technical support services, put the company products and services on the web, and provide recognition and personalized fulfillment, they could build loyalty, reduce attrition, and make major long-term improvements in their bottom line.

What has been lacking in database marketing and the web is a sense of how to develop effective strategies to turn a profit with relationship marketing. That is the central purpose of this book: to outline the methods whereby marketers can develop strategies for using a database and the web to build relationships with customers which will make the customers happy and loyal, reduce attrition, boost sales, and increase profits.

2

"The Vision Thing"

As electronic commerce booms, it's not just middlemen who will find creative ways to use the Internet to strengthen their relationships with customers. The merchants who treat e-commerce as more than a digital cash register will do the best. Sales are the ultimate goal, of course, but the sale itself is only one part of the online customer experience. Some companies will use the Internet to interact with their customers in ways that haven't been possible before and make the sale part of a sequence of customer services for which the Internet has unique strengths.

BILL GATES
Business @ The Speed of Thought,
Warner Books, 1999, p. 91

What is database marketing, and how does database marketing work? How does it relate to the Internet? This chapter is aimed at answering these questions. We will be taking a broad look at the customer's situation today, in contrast with the situation in earlier times—decades and centuries ago. We are going to attempt to place database marketing and e-commerce in their historical perspectives as evolutionary forward steps. This chapter is what former President George Bush would have called "the vision thing."

If former President Bush were to read this book, he might skip this chapter entirely. Compared with the rest of the chapters, which describe practical applications of database strategy and the web, this chapter is filled with history and philosophy, and my personal views, which may well be wrong. I, personally, love to explore the ideas of the past, wonder about how we got where we are now, and speculate about what future generations will think about what we marketers are doing today. So that is what we will be doing.

Let's settle back, therefore, and see ourselves as painted figures on a grand historical canvas leading from the earliest Sumerian traders of 5000 B.C., up through the Industrial Revolution, past the electric age, the automobile age, the nuclear age, the jet age, the computer age, and on into the twenty-first century.

What Drives Industry?

We begin with some basic questions. What drives industry, production, or marketing? In general, are products manufactured first and then marketed? Or are they marketed first and then manufactured to meet the needs of the market?

These are important questions for economists and for marketers. They go to the heart of the whole philosophy of marketing, and particularly of database marketing and e-commerce. To find answers, we need to go back to the Industrial Revolution—an epoch that changed the production system and led to our present affluence. Let's examine the role of marketing in this revolution.

The Industrial Revolution

For thousands of years before 1760, productivity in industry and agriculture was stagnant. Roughly the same number of bushels of grain per acre, or bolts of cloth per worker per year, were produced in A.D. 1700 as were produced in 1700 B.C. Things stayed the same from year to year, and from century to century.

In the period after 1760 in England, however, an unusual series of events occurred that changed the world forever. For the first time, entrepreneurs began to combine significant amounts of capital—machinery and raw materials—with labor, in large factories devoted to the mass production of goods. By 1800, thousands of people were organized into enterprises that mass-produced cotton thread, pottery, iron products, and other items. For the first time in human history, mass production, making extensive use of capital, both increased productivity and brought the price of consumer goods down dramatically. It led to England's dominance of world trade for a century. Due to the system developed in the Industrial Revolution, the average person in developed countries today can expect to live a longer and much more satisfying life than the average person had ever been able to achieve since the world began.

The Central Role of Marketing

Why have we become so wealthy in the last two centuries? Is it our production methods or our marketing skills? Most writers have concentrated on the factories as the places that have produced the wealth. In concentrating on products alone, however, they have overlooked the main reason that the Industrial Revolution was possible: the expansion of the market system and trade.

Adam Smith pointed out in 1776 that mass production was the product of the division of labor: many people working together successfully in a common enterprise, producing much more than the same people could produce working independently. But Adam Smith said something else: "The division of labor is limited by the extent of the market." Where the market is small, the gains from the division of labor are correspondingly small. The larger the market, the more efficiencies are possible, the greater productivity, the greater profits, the greater affluence.

Marketing is the key. Producing a million pounds of cotton thread would not have been possible if marketers had not found a way to sell a million pounds of cotton thread. Marketing is not something that happens after the goods are produced. Marketing is the reason the goods are produced in the first place.

The reason why cellular phones, fax machines, VCRs, and personal computers have been manufactured in the hundreds of millions is not primarily because of the activity of inventors and investors—although they are essential to the process—but primarily because of the activities of the marketers that have made the public aware of the products, created the demand for them, and set up the distribution channels.

New and unknown products—plus new versions of old ones—have to be introduced to the public in a way that creates the orders for the factories. Marketing comes first.

The American Market

From 1900 to the present time, America has had the largest single market on earth. Everywhere else, cultural restrictions, political systems, or physical boundaries combined with poor transportation to limit most markets to comparatively small areas. America has spent the last 200 years breaking down barriers—building waterways, railroads, telegraph networks, telephone and electronic communications systems, superhighways, airports, and massive delivery systems that link all parts of our market together in a freely competitive order.

The result has been the greatest outpouring of production, affluence, and personal freedom ever known. The process has not been directed or controlled by government. Instead the driving force has been free, competitive market activity, each entrepreneur trying to satisfy the public best so as to realize his or her own personal dream.

Marketing has been the means whereby the division of labor has expanded. Individual marketing heroes have provided the leadership. From 1812 to 1860 Frederic Tudor, one of our first mass marketers, built his fortune by shipping blocks of ice from Boston to the South and to the outside world. He taught the middle class how to store ice and to preserve food. He changed the way people ate and drank. A hundred years later, another hero, Frank Perdue, taught us that "It takes a tough man to make a tender chicken." His chicken empire was not so much a triumph of production—which was superb—but of marketing, which was even better. Jeff Bezos, the creator of Amazon.com, figured out how to sell books, and scores of other things, on the web—before most people even knew what the web was. Americans as a people are master marketers. Our marketers have educated the public, and provided the means whereby fantastic new products can be developed, mass-produced, and delivered at lower and lower prices.

The Growth of Mass Marketing

From 1950 to 1980, mass marketing predominated. The growth of television built on the solid foundation of national print ads and radio to create mass audiences for national advertising. National brands, sold in supermarkets, department stores, fast-food restaurants, and franchised outlets everywhere, homogenized the contents of the American home.

Mass marketing makes mass production possible. This combination resulted in a constant reduction in the cost and a constant improvement in the quality of most products, and a vast increase in the real income of the average American consumer.

Look at Figure 2-1. This graph shows real income in constant 1992 dollars. Inflation has been squeezed out. What it shows is that the American consumer was steadily becoming quite affluent. The market was changing, and our marketing methods had to adapt.

The growth in real income shown on this chart conceals another trend, one that is hard to display in graphic form: The products that Americans were buying with their income got a lot more efficient, and sophisticated.

Products today work better than they did. Computer chips are built into everything. Automobiles work much better than they did 40 years ago. Tires last longer and rarely get flat. Toothpaste has essentially ended cavities as a problem. Television sets rarely need repair. Xerox machines, fax machines, computers, air conditioning, and the Internet make offices much more pleasant to work in, and much more productive. Life expectancy has grown. Many diseases have been virtually eliminated from the average person's life: pneumonia, measles, mumps, chicken pox, diphtheria, tuberculosis, smallpox, malaria.

One result of this productive system is that the middle class has grown from being about 15 percent of the population in 1920 to being 86 percent of the population in 2000. While some of the population always seem to live at the poverty line, the vast majority of Americans today are affluent compared with their grandparents. They have the money to buy the products produced by American industry.

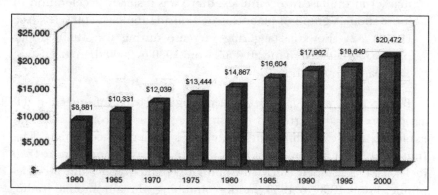

Figure 2-1. Real per capita disposable income in 1992 dollars.

We have arrived at the situation where more than 80 percent of the American households have discretionary income: Not all of their take-home pay is required to pay for food, clothing, rent, and transportation. In 1950, the average American family was spending 31 percent of its household income on food. Today the average family is spending less than 14 percent on food, and the food it is getting with that 14 percent is better in quality and quantity than what the average family was spending 31 percent for in 1950. We have all gained. Our basic needs are met. We want something more.

What the Market Consists of Today

We are not at the end of a long evolutionary process. Instead, we are, today, right in the middle of a vast program of change that is leading us on to new levels of wealth and affluence. Our market is still expanding. Look at some of the features of this market:

- *Consumers became owners of the economy.* An amazing development took place in the 1990s. The average household acquired mutual funds. By the end of the decade, almost 60 percent of American households owned stocks, either directly or indirectly. Consumers began to look on American industry from the standpoint of being owners of it, rather than as supplicants. It changed their attitude as shoppers. They were not tied down to their neighborhood. They began to use the Internet to see what was available.

- *New products were created at an accelerating rate.* If you look at the U.S. market in the last two centuries, there was a steady acceleration in innovation. A graph of patents issued during the past 200 years (see Figure 2-2) shows a staggering increase during the 1990s. More patents were issued in the 20 years from 1980 to 2000 than in the first 150 years of our nation.

Before 1850, we began the American age of steam and mechanized agriculture. Early progress in industry was slow as we concentrated on exploring and extending our nation over the entire continent. The Industrial Revolution was just beginning to take root here. From 1850 to 1900 we developed electricity, railroads, photography, and the telephone. From 1900 to 1950, indoor plumbing, the automobile, radio, and washing machines changed our way of living. From 1950 to 2000,

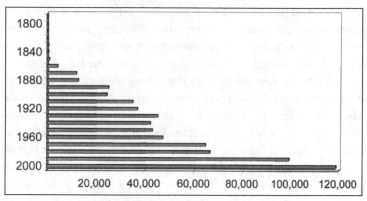

Figure 2-2. Patents issued per year.

the progress was amazing: air conditioning, microwaves, television, VCR, fax, Xerox, jet travel, interstate highways, computers, tremendous advances in medicine, nuclear power, the Internet.

The pace of new-product introduction and expansion was staggering. It is not possible for anyone to keep on top of even a small percentage of the new developments today. As a result of this constant innovation, the market is much more complex for the consumer than it once was.

Why the U.S. Economy Is So Successful

As of the last millennium, America went through an unprecedented boom that never seemed to stop, while the rest of the world did not do as well. Why was that?

- *Freedom to produce.* We are successful primarily because of freedom. Unlike most of the rest of the world, which is burdened with high taxes and heavy governmental regulation at all levels, American business is freer to innovate, to hire and fire, and to produce. We learned to understand the customer, and to design products and services not only to meet the customer's needs, but continually to delight the customer with new products and services that the customer hadn't even imagined.

- *Freedom to market.* In the Preface, I described our astonishment at the governmental restrictions on the marketing of products and services in Germany. Stores are closed on Sundays and holidays and at 6:30 every evening *by law!* In the United States, our biggest sales come on weekends and holidays. Every evening billions of dollars change hands when American shoppers visit shopping malls. Why are the German stores closed during these peak shopping days and hours? *Because of the workers!* German stores are not run for the customers; they are run for the workers in the stores. American stores are run for the customers. We keep the stores open at all hours to make our customers happy. By having two shifts we provide more jobs and money for our workers and convenience for the customers. In Germany, keeping the stores closed means fewer jobs and less money for their workers, and great inconvenience for the customers. Marketing freedom is central to our prosperity. Anyone can manufacture products. Only Americans know how to market them. We let workers in other countries make our products. We sell them.

■ *Low inflation due to our trade deficit with the rest of the world.* The trade deficit came about because Americans bought more every year from abroad than foreigners bought from us. *The result:* Prosperity for America. Here is how it worked. When an American company bought a billion dollars' worth of automobiles from Japan, for example, it paid by giving some Japanese firm a billion-dollar check, which resulted in the Japanese having a billion-dollar balance in a New York bank. Eventually, some Japanese firms bought some American products and used some of these dollars in New York to pay for them. But at the end of the year, a lot of money was still left in the New York banks since the Japanese bought less from us than we bought from them. This also happened in the case of China, Korea, Taiwan, Singapore, and many other countries. It was a wonderful system! We gave them dollars which were created by our banking system and really cost us almost nothing. They gave us millions of valuable products which they had to work very hard to produce and ship. How did this system result in American prosperity? The flood of inexpensive foreign goods allowed us to hold inflation in check here for many years. Low inflation was central to our success. Some American workers were displaced by the flood of imports, of course, but most of them soon found jobs in an economy that had almost no unemployment.

■ *High investment.* A second benefit from the foreign trade deficit accrued from *those foreign-owned dollars in New York banks.* The foreigners were not content to let the dollars just sit there. From the first moment, they wanted their dollars to earn interest. So they invested the dollars in American business: stocks, bonds, mutual funds, and other investments. These were not temporary investments. The trade deficits went on for decade after decade. They fueled the boom in the Dow Jones and American industry.

Meanwhile, American consumers, benefiting from this prosperity, became affluent and changed their buying habits—in no small measure due to the fact that they had very little time to spare.

Consumers Have Very Little Time

In most households today the adults and many of the children are all working. As a result, people search for repair personnel who will do their work without someone having to take a day off from work to wait for them. As well, few people have the leisure to shop around to find the latest products at the lowest prices. Nor do most people have adequate information about the products available. Furthermore, leisure time has a high value to most people. They will pay money to avoid having to waste it in the search for products and services. They are increasingly looking to the Internet to get answers and to contact suppliers directly.

In short, we have created in America a marketing paradise that has resulted in unprecedented prosperity. The key focus: the customer. By giving companies freedom to produce and by making the consumer the decision maker, we have built a powerful engine that runs by itself, and runs very fast. Mass marketing, leading to customer database marketing, has done it.

What Motivates Customers?

To summarize what we have discovered: We have affluent consumers, most of whom work very hard, have little time to shop, and expect and are prepared to pay handsomely for new, high-quality products.

To understand the market, we must understand the customers. What is motivating them to buy or not buy?

Customers Buy Products to Reduce Uneasiness. Why, after all, does anyone buy anything? There is one basic reason that is always true: People purchase products because they think that their life will be better with the products than without them. This is true of both consumer and business customers. They don't *know* that their life will be better with the products. They just make that assumption. Sometimes they are wrong.

The Value of Products Is Subjective. The market value of products and services is determined primarily by the customers. A computer, for example, has no value at all unless someone wants it. The money that went into its production is totally ignored by potential customers. They simply see it as a way to relieve uneasiness. If it will not relieve their uneasiness more than some competing product of which they are aware, they will not buy it, and it will have, essentially, no value for them. Obsolescence is an ever-present worry for any business holding inventory. Constant obsolescence is the result of constant innovation.

Customers Experience Diminishing Marginal Utility. Every time a customer acquires a new product, it normally tends to reduce that customer's need for more of that same product. The satisfaction, utility, or uneasiness reduction power of the next computer, for example, is less than was the utility of the previous computer purchased. This is a limiting factor on buying behavior.

At the same time, as the customer buys one product, the relative utility of other possible products tends to go up (in relation to the one purchased). Suppose the customer wants to acquire, say, a computer and a camera. The utility to her of each one is about equal. If her desire for the computer is slightly greater, she will buy that. After the purchase, her desire for the camera (its marginal utility for her) is now greater (relative to another computer) than it was. As a result, her next major purchase will probably be a camera.

Money Has Marginal Utility Also. Every time you buy something, your stock of money is reduced. The marginal utility of the money you have left (in relation to the usefulness of possible goods and services) tends to go up. When the utility of the money you have left is greater to you than the utility of any possible purchase, you will stop buying.

In Free-Market Exchanges, Both Parties Make a Profit. It is often overlooked that the consumer makes a profit as well as the supplier. Each party to a trade gives up less than he gets—or why would he trade? Money has exchange value. Purchased products seldom do. If you sell a consumer a computer for $1,000, it must be worth more to the consumer than $1,000, or he would never buy it. By doing so, he gives up $1,000, which he could use to buy anything he wants, for a computer that will be hard to trade for anything. For you, the computer must be worth less than $1,000, or why would you sell it? The fact that both parties always must make a profit is essential to understanding the market, and particularly to understanding the strategy for database marketing.

Purchase Decisions Cause Internal Conflicts in Potential Customers' Minds. All customers are torn between their desire to obtain a product or service on the one hand and their desire to retain their money stock on the other. Acquiring a product tends to reduce uneasiness; dissipation of one's personal money stock tends to increase uneasiness. Life is a balancing act between the two desires.

The Internal Struggle Affects Different Sides of the Brain. Research on the hemispheres of the brain has made us aware that we possess two different and complementary ways of processing information— a linear, step-by-step style that analyzes the parts that make up a pattern (the left hemisphere) and a spatial, relational style that seeks and constructs patterns (in the right). It is the left hemisphere that controls our language. It is here that we do our mathematics and calculate prices and bank account balances. (See Figure 2-3.)

Because the right side of the brain constructs patterns and recognizes relationships, it is most efficient at visual and spatial processing. It is here that we visualize what our life would be like if we were to acquire a new product. It is the source of our imagination and our *desire*.

It is the complementary functions of both sides of the brain that gives the mind its power and flexibility. We do not think with one hemisphere or the other; both are involved in the decision-making process. Any significant decision is often preceded by a good deal of logical, linear

Right Hemisphere		Left Hemisphere
Patterns and relationships. Visual and special processing. Imagination and desire.		Language, linear thinking. Mathematics, accounting, and logic.
"If I had that product, I would be handsome, cultured, sophisticated, and popular. I must have it."		"I have only $X in my bank account as a result of yesterday's extravagance. I must resist the right side's customary exuberance."

Figure 2-3. The purchase decision process.

thinking as a person defines and redefines a problem. This linear verbalized thinking goes on in the left hemisphere. Then there comes a moment of insight when an answer presents itself. This answer occurs when the right side combines all the pieces together into an image of the solution to the problem. Finally the mind tackles the difficult job of evaluating the insight and putting it into a form in which it can be communicated and applied to the problem.

Advertising Can Appeal to Either Side of the Mind. It is well known in retailing that "Buy one, get one free!" outpulls "50 percent off!" Why should that be? There seem to be several reasons:

- One reason is that you can get the 50 percent reduction by buying only one, instead of two, so people might tend to buy fewer items.

- The second reason is that, even today, many people are insecure about the meaning and method of computation of percentages. Everyone, however, understands the meaning of free! It's a wonderful word.

- The third reason is basic to database marketing. Wanting products is a right-brain function. Calculating money is a left-brain function. But *50 percent off* requires a left-brain calculation plus a right brain stimulus: a complicated mental sleight of hand, which is hard to process. *Buy one, get one free* is pure right brain. Not only do you get what you want—you get two of them.

Recapitulation

Let's summarize where we are thus far:

Affluent consumers with very little leisure time face a rapidly changing marketplace containing ever-improving new products without adequate knowledge or information about what is available. They purchase products to reduce feelings of uneasiness, but are torn between the desire for goods and the desire to maintain their cash balances. The decision-making process goes on in their mind, which divided into a left brain that keeps track of the money and a right brain that visualizes the benefits that can come from acquisition of new products and services.

Marketers are faced with a dilemma on their approach. Should they base their message on the price (a left-brain argument) or on the benefits of the product (which appeal to the right brain)?

Prices and Products Tend to Be the Same

There is a problem with both marketing approaches today. Prices tend to become similar as each airline, computer company, and automobile manufacturer rushes to match every price move of the competition. The consumer knows that price changes are temporary, and seldom fundamental. Many consumers, moreover, being affluent, are less interested in price than in quality and service.

Product quality also tends to be uniform. Avis, Hertz, National, Budget, Dollar, and Alamo all rent brand-new cars. Detergents, yogurts, canned goods, tires, televisions, phones, and toilet paper are all becoming more and more perfected and similar. Each manufacturer produces equally good, high-quality products that do the same thing. Every improvement is immediately matched by the competition.

The Importance of Time

Price and quality—these have been the staples of marketing for years. However, today, a new dimension is entering into consumer decision making, which is of equal importance. It is time. People have less and less time available for shopping (or for anything).

Products that can be purchased for $100 and a one-hour round-trip to the supermarket or the mall are perceived to cost more than the same products that can be purchased for $120 and a telephone call or an Internet click. Our leisure time has acquired a monetary value that it never had before. To the monetary cost of any transaction, therefore, we must add the cost of the time involved in completing the transaction.

If we can make a purchase more convenient and less time consuming for customers, we make the product more attractive to them. They are more likely to buy it. In many cases, making this purchase more convenient costs us less than the increased value to the consumer: Both of us make a profit by the change in delivery methods.

> Self-service gasoline stations made a quiet revolution in the 1990s. At first, it was thought that the public would not be able to (or willing to) pump their own gas. (Hence the popular humorous book *Real women don't pump gas*.) That thought proved to be entirely wrong. Most gas today is pumped by the customer.
> Self-service gas is less expensive in two ways: it is about four or five cents cheaper, and it usually takes less time than waiting for an attendant to show

up and do his thing. Time, today, is worth more. Self-service gas soon grad-uated to self-pay gas. A credit card gas purchaser swipes his card through a slot, and pays for self-service gas without ever talking to anyone. The advan-tage to the customer: another three or four minutes' reduction in the time required to fill a car with gasoline. People used to this service seek out such stations. It beats waiting in line at the payment window. The service also reduces labor costs for the gasoline company: both parties make a profit.

Mobil took this process one step further with their "Mobil Speed Pass," a small plastic icon, which attaches to your car key ring. Wave the speed pass anywhere near the gas pump, and it recognizes who you are. You pump gas without a credit card or cash. Many tollbooths on highways now recognize computer chips on the windshields of cars. They automatically deduct the toll from the driver's credit account stored in a computer somewhere as he whizzes through the tollbooth at 30 mph.

What we marketers are selling today, therefore, is more than the product. It is the product *plus* the delivery method. Convenience and service are part of what we are selling. The real decision-making process required for a purchase (from the customer's point of view) looks some-thing like this:

$$\text{Customer profit} = a \text{ (utility of product)} + b \text{ (value of brand)} - c \text{ (money cost)} - d \text{ (time)}$$

The letters a, b, c, and d are *weights* that vary with each customer. Lower-income customers place a higher value on c, and a lower value on d (since money is worth more to them and time is worth less). Busy peo-ple place the highest value on d. This was illustrated in the 1970s dur-ing the energy crisis. Gasoline prices were controlled at low levels by the government, which was making a mess by creating a gasoline allocation system. As a result there were regional gasoline shortages and long lines at the gasoline stations. Across the Texas border in Mexico, gasoline cost much more, but there were no lines and unlimited supplies. For a number of months, Texans drove south of the border to fill up their gas tanks at high prices, while Mexicans came north across the border to wait in lines for the cheap gas.

Why the Mass Marketing Process Changed

Mass marketing became dominant from 1950 to 1980 because we had newly affluent consumers, many of whom had lived through the bleak-ness and despair of the Depression and the shortages and rationing of

World War II and the Korean War. For the first time in two decades, consumers had jobs and money and were in a position to spend. The consumers were so grateful to find full shelves in the stores, as well as new homes, automobiles, washers, dryers, telephones, and televisions, that they took what they could get—and loved it!

Why did mass marketing lose its effectiveness for some products? Because of diminishing marginal utility. We have finally reached the point where most people have acquired the minimum. They have enough food, clothing, and medical care, plus a home, a car, a phone, a TV, a VCR, a washer and dryer, and air conditioning. The basics are covered. People have become more discriminating. In effect, they have discretionary income, and they have decided to use their discretion in spending it.

For the producers of some products, the mass market, as we have known it, seems to be slipping away. While there are still emerging minorities moving up to the middle class, who will respond to straight mass marketing during their journey, they are still minorities. The majority of our consumers today have grown up with an abundant economy. They know that they can get anything they want. What they want is something quite different from what previous generations have wanted. They are looking for more than the basics, which they already have. What they seek are recognition, personal attention, service, diversity, and information. They are prepared to pay for these things.

Providing Information

Today's market—filled with change, uncertainty, lack of information, and ignorance—is a wonderful opportunity for marketers. I refinanced my condominium for 7 percent, down from 8 percent. I felt that I had made a profit even though I had to pay 2 points. I learned later that I could have gotten 6.6 percent and paid no points if I had waited 2 more months. "If I had only known" was my thought. How many of us have had that same thought about market transactions. It is universal in any free market. If you were selling refinancing arrangements, you could happily make a profit by educating me, and I would make a profit by listening to you. This is what is happening today through the Internet.

How do you find out about real estate in a new area that you have never been to? Before the Internet, this was a difficult problem. The web has changed everything. Helena and I, sitting in Arlington, Virginia, were looking for a place in Miami, Florida. In a few minutes we found a map of Florida and located a condominium on the beach that exactly fitted our dreams.

The American market is not only huge; it is gigantic. It is filled with millions of businesses and millions of consumers, all looking out for themselves, pursuing subjective goals of their own. Before the web came along, no one could possibly know all the commodities and services that were available, their respective benefits and features, and the prices at which they could be obtained. Now much of that information is at your fingertips. But it will be available only if marketers are smart enough to create interactive web sites like those available to home buyers.

You, as a marketer, have available to you a lot of vital information that your customers need in order to make decisions about their purchases and their lives. Through well-organized marketing activity, not only can you help customers to make a profit, but you can also relieve them of some of their anxiety about the marketplace—what is available, what they are missing out on, and how much it costs. You are an information provider. If you concentrate on giving customers information that they need, you will make them happy, they are more likely to purchase, and you will be successful.

Providing an Institution to Be Loyal To

People *like* to be loyal. Look at the support given to local baseball and football teams. Look at the fans rooting for basketball teams. The loyalty of military personnel to their units is legendary. The dedication of alumni to their colleges is often lifelong.

For years, my father bought nothing but Fords. He was intensely loyal to Ford. Was Ford loyal to him? The company didn't know about him or care about him. That didn't matter. He loved Fords. We all know many people like him: people who love their Steinway piano, their Adidas shoes, their Rossignol skis, their American Airlines flights. And why not? In an increasingly pulverized society, it is wonderful to have something that endures, that lasts, that you can believe in and hang onto, that you can identify with.

What does this mean for U.S. corporate enterprises? They can either play ball or sit this one out. Database marketing and, particularly, the Internet provide mechanisms for taking advantage of this urge to identify by giving your customers a warm, friendly, stable institution to identify with. "Like a good neighbor, State Farm is there." It is easy, and inexpensive, and it builds loyalty. Why reject it?

How Database Marketing Solves the Customer's Problems

Database marketing and the web came along just when they were needed. They solved the information problem; they provided recognition, personal service, and a profit to the customer. The web is an extension of that database, providing recognition and helpful information.

Database marketing is possible, of course, because of the development of computers with advanced software. We can store thousands of facts about every customer, and retrieve those facts in seconds when we need them to provide information and services to each customer. This information is badly needed by the customers. It is worth money to them. They will reward you for it. At the same time, being the one to provide that information to the customer is very profitable for you. Let's take a concrete example. Read this letter (originally created by Thomas Lix):

Ridgeway Fashions
404 Main Street
Leesburg, VA 22090

Dear Mr. Hughes:
   I would like to remind you that your wife Helena's birthday is coming up in two weeks on November 5th. We have the perfect gift for her in stock.
   As you know, she loves Liz Claiborne clothing. We have an absolutely beautiful new suit in blue, her favorite color, in a fourteen, her size, priced at $232.
   If you like, I can gift wrap the suit at no extra charge and deliver it to you next week so that you will have it in plenty of time for her birthday, or, if you like, I can put it aside so that you can come in to pick it up. Please give me a call at (703) 754-4470 within the next 48 hours to let me know which you'd prefer.

Sincerely yours,

Robin Baumgartner, Store Manager

What's my reaction to this letter? Hallelujah! Helena is a Catholic. She has two birthdays a year: Her saint's day is August 18, and her birthday is November 5. I have to buy her something for both days. What should I get for her? She is a very stylish, fashion-conscious businesswoman who always wears the latest clothes. I, on the other hand, am color blind and hate to shop. I wander around the malls, "What? What? What?" These people know. "Liz Claiborne"—what is that? I don't know, but Helena does, and she likes it. If the database has the correct information in it (about Helena's tastes and my pocketbook), I will snap at this opportunity to remove my uneasiness and save me time.

This letter can also be quite effective as an e-mail on the Internet. Scores of stores and catalogers are now encouraging consumers to record their important events. They provide reminders, like this one, in time to help the consumer make up his or her mind before the event. This is classic one-to-one marketing. This is strategic database marketing. This is what it is all about.

Database marketing and the web are designed to reduce ignorance and lack of information, bringing a very particular buyer with unique subjective goals together with a specialized solution to the customer's problem.

Database marketing and the web, of course, are not universal solutions. They will be effective only in situations in which a continuing relationship between a seller and a buyer is *profitable for both parties*. If either one or the other finds that he or she can do better without the relationship, the database or web project will fail—and it should.

Collecting Information

How would Ridgeway Fashions get the information necessary to send me such a personal letter? It should not be from analyzing purchases. That is too much like the CIA, snooping through personal files. It would be an invasion of privacy. To collect this information, a Ridgeway clerk, when Helena was shopping, should ask her, "Would you like to be in the Birthday Club?"

"What is the Birthday Club?"

"Well, you tell us your birthday, your preferences and sizes, and your husband's business address. Then a couple of weeks before your birthday, we will write to him and give him some hints on what to buy."

"Hints? He needs hints. OK. Where do I sign up?"

Additionally, Ridgeway could collect the same information by listing its Birthday Club on the Internet.

The information is stored in the customer's database file. The data go to the merchandise buyers who have to buy clothing that the customers want. Then, once a month, the computer scans the file for people who have a birthday coming up. They check the warehouse to see if what the customers want is in stock. Then the store marketers can write these one-to-one, powerful, personal letters.

Event-Driven Personal Communications

What do you need to keep in the database? To produce this type of customer service selling, the birthday club data have to include such things as:

Suitable gift: Women's apparel

Tropical-weight business suits

Casual outdoor clothing

Decision algorithms:

Quality conscious

Price conscious

Fashion conscious

Magical dates:

Birth dates, anniversaries, graduations

Trips planned, moves in progress

Personal specifications:

Dress and suit sizes

Color preferences

Style and manufacturer's preferences

Personal coloring

Measurements

Face and body shape

Demographics:

Gender, date of birth, education

Income, financial situation

Home ownership

Children

Sociographics:

Shopping role

Occupation and marital status

Spouse's name and birth date

Shopping history:

Shopping behavior

Dollar expenditures in total and by department

Store and brand preferences

Hobbies, interests, activities

Lifestyle characteristics

The database software will:

Sweep the database weekly to determine relevant targets for communications

Determine which product type represents a match

Calculate the expected value of each target, recipient, piece of merchandise, and occasion combination

Select the winning possibility

Generate inputs for the communication package

Monitor the results of each communication and update the database with the results

Lifetime Value

To know if this club is going to work, you have to compute the lifetime value of each customer. This helps you to figure out the amount of money that is practical to expend on maintaining your relationships with your customers.

Building the database necessary to send that letter to Arthur Hughes was not cheap. The store had to collect a lot of information about Helena and me: sizes, styles, birthdays, budgets, ages, fashions, interests, and preferences. The software had to use all that information to match the data with the products that Helena has already bought at the store, and the thousands of products currently available, so as to produce the perfect letter at the right time to the right person.

Capturing the information has a cost. Maintaining the database and producing the monthly output has a cost. Mailing the letters has a cost. E-mail would be much cheaper. Most of the letters or e-mails will not result in a sale. Balancing all these costs are the potential profits that will come from the actual sales (less the returns) which the system produces.

The way to know whether you have built a successful database marketing system is to compute the lifetime value of the Hughes family, and all of the other families on your database. Each time you introduce another innovation (sending out a gift suggestion before a wedding anniversary or child's college graduation, for example), you recompute the lifetime value. If the value goes up, you should do it. If it goes down, you should not.

In the next chapter, we will build a lifetime value table for Ridgeway Fashions to show how you would go about costing out the Birthday Club to determine whether it will pay dividends.

Do Database Marketing and Web Commerce Always Work?

No, they definitely do not. There are tens of thousands of products, particularly packaged goods, where database marketing or the web will never work. Too many articles have been written which imply that database marketing or web sites are panaceas, and that those who fail to use them are blockheads. Don't be fooled. Work out the economics. The next chapter, on lifetime value, will give you a solid tool to determine whether database marketing and a customer web site will work in your situation.

Is Mass Marketing Ending?

Of course not. It is alive and well. Smart mass marketers will include a web site in their ads so customers can get more information, locate dealers, or buy products directly. Mass marketing will always be essential to make the public aware of new products, and old products for which database marketing and the Internet will not work well. Will most toothpaste ever be sold by database marketing or the World Wide Web? Never. Manufacturers of packaged goods will be using mass marketing plus retailers' shelf space long after the people reading this book have been shipped off to a nursing home (located through the Internet).

Summary

- America is unique and fortunate. Working in a land of freedom and opportunity, a nation of immigrants built a continental market with few political and economic restrictions. For the last century we have had the largest and freest market on earth.

- In this free market, entrepreneurs and marketers seek better and better ways of making the customers happy. Customer happiness means purchases, and purchases mean profits for both the buyer and the seller. The size of our market has resulted in economies of scale from mass marketing, mass production, constantly lower prices, and constantly increasing per capita income.

- Mass marketing came about because of a unique combination of circumstances. A whole generation, deprived from a decade of depression, followed by a decade of war, was finally able to produce and purchase in peace. This coincided with the birth of television as a marketing medium. Mass marketing assumed that everyone wanted the same things. From 1950 to 1980 that was a correct assumption.

- Since that time, the very success of mass marketing has brought about its decline for certain products. Most people today have all the basics. Today customers are using their massive discretionary income to buy a wider variety of products. With all adults working, there is less and less time to shop. With the expanding marketplace, there is so much more to know and so little time to learn about it all. Customers today value service, saving of time, and information as highly as they used to value quality and price. Competition has pushed quality of most products up to a uniformly high standard. Competition continues to push prices down to uniformly low levels.

- Now that consumers today have all the basics, what they want is recognition, service, diversity, information, and identification.

Database marketing and the web are the most efficient ways of providing all these things.

- Database marketing and the web are aimed at the customer's right brain hemisphere. Instead of being bombarded with discounts, the customer is showered with attention, recognition, friendship, and service. Why these things? Because that is what the customer wants. Furthermore, database marketing and the web provide the only way to start a two-way dialog in which the customer is able to tell you what is on her mind and you are able to react to her thoughts by varying your services and product mix.

- Database marketing and the Internet work for some products because they are uniquely qualified to meet the requirements of today's customer, just as mass marketing was the ideal marketing solution for these same products in previous decades. Companies that recognize this shift and take advantage of it will prosper. The others may be consigned to the dustbin of history.

- We Americans do have a "vision" which directs our market and our economy. The vision is freedom and control by the consumers. It works.

Executive Quiz 1

"What are these quizzes doing in this book?" you may ask. "Is this supposed to be a textbook?" No it is not. Database marketing is supposed to be fun for the customers. If you don't like quizzes, ignore them. The quizzes are included here for fun. Some people like to do crossword puzzles. Some people like quizzes. If you are one of them, then try your luck. The answers can be found in Appendix B. Choose the best answer to complete each statement.

1. Mass marketing today:
   a. Is ending
   b. Is being replaced by database marketing
   c. Is the best way to sell certain products
   d. Is growing in importance
   e. Provides recognition and diversity

2. The left side of the brain:
   a. Computes mathematics
   b. Sees spatial relationships
   c. Does most of our thinking
   d. Controls the right side of the brain
   e. Is poor at languages

3. In free-market transactions:
   a. Buyers often fail to make a profit
   b. Sellers often fail to make a profit
   c. Information is often lacking
   d. Price is more important than quality
   e. Government sets price guidelines

4. Most stores in Germany:
   a. Are run for their customers
   b. Are open on holidays
   c. Open late to help their customers
   d. Are run for their employees
   e. Are open on weekends

5. From 2000 B.C. to A.D. 1700, the annual rate of productivity gain in industry was closest to:
   a. 0 percent
   b. 0.1 percent
   c. 0.5 percent
   d. 1 percent
   e. 1.5 percent

6. Of all of the following, the key reason why the American economy has been so successful is because of:
   a. Natural resources
   b. Protective tariffs
   c. Our monetary system
   d. Environmental regulations
   e. The extent of our market

7. The average Americans today:
   a. Have a higher income than their parents had
   b. Can no longer afford the housing of their parents
   c. Live increasingly in poverty
   d. Resist innovation
   e. Have the same income as previous generations

8. A trade deficit with Japan
   a. Reduces American prosperity
   b. Fuels domestic inflation
   c. Requires urgent government intervention
   d. Increases investment in American businesses
   e. Damages our economy

9. The value of most products:
   a. Is set by the cost of production
   b. Is set by the cost of imports
   c. Does not change from day to day
   d. Is determined by the customer
   e. Is set by government regulations

10. Diminishing marginal utility means that:
    a. Products become obsolescent
    b. Money is being replaced by plastic
    c. You stop buying some products after acquiring a few
    d. Some products are always scarce
    e. Companies cannot count on sales

Strategy Development

3

Lifetime Value—
The Criterion of Strategy

*Accountants have developed sophisticated techniques
for appraising capital assets and their depreciation;
they have learned how to monitor the constantly
changing value of work-in-progress; but they have not
yet devised a way to track the value of a company's
customer inventory. They make no distinction between
sales revenue from brand-new customers and sales revenue from long-term, loyal customers, because they do
not know or care that it costs much more to serve a
new customer than an old one. Worse, in most businesses, accountants treat investment in customer
acquisition as one more current expense, instead of
assigning it to specific customer accounts and amortiz-
ing it over the life of the customer relationship.*

FREDERICK REICHHELD
The Loyalty Effect

Most marketers today talk about lifetime value. A growing number are
calculating it and using it in their marketing strategy. You don't need to
feel badly if you have not used it yet. It takes an understanding of some
basic concepts that—once you know them—are not difficult, but until
you do, may seem quite mysterious.

In this chapter you will find a complete explanation of how lifetime value can be worked out. Once you get through it, you will be able to use it in your marketing planning. This chapter is detailed. If you stick with it to the end, however, it will change your life as a marketer and make you a better person. Who could ask for anything more?

Definition of Lifetime Value

First, a definition. *Lifetime value is the net present value of the profit that you will realize on the average new customer during a given number of years.* Lifetime value can be used in the development of marketing strategy and tactics. At any given time it is a specific number, but it will change from month to month. There are many different things that cause lifetime value to change, some of which are under your control, many of which are not.

One of the experts on lifetime value is Paul Wang, associate professor of database marketing at Northwestern University. Paul serves as a consultant to a number of companies, and has joined me for many years in giving two-day seminars to marketing executives of major companies for the Database Marketing Institute. Many of the ideas in this chapter and throughout this book are based on Paul's concepts. This method is now being used by thousands of companies throughout the world, such as Fleet Bank, Sears Roebuck, and Allstate Insurance.

Why Lifetime Value Was Not Widely Used in the Past

In the past, few marketers were using lifetime value for a number of reasons:

- *They did not understand it.* That problem is easily solved. In fact, we will solve it in this chapter. In general, marketers didn't understand lifetime value because it involves several marketing and financial concepts that people with an advertising background had not learned in school. Those concepts are not difficult to learn.

- *They did not have a database.* This problem has been largely solved. In the 1990s almost every major corporation found a way to create a customer marketing database, which includes purchase and promotion history. Lifetime value cannot be converted into a concrete number without a database that keeps track of customer behavior over a period of time. If you have not yet gathered customer data and stored them in a database, which provides you the ability to count and select, you really cannot come up with a valid lifetime value number, although you can use the concept in your planning (as we shall see below).

- *They were under pressure to produce.* This was the hardest problem. To get any sort of specificity in lifetime value, you usually have to do some testing. You have to keep track of customer behavior over a period of time. The problem that marketers have to face is: "What marketing programs are we going to carry out right now?" Management expects action from its marketing staff, not just a series of extended tests. If you use the methods in this chapter, however, you will find that it is possible to use lifetime value in planning your current marketing strategy. You will have the time.

What a Lifetime Value Table Looks Like

Let's begin with a basic lifetime value table. After you understand it, you will learn:

- How you can modify it
- How you can use it to test strategy
- Some of the technical details

For this table, we are going back to Tom Lix's example at the end of the previous chapter. We will look at Ridgeway Fashions before and after it adopted the new strategy of writing letters to husbands before their wives' birthdays. We will see how Ridgeway costed out the Birthday Club, and determined whether the strategy would work, using a lifetime value table. While this is a retail example, the principles apply to any type of industry: financial services, telecommunications, business-to-business situations, as well as consumer marketing. Lifetime value is a universal measurement system. This book contains more than a dozen different lifetime value tables for a variety of industries. You will probably find your business represented on one or more of these charts. For now, however, study the table in Figure 3-1, because you will learn the basic principles of lifetime value from it.

	Year 1	Year 2	Year 3
Customers	20,000	8,000	3,600
Retention rate	40%	45%	50%
Spending rate	$150	$160	$170
Total revenue	$3,000,000	$1,280,000	$612,000
Variable costs %	60%	50%	45%
Variable costs $	$1,800,000	$640,000	$275,400
Acquisition cost ($40)	$800,000	$0	$0
Total costs	$2,600,000	$640,000	$275,400
Gross profit	$400,000	$640,000	$336,600
Discount rate	1	1.16	1.35
Net present value profit	$400,000	$551,724	$249,333
Cumulative NPV profit	$400,000	$951,724	$1,201,057
Lifetime value	$20.00	$47.59	$60.05

Figure 3-1. Customer lifetime value.

In the table we are looking at a group of 20,000 Ridgeway Fashions customers over a three-year period. Let us assume that before this time, Ridgeway Fashions issued a plastic membership card to many of its customers, or with customer permission, recorded the customer's credit card numbers so that the company could find out who was buying what, and could store those data in its database. This chart is based on the data available on these customers in the database. It does not include other Ridgeway Fashions customers who pay cash or otherwise cannot be tracked. Year 1 is the year the customer was acquired. Year 2 is the year after that. Year 1, therefore, includes customers acquired in several different years. This is the way lifetime value tables are constructed.

The Retention Rate

You will note that of the 20,000 customers who were acquired in Year 1, only 8,000 of them came back to make purchases in Year 2. That means that Ridgeway retained only 40 percent of the customers that it acquired in Year 1. *The retention rate is the single most important number in a lifetime value table.* It is a measure of customer loyalty, and is something that you, as a marketer, can modify by your marketing strategy and tactics.

The retention rate is easily calculated by a simple formula:

$$RR = \text{year } X \text{ customers} / \text{Year 1 customers}$$
$$RR = 8,000 / 20,000 = 40\%$$

Year X customers represent those Year 1 customers who are still buying in the later year. In the appendix to this chapter, we cover the interesting problem of computing the retention rate of people who don't buy from you every year—such as automobile purchasers. There is a simple formula that converts their spending pattern to an annual figure.

What do we do with new customers who wander into the store and begin shopping in Year 2? We redo the table and put them into Year 1. This is their year of acquisition. In your table, you don't need to select 20,000 as your group for study. You could select 213,102, or any number that you might have in the database. The only requirement is to take snapshots of the performance of a specific group of consumers or companies over its first several years as a customer. Later, we will develop the lifetime value of customer segments, not of all customers, as we are doing here. For now, however, let's stick with looking at all the customers in the database as a group, to see what we can learn about them.

What do we do with lapsed customers who did not buy in Year 2 but came back in Year 3? They are in there. They are part of the 3,600 who are shopping in Year 3. The fact that some of the lapsed customers may be reactivated leads companies to keep these customers on their books for a couple of years. There is always hope. Of course, since they are on the database, we will have to keep track of them and send them occasional messages. This costs money. Database marketing is not free.

The Spending Rate

The spending rate is the average amount spent by the average customer each year. This amount can be computed easily by dividing total sales for the group being studied in a given year by the number of customers in the group. In this example, Ridgeway's annual sales per customer increases over the three years from $150 per customer to $170 per customer. You will have the same experience. Typically, the longer customers are with you, the more they will spend per year, per visit, per order. The Year 2 spending rate represents the total revenue *from the customers who are still active* out of the original group acquired in Year 1. The total revenue is the number of customers still buying in the year times the spending rate in that year.

Variable Costs

Direct costs are computed in a wide variety of ways in different industries. To determine costs in your industry, you should consult the finance department in your company. These costs include the cost of the products or services provided, plus the variable administrative costs such as customer service, debt collection, deliveries, returns, and credits. Variable costs do not include fixed costs such as overhead, utilities, or debt services, costs that do not vary with the number of customers.

What you will notice, and will be true of your situation as well, is that the costs of servicing a customer tend to decrease with the number of years that the customer has been buying from you. This applies to business-to-business as well as most forms of consumer marketing situations. If you are selling software, for example, the customers are likely to tie up your customer service lines during the first 60 days until they learn how your software works. For the next 60 months, you may never hear from them again. This is true in a wide variety of industries, and helps to reduce costs and increase lifetime value.

Computation of costs should not be made into a major problem. If you develop a consistent system and stick to it consistently, that is all you need. The reason? We are going to look at the effect of a *new strategy* on lifetime value. If both tables use the same cost percentages, what that percentage is may not be of crucial importance.

The Acquisition Cost

Most companies are geared for acquisition. They spend a lot of money to get customers. To compute the acquisition cost, simply add up all the money you spend on your advertising, marketing, and sales efforts during the year (exclusive of retention programs, which we will discuss later). Then divide this total by the number of new customers who actually make purchases from you each year. That is your cost of acquisition.

Computing this number is very important. It may drive your whole marketing strategy. You will find that money spent on acquisition does not pay as well as money spent on retention. Lifetime value computation is the first opportunity we have to find that out.

Gross Profits

Gross profits are easy to compute. They are equal to the total revenue less the total costs. We need to spend some time on the discount rate, however, since that is the most complicated part of the entire lifetime value analysis.

The Discount Rate

The reason why we need a discount rate is simple: The profits you receive from your customers come in over several years. Money received in future years is not worth as much *today* as money received today.

If I owe you $1,000 right now, but pay you the $1,000 a year from now, I have cheated you out of the interest you could have earned on that $1,000 if I had paid you right away. Future money is worth less than present money. To estimate the value of future money, we must *discount* it by a certain percentage so we can equate it to present money, and then add the two amounts together.

How much should you discount future revenue? There is an easy answer: You use the market rate of interest. As I write this today, 7 percent seems like a reasonable market interest rate. Ten years ago, 12 percent was what businesses were paying. The amount varies with the general market conditions. You should use a number that corresponds with your current situation. In this book, I am using 8 percent throughout, its being a nice, round average number.

In reality, however, I am doubling that 8 percent to get 16 percent. Why is that? Because I am including *risk*. In any long-term business transaction, like lifetime customer value, there are always serious risks. What are they?

- *Interest rates*. They could go up.
- *Obsolescence*. Your product could become obsolete in the next few years and wipe out your expectation of further sales.

- *Competition.* In most industries, competitors always make marketing a risky business. They could steal your expected customers.
- *Other business risks.* In each business situation, there is many a slip twixt the cup and the lip. Your business is no exception.

For these reasons, in this example, I have doubled the interest rate to get the discount rate. The risk factor (rf) is 2. You may be able to develop more sophisticated risk factors than rf = 2, based on your business history. We will discuss the risk factor further in Chapter 12 on business-to-business marketing.

Computing the Discount Rate from the Interest Rate

Once you have decided on a market interest rate—such as the 8 percent that I have used—you need to compute the discount rate that applies to amounts to be received in each year. The formula used to compute the discount rate is

$$D = [1 + (i \times \mathrm{rf})]^n$$

where D = the discount rate, i = the interest rate , rf = the risk factor, and n = the number of years that you have to wait. The discount rate in Year 3 (2 years from now), for example, is computed like this:

$$D = [1 + (0.08 \times 2)]^2$$
$$D = (1.16)^3 = 1.35$$

It is possible to be much more precise in your discount rate calculation. You can worry about whether you have to wait several weeks or months, on the average, to be paid. This is true in most business-to-business operations. In this case, we can make n into a fractional amount, like 3.25. We will use this type of system in calculating lifetime value for a business-to-business situation in Chapter 12.

Net Present Value Profits

Once you have the discount rate, each of your expected profits must be discounted so as to arrive at the net present value (NPV) of these future profits. The process is a simple one:

$$\text{NPV profits} = \text{gross profits} / \text{discount rate}$$

The net present value of the $336,600 profits expected in Year 3 is $249,333, which is the result of dividing $336,600 by the discount rate of 1.35.

Cumulative NPV Profit

We must now add together the net present value of all the profits in the present year and each previous year. The net present value of profits realized by Year 3, for example, is equal to sum of the net present value of the profits in Year 1 + Year 2 + Year 3.

Lifetime Value

The lifetime value is simply the cumulative (CUM)-NPV profit in each year divided by the original group of customers (in this case 20,000). The NPV lifetime value represents the average profits that you can expect to receive, after a given number of years, from the *average new customer* whom you can sign up. The lifetime value (LTV) of the average new customer for Ridgeway Fashions in the third year is $60.05:

$$\text{LTV} = \text{CUM-NPV} / \text{acquired customers} = \$1,201,057 / 20,000 = \$60.05$$

This is a very important number. It is the most important number in your entire database. It can be used to develop your entire marketing strategy. We will be using this number throughout this book.

Strategy Development

Developing your customer lifetime value table is the first step in the development of strategy. The second step is to get a great idea and test it out—in theory—using your lifetime value table as the measuring stick. Let's do this right now.

Strategy always begins with some assumptions. "If we do this, then the customer will do that." We will learn that the strategy for building customer relationships can affect five (and only five) basic things:

1. *Retention rate.* Building relationships increases customer loyalty and augments the retention rate. Increases in the retention rate will reduce the costs of servicing customers and increase the revenue per customer.

2. *Referrals.* Relationship-building activities can turn your customers into advocates and lead them to suggest your company to their friends, coworkers, or relatives. This works in business-to-business as well as consumer marketing. Referrals typically have higher retention rates and spending rates than other newly acquired customers.

3. *Increased sales.* Database activities can lead to increased cross-selling, upgrades, or simply more purchases by existing customers.

4. *Reduced direct costs.* Database activities can reduce costs, in some cases, by changing the channel of distribution. Once you have customers on your database, you can learn more about them and can increase your channels to reach them.

5. *Reduced marketing costs.* Well-planned database activities are often much more cost effective than mass advertising. Once you have your customers on a database, you will develop innovative ways to market to them. For example, you will find that some customers have a negative lifetime value. They are costing you profits. Why spend a lot of money trying to build a relationship with these losers? Save your marketing money for people who can do you some good.

For Ridgeway Fashions, let's imagine a creative director of database marketing whom we will call Robin Baumgartner. Robin decides to test out the idea of a Birthday Club: to ask women customers to provide information about their sizes and preferences, their birthday, and their husband's business address. This information will be put into the database and supplied to the merchandise buyers who have to buy what the customers want. Then, each month, Robin will send letters to husbands about their wives' birthdays providing hints on what to get.

Figure 3-2 shows what Robin's idea might do to the lifetime value of customers who decide to join the Birthday Club. This table is just like the previous one, but there have been some significant additions.

Referral Rate

Almost any company can get some satisfied customers to become advocates. In this case, Robin is assuming that the Birthday Club will be so successful that she can persuade (or incentive) 5 percent of her customers to recommend Ridgeway to their friends or relatives. As a result, we will have 5 percent more customers in Year 2 than we otherwise would have had. The referral rate will grow in subsequent years, as more and more loyal customers turn into advocates.

Is Robin correct? Can she really increase her customer base by 5 percent in Year 2 through a referral program? Who knows? That depends on many things, including the success of Ridgeway as a store, the execution of the marketing plan, etc. But it is certainly a reasonable goal to build into a marketing plan. It is also a testable proposition. If the plan does produce 5 percent new customers, the database will show it. If it brings in 12 percent, or only 3 percent, the plan can be modified. This

	Year 1	*Year 2*	*Year 3*
Referral rate	5.00%	6.00%	7.00%
Referred customers	0	1,000	660
Retention rate	50%	60%	70%
Retained customers	0	10,000	6,600
Total customers	20,000	1,000	7,260
Spending rate	$180	$190	$200
Total revenue	$3,600,000	$2,090,000	$1,452,000
Variable costs %	60%	50%	45%
Variable costs $	$2,160,000	$1,045,000	$653,400
Referral incentive ($12)	$0	$12,000	$7,920
Birthday Club costs ($15/3)	$300,000	$60,000	$60,000
Acquisition cost ($40)	$800,000	$0	$0
Total costs	$3,260,000	$1,117,000	$721,320
Gross profit	$340,000	$973,000	$730,680
Discount rate	1	1.16	1.35
Net present value profit	$340,000	$838,793	$541,244
Cumulative NPV profit	$340,000	$1,178,793	$1,720,038
Lifetime value	$17.00	$58.94	$86.00

Figure 3-2. Lifetime value with the Birthday Club.

is the beginning of good strategy development. The MCI Friends and Family program was one of the most successful referral programs in the history of marketing. It showed what can be done.

There is one issue here that we should note. These referred customers are really new acquisitions. Why don't we just tuck them into the numbers in Year 1 the way we do with other new acquisitions? Why do we show them as a separate category on a lifetime value chart? There is a very important reason. Research shows, and *your database records will prove it,* that referred people are more loyal, and have a higher retention and spending rate, than the average new acquisition. They are *better people* than the average customer. Why this is so, no one really knows. But the fact that they are linked to an existing customer results in their being more valuable than many other customers. You list them separately because you want to track them, measure their purchasing habits, and devise special programs to increase their number. You may want to create a special lifetime table just for them. Don't lose track of them. In your database, you put the ID number of the referred person in the referrer's record, and vice versa. That way you can track referred people and those who refer them, to determine their lifetime value. Some people also suggest that those who refer other customers are also better customers. They spend more and are more loyal. If you have enough of them, you may want to create a special "advocates group," giving them special attention.

Retention Rate

In the previous example, the retention rate for Ridgeway began at 40 percent. In drawing up this new table for the Birthday Club, Robin makes the assumption that her programs can increase that to 50 percent—with further increases as the remaining customer base becomes composed of more and more loyalists. We show totals for referred, retained, and total customers. Where did she get the 50 percent number for retention rate? She made it up, based on some tests that she had conducted. Certainly, one objective of any new strategy will be to make customers happier, and thus to increase the retention rate. What that increase will be is your job to estimate. Lifetime value is a *forward-looking* concept. You use it to predict your future revenue and profits.

What determines the retention rate? A great many things, only some of which are under the marketer's control. Factors that marketers usually cannot control include:

- The strength of the competitor's marketing strategy
- The saturation of the market for their product
- Macroeconomic events like recessions, booms, or changes in interest rates, which affect the overall demand for most products

The factors that marketers *can* control that affect the retention rate, however, are quite impressive:

- The type of customer that you acquire in the first place
- The price charged for the product
- The efforts made to build a relationship with the customers
- The way you treat your customers

The Spending Rate

Robin is assuming that the Birthday Club will increase spending by its satisfied members. She estimates that Birthday Club members will buy an average of $180 worth of clothing in Year 1 instead of $150. How does she know that it will be $180? She can do little tests. Database marketing offers a tremendous opportunity to conduct miniexperiments prior to your major rollouts. Robin has done her homework. Her estimate is, clearly, a testable proposition.

Her assumptions in the next two years also follow from database marketing theory. Loyal customers always buy more than new customers. As customers drop out, those who are left are the more loyal customers. It is safe to assume that the average annual purchases will go up. If you keep track of customer spending in your database, you can prove, easily, to yourself that loyal customers tend to make more purchases per year, that they buy more on each visit, and that they tend to buy higher-priced items.

Birthday Club Costs

In planning her variable costs, Robin assumes the same cost structure that applied for her customers in general. The costs for the Birthday Club can be calculated with some precision. To set the club up in the first year will cost $15 per customer. This includes the cost of training the clerks to ask people to join the club, giving the clerks a commission of $5 per customer signed up, getting the survey data, entering the data, putting it into the database, creating the Birthday Club software, and writing one letter to each member's husband at birthday time. In Years 2 and 3, the costs are set at $3 per year. This covers the generation of the birthday letters. You will note that she is sending out birthday letters to all club members, even though many have already stopped buying in the store. This is excellent strategy. The club communications, alone, may serve to reactivate some lapsed customers and so are well worth the investment.

Resulting Lifetime Value

Lifetime value for club members is computed exactly as it was for regular store customers. It shows that lifetime value in the third year rises to $86. To show what has happened, look at a third chart, Figure 3-3, which compares the bottom line on both tables. This shows that in the first year the Birthday Club will reduce lifetime value. In old-fashioned direct marketing programs, one might use this initial loss as a reason to abandon the club as being a loser. But with database marketing we can look at the impact of a new strategy several years ahead. And in this case it shows that by the third year the Birthday Club will increase Ridgeway profits by more that $5 million. Bear in mind that this $5 million is not sales; it is net profit, after all costs have been subtracted. It is a real number that can be measured. It shows that the Birthday Club is a profitable strategy for Ridgeway Fashions.

	Year 1	*Year 2*	*Year 3*
Old LTV	$20.00	$47.59	$60.05
New LTV	$17.00	$58.94	$86.00
Change	($3.00)	$11.35	$25.95
With 200,000	($600,000)	$2,270,690	$5,189,801

Figure 3-3. Gain from the Birthday Club.

Lessons Learned

What lessons can we draw from what we have learned already?

- *Lifetime value is a practical, hardheaded technique* for determining the effectiveness of various marketing strategies. It can, and should, be applied to any marketing program to test it before any significant amount of money is spent. Before we act on our hunches and prejudices, we can do our homework and prove to ourselves, at least theoretically, whether any proposed program has the possibility of success.

- *Lifetime value is future net profits* computed in today's dollars using the net present value calculation method.

- *Lifetime value grows* with the number of repeat customers and referrals.

- *Lifetime value increases* with the number of years that customers continue to buy.

The basic idea is to come up with strategies that increase lifetime value by as much as possible. If we set up a matrix showing lifetime value each year for three years (as we have already done), then we can use our imagination and do "what-if" analysis to see what we can do to increase lifetime value. The results of each possible action can be calculated to determine whether the effect on lifetime value is worth the effort and resources that went into it.

Looking at Customers as Assets

Most businesses list buildings, machinery, and cash as assets. But when a business is sold, "goodwill" is often what the buyer pays the most for. Goodwill is nothing other than the value of the customer base that the company has built up over the years, and currently is holding on to. Lifetime value is a way of quantifying the value of the goodwill represented by the existing customer base.

Economists and accountants often talk as if the main problem of any business is to find the most efficient way to *produce* products and services. It's not. The main problem of any business is to find the most efficient way to *sell* its products and services. Customers provide the cash flow that keeps any business alive.

By building up customer lifetime value, we are building up the key assets of the business—assets that are essential to the survival of the business itself.

The Computation Period

In this example, we have shown the results of lifetime value after one, two, and three years. Why stop there? Why not compute it over ten years? Which is the right number of years to look at? Throughout industry there is a lot of confusion over this question. When you think about it, however, it is not that complicated.

Some customers stay with you for years. Others buy once and drop out. The remainder drops out at various intervals—and some drop out and then come back. The lifetime value is a function of the length of time that you use for measurement. The longer period of time you use, the greater the lifetime value. That being the case, which is the correct length of time: one, two, three, five, or ten years?

Paul Wang has what I consider to be the best answer: *All of them are correct.* Lifetime value, for Paul, is always tied to a number of years: Lifetime value after two years is *X;* lifetime value after three years is *Y.* You look at all the numbers and say to yourself: "How long is a reasonable period for our business?" If, for instance, you are a consumer cataloger, long-term lifetime value may be self-delusion. Catalog customers tend to come and go quite rapidly. If you are a bank or an insurance company with long-term retention rates in the 90 percent range, a ten-year LTV table may be quite feasible.

You have to look realistically at your product, your competition, and the market and say, "How long are customers likely to stay with us?" After that you can ask, "How long can we afford to wait?" The answer will be quite different for each product in each industry.

The lesson: Compute lifetime value for each of several years. Use the period of time that makes the most sense to you based on your particular product situation.

How Do You Calculate LTV for a Single Customer?

Lifetime value is always calculated for a group or segment of customers. You cannot calculate it directly for a single customer. Why not? Because LTV includes such factors as the retention rate and the referral rate. I cannot pick out one customer and tell you that she will be here next year. But I can pick out 1,000 customers and say, with some confidence, based on recent trends, that 600 of them will be here next year. This is what insurance actuaries do. To determine the LTV of a single customer, you include her in a segment or group; determine the LTV of the group, and then attribute to her the LTV of the group members. This can be varied with the individual customer profitability or spending rate.

For example, assume that we have determined the lifetime value of our teenage customers. Their spending rate is $100, and their LTV in the third year is $56. What is the LTV of Eliza Hughes, a member of this group, whose personal spending rate is $150? Based on the group she is in, we can redo the LTV chart using the group's retention, rates, referral rates, and cost structure, but using Eliza's spending rate. We can then determine that Eliza's LTV in the third year is $78. We can tuck this number into her database record and use it in future marketing strategies involving Eliza.

Does LTV Predict Success?

In this chapter, we compared the lifetime value of all Ridgeway Fashions customers with those who joined the Birthday Club. This is an excellent use of LTV, since it tells us whether the Birthday Club *can be* a success. It does not, of course, tell us that the Birthday Club *will be* a success. Success depends on execution and on guessing the situation in the market at the time. Maybe the competition already has a Birthday Club. Lifetime value analysis will tell us that the club could be a success if all other factors are favorable. There are plenty of marketing strategies that could not work out even in theory, because the costs would exceed possible increased profits. The LTV table will show this clearly, and should be calculated before any new strategy is undertaken.

What Is Your Product and Who Is Your Customer?

Lifetime value can also vary depending on how you define your product. If you are selling gasoline or heating oil, the product and the customer are pretty obvious. If you are a department store, it is not as clear. Do you determine the lifetime value of all customers or just women's wear customers? By lumping them together, you may miss a lot of detail that would be important to your marketing program. Upper-income women may be attracted by the style of your clothing; lower-income shoppers may like the values; do-it-yourself types may like your hardware department. Lumping them all together at once to determine the lifetime value of all of them may lead you to false strategies that may turn off some while turning on others.

In Chapter 8, on segmentation, we will explore various methods of dividing your customers into segments and determining the lifetime value for each segment.

Possible Strategies

What can you do to increase your profits by increasing customer lifetime value? Throughout this book, we will explore a number of techniques, including retaining existing customers and adding new ones.

Retain existing customers:

- Increase the number of efforts to get customers to renew.
- Build a relationship with customers to make them more loyal.
- Segment the database and target the company's relationship to the appropriate groups of customers, rather than treating them all alike.
- Establish special groups: a President's Club, a Gold Card Group to build loyalty and encourage people to buy more to belong.
- Set up a frequent buyer/flyer/traveler/shopper club.
- Increase renewal or reactivation efforts.

Add new customers:

- Attract the type of customer most likely to stay with you.
- Determine the customer acquisition budget with more precision.

- Profile existing customers and use the profiles to find new customers.
- Use the database to qualify prospects.

Increasing Retention Efforts

Magazine owners have renewal down to a science. *Newsweek,* for example, grips onto its customers like a pit bull. Before the subscription is due to expire, it sends a series of reminders and increasingly strident warnings of impending doom. After the subscription has expired, it issues a continuing series of reactivation messages. It just cannot accept the idea that customers would ever want to drop their subscription to *Newsweek.*

This is great marketing. Most companies don't do this because they don't know how to do it. Magazines do it because they are in the habit of corresponding with their customers, and have developed lifetime value down to a fine science. We explore magazine marketing further in the next chapter.

How to Do Your Own Calculation

Lifetime value calculation as a base for strategy development is not as difficult as you may have thought. Follow these simple steps:

1. *Use your database* to select a group of customers, all of whom came on board at about the same time in the past. Depending on the size of your customer base, you could use any number from 1,000 to 1 million or more.

2. *Determine* how many of these customers are still buying a year later to figure your retention rate. If you have enough data, determine the second-year retention rate as well. If not, estimate it for subsequent years. An attrition rate of 50 percent is not unusual. If you have a rapidly moving type of business, you can compute LTV based on quarters or half years rather than annual numbers.

3. *Estimate* the money that you spent in acquiring these customers by advertising, direct mail, promotions, etc. This is your acquisition cost.

4. *Determine* the average amount of money that these customers spend with you in a single year so as to compute their spending rate.

5. *Determine* the discount rate that applies to your business. Adjust this rate for risk.

6. *Put all these data into a spreadsheet,* projecting your customer lifetime value out for three or more years.

7. *Try out some what-if scenarios,* experimenting with the costs and effects of relationship-building activities, with the goal being to build the long-term customer value to as high a level as possible. Predict the results of each major marketing initiative *before you implement it.*

8. *Keep your LTV spreadsheet active.* After you have tried a few marketing initiatives, check their results against your spreadsheet. Improve your predicting ability. Become a master marketer. If you need help in creating your spreadsheet, you can download a sample lifetime value spreadsheet from the Database Marketing Institute's *www.dbmarketing.com.* It's free.

Selling Your Marketing Program to Management

Every year you have to justify your existence to some flinty-eyed CFO. Now that you have calculated lifetime value, it will become the centerpiece of your budget justification. Suppose you are Robin Baumgartner, trying to get the money for her Birthday Club from her management. What she will do is to say, "If you can give me this budget, I can turn the club into a $5 million profit in the third year."

The CFO will be skeptical. "Prove it to me," he will say.

Robin then produces her revised lifetime value chart, showing the referral rate, the retention rate, and the spending rate once the Birthday Club is in full operation.

"Where did you get these numbers?" he will ask.

"I ran some tests in our stores in Braintree and in Danbury. The numbers are the result of these tests. Do you want to see the details?"

If the CFO finally gives Robin the money she needs, there will be a problem. The CFO will save her revised spreadsheet in his desk drawer. Next year when Robin comes up for a budget review again, he will produce the sheet and ask: "OK, now tell me. What was your actual reten-tion rate with the club? What was your referral rate and your spending rate?"

The problem, of course, is that lifetime value represents real num-bers that can be audited by any accountant. Database marketing is an accountable art. It is not like mass marketing where you use "awareness" as a measure of success. What is awareness? It is a sloppy, indefinable number, which may be in no way related to real sales. Lifetime value is a solid, testable number. You can use the database to prove whether your numbers are valid or not.

Because of this, Robin should be cautious in providing spreadsheets to management. If I were she, I would prepare the sheets, but then *dis-count them* before she makes them public. If she is sure that her retention rate will be 50 percent, she should put 48 percent on the chart. If she is sure that the spending rate will be $180, she should say it would be $176. Always underpromise and overdeliver. That way, next year, she will come off as a heroine when her actual performance beats her projection.

Keeping Management Informed

Now that you know how to compute lifetime value, you should create meaningful customer segments, compute the lifetime value for each of them, and then append lifetime value to every record in your database. You should let top management know what the overall retention rate is for your customers as a whole and for each segment. Let the CEO know what the LTV and retention rates are on a monthly basis. These num-bers are more important to the company than the stock value or any of the other measures that are currently on the CEO's desk. You, and you alone, can produce such numbers. It will make you an information pow-erhouse within the company.

Summary

- More and more marketers today are computing the lifetime value of their customers as a basis for their marketing programs and strategic planning.

- *Net present value* is a way of determining the value *today* of money that you will receive or expend at some dates in the future. It discounts future money by the assumed market rate of interest plus risk. The formula is NPV = amount / D. $D = (1 + i)^n$ where i = the interest rate plus risk and n = the number of years.

- *Customer lifetime value must be recalculated from month to month,* because conditions are always changing: Competitors come up with new initiatives, products become obsolete, and the market becomes saturated. The marketplace is always filled with uncertainty and lack of information. There are no eternal truths.

- *The retention rate* is a measure of how many of last year's customers are still buying from you this year. It varies with things you cannot change, like type of product, competitor's strength, public perception, and macroeconomic trends. There are many things you can do to affect your retention rate: type of promotions, pricing, renewal efforts, relationship building.

- *The computation period* defines how far out you must go to define the lifetime customer value. It varies by industry. The longer the period, the greater the lifetime value.

- *Calculate lifetime value for different customer segments.* Lifetime value may be different for different types of customers. You should think this through before you lump all customers together.

- *For lifetime value purposes, you need to estimate your variable costs.* The easiest method is to compute them as a percentage of revenue. The amount depends on your industry. Variable costs (for this purpose) include everything except marketing costs and fixed costs.

- To compute lifetime value for a given group of customers, add together the net profit from prior years and the net profit from the current year. This gives you the cumulative profit up to that year. This number is divided by the original number of customers.

- Customers are assets, the same as buildings or cash. Another name for lifetime value is goodwill. LTV is a way of measuring the value of your customers.

- Customer lifetime value calculations will also help to determine how much effort to put into acquisition, referral programs, and reactivation programs.

- *Customer lifetime value* also helps to determine the cost and the value of efforts to build database marketing relationships.

- *New strategies,* such as gold cards, president's clubs, and newsletters, can and should be tested by measuring lifetime value before and afterward. If your calculations do not show an increase in future years, drop or modify your strategy before it is too late.

Technical Appendix A: Computing the Retention Rate for Infrequent Purchasers

Background

The retention rate is the most important single number in a lifetime value table. It is typically calculated on an annual basis. A 60 percent retention rate means that of 10,000 customers acquired in Year 1, only 6,000 customers will still remain as active customers in Year 2. This is easy to compute for cellular phones or credit cards. But what is the annual retention rate if 50 percent of the customers buy the same make of automobile after 4 years? Here a formula is necessary. The formula is

$$RR = (RPR)^{(1/Y)}$$

where RR is the annual retention rate, RPR is the repurchase rate, and Y is the number of years between purchases. Here are several examples of the use of the formula.

Automobile Purchase by One Segment. A segment of Buick owners buys a new car every 4 years. About 35 percent of them buy a Buick, and the balance buys some other make of car. What is the annual retention rate?

$$RR = (RPR)^{(1/Y)}$$
$$RR = (0.35)^{(1/4)}$$
$$RR = 76.9\%$$

Automobile Purchase by Several Segments. Buick owners can be divided into four segments: those who buy a new car every one year, two years, three years, and four years. Their respective repurchase rates are shown in the chart in Figure 3-4. This chart provides some interesting information. The repurchase rate of those who buy a Buick every year seems much higher than that for those who wait four years between

Segment	Years Between Purchases	Repurchase Rate	Annual Retention	Acquired Customer	Retained Customer
A	1	55.00%	55.00%	90,346	49,690
B	2	45.00%	67.08%	170,882	114,631
C	3	40.90%	73.68%	387,223	285,308
D	4	35.00%	76.92%	553,001	425,347
Total			72.83%	1,201,452	874,976

Figure 3-4. Repurchase rate and retention rate.

automobile purchases. Their annual retention rate, however, is far lower.

Restaurant Patrons by Week. A businessman's restaurant had a regular clientele of patrons who ate there almost every day. The restaurant owner decided to try database marketing. He set up a system to gather the names of the restaurant's customers and gave points for each meal. He discovered that the restaurant was losing about 1 percent of its clients every week. What was the annual retention rate? The formula is the same as above:

$$RR = (RPR)^{(1/Y)}$$

In this case, the repurchase rate is 99 percent, and the period involved is 1/52 of a year. So the formula becomes

$$RR = (0.99)^{[1/(1/52)]}$$

$$RR = 59.3\%$$

This tells us that the restaurant's annual customer retention rate was 59.3 percent.

Technical Appendix B: Including Payment Delays in the Discount Rate

The complete formula for the discount rate, including payment delays, is

$$D = [1 + (i * rf)]^{n+pd}$$

where i = the market rate of interest; rf = the risk factor (rf = 1 means that there is no risk factor); n = the number of years to wait for payment; and pd = the fraction of a year delay in customer payment. Assume the market rate of interest is 7 percent, the risk factor is 1.5, the number of years to wait is 3, and customers typically pay in 90 days. The formula becomes

$$D = [1 + (0.07 * 1.5)]^{2.25}$$
$$D = 1.25$$

Executive Quiz 2

Answers to quiz questions can be found in Appendix B.

1. Compute the missing values in the table in Figure 3-5:

   a. _____

   b. _____

   c. _____

   d. _____

   e. _____

   f. _____

   g. _____

   h. _____

   i. _____

2. What is the net present value of $4,000 to be received in three years? The rate of interest is 8 percent, including risk.

   a. $2,175.33

   b. $3,175.33

   c. $4,000.00

   d. $4,175.33

   e. None of the above

	Year 1	Year 2	
Customers			
Referral rate	8.00%	9.00%	
Referred customers	0		a
Retention rate	50.00%	60.00%	
Retained customers	0		b
Total customers	16,988	9,853	
Spending rate	$200.00,	$220.00	
Total customer revenue	$3,397,600		c
Expenses			
Variable cost percentage	60.00%	55.00%	
Variable costs	$2,038,560		d
Acquisition cost $40	$679,520	na	
New strategy $15	$254,820		e
Referral incentive $20	0		f
Total costs	$2,972,900	$1,367,194	
Profits			
Gross profit	$424,700	$800,475	
Discount rate	1.00	1.20	
NPV profit	$424,700		g
Cumulative NPV profit	$424,700		h
Lifetime value	25.00		i

Figure 3-5. Sample LTV table.

3. The rate of interest including risk is 14 percent. You have to wait four years for your money. What is the discount rate ?

   a. 1.00

   b. 1.22

   c. 1.69

   d. 1.82

   e. 2.07

4. What is the reason for including a risk factor in computing the discount rate?

   a. Demand for your product may weaken.

   b. Competition could cut prices.

   c. The product may become obsolete.

   d. Interest rates could go up.

   e. All of the above.

5. The retention rate is calculated by dividing the number of customers at any one time by:

   a. The number of customers in some original period several years ago

   b. The number of customers last year

   c. The market rate of interest plus the risk

   d. The expected referral rate

   e. None of the above

6. You began with 2,000 customers last year. This year you have 1,060. What is your retention rate?

   a. 43%

   b. 53%

   c. 63%

   d. 73%

   e. 83%

7. In Year 4 the discount rate is 1.8. The revenue is $142,846. What is the net present value of that revenue?

   a. $257,122

   b. $157,122

   c. $142,846

   d. $79,359

   e. None of the above

8. The revenue is $50,000. The variable cost ratio is 80 percent. What are the variable costs?

   a. $10,000

   b. $20,000

   c. $40,000

   d. $50,000

   e. $60,000

9. One thousand customers were acquired in Year 1. By Year 4 there are only 200 still active purchasers. The cumulative NPV profit in that year from this group is $48,210. What is the lifetime value per customer in Year 4?

   a. $241.05

   b. $141.05

   c. $96.42

   d. $46.42

   e. $48.21

10. A group of customers buys trucks every three years. Their repurchase rate is 40 percent. What is their annual retention rate?

    a. 43.68%

    b. 33.68%

    c. 73.68%

    d. 63.68%

    e. 53.68%

4

Designing a Successful
Customer Strategy

The greatest obstacle to growth is not ignorance, but the illusion of knowledge. To sound a bit radical, the information age as we know it does not exist. What does exist is the non-information age, the age of information anxiety and information overwhelm. We have so much data and information available to us that instead of making better, more informed decisions, the exact opposite is occurring. Guesswork is the norm and success the exception. We are trying to keep up with an endlessly increasing base of information. And the fact is, we will never keep up. . . .

The illusion of knowledge exists because large amounts of data provide security. The reality, though, is that the data is never looked at or used. Why? Because most times there is no technology in place that can do anything meaningful with the data or find the patterns in the data that will energize it and make it come alive to answer our questions. Data alone is not enough. This suggests strongly that we need to change the way we think about and look at information.

By thinking of database-marketing in broader terms, you can integrate into your business decision-making based on new technology that finds the patterns in your information, that gives you, with laser-beam precision, a complete understanding of where you are in your marketplace, what your prioritized opportunities are, why they are best for you and how and who to target for maximum return. And maybe most importantly, you get the ability to answer those questions now!

ROBERT POSTEN

The Landis Group

The ideal customer is one who is highly profitable and stays with us for a lifetime. The best marketing strategy is to attract such customers and to keep them loyal. In the real world, such customers are hard to find. We make our success by managing the customers we have, using marketing strategies that help to nudge them into behavior that is satisfying for the customer and profitable for us.

There are really two behaviors that we can influence here: profitability and loyalty. They are not the same.

- Some customers are highly profitable, but disappear after a single purchase. One example is new home buyers. No matter how satisfied these buyers may be, it is almost impossible to maintain a profitable long-term relationship with these customers so that we can sell them their next home, 10 or 15 years later when they retire, get promoted, or have another child.

- Some customers are only mildly profitable, but they are very loyal. They continue to stay with us for years and years. Banks and utilities have thousands of such customers. Many of these customers will never be very profitable, but they can be very loyal.

In between these two extremes are the vast majority of customers who exhibit behavior that can be modified by conscious customer management strategies. Some are profitable, and some are very unprofitable. Some are loyal, and some are very disloyal. The combined measure of both characteristics is customer lifetime value, which we explained in the last chapter. In this chapter, we will discuss strategies and tactics for managing customer behavior to improve lifetime value. Let's begin with profitability.

Measuring Profitability

Profitability usually measures activities in the recent past, whereas loyalty measures future long-term activity. Profitability is measured by adding up recent receipts from a specific customer and subtracting the costs incurred by this customer in the corresponding period. We measure profitability by saying, "Did we make money on this customer last month? Or last year?" In Chapter 13, we cover in some detail how banks measure profitability. Insurance, transportation, utility, and telecommunication companies can do the same thing. Most other companies, however, cannot do profitability analysis on a customer-by-customer basis because of the difficulty of allocating costs to each customer. How can Sears Roebuck, or Buick, or Dow Chemical allocate its costs back to each customer? These companies can't. For the vast majority of customers, therefore, companies have to use net revenue balanced off against a rough cost percentage as a measure of profitability. That's OK, however, and works just fine.

When they do this, however, they discover something very interesting. Most companies break their customers down into five groups, based on profitability or net revenue. The top group—the Gold customers—usually produces 80 percent or more of the profits or net revenue. The bottom group—the losers—often produces zero profitability or a net loss. Figure 4-1 is a typical layout, which we first saw in Chapter 1. The number of customers in each group does not have to be equal to the other groups. Typically, the number in the top group is quite small—sometimes as small as 5 or 6 percent. The number in the bottom

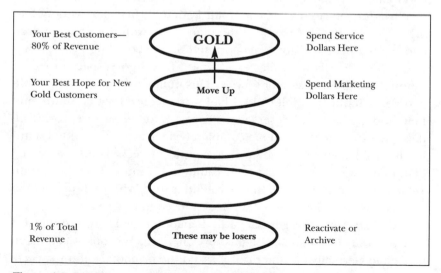

Figure 4-1. Dividing customers into LTV segments.

group can be 35 percent or higher. You will have to decide how to make the divisions based on lifetime value, revenue, or some other measure.

My experience with American Airlines serves to illustrate the chart in Figure 4-1. I do a lot of traveling making speeches. When I started out, I had never made Gold status on an airline. So I picked American Airlines to get Gold status. To achieve Gold on American you have to fly 25,000 miles in a calendar year. January 1, the clock starts all over again and you lose the Gold qualifying miles you had the year before. That year, I flew everywhere on American. I went several times to Orlando via Miami, for example. It is the wrong way to go and takes much longer, but you get more miles that way. On Christmas day I called American Airlines to see how many miles I had.

"Mr. Hughes, you have 24,600 miles."

"I'm so close! You are going to give me the Gold, aren't you?"

"No, Mr. Hughes. You have to have 25,000 miles."

"But I have only a few days left. Can I pay you for the 400 miles?"

"No, Mr. Hughes. You have to fly them."

So the day after Christmas, I went to American Airlines, and for $44 I bought a round-trip ticket to Raleigh-Durham because it was close and inexpensive and would give me the miles I needed. At 7 a.m. I flew down there. At 9 a.m. I flew back. I was in my office in Reston, Virginia, by 11 a.m. Since then I have been Gold, or higher.

What did it mean to me to be Gold? I got to fly first class without having to pay for it. I got to go on the plane first, with the little children and the old people. I got "gold" printed on my boarding passes. I was given 25 percent bonus miles every time I flew. I got a special toll-free number to call for customer service. This number was just for the Gold people. And, finally, I felt Gold. I had worked hard for that status, and I enjoyed it. I felt that I deserved it. American found ways to provide little services for me that had me completely dedicated. It provided status levels that I could work toward. A couple of years later, I achieved Platinum status, and finally I became a Platinum Executive, with 100,000 miles on American in one calendar year. With each upgrade in status came special additional services. I loved it.

What did American get out of it? It had Arthur Hughes hooked. I flew all of my discretionary flights on American. We took vacations in Chile and Germany on American. I asked the promoters of my speeches in Brazil, Tokyo, Australia, and London to let me fly American. I flew American with stopovers in Dallas or Chicago, taking a couple of extra hours in the process, when I could have taken shorter direct flights on other airlines. I dreamed about the miles. Without my fixation on airline status, I would probably have flown half as many miles on American as I actually did.

Gold Customers

Every business has Gold customers. Most companies have not identified them. This is a pity. These customers are the backbone of any business. You absolutely must maintain this group if the company is going to be a success. Many marketers who have identified their Gold customers think that they should single them out for special marketing promotions. This is a terrible mistake.

Gold customers are often maxed out. Many of them are already giving you all their business in your category. That was certainly true of me with American Airlines. I could not possibly have flown more with American, no matter what offers it might have made. What should you do for Gold customers? Find ways to reward them, to let them know that they are important to you. Make it so attractive for them that they would not think of switching.

Fleet Bank did an analysis of its customers, and divided them into segments similar to the chart in Figure 4-1. Fleet discovered that it was almost impossible to profitably cross-sell its Gold customers. Most new sales to this group cannibalized profitable existing business. Fleet Bank decided that its marketing efforts to its best customers should be restricted to retention-building programs.

Take heed of Fleet Bank's findings. Decide whether you should market to your Gold customers. Provide special services for them.

Marketing to Those Just below Gold

This is where your marketing dollars should be concentrated. These are the people with 24,600 miles. You should let them know that they are on the verge of qualifying for Gold status. Just buy a few more times, and they will be up in Gold heaven, getting all the rewards that come with that status.

As shown in Figure 4-2, the three middle segments are where your marketing programs can do the most good. This graph was developed

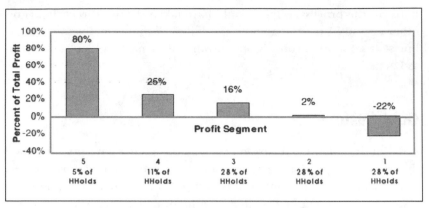

Figure 4-2. Household profitability segments.

by a bank in the Southeast. It shows the profitability of the bank's retail customer households. The chart shows that 105 percent of the bank's profits came from the top two quintiles. These high profits are dissipated by losses from other customer segments. The bottom group represented a loss of 22 percent of its profits. The bank's marketing goal, as a result, was to increase its profits from the middle three quintiles, and to reprice the services rendered to the bottom quintile.

The bank has discovered, like Fleet, that marketing to the Gold customers is an unproductive exercise. Fleet found that:

- Nearly half of its customers were unprofitable. The bottom 20 percent were very unprofitable. Half of the customers currently being acquired would never be profitable.

- However, there was considerable profit potential among many of the low-profit customers. Fleet could gain an increased share of wallet from some of them. Others could be converted to other products that were more profitable for the bank, and more satisfying for the customers.

Dealing with the Losers

What can you do with the bottom segment—the group that, in most industries, not only does not pay their way, but also robs you of your profit?

The first step is to have knowledge of what is going on. Few industries today have that knowledge. You can gain the knowledge only by building a customer database, which includes keeping a purchase history and grouping customers into revenue segments. Next you determine the lifetime value of each segment, using the methods found in the previous chapter.

Once you have isolated and identified the profit losers, what can you do about them? You need analysis and strategy.

The analysis will help you separate those who are unprofitable for temporary reasons from those who are going to be permanently unprofitable. What are the temporary reasons?

- Some losing customers may actually be doing a lot of business with your competitors. You have a small share of their wallet in your category. If you can learn this fact, then your goal is to find those hot buttons that will shift their business to you. The money is there. You just have to get it redirected. Don't give up.

- Others are losers because they are just starting out in life and currently have a small income. They may consist of small but growing companies that will soon be able to buy much more from you. Find this out, and develop a long-term strategy to wait until they are profitable, but avoid losing much money while you wait.

- Still others may be losers because they are buying the wrong products. You may be able to change their price plan, or product mix, in a way that will make them happier and improve your profits.

The permanently unprofitable group contains the true losers. These may be transaction buyers who only buy from you when you are running a sale. They may be people with bad credit, or those who have excessive claims or returns. What can you do about these people? One strategy is to give them your competitor's 800 number. You might even call your competitor and say, "We are really swamped with work here. Can you handle some of our overflow?" They will take your customers, and thank you for it.

Your employees can be very helpful in solving the loser problem. Once you have identified your profit quintiles, let your employees know who the Gold customers are and also the profit quintile of the other customers. Let your employees help by providing superservices to the Gold customers.

Another option is to reprice the services given to the losers. For example, if losers tie up your customer service lines, or waste time in branch visits, offer them a reduction in price if they buy through the Internet or use an ATM.

Choosing a Marketing Strategy

All marketing involves some strategy, even if it is as simple as providing quality merchandise at low prices in a convenient location. For many years Troy-Bilt had the strategy of coming out with a new model rototiller each year, concentrating on a better and better product with more and more features. The strategy failed. The company went on the rocks in the late 1950s. In 1962 the new managers developed a different strategy—focused on what the customers can do with the product, reaching them directly. The new strategy, based on database marketing, turned the company around.

How can you decide what is the best marketing strategy for your product? There is no single answer that has universal validity. For some products, mass marketing through retail stores is the best possible strategy. For some business-to-business products, a web site that lets customers rummage through the inventory and warehouses beats all other methods.

There are thousands of situations where database marketing—relationship building—in conjunction with other methods, is the most profitable solution. If you have such a product or service, you must devise an effective method of using your database to build profits. This chapter contains guidance on the development of this strategy.

To develop a workable strategy, each marketer must come up with clever ideas, using, among other things, the hundreds of ideas being tested by others. Each clever idea should be examined to determine to what extent it would modify customer behavior to improve lifetime value.

Strategy Development Steps

The steps in strategy development are these:

- Group your customers into profitability or revenue segments.
- Determine the lifetime value of each segment.

- Determine the customer segments whose behavior you could profitably modify, by getting them to spend more or to be more loyal.

- Put yourself in the shoes of the members of the segments whose behavior you want to change. Think to yourself, "What would I want to receive from my company? What information or services could they provide to me that would make me spend more money, or be more loyal?"

- From the answers to these questions, write up a list of possible benefits, or rewards, or premiums, or relationships that you could develop with the customers in the segment which the customers would value, and which would nudge them toward greater lifetime value.

- Imagine that you have implemented the new strategies. Visualize how the strategies would affect the customer's spending habits, retention habits, or referrals. Put those changed behaviors and their costs into a lifetime value table. See whether lifetime value goes up or down. Play with the benefits until you have maximized lifetime value.

- Run little tests to make sure that you are right: that the rewards and relationships really do change customer spending and retention. Make sure that you test before you do a rollout.

Designing a Strategy

Let's apply these principles to the marketing of American magazines. The magazine business in America exploded in the 1990s. Hundreds of new magazines appeared (see Figure 4-3). They almost all had the same problem: high renewal costs and low retention rates. Most of them were in a discount trap. They offered substantial discounts to new subscribers

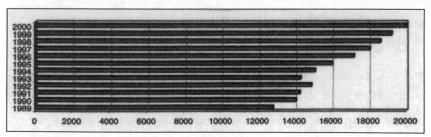

Figure 4-3. Growth of the magazine industry.

and then attempted to get them to renew at the higher (regular) rate. Most subscribers were too smart for that. They realized that they could let their subscription lapse and then renew at the discounted new-subscriber rate. Magazines spent considerable sums on mailings before and after the subscription expired offering more and more frantic "your last chance!" appeals to renew.

Meanwhile, some magazines, for example those sponsored by American Express, were having a much easier time of it. They billed their subscribers one time per year on their American Express card. To avoid renewing automatically, subscribers had to contact the magazine in advance or when they saw the renewal on their American Express monthly bill. Most people did not bother, and let the renewal stand. *Result:* Renewal costs and hassles were almost eliminated, and the retention rates were way up. Outside of American Express, however, most magazines used the old-fashioned system, asking subscribers to send in a check or call a toll-free number with their credit card to renew.

How profitable would it be for a magazine to shift to the negative option system, letting readers pay with an American Express, Master-Card, Visa, or other credit card? Let's look at a typical magazine, and analyze its lifetime value before and after adopting this and some other strategic database marketing strategies.

To begin with, let's take a look at the lifetime value of the typical magazine. As you can see in Figure 4-4, we have 100,000 subscribers acquired from a variety of sources at a heavy discount from the regular price of $40 per year. Subscriptions and new rentals represent about a quarter of the magazine's regular revenue, with advertisers making up the remaining 75 percent. Most magazines derive revenue from renting the names of subscribers to other businesses. The renewal rate is about 30 percent, at a cost of about $8 per renewal, including a series of letters and, in some cases, frantic phone calls. The resulting lifetime value is very low in the first year, rising to about $12 in the third year.

New Strategies

Let's apply some of the ideas developed in this book, many of which are practiced by advanced magazine marketers.

The Web Site. We will create a web site for the magazine which:

■ Has a personalized page for each subscriber, using her name

	Year 1	Year 2	Year 3
Subscribers	100,000	30,000	12,000
Retention rate	30.00%	40.00%	50.00%
Price paid	$25	$40	$40
Advertising (3 ¥ rate)	$120	$120	$120
Name rental & misc.	$20	$22	$24
Total revenue	$16,500,000	$5,460,000	$2,208,000
Cost percentage	75.00%	68.00%	66.00%
Direct costs	$12,375,000	$3,712,800	$1,457,280
Acquisition cost $40	$4,000,000	$0	$0
Renewal costs $8	$0	$800,000	$240,000
Total costs	$16,375,000	$4,512,800	$1,697,280
Profit	$125,000	$947,200	$510,720
Discount rate	1	1.2	1.44
NPV profit	$125,000	$914,333	$1,269,000
Cumulative NVP profit	$125,000	$914,333	$1,269,000
Lifetime value	$1.25	$9.14	$12.69

Figure 4-4. Magazine subscriber lifetime value.

- Takes credit cards and new subscriptions
- Sells additional related and unrelated products
- Provides access to the archives of back issues of the magazine going back for several years
- Partners with other magazines owned by the chain, selling subscriptions to these magazines as well
- Partners with advertisers to the magazine, linking to their web sites and featuring their products

To do it right, the magazine assigns a unique PIN to each subscriber, printed as a part of the label affixed to each copy of her magazine. We post the web site name (URL) all over the magazine: on the cover and at least once on every page. We provide incentives for the reader to go to the web site. After every magazine article, we tell the reader that there is more information about the article or the author available on the web site. This will drive some readers to visit the web site.

When the reader logs onto the web site, using her PIN, she sees a page that says:

Welcome Susan! If you're not Susan, <u>click here.</u>

Once Susan has logged on, we will use cookies to identify her in the future. Cookies are better than a PIN, because they are more like the old corner grocer. He did not ask the customers for their PINs when they came into his store. He knew them by sight.

The page is designed for Susan with the results of any survey and preference information that she filled out in the past, or a new survey for her to complete in case she has not already filled one out. She will receive something free (provided by an advertiser) if she completes the survey. The page will have the features that Susan wants.

Her page becomes the entrée to a whole new web magazine, created especially for her. For each article in the regular magazine, there is a brief bio of the author with a picture. There is material that was left out of the article because of space limitations—there are few space limitations on the web. There is a search button to look for similar subjects covered by the magazine in the past. There are things for Susan to do and to buy.

How expensive is it to create personal pages? It is not expensive at all. Once you have a web site, programmers can quickly add the software that creates personalized pages based on subscribers' preferences on web survey forms. If Susan never looks at her web site (which is the case for a high percentage of the magazine readers), nothing is lost. Susan's page was a couple of lines of computer code that were created automatically when she subscribed. Susan's page never actually exists until she logs onto it for the first time. Even then, it disappears into cyberspace when she logs off, with the results of her visit stored in her database record. Her database data become more and more valuable and sophisticated the more she uses the magazine's web site.

Negative Option Renewal. When Susan's subscription was taken in the first place, the agent took her credit card number. She was told that the renewal cost is billed automatically to the credit card when due unless she notifies the magazine by phone or through the web site in advance (or right afterward). Experience in other magazines shows that when presented in the right way, this negative option system was accepted by between 70 percent (American Express) and 90 percent (*Toronto Globe and Mail*) on the first telephone call.

The significance of this initiative is that the renewal process and problem almost completely disappears. No more threatening or plaintive letters exclaiming "This is your last chance, Arthur Hughes!" Furthermore, the renewal rates in many cases zoom from 30 percent or lower to 60 percent or higher. The system really works.

Referral System. We will set up an organized referral system on Susan's page on the web. We encourage Susan to nominate other people as subscribers to the magazine. There is a simple web form for her to fill out. We can send Susan's friend a letter, or if Susan provides an e-mail address, we can send an e-mail to the person (shown to Susan in advance on the web site so she can edit it), saying:

> Susan Webber suggested that you would be interested in reading *Arizona Highways*. As a result, we would be delighted to send you a free trial copy. If you are interested, click here. We hope that you will try our great magazine, but even if you don't, Susan says Hi!

If Susan's friend signs up, we will give Susan a $15 gift. Perhaps we should be even more generous to Susan. After all, new subscribers are costing us $40 each. Referred subscribers have a higher retention rate, spending rate, and referral rate than the average new subscriber, so they are worth more.

Why do we encourage Susan to edit the letter? This will make Susan happy and may make the letter much more powerful. Susan may take the opportunity to add some personal greeting which may make all the difference.

Additional Products. We will go all out to sell Susan some new products associated with the magazine. What could they be? Let's provide a list:

- Books related to the subject of the magazine.
- Subscriptions to publications from the same chain.
- Related products: Health magazines sell vitamin pills, sports magazines sell sports clothes, travel magazines sell cruises, etc.
- Emblems of the magazine—hats, scarfs, pins, tee shirts, etc., with the magazine's logo on them.

Why is it so important to sell Susan these additional products? Because we know, from prior experience, that the subscriber's retention rate is a direct function of her participation in the subjects of the magazine. The more products subscribers buy related to the magazine, the more likely they are to remain as committed subscribers. It doesn't matter if we make a lot of money or very little from these extra products. They will help us achieve our overall objective of building the retention rate and therefore making the magazine a success.

Personal Communications. We will send Susan a birthday card on her birthday. In addition, we may send her a Thanksgiving Day card, or a Christmas card, or a Valentine's Day card. Most important, we will send her a simple thank you after the annual renewal. Not a pitch for more money, or anything commercial. Just a simple letter on company stationery signed by the publisher or editor that says:

> I want to thank you for renewing your subscription to *Better Homes and Gardens*. You have been a loyal subscriber since 1994. I want you to know that we really appreciate having you as a reader. It is good people like you who make our magazine a success. Thank you, Susan.

Discounts Abolished. We are going to abolish subscription discounts as a policy. If you want *Architectural Digest,* you will pay full price, or you can't get it at all. "Won't that kill our acquisition program?" you might well ask. *Answer:* Of course, it will ruin any program that is based on discounts. But let's see what is wrong with discounts as an inducement for subscribers.

- *Discounts bring in the wrong kind of subscribers.* Some people are interested in buying magazines cheap. Some people want the magazines to read them, and possibly to see what is advertised in them. The first kind of people will not stay with us. The second kind, if they like the magazine, will stay for a long time.

- *Discounts send the wrong message.* We want readers to concentrate on the value of the magazine to their lives, not to their wallets. We don't want them to begin comparing magazines based on price, but based on content.

- *Discounts cost a lot of money.* Millions of dollars are wasted in attracting and signing up the wrong kind of people. Good, serious readers subsidize temporary, disloyal readers. This is wrong.

If we end the discount policy, subscriptions will decline at first. We will have to change our whole approach to acquisition to stress the value of the magazine, the web relationships, and additional benefits and bonuses, which come with subscriptions. There is, for example, nothing wrong with premiums for subscribers. A premium does not discount the value of the magazine. It is something extra. Also, we can give premiums to subscribers who adopt the negative option. But we will never offer discounts.

Effect of the New Strategies

In Figure 4-5 we are looking at the same 100,000 subscribers as in Figure 4-4, but assuming that the new strategies have been applied to them. A number of significant benefits have come from these strategies. In the first place, the renewal rate has gone up from 30 percent to 60 percent. A dramatic gain of this sort is often the result of shifting to a negative option. The *Toronto Globe and Mail* went from 12 percent to 69 percent renewals with the negative option. American Express had even higher rates.

Since we have abolished discounts, the price paid is the standard price, not a discounted price. This will save us $15 per subscriber, or $1.5 million. We can spend the extra money on premiums for subscribers. Most of the premiums, however, are paid by advertisers through a partnership program.

Our cost of acquisition has gone up from $40 to $50. Why? Because, without discounts, getting 100,000 subscribers is more difficult. We have to be very creative in our messages to surmount the difficulty of not buying the subscribers' votes.

We have added a referral program that will bring in 5,000 new subscribers in Year 2. These referred people will have a higher renewal rate than the average new subscriber. How do we know that? Keep track of them, and we can prove it in subsequent years. We will incentivize our referrers an average of $15 each.

We have sold some new products to subscribers. These new products, as already noted, are not so valuable as revenue earners as they are in building the renewal rate. Every new product sold binds the average reader to the magazine more.

Many of these new benefits are balanced by new expenses. The web site is not free. Credit card processing costs have to be accounted for.

Revenue	Year 1	Year 2	Year 3
Referral rate	5.00%	7.00%	9.00%
Referred subscribers	0	5,000	4,200
Retained subscribers	100,000	60,000	42,000
Retention rate	60.00%	70.00%	80.00%
Total subscribers	100,000	65,000	46,200
Price paid	$40	$40	$40
Advertising × 3	$120	$120	$120
Name rental & misc.	$20	$22	$24
New products $15	$15	$20	$25
Total revenue	$19,500,000	$13,130,000	$9,655,800
Cost percentage	70.00%	68.00%	66.00%
Direct costs	$13,650,000	$8,928,400	$6,372,828
Acquisition cost $50	$5,000,000	$0	$0
Renewal costs $0	$0	$0	$0
Credit card costs 3%	$120,000	$78,000	$55,440
Web site costs $4	$400,000	$260,000	$184,800
Relationship bldg. $5	$500,000	$325,000	$231,000
Referral incentives $15	$0	$75,000	$63,000
Total costs	$19,670,000	$9,666,400	$6,907,068
Profit	($170,000)	$3,463,600	$2,748,732
Discount rate	1	1.2	1.44
NPV profit	($170,000)	$2,886,333	$1,908,842
Cumulative. NVP profit	($170,000)	$2,716,333	$4,625,175
Lifetime value	($1.70)	$27.16	$46.25

Figure 4-5. Lifetime value with new strategies.

Referrals have to be paid for. The relationship-building cards and messages cost money. When we get finished, lifetime value in the first year has gone down. But then the trend reverses—dramatically!

	Year 1	Year 2	Year 3
Current LTV	$1.25	$9.14	$12.69
New LTV	($1.70)	$27.16	$46.25
Difference	($2.95)	$18.02	$33.56
With 100,000 subscribers	($295,000)	$1,802,000	$3,356,175

Figure 4-6. Gains from the new strategies.

The total impact of the changes we have suggested will be to increase customer lifetime value by more than $3 million in the third year (see Figure 4-6). This is $3 million pure profit. All the costs have been subtracted. If we had been doing direct mail alone, the loss of $300,000 in the first year would have ruled out such a program. Since we are doing database marketing, we can look two years ahead and see the value of this program.

What to Do with the Charts

Once you have thought up your great new strategies and developed lifetime value charts that cost them out, you have several additional steps you can take.

- Try adding some customer benefits (and associated costs) and see if LTV goes up or down. Maybe there is more you can do.

- By testing, see if you can eliminate some customer benefits (and costs) and still keep LTV up. We are trying to build profitable relationships here. But keep the word *profitable* in mind. That is the point of the relationship-building process.

- When you have developed a benefit (and cost) package that you think is a winner, then discount your resulting LTV growth estimates by a percentage.

- Use these charts as a basis for getting your marketing budget approved. Explain the retention and referral rates to management. Explain the basis of the numbers. Show that with the budget you have requested, you will generate $3 million in increased profits in the third year.

Summary

- Profitability and loyalty are different customer attributes. They can come together in lifetime value.
- Banks and insurance companies can measure customer profitability exactly. Most companies cannot. They have to estimate costs.
- Customers should be segmented into at least five groups, from Gold down to the losers at the bottom.
- Gold customers are very valuable. Efforts should concentrate on retaining them, not marketing to them.
- Concentrating on the losers can have a big impact on the bottom line. Reprice their services, move them up, or get rid of them.
- Magazines offer an ideal example of advanced database marketing, including the Internet.
- Magazines can boost lifetime value using web pages, negative option renewals, referrals, sale of secondary products, personal communications, elimination of discounts, and advertiser premiums.
- LTV charts can be used to sell management, but only if they have been discounted first.

Executive Quiz 3

Answers to quiz questions can be found in Appendix B.

1. In segmenting customers by lifetime value:
   a. The segments should be of equal size.
   b. Profitability is the same as lifetime value.
   c. Gold customers offer the greatest marketing opportunity.
   d. Most companies can compute profitability.
   e. None of the above.

2. The bottom LTV segment may contain all but one of the following:
   a. Transaction buyers
   b. People who are just starting out in life
   c. Your most profitable customers
   d. Your competitor's Gold customers
   e. Temporarily unprofitable customers

3. Selling additional products to a customer is usually a good move because:

    a. The sale improves the retention rate.

    b. The sale improves the referral rate.

    c. The sale reduces the cost to serve.

    d. The sale is usually more valuable than the initial product.

    e. All of the above.

4. What is the best way to personalize a web site for each customer?

    a. By asking customers to enter their name each time they log on

    b. By using a PIN

    c. By using cookies

    d. By creating a unique URL for each customer

    e. By using e-mail

5. The negative option has all but one of these advantages:

    a. The retention rate is increased.

    b. The renewal problem is reduced.

    c. It is more profitable.

    d. It improves the acquisition rate.

    e. It increases the lifetime value.

6. What is the best way to improve referral messages?

    a. Provide a discount on the product.

    b. Let the referrer edit the message.

    c. Thank the referrer in advance.

    d. Sell additional products in the same message.

    e. Use fax rather than e-mail.

7. Referred customers tend to have all but one of the following:

    a. Higher retention rate

    b. Higher spending rate

    c. Higher acquisition costs

    d. Lower costs to serve

    e. None of the above

8. Why is discounting your product a bad idea?

  a. Your competitors can copy it.

  b. It focuses customer attention on price, not value.

  c. It costs money.

  d. It brings in the wrong kind of customers.

  e. All of the above.

5

Building Profits with Recency, Frequency, and Monetary Analysis

*Being measured continually is a tough lesson. In-
directly, it's cost-per-lead, or cost-per-sale, not some art
director's squinty-eyed aesthetic standard that counts.
And you learn very quickly that you can be wrong
about how you think people will react. When you put
it on the line this way, you become a different kind of
creative person.*

MIKE SLOSBERG
Wunderman Worldwide

Direct marketers have been using recency, frequency, and monetary
(RFM) analysis to predict customer behavior for more than 50 years. It
is one of the most powerful techniques available to a database marketer.
It is the basis for any model of customer behavior, and yet differs from
traditional modeling in that it requires no knowledge of statistics. It
does not require any appending of data. If you have a database of your
customers, with their purchase history, you can use RFM analysis right
now at virtually no cost. You don't need to hire a statistician.

There are two types of facts that you can learn about customers: who
they are (demographics) and what they do (behavior). In marketing, we
are trying to predict behavior. Accurate behavior predictions are essential to making profitable marketing decisions. The best predictor of
future behavior is past behavior. It beats demographics every time. If
you are planning to sell something to your customers, knowing that

some of them have bought several items worth $100 by mail recently is worth much more than knowing their age, income, home value, presence of children, or any other demographic information. RFM is pure behavior.

RFM only works with customer files. It cannot be used with prospects, because it requires knowledge of the customer's prior purchase history with you. Prospects, by definition, have no such history. Use of RFM to guide your communications will *always* improve profits over any other method. RFM works with consumer and with business-to-business customer files. It works with any type of industry in which you communicate with your customers for marketing purposes.

In this chapter, we will cover everything you need to know to make serious money using this technique. If you don't already use RFM, you will emerge from this chapter a much more professional marketer who can make your company a lot of money. We will begin by describing each of the three components of RFM, and then show you how you can increase your profits by segmenting your database into RFM cells and using these cells to direct your customer communications.

How to Code Your Customers by Recency

To code your customer base for recency, you need one vital piece of information in every customer's database record: the most recent purchase date. Every time you update your database, be sure that this date is updated as well. To create the recency code, you sort your entire database by this date, with the most recent at the top. Then you divide the database into five exactly equal parts—quintiles—which you number from 5 (the most recent) down to 1 (the most ancient). The coding process is shown in Figure 5-1. Once you have divided the database, you append a "5" to every record in the top group, a "4" to the records in the next group, etc. Every record in your database is now coded as a 5, 4, 3, 2, or 1 for recency.

This method of creating five divisions of exactly equal size (each equals 20 percent of the entire database) is called *exact quintiles*. However, there is another way of doing RFM, which has been around for a long time. This method is called *hard coding*. With hard coding, the top quintile is assigned an arbitrary date range, such as zero to three months. The next is three to six months, etc. Hard coding works, and is in active use in direct marketing operations all over the world. The

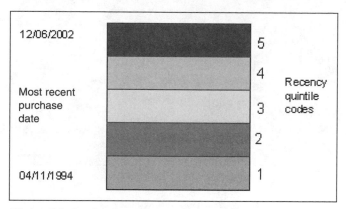

Figure 5-1. Sorting by recency.

exact quintile method, though, is a more accurate method, which you will see produces RFM cells of exactly equal size.

With exact quintiles, there is a certain arbitrary quality in the divisions. The dividing line between 5 and 4, for example, may occur on February 12. Because of the sorting process, some customers with a most recent date of February 12 may show up as 5s. Yet others with the same date can show up as 4s! Don't worry about it. Just do it. We are going to recalculate RFM codes every month, so any arbitrary number assigned this month will be corrected next month. Adjusting the boundaries every month is not worth the effort and ruins the accuracy of the result.

Now that your file is coded for recency, go ahead and do a promotion to your customer base. Not a special test promotion, but some communication that you had planned to do all along which calls on customers to respond or make a purchase. Keep track of which quintile every customer is in and which customers respond. If you do, you will have a response picture that will look very much like the one shown in Figure 5-2.

The customers coded with a 5 will respond much better than the 4s, who will be better than the 3s, etc. The recency code will accurately predict who is most likely to respond. These numbers, and all those used in the first part of this chapter, are from an actual promotion done recently by a database marketer who had a customer database of 2.1 million names, going back over a 5-year period. The customers were offered a video package that cost them about $100, including shipping and handling charges. The graph represents the responses to a test mailing to 30,000 of these 2.1 million names.

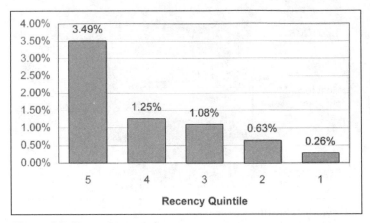

Figure 5-2. Response rates by recency.

If you add these response rates together, you will note that only 402 people, or 1.34 percent of the customers, responded to the offer. The percentages in the five columns add up to 6.71 percent. Dividing this by 5 gives you the 1.34 percent for the overall response. This means that 98.66 percent of the customers did not respond. This is normal. You will almost always experience the same type of response rates, somewhat better or worse, unless you have a highly unusual offer. What this marketer found, and you also will find, is that recency is a very powerful predictor of response. The 5s responded almost three times better than the 4s.

Why is recency so powerful in predicting behavior? Think about it. I recently bought a new Honda Odyssey—a really great car. I am out on my first day on the road in this wonderful vehicle. I am looking all around. What am I looking for? Another Honda Odyssey. If I see one, I want to honk my horn and wave. "Hey, I've got one too! Aren't they great?"

Everyone in the world feels a rush of enthusiasm when purchasing a new car, house, suit, or dress. The feeling lasts for a while. If you were to open a checking account with the Fleet Bank this week, and next week you get a letter from the Fleet Bank, you are going to open that letter. Maybe it is something about your new account. But if you have had an account with Fleet for the past five years, and next week you get a letter from Fleet that is obviously not your monthly statement, you may well chuck it out. It is just another credit card solicitation. In other words, recent buyers will respond. Ancient buyers may not. Recency works. It is a universal human emotion that we may count on in designing our marketing programs.

So we have learned how to code our database for recency. Just sort the file by most recent date, divide it into five exactly equal parts. Code them as 5, 4, 3, 2, and 1, and check the codes on the responses after any promotion. We have learned something. But before we devote more time to exploring recency, let's explain frequency.

How to Code Your File for Frequency

To code a database for frequency we need another piece of information in every customer record. It is a number: the total number of times that the customer has made a purchase from you.

Figure 5-3 shows an example of sorting by frequency. This chart is compiled from sorting the database by the total purchases made by each customer from you. There are many ways to measure frequency: by the average number of purchases per year, the average number of products bought per year, the average number of telephone calls made per month (for a phone company), the total number of checks and deposits made during a month (for a bank). You may experiment to find the best measure for you. What you are looking for is a measure of how important doing business with you is in the minds of your customers, measured by frequency of use of your products or services. Once you have added such a code to each customer record (and updated on a regular basis), you should sort your database by that number, divide it into five

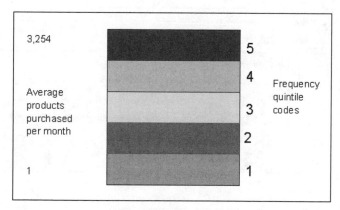

Figure 5-3. Sorting by frequency.

equal parts, and put quintile codes into each database record. The process is identical to that for recency.

If, then, you do a promotion to your existing customer base and keep track of the frequency quintile that each customer belonged to at the time of the promotion, you will get a graph of response rates that looks like the one shown in Figure 5-4. This figure shows the same 402 customers whom we graphed by recency in Figure 5-2, here graphed by frequency quintile. What this illustrates is that frequency is also a good predictor of behavior, but much less so than recency. If you look at Figure 5-2, the graph of the recency response, you will see how dramatic the response rate of the 5s was. In Figure 5-4, the frequency slope from 5 down to 1 is much more gentle. This is generally true of frequency codes. That is why RFM is RFM instead of FRM or FMR.

Something else is interesting here, shown by the diagonal line on the graph. Something is wrong with the lowest frequency quintile. The response rate is 0.93 percent. But if it were to follow the trend of the other frequency divisions, the response rate should be less than 0.5 percent. This is not an accident. You will undoubtedly have the same result when you graph your own customer response by frequency. Why do the 1s on a frequency graph respond better than one would suppose?

The answer is that the lowest quintile on a frequency chart contains an abnormal number of recent buyers. A customer who just joined you yesterday is your most recent buyer. So that customer's recency code is 5. Recent buyers are your best responders. But this recent buyer, being brand new, has not had a chance to become a frequent buyer yet, so the

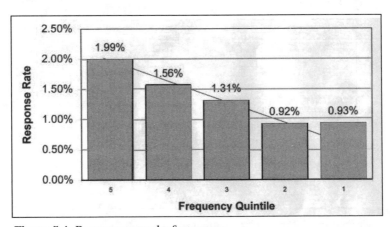

Figure 5-4. Response rates by frequency.

buyer's frequency code is 1. You probably can't make any money with this universal fact, but it does serve to prove to you that you have done your RFM coding correctly. If your lowest quintile on frequency is not higher than the trend, as shown in Figure 5-4, then you have probably done something wrong.

Response by Monetary Amount

Finally, let's graph these same people by their monetary spending. The method is the same. We keep in everyone's database record a single piece of information: the total amount spent on our products or services, either per month, per year, or in some other way. We are trying to determine the monetary significance of our company to each of our customers, as measured in dollars. We will take these data, and sort the entire database by this number, divide the database into five equal groups, and assign code numbers: 5, 4, 3, 2, and 1.

As shown in Figure 5-5, we have sorted the entire file of customers arranged by monetary amount and assigned monetary codes. The best customer has purchased an average of $12,456 per month. The customer spending the least has bought only $10 per month. These amounts are stored in the customer's database record every time the customer makes a purchase. We sort the entire file by this amount. Let's

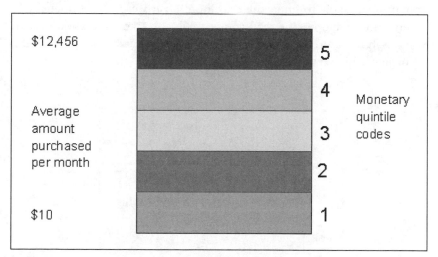

Figure 5-5. Sorting customers by monetary amount.

see what happens when we look at the monetary response rate of these same 402 people whom we already graphed by recency and frequency. The results are shown in Figure 5-6.

When you look at Figure 5-6, remember that the 5s represent people who spend a lot of money with your company. The 1s spend very little. Monetary coding is far less predictive of behavior than either recency or frequency. While there is a gentle slope from the 5s down to the 1s, it is not really very dramatic. It is almost flat. What this means is that on small-ticket items, monetary amount is not very predictive. In today's market, a small-ticket consumer item would be something that sells for about $120 or less—say, a video. A big-ticket item would be something that sells for $1,000 or more. Let's take the case of the video. Suppose this small-ticket item sold for $100. The monetary response rate would look like that shown in Figure 5-6.

Imagine two of your customers: one who spends a million dollars a year on your category of products and one who spends only a thousand dollars per year. Is there any reason to believe that the million-dollar customer would be more likely to open your envelope containing your promotions than the thousand-dollar guy? No. In fact, I would say that the million-dollar customer would be less likely to open the envelope. Why? Because, as a million-dollar guy, he is on everyone's list. Everyone writes to him. He, or his secretary, checks his mail with the wastebasket near at hand. The thousand-dollar guy gets far less mail. He is probably much more likely to open the envelope. So if we go by propensity to open your envelopes (or read your e-mails, or take your phone calls), the graph in Figure 5-6 would have exactly the opposite shape, with the 1s having a higher response rate than the 5s.

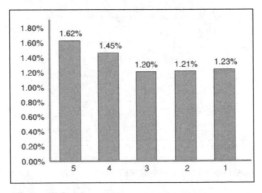

Figure 5-6. Monetary response rates.

But once the envelope is opened, the million-dollar guy can write out a check for whatever is in that envelope, but the thousand-dollar guy will have to think it over. It may not be within his budget. So if we are going to go by ability to pay, the 5s will have a very high response rate, and the 1s will be very low. Thus the final monetary graph is a combination of two opposite human emotions: willingness to open the envelope and ability to pay. That is why the monetary graph for low-ticket items tends to be almost flat. The money does not matter.

That is not true of big-ticket items. If you are selling something for, say, $5,000, then the ability to pay will overwhelm the opening of the envelope and give you a completely different monetary graph. Figure 5-7 shows the response rate of a bank in New York, which made a $5,000 certificate of deposit offer to its 250,000 most affluent customers. In this graph, the monetary response rates look almost like recency response rates. You will have the same experience. If you offer customers a commodity or service with a high price, the high monetary quintiles will respond much better than the low ones.

Putting It All Together

Thus far, we have learned the theory of RFM, which is based on three aspects of customer behavior. The theory does not show how we can make money with this knowledge. That is what we are going to do right now.

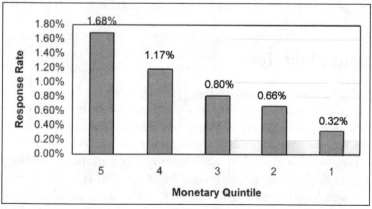

Figure 5-7. Response to bank CD offer by monetary quintile.

When the coding process is finished, every customer should have in his or her database records three single digits: one for recency, one for frequency, and one for monetary. Every customer is either a 555, 554, 553, 552, 551, 545, 544, . . . , down to 111. There are 125 RFM cell codes in all. (Later in this chapter, you will learn that you can work with higher or lower numbers than 125.)

When you do promotions to your customers, therefore, you keep track of the RFM cell code that each is occupying. The results can be very interesting. Let's see how the company we have been following so far in this chapter coded its database for RFM and did a test of its offer to 30,000 of its 2.1 million customers.

Selecting an *N*th

The test group was selected using an *N*th. An *N*th is a test group that is an exact statistical replica of the full database. For example, if a database had 300,000 customers, and we wanted to select a test group of 30,000 using an *N*th, we would divide the 30,000 into the 300,000, giving the result of 10. We need to select every tenth record from the master database to create the test group. We will select record 1, 11, 21, 31, 41, 51 . . . taking every tenth record. The resulting test file will have 30,000 members and will exactly mirror the main database. It will have the same percentage of people whose zip code is 22203, whose income is over $100,000, who have two children, etc., as the main database. It does not matter whether the main file is sorted in alphabetical order, in zip code order, or in customer number order; the results will be the same, providing we are dealing with large numbers, such as 30,000.

Results of the Test

When the company mailed the $100 offer to its 30,000-person test group, it got the results shown in Figure 5-8. In the figure, the horizontal (*X*) axis represents the RFM cell codes of each of the 125 cells mailed in the test. The vertical (*Y*) axis represents the breakeven index of each cell. Breakeven is explained in the following paragraph. From the graph in Figure 5-8, we can see that only 34 of the 125 cells did better than breakeven. The remainder lost money. Let's take a moment to explain breakeven.

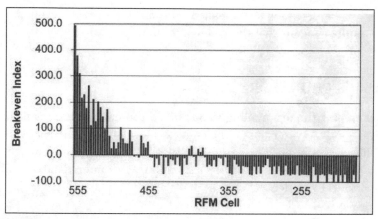

Figure 5-8. Results of test mailing to 30,000 customers.

How Breakeven Is Calculated

Breakeven in direct marketing means that the net profit from sales to a test group exactly equals the cost of promoting that test group. If, for example, we mail 400 people at a cost of $0.50 each, or $200, and the net profit (after credits, returns, cost of goods sold, shipping, etc.) is $200, then we have just broken even. Before we begin a promotion, we can calculate the response rate we will need to get from each cell to breakeven. There is a neat little formula that tells us this breakeven (BE) response rate. It is

$$BE = (cost per piece) / (net profit from a single sale)$$

In the case of the $100 video offer, the company calculated that it made $40 on each successful sale. The cost per piece of the mailing was $0.55. So the rate needed for breakeven on each RFM cell was

$$BE = (\$0.55) / \$40 = 1.375\%$$

The *breakeven index* (BEI) is calculated by another neat little formula:

$$BEI = [(r - BE)/BE] \times 100$$

In this formula, r = the actual response rate of the RFM cell. So if the response rate of one cell is 2.5 percent, then the breakeven index is

$$BEI = [(0.025 - 0.01375) / (0.01375)] \times 100 = 81.82$$

A breakeven index of 0 means that the cell just broke even. A negative number means that the cell lost money.

Results of the Test

In summary, the test mailing to 30,000 customers had the result shown in Table 5-1. As you can see, the company lost $420 on the test. Was that a failure? Not at all. For a net cost of $420 the company learned how 30,000 customers, an *N*th of its 2.1 million customer database, would respond to this offer.

Table 5-1.

	Number	Rate	Dollars
Sales	402	$40	$16,080
Mailing	30,000	$0.55	$16,500
Net loss			($420)

Since the 30,000 was an *N*th, these customers were completely representative of how the entire database would have responded to this same offer. The company then knew which RFM cells would be profitable and which RFM cells would be losers. As a result, it did not mail the offer to the entire database of 2.1 million. Instead, it selected customers from the 34 profitable RFM cells on the rollout. (It also selected a small number of customers from each of the unprofitable cells just to be sure that it had done the coding correctly.)

Table 5-2 shows the selection process. The first column is the test file results. The second column shows what would have happened if the company had mailed the full database of 2.1 million. It would have lost about $164,000. The appendix to this chapter explains why the response rate to the full file is estimated at only 1.17 percent instead of the 1.34 percent achieved on the test. The third column shows what the company actually mailed on its rollout. The company selected customers out of the 2.1 million who were in the 34 RFM cells that were shown to be profitable on the test. There were 554,182 of these folks. Mailing only to them, the company got an overall response rate of 2.76 percent and a net profit of $307,000. This shows the full power of RFM. You profit by *not promoting* people who you have learned are unlikely to respond.

Table 5-2.

	Test	Full File	RFM Select
Response rate	1.34%	1.17%	2.76%
Responses	402	23,412	15,295
Average profit	$40	$40	$40
Net revenue	$16,080	$936,480	$611,800
No. mailed	30,000	2,001,056	554,182
Cost per piece	$0.55	$0.55	$0.55
Mailing cost	$16,500	$1,100,581	$304,800
Profits	($420)	($164,101)	$307,000

What happened when the company mailed these 544,182 people? That is the most exciting result of this entire case study. Look at Figure 5-9, which compares the actual response rates of the 30,000 people in the 34 successful RFM cells on the test with the 554,182 people mailed on the RFM selected rollout.

Each bar on this graph (the X axis) represents one of the RFM cell code numbers of the 34 cells mailed on the test which were profitable. The percentages on the left (the Y axis) of this graph are the actual response rates of the profitable cells on the test and the corresponding cells mailed in the rollout. The vertical bars are the response rates of the 34 profitable cells in the test. The lines and dots are response rates of the 544,182 people from those same profitable cells which were mailed

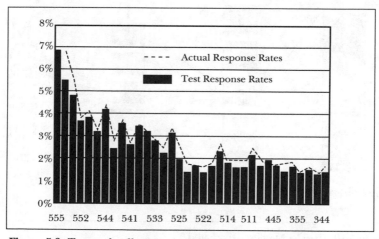

Figure 5-9. Test and rollout response rates.

on the selected rollout. It is uncanny how accurately RFM predicted the response of these people. This is why RFM through the years has been selected as the most profitable method for doing customer promotions. It works. And it costs almost nothing to use. All the graphs and methods explained so far in this chapter can be understood by any marketer with no knowledge of statistics. We do, however, have to let you in on a secret that we have been withholding up to this point.

How RFM Sorting Is Done

The RFM sorting is a little more complicated than the earlier sections of this chapter have implied. From the early sections, you got the idea that you would sort your database once for recency, once for frequency, and once for monetary. That is true, and it will work to produce the results shown on the R, F, and M graphs presented in this chapter. But when you come to create the three-digit RFM cells used in the test and rollout shown previously, you use a slightly more complicated RFM sorting scheme. You have to sort your database 31 times. Figure 5-10 shows how.

To create RFM cells, you sort the database once by recency, dividing the database into five equal parts. Assign a 5, 4, 3, 2, or 1 to all the members of each of the recency quintiles. Then sort each of these 5 quintiles

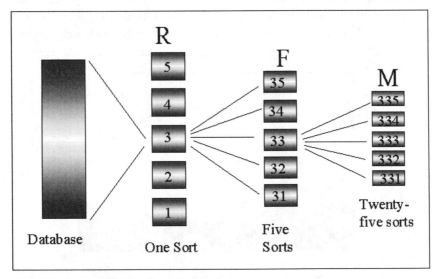

Figure 5-10. How RFM cells are created.

by frequency, dividing each into 5 groups, and assigning the members of each group a 5, 4, 3, 2, or 1. Finally, each of these 25 groups is sorted again by monetary. It seems complicated, and it is. But computers can do this with ease. The result of this process is that every RFM cell has exactly the same number of customers in it as every other RFM cell. This becomes very useful for comparing RFM performance and selecting the appropriate customers for promotions.

Paul Wang and I have been teaching database marketing principles, including RFM, in two-day seminars for the Database Marketing Institute since 1993. In each seminar, marketers ask us, "Is there software that does this RFM sorting job?" At first we said no, and told them to ask their MIS departments to do the job. But after a while it became obvious that many marketers could not get sufficient help to create RFM cell codes. We decided to create some software to help them out. The result is *RFM for Windows*, which is available from the Institute. Many alumni of the Institute use this software in their work. They share with us reports of their promotions to customers. From these reports, we learn a great deal about customer response. The data for all of the graphics in this chapter have been obtained from alumni who are users of this software. You can get a free copy of this software on the Internet by clicking on www.dbmarketing.com and downloading it.

RFM with a Consumable Product

One alumnus of the Institute worked for a company that sold personalized checks. The company had a database of 600,000 customers. The alumnus coded the database for RFM using the methods shown in this chapter. Then he did a promotion to 45,000 customers selected using an Nth. The results, shown in Figure 5-11, were very surprising. As you can see, the response rates for the most recent quintile were lower than those for the second quintile. When I saw that, I wondered if there was something wrong with the theory. How could this be? Then I realized that this company sells a consumable product. The most recent buyers had not yet run low on the product, so they did not order as many. So, I wondered, did the company mail too soon? Should it have waited for these recent buyers to run low?

To verify that, I looked at the total sales by recency quintile. Once more I was surprised by the results, shown in Figure 5-12.

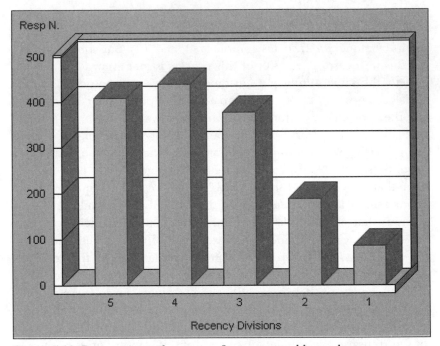

Figure 5-11. Response rates by recency for a consumable product.

The graph represents the same people, arranged differently. The most recent buyers purchased even more than the next quintile, even though their response rate was lower. What I had not counted on was that recent buyers tend to place larger orders. Since then, I have verified this finding with other alumni. Recent buyers not only have higher response rates, but tend to buy more per order, and tend also to buy higher-priced options. Further analysis showed that both frequency and monetary could be used to increase profits for this company. We discovered that, in general, for most products:

■ The highest frequency quintile buys much more than the lower quintiles.

■ The highest monetary quintile places much bigger orders than lower quintiles.

This company's breakeven rate by RFM cell was quite different from that of the company with the video offer. The company with the consumable product had 72 profitable cells out of 125, as shown in Figure 5-13.

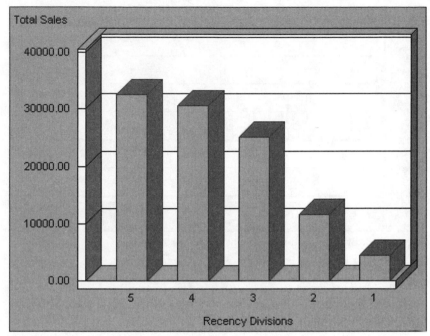

Figure 5-12. Total sales by recency for a consumable product.

At this point, you understand the theory behind RFM. RFM helps you to determine which of your customers will respond and how much they will buy. It is a wonderfully powerful tool.

RFM for Business-to-Business Files

RFM was originally invented primarily for consumer database files. It works well there. It also works with most business-to-business files. Federal Express, for example, has made highly profitable use of RFM in segmenting its business customers. Most business-to-business files are much smaller than consumer files. Many business customer files are well below 20,000. How can such a company make profitable use of RFM? There are two factors to consider.

- *For a small file, 125 cells are too many cells.* The number 125 comes about by multiplying 5 recency divisions by 5 frequency by 5 monetary. Dividing a small business file of 20,000 records by 125 gives you

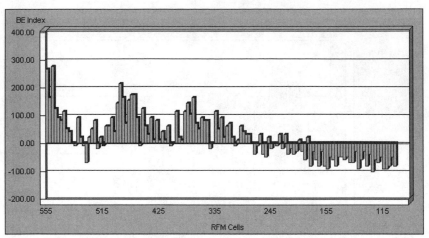

Figure 5-13. Breakeven index for consumable product test.

only 160 customers in each cell. This is too small for accurate statistical results. For a business file of 20,000 records, therefore, there probably should not be more than 20 RFM cells, each one having about 1,000 companies in it. To get down to 20 cells, the RFM should be created by reducing the frequency and monetary divisions like this:

5 recency × 2 frequency × 2 monetary = 20 RFM cells

If experience shows that monetary is very important in the sales of the business (the company sells big-ticket items), then the division might be changed to

4 recency × 2 frequency × 3 monetary = 24 RFM cells

There are many ways of doing RFM. Users will have to experiment to see which works best for their situation.

■ *RFM does not beat a sales visit.* RFM is not too useful for those customers being called on by the sales force. The sales force knows far more about the customers than can be learned from an RFM analysis. However, most businesses have their sales force calling on only the top 20 percent of their customers, leaving the remaining 80 percent to be dealt with by catalogs, letters, e-mail, and phone calls. If this is the situation in your company, RFM is perfect for helping to manage the 80 percent that do not rate a sales visit. It will tell you which customers are most likely to respond to a phone call, an e-mail, a fax, or a letter.

RFM and Modeling

How does RFM compare with modeling? A while ago I had a public debate in *DM News Magazine* with Jim Wheaton, an expert on modeling. Jim maintained in an article that RFM was kudzu, meaning that it was crude and unsophisticated compared with modeling. He pointed out, correctly, that most models do a more accurate job of finding responsive customers than straight RFM.

My response was this. Any good model of customer behavior always includes recency, frequency, and monetary amount. They are the most important available measures of customer performance. Models, however, go beyond RFM to include demographics, product selection, and other factors. Some of these other factors do help in predicting customer response, so a good model, properly run, can outperform RFM. The problem is that models are expensive and difficult to run. To run a model you usually have to hire a statistician (or use one on your staff). You have to buy or obtain demographic data and append them to your file. A good model takes a week or two to run—some companies have spent more than six weeks to get a perfect model run. The cost of the modeling professional, the data appending, and the modeling software, plus the time involved, may run the cost of a model from $25,000 to $200,000, depending on who is doing it and what is involved.

To decide which is better, you have to consider the economics. The purpose of both modeling and RFM is the same: to increase profits. Modeling is usually expensive. RFM is almost free of charge. Any marketing professional can understand it and use it. The software for creating the RFM cells can be bought for permanent use for as little as $1,500. You can use it over and over again without paying a fee to anyone. Models quickly get out of date. A $25,000 model needs to be run every six months or more often as the market changes and competition heats up. So to determine whether to use a model, you must accept the idea not only that the model has to be more accurate than RFM (which it probably is) but also that it gives you enough lift in response to pay for the model, plus beating the RFM lift. Except in the case of very large databases, this is seldom true.

Elsewhere in this book, you will find a number of case studies of companies that make major use of RFM in their marketing program. The studies include Sears Canada and Federal Express. RFM is being used by catalogers, retailers, hotels, airlines, banks, insurance companies, cellular phone companies, and high-tech manufacturers. There are tens of thousands of active users in the United States and Canada. If you have not used it yet, you should look into it, because it will definitely improve your response rates and build your profits.

When Not to Use RFM

Using RFM is like taking drugs. It gives you such a high that you want to use it all the time. That would be a mistake. If you use RFM to decide whom to write to or whom to call, some of your customers will never hear from you at all. On the other hand, the more responsive customers may suffer from file fatigue: You will communicate with them too often.

You should develop a customer contact strategy. Figure something valuable that you want to communicate to your less responsive customers once or twice a year just to let them know that you haven't forgotten them. Birthday and holiday cards are useful. Thank-you cards are always in season. But don't bother nonresponsive people with continual offers.

Database marketing is meant to be profitable for both the buyer and the seller. If you lose money, it is not profitable for you. If your customers do not respond, you have wasted their time sending them something that they do not want. You have cheapened your reputation and relationship with them, forcing them to reject you. Save your promotional dollars for situations in which both you and your customers are likely to win. It is a favor to both the buyer and the seller.

Imagine a friend or an associate at work who tells you about a good thing, perhaps a vacation spot that you visit. Later, however, he begins to suggest other things that are not so helpful. He invites you to play poker every Thursday night. He tries to convince you to buy a time-share condominium. His wife tries to sell you life insurance. He wants to play handball or golf two times a week. You politely turn down each of these offers, but you are getting a little sick of them. You try to avoid eye contact when you run across him, and dread that it is he who is calling when the phone rings. This isn't a relationship; it's a damn nuisance.

This is what it is like to be on the receiving end of a large string of unwanted offers from your company. Don't send them. Use RFM to save money and your customers' time, while building goodwill with other customers by sending them offers that they appreciate.

When Should You Use RFM?

Now that you have learned about RFM and have coded your customer base with RFM cell codes, you are in a position to make serious money any time that you want. If management comes to you and asks you to introduce a new product, you know exactly which customers are most likely to respond to your offer, and which are less likely. You can amaze your management with your success rates.

Another time to use RFM is during budget season. Once a year, database marketers typically have to justify their marketing program to management for the coming year. One of the best ways to do that is by customer lifetime value analysis, described in Chapter 3. Another useful step is to do a customer promotion to high-responding RFM cells a couple of months before your budget comes up for review. You can bring in a lot of sales with very little promotional expense if you just promote the highest-ranking customers. RFM can open a whole new world for you, at very little expense.

Summary

- Recency, frequency, and monetary (RFM) analysis is based on customer behavior. It is used to predict which customers will respond to a promotion and which will not. It is easy to understand, easy to use, and very inexpensive. No knowledge of statistics, or models, or appending of purchased data is required. It uses your own customer purchase data. It works only with customer data, not prospect data.

- Recency is the most powerful predictor of customer response, Frequency is next. Monetary does not predict well with small-value items. It predicts well with expensive products and services.

- To make money with RFM, you code your customer base with RFM cell codes using software that you can write yourself, following the rules given in this chapter. If you don't have a programmer available, you can obtain RFM software from the Database Marketing Institute at www.dbmarketing.com.

■ The profits from RFM come from *not* mailing (or calling) customers shown by the RFM analysis as unlikely to respond. Your profits come from a reduction in mailing or telemarketing costs.

■ RFM is widely used in industry, particularly in cataloging, insurance, banks, telephone services, and manufacturing.

■ For business-to-business marketing, RFM must be modified, since the customer files are much smaller. Instead of 125 RFM cells, you can have as few as 20 or less. The principles, however, are exactly the same, and just as profitable

■ There are formulas for the breakeven response rate and the minimum test cell size.

Appendix: Frequently Asked Questions about RFM

How Big Do RFM Test Cells Have to Be to Get Accurate Predictions?

There are two contradictory goals in creating RFM cells. You want them as large as possible so that tests with the cells will be statistically accurate. On the other hand, you want them to be as small as possible to keep the costs of tests down.

To put this question into perspective: If each cell contained 100 people and you had 20 cells, you could conduct tests of 2,000 people and use the results to predict the behavior of a database of 1 million. Since profitable response rates are often 2 percent or less, the accuracy of the 100-member cells would rest on the responses of 2 people. That is much too small for accurate predictions. The 2 people involved could be on vacation that week and throw off your count.

On the other hand, if each cell in a test contained 6,000 customers, then each test would be highly accurate. But an RFM test that used 125 cells at 6,000 each would involve mailing to 750,000 people. It would cost you $300,000 at $0.40 each. That type of test is too expensive for even the largest mailer. Somewhere in between 100 and 6,000 is the right size for each single RFM cell. There is a simple formula that tells you the right size.

To begin with, you must assure that your overall test is large enough to test the offer. Such a test would usually involve enough responses to be sure you had a winning proposition. For a business-to-business situation, that size could be as small as 5,000. For a consumer mailing, the test might be 30,000 or more. But the question we are dealing with is, how large should each cell within the test be? Based on the breakeven rate already explained in this chapter, the formula for the minimum test cell size is

$$\text{Minimum RFM test cell size} = 4 \ / \ \text{BE}$$

where BE = breakeven response rate. What is the "4"? It is a rule of thumb. Use it. It works. If your breakeven rate on a promotion is 1.76 percent, then your minimum test cell size is

$$\text{Test cell size} = 4 \ / \ 0.0176 = 231 \text{ customers}$$

Why Use Quintiles for RFM Cells? Why Not Deciles?

Deciles (creating 10 recency divisions, 10 frequency divisions, and 10 monetary divisions) are a possible RFM method that some have used. It makes for a very large group of RFM cells ($10 \times 10 \times 10 = 1,000$), which can be used only for the largest consumer files. It has certain obvious drawbacks. Each test is very expensive. If your minimum test size is 231 customers in each cell, as shown above, then each test will require mailing to 231,000 people. That is too expensive a test for anybody. So the answer to the question is that deciles are great for scientific accuracy, but useless for practical testing purposes. Stick to something simple that works. Use quintiles, or smaller numbers.

For many files, quintiles may be too large. As already pointed out, for a business-to-business file of 12,000 names, for example, you would not want to have more than about 20 cells, not 125. You can figure out your distribution by seeing which of the divisions (R, F, or M) turn out to be the most predictive for you. If monetary amount is very important, then $2 \times 2 \times 5 = 20$ might be the way to go.

I like to use a budget calculation. If you have a large file but management has given you a test budget of only $12,000, then you would figure your RFM cells this way. Suppose your mailing costs are $0.50 each. For $12,000 you can only mail 24,000 pieces. If your minimum test cell size is 240 customers, then you can have only 100 cells (24,000 / 240 = 100). So you would create your RFM divisions as 5 × 5 × 4 = 100.

How Do You Measure Recency with Continuity Products?

Most people use their telephones, electric service, bank accounts, credit cards, and newspapers every day. Most people pay their bills once a month. What constitutes recency in such situations? The answer is different in each case. What we are trying to get at is "The last time that the customer made a business decision concerning your company's services." It could be the last time that the customer opened a new product account, or changed his or her service, or moved. Keep your eye on the goal: We are trying to predict behavior. You will have to experiment with various events to determine which is the most predictive of response rates.

How Do You Measure Frequency of Purchase?

Frequency is the stepchild. Recency is independent. Monetary is independent. But frequency is closely related both to monetary and to recency. It is halfway in between. One customer spent $2,400 two years ago and has not bought since. Another spent $100 per month for the last 24 months. They have both spent $2,400 with you. Which is the best customer?. I would say that the second customer is far better. You are maintaining contact and have hope for future sales, and increased sales.

How is frequency measured? What units should be used? There are many possibilities:

- A cataloger or retailer can measure the number of purchases in a year or the number of items ordered.
- A bank can measure the number of checks written and the number of deposits made.

- A hotel can measure the number of trips or the number of nights stayed.

- A telephone company can measure the number of calls or the number of minutes talked.

- An electric utility can measure the number of months in service or the number of kilowatt-hours used per month.

Each of these industries has several possible ways of measuring frequency. *Which is the best frequency measurement?* There is no universal answer, but there is a universal method of finding the answer. The universal method is this: Test each of several possible methods and see which of them does the best job of predicting actual response rates.

- Identify two or more possible measurements of frequency, such as number of purchases or number of items purchased. Use each method to develop separate RFM scores. File both in your customer database.

- Carry out any regularly scheduled promotion to your customer base, but keep track of the frequency quintile that each customer is located in. When the responses come in, append them to the database, and draw a graph of the results.

- The correct measurement is the one that produces the most predictive graph. A predictive graph is one in which there is a dramatic difference between the response rates of each quintile. Figure 5-7 is very predictive. Figure 5-6 is not.

The cost of testing is almost nothing, and you will get some very interesting results. Take, for example, the New York bank, which sold $5,000 certificates of deposit, and was described earlier in this chapter. The marketing director tested one measure of frequency, and obtained the results shown on the graph in Figure 5-14. The graph seemed to make no sense. Why would the best responders be those whose frequency is in the third quintile, and the lowest response rate be from those in the top quintile? When I saw this graph, I called the marketing director at the bank right away and asked her what she had done to create this monstrosity.

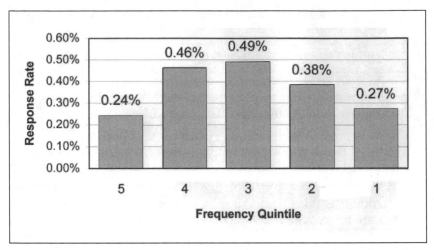

Figure 5-14. Bank CD response rates by frequency with ATM usage.

"I did just what you told me," she said, "adding together the number of deposits and checks written per month. Then, because the data were available, I added in the number of times that the customer had used the ATM each month. That was how I measured frequency."

At first, her explanation seemed to make sense to me, and I wondered if my understanding of frequency was flawed. But after a while, I figured it out. She was selling a product whose minimum price was $5,000. I asked her, "Do people who can afford a $5,000 CD tend to make extensive use of ATMs?"

She pondered this question and did a little research. What she discovered was that higher-income people tend to use ATMs less often than lower-income people. By adding ATM usage as a frequency measurement, she was mixing in a contrary factor: a behavior that was the opposite of the desired response—purchase of a high-dollar CD. After learning this, we redid her calculations, taking out the ATM usage. We ended up with the graph shown in Figure 5-15.

Why is this graph better? Because the measure selected for frequency of use more accurately predicted who actually responded to the offer. These response rates are low: The highest is only one-half of 1 percent. But for the bank, the rates were high enough to make the overall promotion profitable. Use of the correct frequency measurement enabled the bank to drop close to 100,000 customers from its next CD promo-

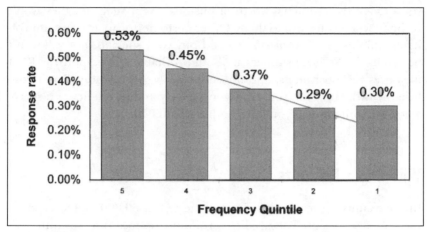

Figure 5-15. Bank CD frequency response rates without ATM usage.

tion, getting almost the same amount of sales, but greatly increasing the profits to the bank.

Does RFM Measure Profitability?

Only very indirectly. There are really two different customer behaviors: responsiveness and profitability (scc Figure 5-16). Some customers give

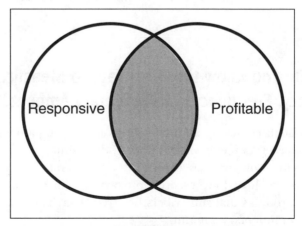

Figure 5-16. Responsive versus profitable customers.

you thousands of dollars' worth of business every year, but they won't respond when you write to them. Other customers who are very unprofitable will answer all your surveys and buy your specials, but still won't be profitable. Some customers are both profitable and responsive. RFM measures responsiveness, and not, necessarily, profitability. Don't confuse the two. However, you can use monetary and frequency as a surrogate for profitability if you have nothing better to use.

Why Don't Rollouts Do as Well as Tests?

In the example given in this chapter, the test of 30,000 had a response rate of 1.34 percent. The predicted rollout response rate was only 1.17 percent. Why was the rollout rate expected to be lower? In fact, most marketers find that rollout rates are quite often lower than test rates. There are a number of valid reasons for this, but the most compelling is that marketers just cannot leave well enough alone. Marketers hate to have unsuccessful tests. So they do things for the test that they could not afford to do for the rollout. They may use the best list, or mail first class, or mail at the ideal time. When the rollout comes, they find that they have to economize, so they get a lower overall response rate.

Because that is so, when you are estimating your response rate after a test, be sure to discount it by a factor of, say, 10 percent. If you do that, and the rollout is better than you predicted, you will look like a hero. If it is worse, people will think that you are not such a good marketer after all.

How Do You Know the Best Ways to Measure Recency, Frequency, and Monetary Amount?

This problem comes up a lot, and leads many companies to abandon RFM because they feel it will not work in their situation. For example, if you are a magazine with a standard subscription rate, everyone pays the same price. So how do you score monetary amount? *Answer:* Keep track of other products that subscribers buy from you. These will create differences in monetary amount.

For recency, electric utilities complain that everyone uses electricity all the time, so their most recent date for everyone is yesterday. No problem. Use other measures, such as the last time that the customer changed his service or bought some new product from you. Either of these will work as the recency date.

Frequency is also a problem in many cases. Use whatever measures you have, such as number of months or years as a customer.

The basic rule is to be creative. You are trying to determine how important the products and services of your company are to each customer. If you are debating between two possible measures, use them both and develop two RFM scores for each customer. Keep them in the customer's record. Then, the next time you run a promotion to your members, see which RFM system does the best job of predicting behavior. That analysis will tell you which method to use.

Executive Quiz 4

Answers to quiz questions can be found in Appendix B.

1. Your cost per piece for a promotion is $0.72. The net profit on the average sale is $60. What response rate do you need to achieve to breakeven in an RFM cell?

   a. 0.012%

   b. 0.12%

   c. 1.2%

   d. 12%

   e. None of the above

2. Which of the following RFM cells will probably have the best response rate to a mailed promotion?

   a. 311

   b. 444

   c. 231

   d. 211

   e. 333

3. If you mail a promotion to 30,000 customers and 510 respond, what is the response rate?

   a. 510%

   b. 58.8%

   c. 1.7%

   d. 2.7%

   e. 170%

4. Which best predicts the response of existing customers to your next promotion?

   a. Modeling based on demographics

   b. Customer satisfaction analysis

   c. Affinity analysis

   d. RFM analysis

   e. Telephone surveys

5. In predicting response using RFM, in most cases, which is the most powerful predictor?

   a. Frequency

   b. Total monetary spending

   c. Recency

   d. Frequency and monetary override recency

   e. None of the above

6. To code your customer file with RFM codes, you must:

    a. Use demographic modeling

    b. Sort and segment the file several times

    c. Discount each RFM cell response rate by a fixed percentage

    d. Determine the breakeven rate for each customer

    e. None of the above

7. RFM analysis:

    a. Is useful with prospect files

    b. Can be used on either prospect or customer files

    c. Is based on customer demographics

    d. Usually requires help from an outside consultant

    e. None of the above

8. In RFM rollouts after a test, the rollout response rate, normally:

    a. Is not as good as the test

    b. Is about the same as the test

    c. Is much better than the test

    d. Cannot be predicted in advance

    e. None of the above

9. If your customer file is 6,000 names, how many RFM cells can you usefully create?

    a. 240

    b. 125

    c. 120

    d. 60

    e. 20

10. What is the best way to measure frequency?

    a. Use a focus group.

    b. Consult a modeling expert.

    c. See which existing data best predict actual response.

    d. Append data from outside files.

    e. None of the above.

6

Communicating with Customers

Any communication, irrespective of whether or not there is a promotional offer, will increase visits. . . . However, the right promotional offer to the right recipient at the right time will dramatically increase response.

JUDD GOLDFEDER
The Customer Connection

Communications with customers can be very profitable. One of the best examples of this was an experiment done with the customers of a manufacturer of lighting products. This manufacturer sold only to contractors and builders. He sent out 45,000 catalogs per year, receiving orders through a bank of operators on a toll-free number. Business was good.

A consultant from Hunter Business Direct in Milwaukee persuaded the manufacturer to try a test. They took the top 1,200 customers and divided them into two exactly equal groups of 600 each. One was the test group, and the other was the control group. They set up a two-person staff to work with the test group. One person was a customer relations specialist, and the other was a lighting engineer. The job of this two-person staff was to contact the decision makers at each of the 600 test companies to build a relationship with them. The two-person staff:

- Followed up on bids and quotes
- Scheduled product training
- Reminded customers of product specials

- Asked about their customers' needs
- Offered product comparison information
- Provided new product information

They did not offer discounts.

The 600 in the control group received none of these things. They got the same excellent treatment that all other customers had always gotten: an alert and helpful inbound order-taking staff.

What was the result of six months' worth of communications with the test group compared with the control group? In the first place, the retention rate of the test group was slightly higher. During the six-month period, 76 percent of the test group placed orders, while only 73 percent of the control group made further purchases. This 3 percent improvement in the retention rate, however, masked other, far more significant differences.

In terms of the number of orders placed during the six-month period, the test group members placed more orders than they had before, while the control group placed fewer orders (see Figure 6-1). Not only that, the test group's average order size was larger than that of the control group (which was 86 percent of previous order sizes), and larger (114 percent) than what the test group members had been ordering before. The net result of the test was a gain of $2,600,000 in orders from the test group as compared with the control group, as shown in Figure 6-2.

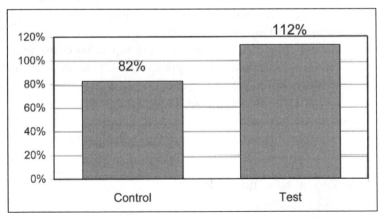

Figure 6-1. Number of orders placed by control and test groups.

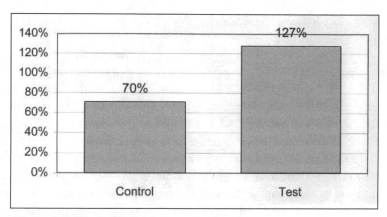

Figure 6-2. Total revenue from control versus test groups.

What a success! You spend $50,000 to put two workers on the phone communicating with customers for six months. As a result, you produce $2,600,000 more in sales. You will have to agree that communications with customers work!

To prove that communications work, you *absolutely must have a control group*. Imagine this test without the control group. How would you be able to prove that the two-person staff had done any good at all? You couldn't. Management usually does not understand control groups. Executives of the lighting firm might say, "That consultant cost us $2.6 million. If we had communicated with all 1,200 customers, instead of only 600, our overall sales would have been $2.6 million higher. We cannot afford such expensive consultants!" In fact, of course, the control group was the only way that anyone could have known that the test was working. Without the test group, the executives might have thought that the entire project was a "feel-good," worthless waste of money.

The Role of Customer Communications

There is no point in building a database, segmenting customers, and computing RFM and lifetime value if you don't communicate with your customers. Database marketing and the web only work if the customer benefits from them. The customer has to say, "I'm glad I'm on that database because . . ." You will have to fill in the rest of the sentence. In communications today, you can use the web, e-mail, mail, and phone. This chapter explains how to go about creating and profiting from excellent customer communications.

Let's start with the web. This medium is exploding with information. Every day, scores of new sites start up. Many of them are quite valuable to customers. When Beta VHR went out of business in the United States, I was stuck with more than 200 tapes I had made of wonderful old movies. When my last Beta VCR conked out, I could no longer play them. I called everywhere in the Washington, D.C., area, trying to find another Beta player, without success. Then, as I was writing this book, I tried www.ebay.com and sought Sony Betamax. To my amazement, I came up with 12 machines for sale throughout the country (see Figure 6-3). I bid $150 on one and was outbid. So I bid on two more at higher amounts. I finally succeeded in buying one.

What are the implications of this system? We are now in a worldwide market. If you have considered yourself a regional store, distributor, or manufacturer, think again. The web has opened up the entire world to you, if you can figure out how to take advantage of it.

For your company, you must use this medium right now to provide information and dialog with your customers. Why is the web important to you? Let me count the ways:

- It is far cheaper than telephone customer service.

- It operates 24 hours a day, 7 days a week.

- It never puts customers on hold.

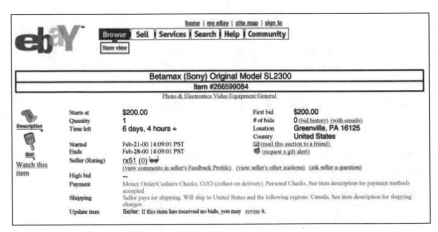

Figure 6-3. Bidding on a Sony Betamax at Ebay.com.

- You can know, instantly, which customer has read your message, and when.

- It enables customers to find out information for themselves—information that your customer service staff may not be briefed on and may not have available.

- It can build a bond with customers that will keep them coming back.

- It can expand your trading area. You will have visitors from all over the country—and all over the world. Some of these visitors can become valuable customers.

In using the web for communications, begin with this idea: "We are going to give our customers the same access we provide to our employees." Let them look into your warehouses to see what is in stock. Let them track delivery of packages. Let them look for discontinued items.

Use of an Extranet

The best way to communicate with customers using the web is to create an extranet for your customers. Anyone can log on to your web site, but good customers are given an ID and password that enables them to see things that are just for them. Dell Computer has created more than 30,000 Premier Pages for its best customers. Amazon says "Welcome back Arthur" whenever I log on. American Airlines knows what my frequent flyer number is when I click on its site. In fact, as soon as I enter my password, the page tells me how many miles I have earned. FedEx lets customers track the status of all packages they have shipped. The thing to realize about web communications with customers is that they are:

- *Interactive.* Customers can talk to you, and you can talk back to them.

- *Inexpensive.* Message by message, the web costs about 10 percent or less than any other communications media.

- *Addictive.* Once people have learned how to use your web site, they become hooked. They don't want to go back to letters, statement stuffers, and phone calls.

Recently, Helena and I visited the Hecht Company to look for a purse for a trip to Prague. Hecht's had exactly what we wanted, but it was the wrong color. The company was out of the right color and would not be getting any more stock in that season. I frantically hunted on the purse label for a web site. There was none. Too bad. If there had been one, we could have ordered the right color directly from the manufacturer. We would gladly have paid a premium to get what we wanted.

To control the lights in our condominium in Arlington, we installed electronic wireless switches made by Stanley Tools. We have about thirty lamp modules and six home controllers. They break down from time to time. We bought them originally at Home Depot. Home Depot does not stock them any more. We were stuck, until we looked closely at the package on the only spare module we had left. It said www.smarthome.com. Wow! We logged on and found more than 300 electronic light products made by Stanley—exactly what we needed (see Figure 6-4). Furthermore, I found a number of other electronic products on the web site that I had never heard of before. I ordered some.

I turned 72 recently. What kept me healthy at the time was a bunch of about ten different pills that I took every day from GeroVita International. The company had an 800 number that I would call to order the pills. But it had no web site. This company had a lot of information about hormones, enzymes, vitamins, minerals, dosages, side effects, etc., which I really wanted. But when I called the toll-free number, all the operators could do was to take my order. The company sent me an expensive newsletter twice a month with some of the information

Figure 6-4. Smarthome.com home automation.

that I wanted. That was good. It was communication, and I bought additional products that I found in the newsletter. Why not put this same information on the web and let me (and everyone else in the world) read it for myself? It would have been cheaper for GeroVita and more satisfying for me. Figure 6-5 shows what GeroVita should have done.

How Travelers Retains Its Best Customers

Long-term loyal customers are more valuable than other customers. They generally buy more often, they buy higher-priced options, they have a higher retention and referral rate, and they are less costly to serve. How do you get customers to be loyal? How do you organize your company and your channel to foster and reward loyalty, and to discourage the other kind of customer? Most organizations are set up for acquisition. Few are organized for retention. That is the problem. This is a story of how Travelers Property Casualty Company worked through its independent agents to use communications to build profitable relationships with its insurance customers.

Home and automobile insurance is a tough business. Because of vigorous competition and high acquisition costs, it takes several years before an automobile insurance customer can become profitable. If the customer leaves a year or two after being acquired, the insurance company loses money. Travelers knew this, but was not able to do much

Figure 6-5. www.drwhitaker.com.

about it. The company worked through thousands of independent agents who handled insurance for many different companies. Then Alison Bond, director of national agency sales and operations, working with Customer Development Corporation (CDC), hit on a system that really paid off. She designed a series of customized communications with insurance customers aimed at building a relationship with them so that they stayed with the company for a lifetime.

From her previous experience, Alison knew that:

- All similar communications programs attempted at Travelers had failed.
- Customers want communications. They like to hear from their insurance agents.
- To be effective, the communication should come from a local agent, not from the national headquarters.
- A 1 percent increase in the customer retention rate would be worth millions of dollars in increased annual profits to Travelers.
- To get this type of increase in retention, she would have to get 15 percent of the agents covering 25 percent of the customers to buy into her plan.

To begin, she had to sell the program to the independent agents. She met a lot of resistance. The agents were not convinced:

- That a retention program was valuable to them
- That direct mail would work
- That communications could affect when or whether a customer would defect
- That the program would have an adequate return on investment
- That Travelers marketing staff knew anything about their customers that they didn't already know

She also had to deal with CDC experience that suggested that the corporate headquarters should subsidize communications programs, and with Travelers management which said "make the agents pay for everything." She followed her management's policies, and they worked very well.

What she developed was a retention program, built from a customer database that provided a systematic program delivering communications at a very low cost. The messages were from the local agent. She provided the agents with a turnkey operation which was simple to buy into, and required almost no work on the part of the agents themselves.

She developed five annual "touches," which varied with the type of insurance that the customer had and the length of time that the customer had been with Travelers (see Figure 6-6). She learned that for each customer, she had constantly to determine the appropriate message, the frequency of messages that the customer wanted, the desired channel, the timing of the message, and the likelihood of defection. She was armed with statistics that showed that 65 percent of the customers who defected had never talked to an agent before they left. But 80 percent of the customers who had talked to an agent during the year did not leave.

What did customers want from their independent agents? The Independent Insurance Agency Association conducted a Customer Retention Survey for Personal Lines Customers to find out. Survey results showed that:

- Customers wanted information about their policies.
- Fifty-two percent of insurance customers described themselves as relationship buyers.
- Customers wanted an annual review of the coverage of their policy.
- Customers were looking for an agent with integrity who had a stable business.

Repetition is not necessarily a bad thing, she learned. Why? Because the average customer got 1,186 mail pieces in a year. Families got more than 5,000 pieces. The five communications from the Travelers agent needed to get noticed in all the clutter. Customers tended to remember the message from their local agent, whereas they would forget a letter from a Travelers VP.

Within 60 days of renewal	An annual review of the policy
Within the 1st quarter	A thank-you card
Within the 2nd quarter	A cross-sell postcard
Within the 3rd quarter	A newsletter
Within the 4th quarter	A seasonal greetings card

Figure 6-6. Five annual touches for insurance customers.

The program was based on detailed analysis of the customer database. Alison used database data and modeling to determine who was staying and who was leaving. She determined customer profitability and lifetime value. She used these to drive her segmentation and retention strategy. Overall, she came up with a measurement of customer desirability. Now that she knew whom Travelers wanted to keep and what they were worth, she could develop and execute a program to modify customer behavior through communications.

To get the agents to sign up for the program, she had to make it easy for them. She sent them a kit describing it. She gave them an 800 number to call, and recommended a standard package. She provided a web site for them to review the status of their program, and provided regular reports. To sell agents on the program, she showed them what happened to agents who bought similar programs in previous years versus those who did not. Agents who did not participate in the program lost 17.3 percent of their customers in the first year. Participating agents lost only 12.2 percent. She could prove with numbers like these that there was a good return on the agent's marketing dollar.

So what did her program accomplish? To measure her success, she compared the retention rates of customers of agents participating in the program with those of customers of agents who were nonparticipants. For auto insurance customers, she was able to increase the retention rate by 5 percent. For property insurance, the increase was 4 percent. The charts looked like the graphs in Figure 6-7.

Why did her program succeed where the others had failed?

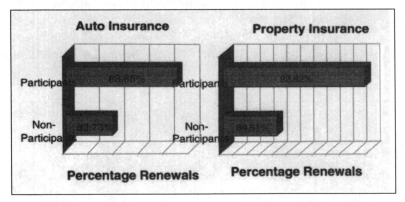

Figure 6-7. Improvements in renewal rate due to communications programs.

- Her program was not centrally subsidized.

- In prior programs, the agents risked nothing.

- In her program, the individual agents were risking their own money. They wanted it to succeed.

This type of customer communications program had all the right attributes:

- It was based on a customer database with purchase and response history.

- It was based on measuring customer profitability, lifetime value, and retention.

- It created custom communications from an agent whom people knew.

- It was sold to the agents, involved them, and enlisted their enthusiastic participation.

- It made customers happy and Travelers profitable.

Getting Them to Eat More

The Customer Connection (TCC) in Escondido, California, developed real proof that customer communications work. Look at these figures on the costs and sales resulting from three communications programs involving restaurants:

Promotion Cost	Resulting Sales
$1,800	$21,800
$16,620	$298,057
$2,700	$102,100

One restaurant had weekly sales of $129,700. TCC set up a special promotional program for it. Weekly sales grew to $464,900. In addition, sales per visit increased by an average of almost $2. How did TCC do it?

Birthday Cards

In the beginning TCC began with birthday and anniversary cards. The cards produced dramatic results. For one 25-unit steak and seafood company, TCC offered a $10 birthday discount to 215,600 customers who filled out birthday club registration cards. A database was created from these registrations. The birthday card mailings, over a year, cost $90,000. Of those cards sent, 41.1 percent were redeemed, producing overall sales of $2.9 million. Each birthday patron brought an average of 1.8 other guests for the party who paid full price.

Building on the success of the birthday program, TCC created permanent frequent diner membership cards for restaurant patrons. One restaurant chain had given its diners paper membership cards. Then TCC ordered plastic cards from a manufacturer. In June, TCC mailed out 24,725 of these permanent plastic cards. During the week before the cards went out, these patrons visited the restaurants 1,050 times. During the 13 weeks after receiving their permanent plastic cards, these same patrons visited an average of 1,400 times per week—an increase of 33 percent. They spent $156,000 more than they were spending before the cards were mailed. What is most significant is that there was no special promotion associated with the plastic cards. There was no additional discount offer. The plastic cards were simply a substitute for the paper cards. They were a form of customer communication. Communications programs work!

Points Programs

The next step above birthday and membership programs, of course, is points. Everyone likes to accumulate miles or points whenever their shopping, and restaurant patrons are like everyone else. TCC set up an on-line real-time frequency program that linked a point-of-sale (POS) terminal and TCC computers. The process was just like credit card verification. Whenever a member presented a plastic membership card, it was swiped through the terminal which dialed the TCC 800 number. TCC's computers posted the transaction, and sent back information that was printed on the diner's transaction receipt. The information included the member's up-to-the-minute point balance, along with offers, rewards, and messages tailored to the individual's past frequency and purchase behavior.

This POS system had a lot of nifty side benefits for the restaurant owner:

- *Information on gift certificates could be retained.* These were similar to a prepaid phone card. When a patron presented a gift certificate at a restaurant, it was swiped through the terminal and the meal was charged to the card. The certificate data were stored on the TCC computer, so if the card were lost, it could be reconstructed.

- *Specific menu items could be tracked.* This provided the restaurant with expanded marketing flexibility for special promotion creation. It was used for a continuity program for tracking the tasting of a variety of beers.

- *Premeal offers could be issued.* By swiping the member's card before taking the order, the restaurant could offer the diner bonus points or special discounts on appetizers or desserts that might not otherwise be ordered.

- *Terminals in reception areas could be used to communicate promotions.* While they were waiting to eat, diners could swipe their own cards to get up-to-the-minute account information. This was an opportunity for promotional messages, incentive purchase coupons, or announcements of future events or upcoming promotions.

"They Would Have Come Anyway"

So how do communications really affect dining behavior? Programs like those run by TCC really permitted managers to measure the impact of their communications in detail. Let's take a specific example.

A restaurant chain wanted to increase frequency and reactivate members who seemed to be "drifting away." TCC selected 4,000 members who had not earned any points during the previous three months. It sent them a letter offering a $5 discount on dinner. The offer was good for 35 days. The letter cost $1,800. What were the results?

- *Average member visits* went from 25 per day before the promotion, to 42 per day during the promotion, and to 29 per day in the 35-day period after the promotion was over.

- *Average visits per card* went from 1.18 before to 1.26 during and 1.22 after the promotion.

- *Incremental sales* were $17,100 during the promotion and $4,700 in the 35 days after the promotion was over.

So by spending $1,800, this restaurant chain reactivated 599 people who were otherwise lost as patrons. Not only was there a gain during the promotion period, but it had a lasting effect, with 147 of the reactivated people visiting the restaurant after the promotion was over. Relationship building works and has lasting benefits.

Boosting Retention through Targeted Communications

What do you do when you have a defection rate of almost 40 percent and falling revenue per customer in a highly competitive industry? This was the problem a large Fortune 50 telecommunications company faced. The marketing staff turned to Craig Wood at KnowledgeBase Marketing, Inc., in Chapel Hill, North Carolina. Craig's first step was to identify strengths, weaknesses, opportunities, and threats. His group interviewed customers and employees. Before Craig arrived, the telephone company had a customer contact strategy that involved five communications per year:

- A welcome message
- A "how are you doing?" cross-sell piece at 90 days
- A retention piece after 6 months
- A referral piece after 9 months
- An anniversary piece after 12 months.

Everyone got the same communications. They cost an average of $7.38 per customer per year. The customer satisfaction indexes showed very high satisfaction, but 4 out of every 10 of these satisfied customers were leaving every year—most of them to the competition.

The company had no marketing database, so Craig set about creating one to meet the needs of an enhanced program. He included in the database both current customers and those who had dropped the service during the past three years. He included calls to customer service and sales, and responses to marketing efforts broken into negative, positive, severe, and mild. Craig also appended demographic data, including age, income, education, and home value. Using this database with billing history going back for several years, Craig's team built predictive churn models that rated customers by likelihood of dropping the service.

A Risk-Revenue Matrix

Once Craig had the database in place and had run the churn model, his team developed a current value algorithm and created a risk-revenue matrix, like the one in Figure 6-8. The basic principle of this matrix was to determine which customers the company should work to retain and which it didn't need to bother with. Those in Priority C either were of low value to the company or had a low probability of leaving. Don't waste money on these folks. Concentrate your resources on the valuable people (Priorities A and B) who might quit the service. This matrix reduced those customers included in the retention program from 100 percent to 44 percent—a tremendously cost-effective technique.

To determine the value of customers to the firm, Craig and his team calculated current lifetime value and potential lifetime value for all the customers, based on their demographics. For example, a woman in her twenties might be currently using 1,200 minutes per year. Looking ahead, as her family expanded and her income grew, her potential might expand to 1,800 or more minutes per year. These calculations were built into a program which stored LTV and potential LTV into every customer's database record.

Now that they knew which customers they needed to retain, Craig's group had to devise a communications and reward strategy designed to keep the customer's loyalty. Essentially, the retention program was composed of four principles:

Lifetime Value	Likelihood of Churn		
	High	Medium	Low
High	**Priority A**	*Priority B*	Priority C
Medium	*Priority B*	*Priority B*	Priority C
Low	Priority C	Priority C	Priority C

Figure 6-8. A risk-revenue matrix.

- *Customer care.* Having good customer service and communications
- *Problem detection and intervention.* Having in place a program to deal with customer dissatisfaction
- *Relationship marketing.* Determining the most valuable customers and building a relationship with them
- *Rewards.* Working to modify customer behavior, and support those whose loyalty was important to the company

A Customer Contact Strategy

The relationship marketing program consisted of a series of two-way (survey and response) communications ranging from zero "touches" up to eight per year, depending on the priority of the customers and their personal preferences and demographics. For those people in the retention program, Craig devised a customer contact strategy that included the same elements the client was already mailing: a welcome package, an anniversary package, a retention questionnaire, and a cross-sell package. In addition, Craig introduced a rewards program for a very select group of high-value customers.

Once Craig had determined the appropriate communications, he had to test various combinations to be sure that they would be effective in modifying behavior. To do this, he created a communications testing matrix, which was tested on a relatively small number of customers. Senior management agreed to test four communication components: A, B, C, and D. There were three types of incentives: none, a few free minutes, and a lot of free minutes. Each of the test programs was compared with the behavior of a control group that received no communications at all.

How Big a Reward Do You Need?

One of the things that Craig and his team discovered in the testing phase was that the number of minutes given as a reward had little impact on behavior. People responded just as well to a reward of a few minutes as they did to a lot of minutes. As a result of this very valuable discovery, they scaled back the rewards to just enough to make a difference. They also learned that in communications, the slickness of the approach didn't matter either. They tried two different creative approaches, one expensive and one inexpensive. Both worked equally well, so they retained the less expensive package.

With the testing completed, they were ready for the rollout, comparing always the behavior of the customers they were trying to retain with those of control groups that received no retention building communications at all.

The Results

In the first place, they were able to reduce churn. They brought the defections of the test group down by 3 percent per year. That increased the retention rate from 38 percent to 39.27 percent annually (see Figure 6-9). This translated into a $2 million annual increase in the bottom line.

Within the target groups, churn reduction was even more dramatic. The overall rate of churn in the control group of the four priority cohorts (A and B) was 24 percent. Of those in these cohorts who were mailed the retention program, the churn rate was 18 percent—a decrease of 25 percent. Most of the retention packages called for a response from the customer. Of those who responded positively—saying that they were happy with the service—the churn rate was only 9 percent. For those who responded that they were unhappy, a SWAT team worked to resolve their problems. Where the team was successful and

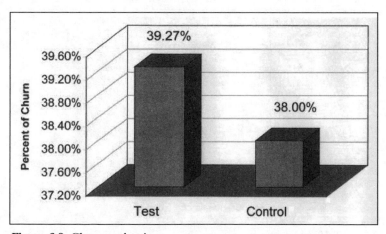

Figure 6-9. Churn reduction.

the problem was resolved, the churn rate was also 9 percent. But response to the communications was not essential to reduce churn. *The churn rate of the nonresponders to the messages was lower than the churn rate of the control group that received no communications at all!*

Increased Annual Revenue

Besides reducing the churn rate, the communications program also had a positive impact on phone usage and revenue. As you can see in Figure 6-10, the average annual revenue from those in the retention program was 5 percent higher: $707 as compared with only $678 from identical people in the control group that did not receive the retention communications. As shown in Figure 6-11, the phone usage for the targeted groups also increased by 15 percent—from 1,300 minutes per year to 1,500 minutes per year.

 Perhaps most surprising of all was the reduced cost of the communications. Previously every customer got five mailings per year for an average cost of $7.38. With the new retention program, the company stopped mailing to everyone in Priority C. The number of people mailed dropped by 56 percent. The highest-value, highest-risk customers, Priority A, received eight messages a year, while Priority B customers received fewer. The overall cost per customer of the communications, therefore, in the third year came down to only $1.38 (see Figure 6-12). In other words, the telephone company got these great retention benefits *and at the same time* reduced the cost of the retention program!

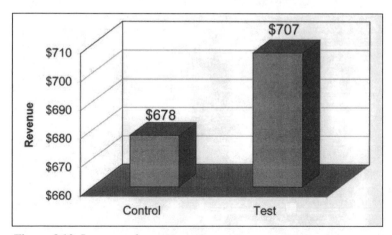

Figure 6-10. Increase phone revenue.

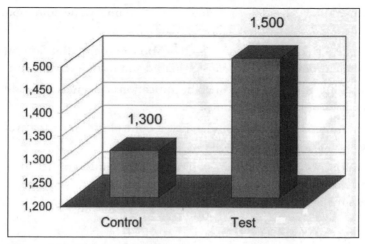

Figure 6-11. Increased minutes usage.

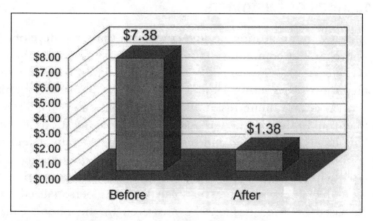

Figure 6-12. Reduced cost of communications.

We can sum up the central lessons learned about customer communications from this program developed by KnowledgeBase. To succeed you must:

- Interview customers and employees to come up with a plan that would work in the circumstances.
- Build a database that contains enough data so that you can determine two things: likelihood to churn and lifetime value to the company.

- Run a churn model, and determine lifetime value and potential value.

- Create a risk-revenue matrix so that you can focus attention on only those customers who are most valuable and most likely to churn.

- Develop a winning series of communications designed to modify the behavior of the target groups.

- Test those communications against a control group so that you can be sure of what you are doing.

- Measure your success every step of the way against control groups so that you are sure that what is happening to churn, to usage, and to revenue is due to your efforts, and not to some market shift.

One-to-One with Hundreds of Thousands of Customers

MicroMass Communications in Raleigh, North Carolina, developed an innovative two-way communications program for smokers who had purchased *Nicorette* nicotine gum or *NicoDerm CQ* patches. When the smoker bought a *Nicorette* starter kit at a drugstore, he found a Committed Quitters program outline inside the package, with an 800 number to call to enroll. In the call, he was asked 27 personal questions about his smoking habits, his lifestyle, and his goals in the program. There were 63 possible data responses which were entered into the data record on each participant. Right after the call, the smoker received a free Committed Quitters stop-smoking plan that was personalized to his needs, based on the questions he answered in the phone call. He received a 12-week calendar addressing barriers, motivations, high risk situations, and coping strategies. The next week he got a personalized newsletter explaining high-risk situations and providing social support, plus a reminder to buy his first Nicorette refill. A week later, he got a reinforcing postcard. Some program members elect to receive their reminders and materials by e-mail.

Meanwhile, the former smoker was chewing away or applying patches and trying to keep from dreaming about a cigarette. If he felt the need, he could call an 800 number where a trained antismoking counselor listened and provided helpful advice. In the sixth week, he received a trifold mailer with additional advice on how to cope with his problems, plus a reminder to begin tapering off. If the program were to be successful, at that point the smoker should be able to do less chewing and patching, and still stay smoke-free. Week 9 brought a congratulations packet, and at the end of the treatment program, he was given an award packet. (See Figure 6-13.)

How effective was the Nicorette system? Dr. Saul Shiffman of the University of Pittsburgh reported on a study of 3,807 smokers who were randomized into three groups, all of whom bought Nicorette nicotine gum:

- Those who got no outside assistance
- Those who got the standard Committed Quitters program
- Those who got the "enhanced" CQ program with a phone call from a counselor

More than 75 percent of those smokers who received no assistance were back smoking again after 28 days. But only 64 percent of those who received the standard CQ program had resumed smoking (see Figure 6-14). In other words, the CQ contact program boosted the success rate by 50 percent. "The study demonstrates the potential for low-cost, tailored printed materials to have a significant impact on cessation, even among smokers who are already receiving nicotine medication and basic written behavioral advice," said Dr. Shiffman. The study also showed that the personal phone call (enhanced program) was not worth the extra expense since those called had virtually the same success rate as those receiving the direct-mail program alone. This may be a significant finding. Perhaps people don't like to get personal phone calls about their health maintenance programs, and money spent on such efforts might be wasted.

Summary

- Communications with customers can make the customers happy and increase retention and sales. You can only prove that communications work, however, if you have a control group.

Welcome & Calendar	Newsletter	Reinforcing Post Card	Tri-fold Mailer	Congrats Packet	Award Packet
1	2	3	6	9	12

Figure 6-13. Mailings to NicoDerm Committed Quitters.

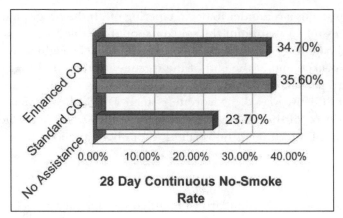

Figure 6-14. Effectiveness of CQ program.

■ One of the fastest-growing, and least expensive, ways to communicate with customers is by use of the World Wide Web. You create an extranet, giving your best customers their own ID, personal page, and password. If you do it right, you will have them hooked for life.

■ The Travelers communications program was successful in increasing customer retention. This program had some key features:

It was funded by the independent agents, not by Travelers.

The communications came from a local agent, not from a Travelers VP.

Its five "touches" a year were personalized for each customer's situation.

It improved the retention rate by up to 5 percent.

■ Birthday rewards from restaurants produce millions of dollars in sales annually at comparatively little cost

■ Points work in building interest and retention. People like to open the envelopes that tell them how many points they have accumulated.

■ A revenue-reward matrix can be very useful in deciding whom to communicate with and whom to ignore. Use of such a matrix can be highly profitable.

■ Giving free minutes as a reward can change behavior. The number of minutes given is not as important as the fact that you are paying attention.

- Slick, expensive communications may do no better than less expensive communications. Don't waste money. Test.

- Successful retention communication programs not only improve retention, but usually increase sales and the average order size as well.

- Regular mailed communications with smokers can improve their success rate in quitting. Telephone calls are not worth the extra money involved.

Executive Quiz 5

Answers to quiz questions can be found in Appendix B.

1. Communications with customers tend to increase:

    a. The retention rate

    b. The average order size

    c. The number of orders

    d. The total sales

    e. All of the above

2. Which is the most important element in any customer communications program?

    a. An extranet

    b. A control group

    c. A points program

    d. Rewards

    e. Discounts

3. In the Travelers Insurance case study, which was not true?

    a. Communications came from a senior VP.

    b. Repetition of the same message did not matter.

    c. The retention rate was increased by 5 percent.

    d. Agents paid for the program themselves.

    e. The program was based on customer lifetime value.

4. In the telecommunications case study, a risk-revenue matrix was used to:

    a. Increase the total number of customer contacts per year

    b. Determine which customers were dissatisfied with the service

    c. Reduce the cost of the communications program

    d. Eliminate the need for a control group

    e. Determine customer lifetime value

5. In the Nicoderm case study, Micromass discovered that:

    a. Half the participants were able to quit smoking for good.

    b. Personal contact by phone beat direct mail as a medium.

    c. Of those who got the communications, 35.6 percent were successful in quitting smoking.

    d. All of the above.

    e. None of the above.

6. The lighting manufacturer case study showed that:

    a. Discounts were the most effective way to change behavior

    b. A control group was not needed

    c. The costs exceeded the benefits

    d. The control group members spent more than they had before

    e. The average order size of the test group increased

7. Web communications with customers has all but one advantage over direct mail:

    a. It is less expensive.

    b. It saves trees.

    c. It operates 24 hours a day, 7 days a week.

    d. It lets customers find out things that they could not do in other ways.

    e. You can use slick graphics in your presentation.

8. Which group should get the most customer communications?
   a. Those with the highest lifetime value
   b. Those least likely to churn
   c. Those who have been with you the longest
   d. Likely churners with high LTV
   e. Likely churners with low LTV

7

Building Customer Loyalty

The first step in managing a loyalty-based business system is finding and acquiring the right customers: customers who will provide steady cash flows and a profitable return on the firm's investment for years to come, customers whose loyalty can be won and kept. Loyalty-based companies should remember three rules of thumb:

1) *Some customers are inherently predictable and loyal, no matter what company they're doing business with. They simply prefer stable, long-term relationships.*

2) *Some customers are more profitable than others. They spend more money, pay their bills more promptly, and require less service.*

3) *Some customers will find your products and services more valuable than those of your competitors. No company can be all things to all people. Your particular strengths will simply fit better with certain customers' needs and opportunities.*

FREDERICK REICHHELD
*The Loyalty Effect**

*From the Loyalty Effect: The Hidden Force behind Growth, Profits, and Lasting Value, by Frederick F. Reichheld. Boston: Harvard Business School Press, 1996.

Loyal customers are more valuable than the average customer. They tend to:

- Have higher retention rates
- Have higher spending rates
- Have higher referral rates
- Have a higher lifetime value
- Be less expensive to serve
- Buy higher-priced options

There is one key measurement for loyalty. It is the retention rate. Retention is more important than the spending rate or the frequency of spending. Why? Because if customers are gone, they're gone. It is hard to get them back. As long as you have them, there is always a possibility of getting them to spend more or trade up to higher options.

Frederick Reichheld's book, *The Loyalty Effect* (see Appendix A for further details), burst on the database marketing industry like a welcome rainstorm. When I read it, I learned a lot. His ideas are so important that they permeate every chapter of this book. If you haven't already read it, you should run right out now and buy a copy yourself.

Reichheld maintained in his book that a 5 percent increase in the retention rate can lead to a massive (up to 75 percent) increase in the lifetime value of customers. Let's compare the lifetime value of the regular customers with the Gold customers of a supermarket, where there is a 5 percent difference in the retention rate.

We are tracing the lifetime value of 100,000 newly acquired customers of a supermarket who can be tracked because they use the supermarket's frequent buyer card (see Figure 7-1). Their retention rate in the first year is 75 percent, rising to 92 percent in the fifth year. The average customer visits the store a little over 6 times in 10 weeks, spending $33 each time. The average customer's lifetime value in the first year is a minus $13.76 due to the acquisition cost of $40 per customer, but it becomes healthy in the later years.

Now let's look at the lifetime value of the top 20 percent of the customers at this same store. These people have a higher retention rate, they visit the store more often, and they spend more when they do. To get these better customers, we have spent a little more on targeted acquisition. Their lifetime value is considerably higher, as Figure 7-2 shows.

	Year 1	Year 2	Year 3	Year 4	Year 5
Customers	100,000	75,000	60,000	50,400	44,352
Retention rate	75.00%	80.00%	84.00%	88.00%	92.00%
Visits/week	0.64	0.691	0.75	0.81	0.84
Average basket	$33	$45	$55	$60	$65
Total sales	$105,600,000	$116,437,500	$123,750,000	$122,472,000	$121,080,960
Cost percent	83.00%	80.00%	79.00%	78.00%	77.00%
Direct costs	$87,648,000	$93,150,000	$97,762,500	$95,528,160	$93,232,339
Labor + benefits 11%	$11,616,000	$12,808,125	$13,612,500	$13,471,920	$13,318,906
Card program $16, $8	$1,600,000	$600,000	$480,000	$403,200	$354,816
Acquisition cost $40	$4,000,000				
Advertising 2%	$2,112,000	$2,328,750	$2,475,000	$2,449,440	$2,421,619
Total costs	$106,976,000	$108,886,875	$114,330,000	$111,852,720	$109,327,680
Gross profit	($1,376,000)	$7,550,625	$9,420,000	$10,619,280	$11,753,280
Discount rate	1	1.14	1.3	1.48	1.69
NPV profit	($1,376,000)	$6,623,355	$7,248,384	$7,167,712	$6,958,885
Cumulative NPV profit	($1,376,000)	$5,247,355	$12,495,739	$19,663,451	$26,622,336
Lifetime value	**($13.76)**	**$52.47**	**$124.96**	**$196.63**	**$266.22**

Figure 7-1. Lifetime value of regular customers.

	Year 1	Year 2	Year 3	Year 4	Year 5
Customers	20,000	16,000	13,600	12,104	11,257
Retention rate	80.00%	85.00%	89.00%	93.00%	97.00%
Visits/week	0.69	0.74	0.8	0.86	0.89
Average basket	$50	$68	$83	$90	$98
Total sales	$34,155,000	$39,960,000	$44,880,000	$46,842,480	$48,840,094
Cost percent	83.00%	80.00%	79.00%	78.00%	77.00%
Direct costs	$28,348,650	$31,968,000	$35,455,200	$36,537,134	$37,606,872
Labor+ benefits 11%	$3,757,050	$4,395,600	$4,936,800	$5,152,673	$5,372,410
Card program $16, $8	$320,000	$128,000	$108,800	$96,832	$90,054
Acquisition cost $60	$1,200,000				
Advertising 2%	$683,100	$799,200	$897,600	$936,850	$976,802
Total costs	$34,308,800	$37,290,800	$41,398,400	$42,723,489	$44,046,138
Gross profit	($153,800)	$2,669,200	$3,481,600	$4,118,991	$4,793,956
Discount rate	1	1.14	1.3	1.48	1.69
NPV profit	($153,800)	$2,341,404	$2,678,978	$2,780,202	$2,838,407
Cumulative NPV profit	($153,800)	$2,187,604	$4,866,582	$7,646,783	$10,485,190
Lifetime value	**($7.69)**	**$109.38**	**$243.33**	**$382.34**	**$524.26**

Figure 7-2. Lifetime value of Gold customers.

Comparing the Two Groups

What is the difference between these two groups of customers? We can graph the increase in the lifetime value. As you can see from Figure 7-3, no matter how you measure it, loyal customers are more profitable.

So how do you get loyal customers? There are really three ways:

■ You can treat loyal customers better.

■ You can reward loyalty with points or benefits.

■ You can vary your customer acquisition methods to attract good customers, and avoid the bad ones.

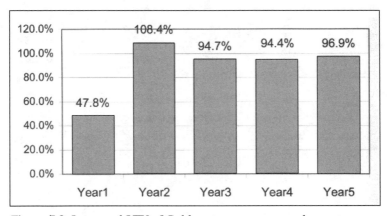

Figure 7-3. Increased LTV of Gold customers over regular customers.

Treating Loyal Customers Better

The 80/20 rule applies in all industries. The top 20 percent of your customers give you 80 percent or some other large percentage of your total revenue. Banks compute this by measuring profitability on a monthly basis. We return to a familiar graph, Figure 7-4, showing how one bank divides its customers into five segments. In this example, the top two segments, totaling 16 percent of the customer households, produced 105 percent of the profits. The bottom 28 percent of the customer households were losers. Most companies have an idea that their customer value looks something like this, but few have taken the time to do the actual analysis and figure out who their loyalists are—and who the others are.

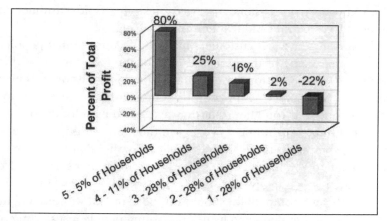

Figure 7-4. Profit contributed by household segments.

Once you have identified them, however, there are many things that you could and should do to retain these good customers. Here is what some people do:

- Offer special customer service lines for Gold customers, putting their best agents on these lines.
- Create advisory panels made up of their best customers.
- Have special member-only nights for Gold customers.
- Have special seminars or reports.
- In business to business, host an annual retreat at a resort for the CEOs of their best customers.

Dropping the Losers

In addition to keeping your loyal customers, you should do something about the losers. If these customers are actually costing you money and eating up profits that other customers are creating, you must do something about it.

The first step is to identify these people. Once you know who they are, you can reprice their services, or move them toward the door. One bank lets all its employees know which segment each customer falls into. For those customers at the bottom, who are losing money for the bank, the employee screens suggest repricing of products. Their loans are renewed at a higher rate. Waivers are not granted. Even more interesting, the call center software makes losing callers wait for five or six rings before anyone from customer service picks up. Gold customers are answered by a special Gold team on the first ring.

Of course, your worst customers may not be undesirable people. It could be that many of them do the bulk of their business elsewhere. They may be Gold customers to your competition, although they are expensive convenience shoppers with you. So what should you do in such a situation? If you know that they are spending a lot in your category, it might be worthwhile trying to win them over. It is for this reason that many companies try to learn the share of wallet that they have with each customer. You may be able to find this out from a survey or from credit bureaus. Certainly customers who spend 90 percent of their money with your competition should not be dropped without a fight.

Some businesses deliberately seek out young people just starting out, in the hopes of keeping them for a lifetime. It is for this reason that credit cards are issued to college students. These students are seldom profitable customers. The bank hopes to earn their goodwill for future business. This assumption is open to question, however. Any company that deliberately loses money now in the hope for future profits should follow these losers in their database for several years to determine if they actually do bring in a profit some day. In an industry as volatile as credit cards or long distance service, I would question the long-run profitability of such a strategy. Helena and I both have Citibank credit cards because they give us American Airlines miles. We dropped our Chevy Chase and MBNA cards that we had had for years when we decided to collect American miles. What Chevy Chase and MBNA should have done was to ask us what airline program we were members of. If they had offered us airline miles, proactively, we would have stayed, happily, as customers. Too bad for them.

Relationship Effects

Sometimes we will want to retain nonprofitable customers, even though their lifetime value may be small or negative. Lynette Ryals, of Cranfield University in the United Kingdom, listed four relationship effects that might cause you to think twice about dropping some unprofitable customers. She describes the effects as reference, referral, learning, and innovation.

Reference Accounts. Reference accounts are the customers who add prestige to your organization simply because you are known to be one of their suppliers. This is often associated with large and powerful companies with stringent supplier selection and monitoring procedures. Sometimes these customers will permit their names to appear on your literature, will give you a reference, will speak at your conferences, or will even allow site visits by other prospective customers. Even if they do not, just being associated with certain companies has a value to you. In the United Kingdom, to be a supplier to Marks and Spencer or Tesco confers a certain standing on the company. In the United States, the equivalent might be to be a supplier to Saks or Wal-Mart. The prestige customer acts like a brand name, reducing the psychological risk of dealing with you ("If they supply Wal-Mart, they must be good"). This encourages other buyers. The value to your company of these reference accounts is greater than the value of your transactions with them.

Referral. An insurance company has a small customer who is renowned for being difficult and time consuming. The insurance company probably makes no profit on its business with that customer whatsoever. Why does this company continue to court this demanding customer? Why doesn't it discourage him, or refuse to deal with him altogether? The answer to this seeming puzzle is that this individual has a great deal of influence in his local region. He is appreciative of the service that his insurers give him, and he tells everybody about it. In fact, he has recruited a significant number of good, profitable clients for this company over the years; he refers others to his favorite supplier. Referral accounts are customers who refer other customers; they may not be intrinsically profitable in themselves, but the business they help to bring in can be very substantial. After all, who are your best salespeople—your sales team or your satisfied customers?

Learning. Some customers are intrinsically valuable in a way that would be difficult to identify through normal accounting procedures. These are the customers from whom you learn. It is said that Toyota is particularly good to have as a customer because it will help its suppliers to install certain systems and processes. The supplier then reaps the benefit of these processes for the rest of its business. Learning from customers might result in better ways of manufacturing products, or better administration or IT. Sometimes the customer is even prepared to train its supplier's staff.

Innovation. The learning benefit from a customer is not always a transfer of know-how from the customer to you; sometimes the process is a shared one of joint learning from which both parties benefit. Jointly funded research and development is one of the best-known examples, as is the use of certain customers as beta test sites for partially developed products or systems. You get the benefit of feedback about your new products or services in use, but before committing massive sums to the venture by rolling it out on a large scale; and the beta test customers benefit from early delivery of the product and often the chance to influence the final design toward one that fits their needs more precisely. This also results in a more efficient use of information. The customer is likely to be informed about what the market wants; the supplier, about what is possible. Jeremy and Tony Hope, in their book *Competing in the Third Wave* (Harvard Business School Press, 1997, p. 57) cited the experience of Chrysler, which offered its suppliers $20,000 for each part they could engineer out of a car. One supplier submitted no fewer than 213 ideas, of which 129 were approved, saving Chrysler $75.5 million. That supplier's turnover with Chrysler doubled.

Bolstering Loyalty with Points

There is no question today that loyalty can be created or increased by awarding points or miles. The basic idea behind points is to avoid discounting your product. Points represent a gift or reward that cannot easily be related to the price of the product or service. There are millions of Americans today, for example, whose loyalty to an airline has been molded by frequent flyer programs. These airline programs work.

Do rewards work for other products and services? The answer seems to be yes, but not as well. There are scores of other programs run by restaurants, retail stores, banks, hotels, credit card companies, long distance services, and others that reward customers with points. Many companies have been able to prove, using control groups, that these programs do build loyalty.

The Hallmark Gold Crown Loyalty Program

There are 5000 independently owned Hallmark Gold Crown stores striving for consumer loyalty. To build long-term, profitable relationships with Gold Crown customers, Hallmark created a program that quickly became one of marketing's greatest success stories.

How the Program Was Developed

The key behavior Hallmark wanted to drive was greeting card purchases. In the early 1990s, Hallmark initiated a store-specific, punch-card loyalty program that rewarded consumers for completing a required amount of purchases. Later, Hallmark developed a direct-mail program for members who indicated that they purchased more than 40 greeting cards annually. Although this program stimulated purchase behavior, it neither offered Hallmark the ability to capture detailed data on consumer behavior nor enabled consumers to earn rewards for shopping at any Hallmark Gold Crown store.

"What Hallmark needed was a universal card that could identify, track, and reward the most loyal card buyers in the Hallmark Gold Crown network," said J.D. Henning, Director of Account Development, Carlson Marketing Group. Hallmark turned to Carlson Marketing Group for assistance in creating and managing a state-of-the-art consumer loyalty program. Working together, Hallmark and Carlson Marketing Group designed a relationship marketing initiative that tracked consumer's product preferences and identified customers with the strongest relationship to Hallmark.

Hallmark replaced the punch-card program with a system-wide electronic points program. Transaction data for each member was captured at the point of sale, using either a personalized bar code or magnetic strip on each member's card. With this electronic program, Hallmark could now track members' purchase behavior across all stores and build a relationship with them through ongoing communication.

The program was tested in more than 60 stores in the Kansas City and Denver marketplaces. Very detailed information was obtained from point-of-sale technology that made it possible to track the actual products consumers purchased. Participating consumers enrolled in the stores and immediately received a sequentially numbered temporary card. They earned 10 points for every dollar spent and received a reward certificate for every 100 points. Once earning 500 points, they received a permanent card, as well as quarterly reward certificates redeemable at Hallmark Gold Crown stores for Hallmark merchandise.

The success of the test was measured by comparing total store sales, numbers of transactions, and the individual average transaction of each consumer with similar statistics from the national average. Based on the findings from a successful one-year test, the program was modified and rolled out nationally to nearly 5000 stores as the Gold Crown Card program in August 1994. The rollout required store owners to "enroll" in the program, fund part of it, install technology to capture the data, and follow executive program guidelines consistently.

Lessons Learned in the Test

Once Hallmark had accumulated enough purchasing data, it was able to create customer segments based on behavior. Some members, it found, came in once a week to buy one card, generating many smaller transactions. Others came in once a year at Christmas, spent a lot, and didn't come back for a year. With this data, Hallmark could treat each segment differently. It didn't need to send a Valentine's, Mother's Day, or summer mailing to consumers who were only Christmas shoppers.

Hallmark also learned the sooner it issued the program's permanent card the sooner the consumer would become actively engaged in the loyalty initiative. As a result, it lowered the hurdle rate for a permanent card to 200 points. Once a member earned 200 points, she was sent a welcome kit that included a 100-point bonus, a permanent plastic card, and a description of the program. On a quarterly basis, she received a mailing that outlined her account activity including points earned, which stores she had shopped, a product brochure announcing new product lines for the season, special bonus offers, and a reward certificate redeemable in-store.

Other significant adjustments were also made. The base reward structure was lowered to 200 points for a $1 reward certificate. For every greeting card purchased, 25 bonus points were added. Unique seasonal bonus offers and ornament offers were included, which still allowed the flexibility to give special offers and stay within a profitable financial reward structure. The quarterly reward certificate was capped at $20. If the consumer earned more points, the points were banked to the next quarter.

Results

The Gold Crown Card program reached initial enrollment objectives in half the time anticipated. The dollars per transaction, the number of trips consumers made, the total store sales, and total store transactions were all up, compared to controls.

After five years, the program grew to the point where a third of all transactions and almost half of all card-shop dollars were made on the card. In addition, 13 million active members (those who had used the card in the last twelve months) were participating in the program. It became the largest active-member database loyalty program in the world at that time. With the data generated electronically through this program, Hallmark was able to track consumer purchase behavior, develop a long-term relationship with loyal customers, and target profitable segments of its consumer base.

Challenges

As the program matured, Hallmark focused on making the program remain fresh to its membership. To answer this challenge, Hallmark utilized the individual consumer data they were gathering to create communication pieces segmented based on members' purchase behavior, demographics, lifestyle, and locations of the stores they visited.

Following the launch, sales and transactions met and, in most cases, exceeded program growth forecasts. Program members were responsible for nearly half of the revenue generated in the Hallmark Gold Crown stores. Formal qualitative research confirmed that members placed a high value on the program and changed their purchasing behavior because of the incentives offered.

The program evolved into the Internet age, and was featured on the Hallmark web site (www.hallmark.com). On line, members could quickly view electronic point balance and transaction details, get answers to Frequently Asked Questions or permanent card inquiries, as well as provide change of address information.

"Our main objective is to offer our members their choice of how they want to interact with us," explained Cindy Jeffries, Director, Hallmark Advertising. "They can choose to receive program information through traditional mail, online, by phoning our call center, or by e-mailing us at Hallmark. It's entirely up to the member. And, these choices will continue to expand in the future."

"The continuing evolution of the Internet will enable Hallmark to make specialized e-mail offers in a cost-effective, efficient manner. We will enhance our ability to reach specific market segments, receive instant responses, and capture that data electronically," said Jeffries.

Its web site and other recent enhancements, together with its far-reaching data-capture capabilities, place the Gold Crown Card program in the forefront of loyalty programs. Through this innovative program, Hallmark tracks individual purchasing behavior, leverages that data to prioritize communications to consumers, and produces outstanding marketing results.

Carlson Marketing Group Loyalty Study

How popular and successful are customer loyalty points programs? The Carlson Marketing Group (see Figure 7-5) did several telephone studies of consumers over 18 years of age to answer this question. What the Carlson group found out was quite interesting. For instance, even though there are hundreds of loyalty programs out there, very few people actually participate in them. Of all consumers,

- 14 percent are unaware of loyalty programs
- 44 percent are aware but decline to play
- 42 percent are aware of the program and do play

The studies showed that 71 percent of people with incomes over $75,000 do play. They are a desirable segment because they have discretionary income. Of consumers over 55, however, only 28 percent are aware of and use the programs.

Effect on Behavior

- *Loyalty programs increase business for companies.* Sixty percent of people participating in the programs say they are spending more with the company that offers their favorite loyalty program. Overall, people estimate that they have increased their spending by 27 percent.

- *Airline and credit card programs are more successful than others in increasing revenue.* Credit card programs increase usage by 46 percent. Sixty percent of telecommunications participants were already using the services at maximum levels before joining the programs.

Figure 7-5. Carlson Marketing Group web site.

- *Loyalty programs encourage consolidation of purchases.* Eighty percent of loyalty program participants shop around before joining their favorite loyalty program. After joining, they tend to buy from just that company. Three quarters of those holding credit cards with loyalty programs use just that card after joining the program.

- *Telecommunications loyalty programs lead some to add services and reduce the likelihood of switching to other providers.* Thirty percent sign up for additional services. Half say they are unlikely to switch.

- *Discontinuing a loyalty program reduces sales.* Sixty percent of participants will spend less if the programs were to be discontinued. Their spending with the company would decrease by 30 percent. Credit card users would use the card 56 percent less.

The Value of Benefits and Rewards

- *Rewards are the most compelling feature of a loyalty program.* Next in importance are special treatment and special discounts.

- *The look and quality of promotional pieces is not considered important.*

- *People expect awards within seven months of joining.* Retail participants want rewards in five months.

Widespread Participation

- *Those who participate typically are enrolled in three loyalty programs.* Airline and credit card programs have the widest participation. Those with incomes over $60,000 strongly prefer these two programs.

- *Three of the four most popular programs relate to travel:* Airlines (65 percent), Hotels (39 percent), and Car Rental (31 percent).

- *Men are more likely to join travel-related programs.* Women join retail programs such as those given by clothing and shoe stores, greeting card companies, and grocery stores.

Communications about the Programs

- *Statements and special offers are the most closely read of all types of communications that loyalty program participants receive.*

- *Few people take full advantage of special offers available to them.* Retail program participants are more likely than others to use the special offers.

■ *Mailings, newsletters, and statements are used to communicate.* Most prefer mail, although a growing number prefer e-mail.

From the survey, it is clear that to be successful points programs have to:

■ Provide real value, "with things I can use, that are important to me."

■ "Give me an opportunity to tell you what I want in the program. Just ask me. Make it interactive."

■ Be simple to participate in. Tracking should be automatic.

■ Not involve any type of telephone solicitation.

■ Be a straightforward, honest, relevant communication, delivered the way I want it.

■ Provide reward choices that are easy to get and easy to use.

■ Understand that consumers, particularly seniors and higher-income groups, are becoming more discriminating about which programs they join and are active in. A good program can have a significant impact on your bottom line. But if the customer doesn't like your program, that will also have a significant impact on your bottom line.

Acquiring the Right Customers

Given that loyal customers are better to have and more profitable than others, what can you do about it? Until Reichheld's book, *The Loyalty Effect*, came along, there was one universal answer: Figure out who the loyal customers are and treat them well. Provide special benefits: Gold cards, President's Clubs, advisory panels, member nights, special toll-free phone lines, and hundreds of special services that will encourage these loyal people to stick around for a long time.

There is nothing in Reichheld's book that disagrees with these recommendations. But there is little to support them, either. Reichheld simply changed the subject. The route to loyalty, he explained, is to recruit loyal people to begin with. "Some customers are inherently predictable and loyal, no matter what company they're doing business with. They simply prefer stable, long-term relationships." (Reichheld, p. 63)

His book provides dozens of examples of companies that have figured out the characteristics of their loyal customers. These companies have developed simple rules that aid them in attracting the right kind of customer, and in avoiding the wrong kinds. A summary of some of his examples:

- An insurance company discovered that, in regard to its products, married people were more loyal than singles. Midwesterners were more loyal than Easterners. Home owners were more loyal than renters. Once the company found this out, it used the knowledge to guide its acquisition strategy.

- MBNA discovered that people reached through an affinity group— such as doctors, dentists, nurses, teachers, and engineers—were more loyal credit card holders than people reached through general direct-mail campaigns.

- Many companies used their databases to learn that customers attracted by low-ball discount offers were more likely to disappear than customers attracted using nondiscounted offers. The former group tended to leave as soon as the competition made them an even lower-ball offer. Were they different people, or had the offer made them think of the company's products in terms of price rather than value? Who knows? It really doesn't matter. Discounting is not a profitable long-range strategy.

Reichheld also pointed out that satisfaction scores may be worthless as a means of measuring customer loyalty. In the automobile industry, American cars typically have satisfaction scores in the 90 percent range, but the repurchase rates hover around 35 percent. Repurchase is the best indicator of loyalty, he concludes.

Reichheld noted further that the compensation given to sales personnel can influence the characteristics of the customer base. If, for example, insurance salespeople are given a 80 percent commission for a new acquisition and a 20 percent commission for the first policy renewal, the salespeople will concentrate on customers who will not necessarily be loyal. If, on the other hand, the salespeople are paid 20 percent for an acquisition and 80 percent for the first renewal, the salespeople's acquisition methods will be entirely different. They will seek out people who will last. The effect of this change will be to boost the company's bottom line, since loyal customers are more profitable than disloyal ones.

Interviewing the Defectors

Probably the most important names on your customer database are those of the people who have recently deserted you. These people are valuable. They provide important clues about what you are doing right and doing wrong. You should set up an ongoing program to interview them to determine why they left. To make the most of the situation, you should determine the lifetime value of each customer and keep it in the customer's database record. When you lose customers, therefore, find out if their lifetime value is higher or lower than the LTV of your existing customer base. You can make up a useful table similar to the one shown in Figure 7-6.

In Figure 7-6, we begin with 100,000 customers with an average lifetime value of $282. The firm value, therefore, is $28.2 million. During the year the firm lost 15,000 customers whose average LTV was $177. This was good, since the people who were lost were less valuable than those who remained. The average LTV went up to $300.

The firm gained 20,000 new customers during the year. Unfortunately, these new customers had a very low LTV, averaging $134. The firm needs to investigate why it is attracting the wrong kind of people, since its acquisitions are reducing the value of the firm.

During the year, 30,000 customers increased their LTV. The average LTV of these gainers was $341. In addition 10,000 customers reduced their LTV. Their average, after the loss, was $163. The final result of the year was a net gain of 5,000 customers, a small loss in average lifetime value, and an overall gain of about $1 million in firm value.

This kind of analysis is not difficult to do once you have developed a good system for calculating customer lifetime value. It is extremely useful in measuring the effectiveness of your acquisition and customer migration and retention programs.

Category	Number	Avg LTV	NPV
Begin balance	100,000	$282.00	$28,200,000
Defectors	15,000	**$177.00**	$2,655,000
Result	85,000	$300.53	$25,545,000
New customers	20,000	**$134.00**	$2,680,000
Result	105,000	$268.81	$28,225,000
Gainers	30,000	**$341.00**	$10,230,000
Losers	10,000	**$163.00**	$1,630,000
Nonchangers	65,000	$268.81	$17,472,619
New balance	105,000	$279.36	$29,332,619

Figure 7-6. Tracking the changes in LTV over a year.

The Reichheld Value Proposition

Over time, you can retain loyal customers by providing them with value superior to what they can get from your competition. The superior value results from two factors. In the first place, long-term loyal customers are less expensive to serve and therefore are more profitable. Some of that profit can be transferred to your loyal customers in terms of higher levels of service. In the second place, long-term loyal customers pay more for their products and services. They buy higher-priced options. They buy more, and they buy more often. This additional revenue can also be returned to the customers in higher value. The result is a win-win situation. Loyal customers give you higher value, and receive higher value in return.

The Importance of Loyal Employees

Another key contribution of Frederick Reichheld is a recognition of the importance of employee loyalty to customer loyalty. He pointed out that many customers are loyal not to the brand or the firm, but to the people who serve them at the firm. When you lose employees, you often lose customers as well. Any marketing program aimed at customer retention must begin with looking at employee satisfaction and retention. This is not normally an issue dealt with in marketing books like this one. It should be. The problem is that employee retention throughout a company is seldom something that the marketing department can influence directly. It they want to retain customers, however, marketers must recognize that customer loyalty and employee loyalty are usually tightly linked.

Summary

- Long-term loyal customers are more profitable than regular customers. They:

   Spend more, buy more often, and buy higher-priced options

   Are less expensive to serve

   Have a higher retention and referral rate

- There are three ways in which you can increase the number of loyal customers:

Treat them better.

Reward loyalty with points or benefits.

Vary customer acquisition methods to attract good customers and avoid the bad ones.

- The first step in treating long-term loyal customers better is to identify who they are. The retention rate is the key measurement of loyalty.

- Since your top 20 percent of customers usually give you 80 percent or more of your revenue, you must develop programs to reward and retain these people.

- You may also want to find ways of dropping the losers.

- There may be reasons for retaining some of your less valuable customers. These reasons include reference, referral, learning, and innovation.

- Airline miles programs have proved to be an excellent method for retaining and building customer loyalty.

- At least as important as customer recognition and rewards is recruiting the right kind of customer to begin with. Reichheld pointed out that the type of customer acquisition system can be a key element in building customer loyalty.

- Reichheld also pointed out that employee loyalty is central to customer loyalty.

Executive Quiz 6

Answers to quiz questions can be found in Appendix B.

1. Which is the best way to compensate agents for attracting long-term loyal customers?

   a. Pay higher commissions for high dollar sales.
   b. Pay higher commissions for renewals than for acquisition.
   c. Pay higher commissions for agent seniority.
   d. Pay higher commissions for new-customer acquisitions.
   e. All of the above.

2. Which of the following is less likely with loyal customers?

   a. They cost slightly more to serve than new customers.

   b. They tend to buy higher-priced options.

   c. They have a higher retention rate.

   d. They are more likely to become advocates.

   e. They produce more revenue than new customers.

3. In the Carlson loyalty study, which of the following was not shown to be true?

   a. Lower-income folks liked loyalty programs more than those with higher incomes.

   b. Older folks liked loyalty programs less.

   c. Of those surveyed, 35 percent wanted more supermarket programs.

   d. Of those who earned $75,000-plus, 43 percent did a lot more business because of the programs.

   e. Younger folks liked the programs more.

4. Regarding consumer loyalty programs, the Carlson study showed that:

   a. More than 50 percent of consumers are not aware of these programs

   b. Forty-four percent are aware of them and participate

   c. Only 36 percent of those with incomes over $75,000 participate

   d. Fifty-three percent of the participators do a lot more business because of the programs

   e. None of the above

5. In the company shown in Figure 7-7, you can see that after one year:

   a. The number of customers has gone down

   b. The firm value has gone up

   c. There were more existing customers whose LTV went down than up

   d. Overall LTV went down

   e. None of the above

6. If you were advising the management of this company, you would
tell them that their first priority should be:

   a. Worry about the defectors

   b. Concentrate on internal migration problems

   c. Focus on acquisition

   d. All of the above

   e. None of the above

7. Why do you think that Reichheld finds satisfaction scores worthless
for measuring loyalty?

   a. Very few companies measure customer satisfaction.

   b. Customers are unwilling to respond to surveys.

   c. The real measure of loyalty is retention and repurchase.

   d. No one has developed a sophisticated satisfaction scoring system.

   e. All of the above.

8. What was a key Reichheld contribution to database marketing theory?

   a. Development of lifetime value theory.

   b. Long-term customer costs are lower than new-customer costs.

   c. Employee loyalty does not affect customer loyalty.

   d. Customer value goes down over the years.

   e. All of the above.

Category	Number	Avg LTV	NPV
Begin balance	100,000	$282.00	$28,200,000
Defectors	15,000	**$343.00**	$5,145,000
Result	85,000	$271.24	$23,055,000
New customers	20,000	**$294.00**	$5,880,000
Result	105,000	$275.57	$28,935,00
Gainers	15,000	**$305.00**	$4,575,000
Losers	15,000	**$182.00**	$2,730,000
Nonchangers	75,000	$275.57	$20,667,857
New balance	105,000	$266.41	$27,972,857

Figure 7-7. Changing LTV over one year.

8

Using Customer Profiles in Marketing Strategy

To develop a relationship program, you still have to put individuals into groups, and develop products and strategies that will keep them loyal. That, in my opinion, is where companies have the most difficulty. We come across this problem every day with our clients. Even when you say to them, "I can help you identify your key customer segments," they respond, "Well, great, but tell me what to do with them once they're identified? How do I manage each segment?" Many marketers are not yet sophisticated enough to know what to do with the information.

STEPHEN SHAW, EXECUTIVE EDITOR
CRM Journal, Toronto

How to Achieve One-to-One Marketing

We talk about one-to-one dialog with each customer, and that has been the goal for many years. In fact, however, with a million customer names on our database, until recently it was not possible to really have 1 million separate and different dialogs.

This situation has changed dramatically with the advent of the Internet. Amazon.com, for example, does manage to have a dialog of a sort with each customer, as you can see from Figure 8-1. What books had I bought from Amazon at the time? Literature: *Closely Watched Trains*. Science: *In Search of the Big Bang*. And business: *Business-to-Business Internet Marketing*. Was this a dialog, or what?

Figure 8-1. Amazon welcomes Arthur back.

Few other web sites have achieved this type of dialog, but many are working on it. Right now there are probably a dozen sites doing an equally good job of creating a dialog.

Why Profiles Are Needed

No one knows yet the full potential of the web to create intimacy with customers. It is very great indeed. But there is still lots of room for customer contact through telephone calls. In addition, we will be using mass marketing and direct mail. The Internet may be more intimate, but is unlikely to completely supplant other database marketing media. If you are reaching your customers by noninteractive media, profiling is essential. Customers are not alike in their profitability or in their preferences. What we seek to do is to develop customer profiles—dividing customers into groups of people with similar tastes and purchasing habits, so that we can offer each group what it is looking for. This, at least, is the way that a dialog can be started.

How do you go about creating customer profiles? There are a number of valid and useful methods. One of the most powerful methods is RFM analysis, discussed in previous chapters. In this chapter, we will discuss three additional methods:

- Product affinity
- Demographics
- Cluster or lifestyle coding

Classification by Product Affinity

Affinity analysis starts from a customer's perspective. You look at what customers are buying, how often and when, and use this analysis as a way of classifying customers.

One obvious type of product affinity analysis would be to check everyone who buys baby diapers and baby food. Here is a household with a single preoccupation. Baby clothes, strollers, and crib toys are likely promotion items. You would be unlikely to offer these people golf clubs or yachting apparel without some other indication.

Another affinity could be people who buy lawn fertilizer, lawn mowers, and garden hoses. Should you try to sell them lawn furniture, shrubbery, weed whackers, and insect repellent? Go to it!

If they buy an executive briefcase, how about a computer? An unlikely offering for such a household would be a food processor or a TV recliner.

If they take out a home equity loan, you might offer them a credit card, auto loan, or traveler's checks. They might not be the best candidates for a CD.

This type of analysis is difficult to do. It demands a lot of thought and requires an analysis of customer purchasing habits. It also requires, of course, data about purchases in a database. Without the data, the analysis is impossible. Banks today create customer databases with display screens that suggest "next product." Their data come from affinity analysis. You profile your customers. See what customers in each profile are buying. Then look for customers in each profile who lack one of the standard products for that profile, and suggest it to them.

Cross-Buying Rates

One of the experts in affinity analysis is Richard J. Courtheoux, President of Precision Marketing Corporation. He shows how the purchasers of one product can be cross-tabulated against the buyers of another product for analysis purposes. For example, look at the table in Figure 8-2. From this table, we can conclude that buyers of product A are 10.5 times as likely to buy product B as people who have not purchased product A. We learn this by dividing 31.53 percent (A—yes, B—yes) by 3.01 percent (A—no, B—yes). We get, 31.53 / 3.01 = 10.5.

A	B-No	B-Yes	Total
No	268,431	8,328	276,759
Row	96.99%	3.01%	100.00%
Yes	27,023	12,444	39,467
Row	68.47%	31.53%	100.00%
Total	295,456	20,772	316,228
Row	93.43%	6.57%	100.00%

Figure 8-2. Cross-buying rates between products A and B.

Affinity Matrix

The computer can be used to calculate the cross-buying rates between any number of products in a similar way to that shown above. Based on these numbers, an affinity matrix can be constructed that shows the likelihood of each group of buyers of one product being buyers of another product.

Once you know the likelihood of people buying a certain product who already have bought another product, you can use this information in your daily contacts with customers. Part of the rationale used in banks to select "next product" comes from an affinity matrix. If you sell more than one product to customers, you can test whether this type of affinity ranking works by setting up control groups. For example, look at Figure 8-3. Using this matrix, if you have done your homework properly, mailings to people offering product B will do better for people who have already purchased product A or C than they will for people who have purchased product D.

How to Go about Affinity Profiling

On the assumption that you have a database that contains purchase information sufficient to do the analysis (which is going to be true on

	Prod A	Prod B	Prod C	Prod D
Prod A	eq	10.5	2.4	4.5
Prod B	10.5	eq	9.0	1.1
Prod C	2.4	9.0	eq	3.0
Prod D	4.5	1.1	3.0	eq

Figure 8-3. Affinity matrix.

only a small proportion of databases), how can you produce the affinity matrix? You can use ad hoc queries from your database to get the data, and enter the results into a spreadsheet. If you don't want to do the work yourself, the normal method is to call in a programmer from your service bureau and ask her to write a program that results in the matrix shown in Figure 8-3. After a day's work, most programmers should be able to do the job. Before the programmer begins, however, there are some problems you might need to address.

1. You have to decide what to do about quantities and prices. If product A is snow tires (at $300 a set) and product B is sewing supplies (at $20 per average purchase), do you equate $300 with $20 and call each one a purchase? It is possible to shift the equations and base the affinity matrix on dollars rather than number of purchases. You might try it both ways and see which one makes the most sense.

2. A more serious difficulty is the sheer problem of numbers. If you are a bank with 10 products, the matrix will be very neat and understandable: You can match home equity customers with credit card holders and savings account owners, and come to some valid and useful conclusions.

If, however, you are a department store with 10,000 products, your matrix may contain 100 million cells, and take tens of thousands of pages to print out. It will be totally useless to you. Beware of letting the computer do your thinking for you. The computer is not an intuitive machine. It cannot think. It will just follow orders, blindly. If you tell it to do something stupid, it will do so, hour after hour after hour.

That is one advantage of doing computations on a PC. A PC printer cannot easily print out 10,000 sheets of paper. It will take days, and wear out the laser printer. Someone will ask you if it is really necessary, before the job is finished. For a mainframe, 10,000 sheets of paper is an hour's work.

How to Handle a Massive Affinity Matrix

What should you do if you have too much data? You have to use your head. Purchases should probably be organized by department, not by product. That could cut the matrix down to a much smaller number, depending on the number of departments. Even that may be too big, though, if it results in more than 50 possible groups. For affinity to be useful, it should be limited to a maximum of about six groups on a side or less. You can achieve that by combining similar departments.

Don't place too much reliance on an elaborate computer-constructed affinity matrix. Common sense can often tell you as much or more. For example, affinity analysis may tell you that:

- People who buy snow tires are more likely to buy hardware than sewing supplies.
- People who have large savings accounts are more likely to open money market accounts than people who have large credit balances.
- People who buy children's books are more likely to buy encyclopedias than people who buy books on sports.

But *you knew all of this already!*

The advantage of an affinity matrix is that it can start you thinking about relationships that might not have been obvious, but that may become clear to you after you analyze the data. For example:

- What do female skiers purchase to wear when they aren't on a skiing trip?
- What is the best product to offer to someone who has just taken out a long-term care policy?

If you have the data, you should always experiment with building an affinity matrix to see what it can teach you. Based on the analysis, you may develop an entire, new marketing strategy.

One of the most creative uses of affinity analysis is Collaborative Filtering developed by NetPerceptions, of Eden Prairie, MN (*www.netperceptions.com*). This company has developed software that is able to compare the purchase preferences of millions of customers stored in a database. Using collaborative filtering software, NetPerceptions can determine "soul mates"—people who have the same set of likes and dislikes that you do. Once a soul mate is identified, the software can suggest additional purchases that your soul mate has made which are very likely to appeal to you. NetPerceptions has hundreds of clients, including eToys, Inc., DVD Express, Home Box Office, Kraft Foods, Publishers Clearing House, and Time Warner. They installed their sofrtware at GUS, the largest catalog house in the United Kingdom. Prior to the installation, GUS was getting one cross sell for every five catalog orders. When someone called up to order an item, the agents were trained to suggest an additional purchase. In 20 percent of the cases, they were able to sell the additional item. Once the Collaborative Filtering software was installed, their success rate jumped to 40 percent—a 100 percent increase in the cross sell ratio—by making recommendations to the agents, while the customer was on the line, of what additional products to suggest.

Profiling by Demographics

Profiling really depends on the comparison of two types of measurable variables: behavior and demographics. Behavior concerns factors like what your customers bought, the recency of purchase, amount of purchases, amount of responses, or length of time as a customer. These are actions of our customers that we can record in the database. RFM and affinity are methods of classifying behavior.

Demographics refers to facts about people that describe who they are and that we can determine, measure, and record. Demographics includes income, age, presence of children, housing type and value, ethnicity, sex, marital status, type of automobile, occupation, and a hundred other similar facts. There are, of course, lots of other things that affect purchasing behavior: for example, whether the parents are liberal or conservative, or whether the children have to earn their own pocket money or receive a lavish allowance from their parents. But these things are more difficult to learn, and so cannot be readily used in marketing analysis.

There are more than 200 different pieces of information about each U.S. household from the 2000 U.S. census which can be inserted in your database. A list of some of them gives you an idea:

Age

Education

Bank balance

Department store average balance

Family members who work

Occupations

Cars per household

Age of housing

Income level

Type of housing

Owned or rented

Property value

Travel time to work

Urban-rural nature of neighborhood

Where else can this demographic information come from?

- Credit history
- Results of direct surveys

Survey data are probably the most accurate. You can ask your own customers questions on satisfaction surveys, on application forms, in contests, and in other ways.

A winter resort collects a lot of data about its skiers in a unique way. Every winter the resort holds a sweepstakes with a Jeep as the prize. Entrants have to fill out a survey form contained in wooden boxes on each table in the cafeterias at the base of the ski lifts. The boxes contain forms, pencils, and a place to put the completed forms. A hundred thousand are filled out (including many duplicates, because skiers like Jeeps). The resort keypunches the information, eliminates the duplicates (following the fine print in the contest rules), and awards the Jeep every spring. In the process the resort builds up its valuable database, loaded with age, income, family composition, skiing experience, and future winter sport plans.

Census data are the second best source. Every 10 years the Census Bureau finds out an amazing amount of information about American households. Everyone is asked his or her age. Every seventh household is given the "long form" to fill out, which asks for about 200 other pieces of information, including income, occupation, type of housing, etc.

To protect the privacy of Americans, the Census Bureau does not release any information about a single household. Instead, it furnishes to the public only the long-form answers from a block (an area of about 14 houses). Marketers use this information, and assume that everyone in the block has the same demographics as the two families that filled out the long form. It is, obviously, wrong in some cases, but probably right in most cases, and better than nothing.

These data are purchased directly from the Census Bureau by private list compilers. These firms package the data attractively, and resell them to marketers for appending to their customer and prospect files. If you haven't looked into buying such data, you should. Demographics is a useful tool in marketing and an essential tool in modeling.

There are many other sources of demographic data besides the census and surveys. The R. L. Polk Company of Southfield, Michigan, the first national compiler of automobile data, purchases driver's license and registration data from the states that sell such data (about half of them do), and has compiled useful information from the other states. Where they have driver's licenses, they have an exact date of birth, which is, probably, as accurate as you can get.

Overlaid data are seldom completely accurate. Take all estimates of age, income, home value, and children with a huge grain of salt. They can be totally wrong. However, they are often all that is available, and in many cases, again, better than nothing.

Applicant Data

Banks and insurance companies are sitting on a gold mine that they rarely make use of. To obtain a loan or an insurance policy, people have to fill out a great deal of information. This information is private, of course, and should not be rented outside of the institution. There is no reason, however, why the financial institution that receives this information from its applicants cannot use it to better target its promotional mailings to these same applicants.

In fact, very few banks enter the valuable data that are submitted on loan applications. The loan processing staff see no point in spending the money to do the data entry (since they are not marketers). When marketers try to get such data, they find that the data are stored away in legal folders in some bank archive and are too costly to extract. Many insurance companies, however, are making effective use of applicant data for marketing purposes.

Is this legitimate? Well, why not? Think about it. If you go to a banker and tell him that you have $100,000 that you want him to put in a savings account, would you think it wrong for the banker to say to you: "You could make more money by putting that same money into a CD." Of course not. It would be a very helpful favor. Why, then, would it be wrong for the bank marketer to do the same thing?

In a free-market transaction, both parties always make a profit. The investor who puts his money into a CD makes a profit. If he didn't see it as profitable for him, he wouldn't do it. At the same time, the financial institution that issues the CD also makes a profit. That's why the bank has CDs. Any time you, as a marketer, persuade customers to buy one of your products, you are doing them a favor and helping them to make a profit. The market is characterized by ignorance. Millions of people pass up profitable opportunities *because they don't know what is available*. You, as a marketer, are playing a key role in the market by reducing ignorance, and hence helping millions to make profitable use of their resources.

The lesson: Use what information you can get your hands on to help your customers and prospects to learn what is available. You are doing them a favor.

How Significant Is Demographic Information?

Are age, income, and presence of children important to develop a profile of your customer? Maybe yes and maybe no. For some products—batteries, tires, wallpaper, dog food, garden supplies—these factors may show no correlation at all. For other products—insurance, bank products, cellular phones, vacation property—demographics may be a powerful profiling tool. In all cases, you should test overlays with a small sample of your file to determine whether there is any correlation between profitability, response, and the demographics.

Cluster Coding

Claritas, Inc., a major source of demographic information for marketing, located in Arlington, Virginia, has gone one step beyond demographics. For some time, it has been grouping demographic data into *clusters*—groups of people who have similar lifestyles. Claritas has grouped everyone in the United States (and Canada as well) into 62 different clusters. Some of Claritas's catchy names have become household words: Shotguns & Pickups, Pools & Patios, Furs and Station Wagons, Money & Brains.

Each cluster has a number, from 01 to 62. The lower numbers are usually the more affluent. Each cluster comes with a useful description that provides a lot of information about how people in that cluster live; what they buy; what media they read, watch, or listen to; what their housing is like; what their education, age, and family composition are. It is much easier to work with 62 different groups than data on 7.5 million census blocks, which is what the census data provide. Table 8-1 shows the 62 Prizm clusters with the percentage of the U.S. population included in each cluster.

Don't assume that people with a high buying power will have a high response rate. Marketers have found that groups with a high buying power often respond very poorly when promoted. Why is that? Probably because, with their affluence, they are subjected to hundreds of unwanted solicitations. They are used to tossing out mail unopened.

Each cluster represents a segment of society which has relatively similar lifestyles and purchasing habits. To illustrate that, here are the definitions of some of them:

Pools & Patios (04) are empty-nester executive and professional couples living the good life in their "postchild" years. Their dual incomes support rich, active lives filled with travel, leisure activities, and entertainment. Many live in the densely populated Northeast Corridor of the United States. Helena and I are Pools & Patios people.

Gray Power (13) are affluent retirees in Sunbelt cities. Found in retirement communities across the United States, these affluent retirees are playing golf, monitoring their health, and tending their hefty investment portfolios.

New Beginnings (24) are young, mobile city singles. Concentrated in the boomtowns of the Southeast, the Southwest, and the Pacific Coast, this cluster is a magnet for many young, well-educated minorities who are making fresh starts. They live in multiunit rentals and work in a variety of low-level, white collar jobs.

Middle America (38) are midscale families in midsized towns—married couples who are busy with kids and dogs. They enjoy fast food, sports, fishing, camping, and watching TV.

Grain Belt (57) are centered in the Great Plains and South Central United States in America's bread basket. Life is tied to the land and ruled by the weather. Mostly self-sufficient, family- and home-centered, these families are poor only in money.

Today, the easiest way to get cluster information appended to a customer or prospect file is to run the names through a program that appends zip + four coding (nine-digit zips). Licensed service bureaus have look-up tables that equate the nine digit zip codes to the appropriate cluster codes. For about $12 per thousand, you can have your entire database cluster-coded.

Don't expect to get a match on all your data. For a consumer list, you can expect to get between a 90 and 95 percent match, depending on the completeness of the vendor's database, the matching logic applied, the recency of your names, and the demographics of your list. Cluster coding cannot be used for a business-to-business file because the census data, on which it is based, counted only residences, not businesses. Don't make the mistake of trying to use clusters where they have no validity.

Table 8-1

Prizm Lifestyle Segmentation

Number	Cluster Name	% U.S. Households	Socioeconomic Rank	Description
01	Blue Blood Estates	1.18	Elite	Privileged superrich families
02	Winner's Circle	2.15	Wealthy	Executive suburban families
03	Executive Suites	1.32	Affluent	Upscale white-collar couples
04	Pools and Patios	1.85	Affluent	Established empty nesters
05	Kids and Cul-de-Sacs	2.93	Affluent	Upscale suburban families
06	Urban Gold Coast	0.59	Affluent	Professional urban single, and couples
07	Money and Brains	1.12	Affluent	Sophisticated townhouse couples
08	Young Literati	0.94	Upper middle	Upscale urban couples and singles
09	American Dreams	1.40	Upper middle	Established urban immigrant families
10	Bohemian Mix	1.48	Middle	Bohemian singles and couples
11	Second City Elite	1.89	Affluent	Upscale executive families
12	Upward Bound	1.83	Upper middle	Young upscale white-collar families
13	Gray Power	2.03	Middle	Affluent retirees in Sunbelt cities
14	Country Squires	1.33	Wealthy	Elite exurban families
15	God's Country	2.63	Affluent	Executive exurban families

16	Big Fish, Small Pond	1.37	Upper middle	Small-town executive families
17	Greenbelt Families	1.48	Upper middle	Young middle-class town families
18	Young Influentials	1.35	Upper middle	Upwardly mobile singles and couples
19	New Empty Nesters	2.06	Upper middle	Upscale suburban fringe couples
20	Boomers and Babies	1.11	Upper middle	Young white-collar suburban families
21	Suburban Sprawl	1.50	Middle	Young suburban townhouse couples
22	Blue-chip Blues	1.93	Middle	Upscale blue-collar families
23	Upstarts and Seniors	1.28	Middle	Middle-income empty nesters
24	New Beginnings	1.19	Middle	Young mobile city singles
25	Mobility Blues	1.48	Middle	Young blue-collar service families
26	Gray Collars	1.97	Middle	Aging couples in inner suburbs
27	Urban Achievers	1.60	Middle	Mid-level white-collar urban families
28	Big City Blend	1.12	Middle	Middle-income immigrant families
29	Old Yankee Rows	1.31	Middle	Empty-nest middle-class families
30	Mid-City Mix	1.08	Middle	African-American singles and couples
31	Latino America	1.23	Middle	Hispanic middle-class families
32	Middleburg Managers	1.72	Middle	Mid-level white-collar couples
33	Boomtown Singles	1.03	Middle	Middle-income young singles
34	Starter Families	1.58	Middle	Young middle-class families

Number	*Cluster Name*	*% U.S. Households*	*Socioeconomic Rank*	*Description*
35	Sunset City Blues	1.68	Lower middle	Empty nesters in aging industrial cities
36	Towns and Gowns	1.39	Lower middle	College-town singles
37	New Homesteaders	1.66	Middle	Young middle-class families
38	Middle America	2.23	Middle	Midscale families in midsize towns
39	Red, White, and Blues	1.80	Middle	Small-town blue-collar families
40	Military Quarters	0.42	Lower middle	GIs and off-base families
41	Big Sky Families	1.48	Upper middle	Midscale and farmland couples, kids
42	New Eco-topia	0.90	Middle	Rural white- and blue-collar farm families
43	River City, USA	1.78	Middle	Middle-class rural families
44	Shotguns and Pickups	1.91	Middle	Rural blue-collar workers and families
45	Single City Blues	1.74	Lower middle	Ethnically mixed urban singles
46	Hispanic Mix	1.56	Poor	Urban Hispanic singles and families
47	Inner Cities	1.94	Poor	Inner-city single parents and families
48	Smalltown Downtown	1.83	Lower middle	Older renters and young families
49	Hometown Retired	1.20	Lower middle	Low-income older singles and couples
50	Family Scramble	2.19	Lower middle	Low-income Hispanic families
51	Southside City	1.97	Poor	African-American service workers

52	Golden Ponds	1.62	Lower middle	Retirement town seniors
53	Rural Industrial	1.70	Lower middle	Low-income blue-collar families
54	Norma Rae-Ville	1.37	Poor	Bi-racial mill towns
55	Mines and Mills	2.24	Poor	Older families in mine and mill towns
56	Agri-business	1.45	Middle	Rural town and ranch families
57	Grain Belt	2.25	Lower middle	Farm owners and tenants
58	Blue Highways	2.04	Lower middle	Moderate blue-collar farm families
59	Rustic Elders	1.88	Lower middle	Low-income older rural couples
60	Back Country Folks	2.18	Lower middle	Remote rural town families
61	Scrub Pine Flats	1.52	Poor	African-American farm families
62	Hard Scrabble	1.99	Poor	Families in poor isolated areas

Overlaying cluster codes may be very useful, or it may be a waste of money. The decision depends on the product you are selling and the size of your customer base. In the ideal situation, you can learn that your product appeals to Young Influentials and Boomers & Babies, but it goes nowhere when marketed to God's Country or Old Yankee Rows. This type of knowledge is dynamite. You can use it to purchase new prospect names from the right clusters, and avoid getting names from the wrong clusters. It should pick up your response rate by a significant amount—by far more than the cost of the appended information.

On the other hand, such breakthroughs are few and far between. If marketing by cluster were that easy, everyone would be doing it. In most cases, the lift from using clusters is marginal, and hardly generates enough additional revenue to pay for the cost of appending the cluster information. Here are two cases in which it really paid off:

■ *A West Coast consumer credit company* offered small, unsecured loans to customers with no credit or less than perfect credit. The company mailed 2.6 million pieces of direct mail every quarter on behalf of its 260 branches. Response rates were dropping, and the cost per loan was rising. The company decided to code its customer file with Prizm clusters, finding, to its surprise, that only about a third of the Prizm clusters were interested in its loans. By concentrating its direct mail on the successful Prizm clusters, the company reduced its mail dramatically, while increasing its response rates. The cost per loan dropped from more than $700 to less than $350.

■ *An East Coast cable marketing council* decided to target some of its "nevers"—35 percent of current nonsubscribers who had never subscribed to cable. From an analysis of this group, the council members learned that about 10 percent were very interested in news and information programming. How could they reach this group? Based on Prizm cluster descriptions, they identified eight Prizm clusters that they called the "info seekers" target group. Matching residents of these eight clusters with their customer database, they identified 300,000 households that were living in the eight clusters, but that had never subscribed. They sent direct-mail pieces to these 300,000 in a creative campaign called "Perception vs Reality," which emphasized the information services such as CNN, CNBC, C-Span, the Discovery Channel, the Learning Channel, and News Channel 8. The results of the campaign surprised everyone involved. Typically the market averaged about 5,100 connects a week. During the two weeks of the campaign, there were 17,440 cable connections, representing a weekly increase of 71 percent. The direct-mail response rate was 43 percent higher than past campaigns. A follow-on campaign generated a 69 percent increase in direct-mail responses.

How can you tell whether you should use cluster data in your situation? There is an easy answer, which is always correct: Test. Get cluster information appended on 50,000 customers or so, and see what you discover. Split your next marketing program into half that are selected using cluster information and half that are selected without using clusters. See which provides more profit (after deducting the cost of the clustering).

Profiling Retail Customers

Modern retailers make extensive use of profiling. Gold customers, who are responsible for most of a retailer's revenue and profit, must be kept loyal. Customers who are not buying as much as they should, have to be encouraged to buy more. The most advanced retailers have learned that money should not be spent on worthless customers who may not even be paying their way.

Here is how some large modern retailers go about the process. A typical large retailer has several hundred stores, and more than a million customers, most of whom are women. To gather data on their customers, they use two methods. Many customers use a proprietary store charge card. Gathering these charge card data is easy. Other customers use a credit card such as Master Card or Visa. The point-of-sale terminals capture the numbers from these cards. For those customers not already in their database, credit companies, such as Trans Union, can provide the names and addresses matching the credit card numbers using a reverse append. For the average chain, this system captures more than half of the customers representing almost three-quarters of the total sales. For customers who pay by cash or check, you are usually out of luck. It is almost impossible to get accurate data on their continued purchases. That is why stores want you to use a credit card, if possible. In the old days, stores gave you a discount if you paid cash, since credit cards charge the merchant a fee. Today, most stores have realized the value of the data (and increased sales) that come from credit card users. It is the rare store today that foolishly gives a discount for cash or check.

The stores then code the household purchase data for RFM, and typically add cluster coding such as that provided by Claritas. The goal of the process is to learn:

- What percentage of my sales do they generate?
- Who are my best customers?
- What is their clothing budget, and what is our share of their wallet?
- What are their demographic characteristics?
- When and what do they buy from us?
- Who pays full price versus only items on sale?
- When and what do they buy from the competition?

Skillful analysis of customer purchase history matched against sale dates and promotions can help to answer these questions so that the profiling process can begin. With this knowledge, retailers typically divide their customers into unique segments based partly on demographics, but mostly on behavior. For example, they can separate their customers into the categories shown in Figure 8-4. Breaking the customers down in this way is very important to customer relationship management and marketing strategy. From these numbers, you can easily compare their lifetime values. Figure 8-5 presents an example of the lifetime value of Gold customers. Each Gold customer is very valuable to the store, representing a lifetime value of more than $2,300 by the fourth year with the chain. The average Gold customer makes almost two visits a month, spending more than $150 on each visit. The store spends $40 per year on special services for each customer, and spends $75 to acquire good customers like this.

On the other hand, occasional shoppers are not very profitable. Figure 8-6 presents a picture of the lifetime value of such a shopper. For the first two years, occasional shoppers don't even pay their way. Notice that the store spends almost nothing on marketing expenses for these customers—$1 per year. This is because of a conscious decision that the

	Number	Revenue
Gold customers	15%	55%
Regular customers	35%	35%
Occasional shoppers	50%	10%

Figure 8-4. Retail store customers by revenue segment.

	Year 1	Year 2	Year 3	Year 4
Revenue				
Customers	280,000	210,000	168,000	142,800
Retention rate	75%	80%	85%	90%
Visits per month	1.40	1.51	1.72	1.81
Average sale	$126.00	$147.00	$165.00	$172.00
Annual revenue	$592,704,000	$559,364,400	$572,140,800	$533,477,952
Costs	70%	60%	58%	56%
Variable costs	$414,892,800	$335,618,640	$331,841,664	$298,747,653
Marketing costs $40	$11,200,000	$8,400,000	$6,720,000	$5,712,000
Acquisition cost $75	$21,000,000			
Total costs	$447,092,800	$344,018,640	$338,561,664	$304,459,653
Profit	$145,611,200	$215,345,760	$233,579,136	$229,018,299
Discount rate 14%	1.00	1.14	1.30	1.48
NPV profit	$145,611,200	$188,899,789	$179,676,258	$154,742,094
Cumulative NPV profit	$145,611,200	$334,510,989	$514,187,248	$668,929,342
Lifetime value	**$520.04**	**$1,194.68**	**$1,836.38**	**$2,389.03**

Figure 8-5. Lifetime value of Gold customers.

	Year 1	Year 2	Year 3	Year 4
Revenue				
Customers	800,000	360,000	180,000	99,000
Retention rate	45%	50%	55%	60%
Visits per month	0.10	0.12	0.15	0.17
Average sale	$67.00	$72.00	$76.00	$84.00
Annual revenue	$64,320,000	$37,324,800	$24,624,000	$16,964,640
Costs	70%	60%	58%	56%
Variable costs	$45,024,000	$22,394,880	$14,281,920	$9,500,198
Marketing costs $1	$800,000	$360,000	$180,000	$99,000
Acquisition cost $40	$32,000,000			
Total costs	$77,824,000	$22,754,880	$14,461,920	$9,599,198
Profit	−$13,504,000	$14,569,920	$10,162,080	$7,365,442
Discount rate 14%	1.00	1.14	1.30	1.48
NPV profit	−$13,504,000	$12,780,632	$7,816,985	$4,976,650
Cumulative NPV profit	−$13,504,000	−$723,386	$7,093,616	$12,070,266
Lifetime value	**−$16.88**	**−$0.90**	**$8.87**	**$15.09**

Figure 8-6. Lifetime value of the occasional shopper.

marketing budget should be focused only on shoppers who are likely to be profitable to the store.

Four important steps are involved in building profiles and profiting from them:

- Collecting and analyzing the data so that conclusions can be drawn.

- Gaining insight through defining the groups, and classifying all customers into the correct group after they have been with the store for six months or more.

- Managing customer relationships—changing your behavior toward customers based on what you know about them. It takes real guts to go to your management and say, "I am going to spend 60 percent of my marketing budget on the Gold customers, who represent only 15 percent of the customers. I am not going to spend anything at all on the occasional shoppers who represent half of all of our customers." Management is going to say, "Are you crazy? You are going to ignore a half a million people?" But without this tough decision making, your profiling exercise is worthless. The whole purpose of profiling is to develop a more profitable marketing strategy than you would have had without the profile. You have to act, and not just sit around and draw graphs.

- Tracking the impact of your strategies and tactics on each segment to be sure that what you are doing is actually affecting customer behavior and company profits.

The goal for the Gold customers, of course, is retention. You have to spend a lot of money on these people to retain them, because they are very important to the store. What can you do for such people? You can provide:

- Loyalty benefits, based on their status
- Private sales with advanced notice
- Personalized gifts with purchases
- Seasonal merchandise previews
- Image-based mailings and catalogs
- In-store recognition and special services

What should you do for your regular customers? These are good solid people. They represent about a third of your customers, and they provide you with a third of your revenue. For these people, you are hoping to see some upward migration. You will spend some money to accomplish this.

What do you do for your occasional shoppers? First, don't spend much money on them. Even though they are half of your customers, they are really worthless when it comes to generating profits. Give them announcements of clearance sales and gift certificate promotions. Spend your marketing dollars on someone else.

How can you measure your success with each of these three groups? You have to set up control groups, which do not get the special promotions given to others in the segment. Armed with these control groups, you can use your database to measure:

- Attrition and retention
- Migration upward and downward
- Incremental sales per program and per season
- Frequency of seasonal purchases
- Dollars spent per trip and per season
- Number of departments shopped per trip and per season
- Number of items shopped per trip and per season
- Share of customer's wallet

Profiling Financial Services Customers and Prospects

Some credit insurance providers used a consumer profile of household financial spending habits. The consumers consisted of over 3,000 households recruited from a nationally representative sample of credit card holders. Every month, each household sent in its credit card statements, plus copies of the credit card and fee enhancement offers that it received from credit card issuers during the month. With these data, the insurers not only knew who bought what, but the offer that triggered the purchase decision.

A segmentation study of American households, from a financial services perspective, was done using these data. The study identified seven basic consumer panel households, as shown in Figure 8-7. Although credit insurance was offered to all these seven groups, only three of them ended up with a significant percentage purchasing the product. The three best segments for the insurance were the white-collar, blue-collar, and lower-income segments, which together represented 33 per-

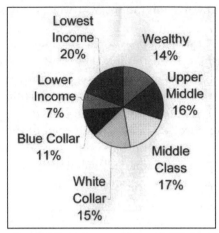

Figure 8-7. U.S. population divided
into seven segments.

cent of all American households. Figure 8-8 shows a more detailed look
at the segments.

Once the credit insurance providers knew who was likely to buy the
product, and who was not, it would have been very profitable, through
profiling, to greatly reduce their marketing costs and increase their
profits by focusing their marketing efforts on those three responsive
segments. By ignoring the other 67 percent of the potential market,
however, it would have reduced overall sales. That was the dilemma.

In Figure 8-9, we show two ways of marketing credit insurance to 1
million households. The first method is to telephone all of the 1 million. The second method involves calls only to those households in the
three most responsive segments. By concentrating on responsive seg-

	% Population	Costs to Acquire	Costs to Serve	Overall Potential	Key Needs
Wealthy	14	High	Medium	Low	Child's education
Upper middle	16	High	Medium	Low	Retirement
Middle class	17	High	High	Low	Leave me alone
White collar	15	Medium	Medium	High	Financial independence
Blue collar	11	Low	High	High	Family protection
Lower income	7	Medium	Low	High	Owning a home
Lowest income	19	Medium	High	Medium	Disposable income

Figure 8-8. U.S. population segments in the credit insurance market.

	Total	*Selected*
Called	1,000,000	330,000
Calling cost	$4,000,000	$1,320,000
Response rate	3.00%	6.00%
Sales	30,000	19,800
Revenue	$4,500,000	$2,970,000
Profit	$500,000	$1,650,000

Figure 8-9. Increased profit from promoting only responsive segments.

ments, profits from a million cardholders would jump from a half a million to $1.6 million. At the same time, of course, overall revenue would decrease by $1.5 million. For an outsider, the choice would have been a no-brainer. Go for the profits. Inside the industry, the choice was a difficult one. Why?

Why Profiles Are Not Always Used

Product managers within financial institutions, like all other product managers, respond to financial incentives. Their performance incentives are often designed to produce sales, rather than profits. A manager who brings in $4.5 million in sales may receive more of a bonus than one who brings in only $3 million, even though his profits to the bank are $1.5 million more. The problem is, how do you prove to bank management that you have increased these profits? Better to just take the bonus based on the sales rather than trying to deal with bank managers who understand sales, but *not* database marketing. Unless the compensation system in banks were to be changed, there would be little point in those in charge of insurance putting this segmentation program into operation.

Summary

- Profiling is a way of dividing your customer base into segments with similar attributes—purchasing behavior, demographics, or lifestyle. It is useful because you can engage in relationship building better if you talk about things that the customers are interested in. It is also useful because you can vary your marketing programs based on the segment you are dealing with and thereby improve your success rate.

- There are several different types of profiling methods—consisting of information or data that you can add to a database to assist in constructing meaningful segments. They include product affinity, demographics, and cluster coding.

- Product affinity is a useful way of classifying customer behavior. By comparing purchasing behavior of different customers, you can create, useful segments (parents of babies, automotive repair freaks, sewing specialists) that can be the start of a dialog, or a way of improved marketing.

- An affinity matrix can be constructed on a computer, which measures the propensity of people who buy certain products to buy other products. Be careful not to go overboard with computer affinity matrixes. Computers can generate thousands of pages of data, which are almost useless in marketing.

- Demographics can be applied to any file. The 2000 census lists several hundred different pieces of data, such as income, presence of children, and house value, that can be inserted into any database record to which a zip + four coding has been applied. The demographics can be used to develop profiles of a customer database.

- Cluster coding can be very profitable for the right product situation.

Executive Quiz 7

Answers to quiz questions can be found in Appendix B.

1. Banks often fail to use customer data from completed loan applications in profiling customers for their marketing programs. Why?

    a. Use of customer data in marketing programs violates federal regulations.

    b. Customer privacy prevents using loan application data in marketing.

    c. The loan application processing branch does not understand marketing.

    d. All loan applications are destroyed as soon as a loan is approved.

    e. None of the above.

2. Why is cluster coding not used in all marketing profiling exercises?

    a. Most marketers have never heard of cluster coding.

    b. Cluster coding works best with business to business files.

    c. Cluster coding only works with a small percentage of products.

    d. Cluster coding is quite expensive.

    e. None of the above.

3. If the main goal for Gold customers is retention, what should be the main goal for regular customers?

    a. Retention

    b. Reactivation

    c. Referrals

    d. Upward migration

    e. None of the above

4. In the credit insurance example, why were banks not interested in increasing their profits from the service?

    a. Banks are a public service.

    b. Managers were compensated for revenue, not profits.

    c. Managers did not understand profiling.

    d. Wrong: Banks were interested in profits.

    e. None of the above.

5. What is the best way to collect data on retail customers' purchases?

    a. Get them to use a store credit card.

    b. Save bank credit card numbers and reverse append names.

    c. Both a and b.

    d. Use focus groups.

    e. Do a survey of customer buying habits.

6. Of the following Prizm cluster families, which probably has the lowest income?

    a. Golden Ponds

    b. Suburban Sprawl

    c. Greenbelt Families

    d. Gray Power

    e. Bohemian Mix

7. In an affinity matrix, which product dimensions would be most useful for marketers?

    a. 100×100

    b. 50×50

    c. 20×20

    d. 10×10

    e. 6×6

8. Breakeven for a direct-mail promotion is 2 percent. A test mailing to 20,000 had an average response rate of 1.2 percent and an overall loss. Overlaying Prizm clusters shows response rates by cluster varying from 5.8 percent to 0.3 percent. What should you do for the rollout?

    a. Give up. The test was a failure.

    b. Mail names in Prizm clusters with 2 percent or better response rates.

    c. Mail all cells, since Prizm cannot predict response rates.

    d. Retest. It may have been a fluke.

    e. Redo the offer, change lists, and rollout.

9

Strategy Verification: Testing and Control Groups

I think that without numbers there is no future. You cannot measure your progress unless you've got benchmarks against which to evaluate costs and profits. So ROI, RFM, and Lifetime Value are the minimal critical benchmarks you must now establish if you want to measure the profitability of your business today. Those same benchmarks then become the standards by which you measure your business' future growth and the justification for the database tools you must have to get that growth. Without the numbers, you don't have a future.

JOHN TRAVIS, MANAGER,
Business Development, Hudson's Bay Company

Why Testing Is Essential

The market is constantly changing. What worked last year does not work as well this year, and may not work at all next year. Capital One pioneered the "teaser rate" for credit cards. It was the first to make an introductory offer of 3.9 percent annual percentage rate to get people to switch their credit cards. The company was wildly successful. Its card memberships and profits grew at a phenomenal rate. Of course, after a few months, the teaser rate expired. The card interest rates for each new member went up to 18.9 percent. Capital One lost some customers, but kept most of them.

Soon, everyone was offering teaser rates. In a couple of years, the idea lost its luster. People were no longer fooled. Capital One, again ahead of the market, shifted to offering a firm 9.9 percent permanent rate, while the rest of the world was still offering teasers.

The object of testing is to learn how well you are doing, so you can modify your marketing strategy. The goal is to constantly be very successful at what you are doing.

Why Management Resists Testing

You have 400,000 customers to whom you can make an offer. You are pretty sure of what that offer should be and which customers should get the offer. But you want to test your theory before you blow your whole budget on a hunch. You want to send two different offers to 25,000 customers each, and then roll out the best offer to the remaining 350,000. Management will resist the idea. "Our goal is to increase sales this quarter. Your tests will delay the results until next quarter. Forget the test, take your best offer, and roll it out. You can test later."

It might seem best not to argue with your managers. But postponing testing could cost you your job. Without tests, you cannot learn anything. If you cannot learn, you cannot improve, while your competition may be learning a great deal. There is real danger in not testing. If you are not really on top of things, you may not be around next year after company profits take a nosedive and management looks around for something to cut.

Fortunately, database marketing is in a much better position to test and prove its contribution to profits than advertising, customer relations, corporate planning, R&D, or most other staff functions. We just have to go about it in an organized way.

Marketing Objectives

The first step in any testing program is to determine what you are trying to accomplish. The goal of database marketing programs is usually to:

- Increase sales to existing customers
- Reduce attrition
- Gain new customers

The statement of objectives should always contain a number and a date (increase sales by 4 percent within the next two years). The reason for the specific number is so that you can relate this objective to your estimated costs *before you start*. A 4 percent increase in sales may represent, for instance, a $1 million increase in gross profits from those additional goods sold. If your total marketing program costs more than $1 million, marketing, as an activity, has lost money for the company, even though sales have gone up. You will have to refine your strategy: Shoot for a more lofty goal, cut your costs, or come up with a better relationship-building idea.

The best method, of course, is to define your customer lifetime value and test the effectiveness of various alternative ways of increasing lifetime value. Building lifetime value thus becomes a measurable goal. Once you have defined consistent goals, one of your next steps will be to set up—in advance—the controls necessary so that whatever marketing program you pursue is properly tested. In this chapter, we will go through the steps necessary to test several types of marketing programs. Let's begin by devising a test for a department store. Many of the concepts in this chapter were developed by Annette Champion of Arthur D. Little, Inc., the international management and technology consulting firm.

Creating a Controlled Test

Let's assume that your department store has a house credit card that is tied in to a customer database. This house card permits you to capture data about purchases. You are planning a new offer to increase sales. The question: How much does the offer actually increase sales, and what is its effect on lifetime value?

To set up a test you need two groups of customers: a test group (which gets the offer) and a control group (which does not get the offer). Without the control group, you really know very little. If you don't have a control group and sales go up, is it because of the offer or because of some other factor unrelated to the offer? You can't be sure. If overall sales go down, perhaps they would have gone down *more* without the offer. Who knows, if you didn't test properly? So we will set up these two groups.

Setting Up Test and Control Groups

Assume that your department store has 400,000 customers who use the store credit card. You have brought in a new line of high-fashion clothes for women. This is being promoted through print ads. You want to test, in addition, the effectiveness of a direct-mail offer to female customers. For the purpose of the test, you have decided to mail your offer to 20,000 women.

As a first step, you query your database to see how many women have credit cards in their name. There are 200,000. You must select two groups: a test group of 20,000 who will get the mailing and a control group of 20,000 who will not get the mailing. Control groups do not have to be the same size as test groups. They could be larger or smaller. But they have to be big enough to give valid results, and they have to be exactly the same as the test group in demographics and purchase behavior. To create these two groups, you use the procedure called an *N*th.

As already described in the RFM chapter, an *N*th is a software function that assures that you get an exact representative sample in each group selected. If your test and control groups are in any way different from each other, you won't get valid test results.

An *N*th works this way: If you have a file of 200,000 records and you want a test file of 40,000 (see Figure 9-1), you would select every fifth record to create your *N*th (200,000 / 40,000 = 5). If you want a test file of 50,000, you will select every fourth record, etc. There is free *N*th software at www.dbmarketing.com.

We will, of course, separate the 40,000 into two groups of 20,000: a test group and a control group. We do this, as well, using an *N*th. Most modern database software systems permit marketers to create these test and control groups with a PC at their desks, storing in each customer's record the information that the customer is in a test group or a control group for a particular promotion. This is not a trivial matter. As a marketer, you

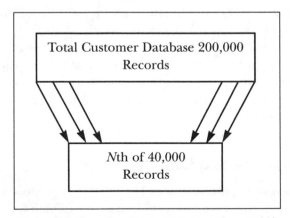

Figure 9-1. Constructing test groups using an *N*th.

will have to come up with an organized coding system so that you can remember who was in which group. You must keep other marketers in the organization from ruining the validity of your test by sending some other promotion to your test or control group during the test period.

How big should a test or a control file be? Cost considerations say, make them small. Statistical accuracy says, make them big. As a good rule of thumb, each group must be big enough so that you can anticipate a minimum of 500 responses from the promoted group. If you anticipate a 2 percent response rate, then your test group must have at least 25,000 people in it. If you have too few respondents, the test may give you invalid results for future predictions. The control group can be smaller than the test group, but still must be large enough for statistical accuracy.

Control Group Substitutes

Sometimes it is not possible to set up a control group. One example is the Travelers Property and Casualty study reported in Chapter 7. In this case, a series of communications were sent to customers of participating independent agents. The control group was designed to answer this question: "Will these communications improve the retention rate of these customers?" The perfect situation would be to select 20 percent of each participating agent's customers and not send them the messages. Independent agents, paying for the programs with their own money, would not willingly participate in such a test. Alison Bond, who ran the Travelers program, used the retention rate of nonparticipating agent customers as the control group. Using the customer data from these agents, she was able to show that her program increased the retention rates by about 5 percent. A statistician might object to this control group. Perhaps the participating agents were more customer friendly than the nonparticipating agents. If this were to be so, their higher retention rates were due to the agent's effectiveness, not the communications. Control groups are almost always a compromise, but that does not mean that you can do without them.

When the groups are set up, a promotional offer is made to the test group. The control group is treated like everyone else, and does not receive the promotion or other related communications. They do, of course, get all normal communications that customers get. In the example we are using here, both groups are on the database and use the store's credit card. Their purchase behavior is registered in the marketing database. A month later, the purchases of the two groups are compared. The effectiveness of the promotion is measured by the difference in purchases by the test group and the control group.

Let us assume that we are promoting a woman's suit that costs $150. Let us also assume that 1,000 of the 20,000 test households (5 percent) took advantage of the offer, buying a net average of $150 of promoted items (the suit) plus $80 of nonpromoted items during the month. The remainder of the test group (19,000 households) bought an average of $30 of nonpromoted items during the same month. Let us further assume that during the same month, the controls bought an average of $2 of the promoted items (the suits—even though they were not promoted to them) and $22 of nonpromoted items. How successful was the test? As Figure 9-2 shows, overall, sales due to the test increased by $320,000 and profits increased by $118,000.

- Why did sales of nonpromoted items increase in responding households? Because when the customers went into the store to get the suit, they saw other items and bought them too.

- Why did sales of nonpromoted items to nonresponding test households increase over sales to control households? Because some of the nonresponding customers went to the store because of the promotion, did not like the suit, but bought something else anyway.

The return on investment from this promotion is 11.8 ($118,000 / $10,000). Since the test generated a clear $118,000 profit over the cost of the promotion itself, the promotion can now be repeated to the other customers with, presumably, equal success. So far, however, what we have done is straight direct marketing using a database. What follows is real database marketing.

In database marketing we consider the long-term effect on the customers of every customer contact. This promotion was a success in that it increased profits by more than the cost of the test. That is not the end of the impact on the customers, however. We must look at the results on the test group in the following months. After all, the test resulted in bringing many more than 1,000 women into the store: the 1,000 respondents plus *an unknown number of nonrespondents*. Many of these women might not otherwise have come into the store. How do we know that? Because most of the women in the control group stayed at home. As a result of this promotion, those women who did respond moved to higher RFM cells. They all became recent buyers, they probably became more frequent buyers, and their monetary scores probably advanced. A woman respondent whose RFM cell was 423 before the promotion

Sales to Control and Test Groups in First Month after a Promotion

Group	Number of Customers	Average Sale of: Promoted Items	Nonpromoted Items	Combined Sales	Total Amount
Responders	1,000	$150.00	$80.00	$230.00	$230,000
Nonresponders	19,000	$0.00	$30.00	$30.00	$570,000
Controls	20,000	$2.00	$22.00	$24.00	$480,000
Total	40,000				$1,280,000
Total sales to test group					$800,000
Total sales to control group					$480,000
Increased sales due to the promotion					$320,000
Gross profit from sales @ 40%					$128,000
Cost of promotion to test group @ $500/M					$10,000
Net profit					$118,000
Return on investment $118,000 / $10,000					$11.8

Figure 9-2. Measuring results of the test promotion.

could have become a 534 because of her purchase of the suit. The same type of thing probably happened to almost all the 1,000+ respondents. In addition, the lifetime value of the respondents probably went up as well. We can see this from their subsequent behavior.

The following months, some of those in the test group who moved to higher RFM cells will probably visit the store again. Why? Because of increased recency, frequency, and monetary scores. These responders (and some of the others) have become recent buyers because of the promotion. Recent buyers (we remember from Chapter 5) are the most likely customers to buy again soon. This is normal behavior. This subsequent behavior can also be measured, as shown in Figure 9-3.

As the figure shows, total sales this month are down. Why were sales to controls only $400,000 during the second month? Who knows? This was a slower month for reasons unrelated to the test. If the controls had not been followed, however, and only the test group measured, one could have concluded that the test promotion *depressed* sales in the following month, which, of course, was not true. The testing shows that even in a slow month, the test in the previous month *helped* overall sales.

■ Why did the respondents buy more than the controls in the second month? They received no promotion. *The reason:* Recency (and pos-

Sales to All Groups in Second Month after Promotion			
Group Name	*Number*	*Sales/ Customer*	*Total Sales*
T1 Test-resp.	1,000	$30	$30,000
T2 Test-nonresp.	19,000	$21	$399,000
T3 Controls	20,000	$20	$400,000
T4 Total (T1+T2+T3)	40,000		$829,000
S1 Total sales to the test group			$429,000
S2 Total sales to the control group			$400,000
S3 Net increased sales from promotion (S1-S2)			$29,000
S4 Marginal profit from sales (@ 20% of S3)			$5,800
C1 Cost of promotion (none)			$0
P1 Net profit from promotion (S4-C1)			$5,800

Figure 9-3. Sales in the second month.

sibly frequency and monetary). They had moved to higher RFM cells. This is the long-term effect of any promotion, and shows the difference between direct marketing and database marketing.

■ Why did the nonrespondents buy more than the controls in the second month? For the same reasons. Some of them had become recent buyers *because of the promotion,* even though they did not buy the suit. Database marketing works!

Good testing programs will follow the test and control groups for the next 12 months to determine the residual effects of the test. In some situations, the residual effects can be even more important than the initial response to the promotion, and can, in themselves, be the justification for the marketing effort itself. The next step, of course, will be to determine the effect on the lifetime customer value from the promotion. Lifetime value, rather than the immediate short-term payoff, should be the real goal of marketing database strategy.

Figure 9-4 shows that the store loses about 35 percent of its average newly acquired store customers in their year of acquisition (retention rate is 65 percent). In subsequent years, the retention rate of the loyal-

	Year 1	Year 2	Year 3	Year 4
Revenue				
Customers	20,000	13,000	9,100	6,825
Retention rate	65%	70%	75%	80%
Visits per month	0.50	0.60	0.70	0.80
Average sale	$65.00	$70.00	$75.00	$80.00
Annual revenue	$7,800,000	$6,552,000	$5,733,000	$5,241,600
Costs	60%	50%	48%	47%
Variable costs	$4,680,000	$3,276,000	$2,751,840	$2,463,552
Marketing costs $12	$240,000	$156,000	$109,200	$81,900
Acquisition cost $45	$900,000			
Total costs	$5,820,000	$3,432,000	$2,861,040	$2,545,452
Profit	$1,980,000	$3,120,000	$2,871,960	$2,696,148
Discount rate 14%	1.00	1.14	1.30	1.48
NPV profit	$1,980,000	$2,736,842	$2,209,200	$1,821,722
Cumulative NPV profit	$1,980,000	$4,716,842	$6,926,042	$8,747,764
Lifetime value	**$99.00**	**$235.84**	**$346.30**	**$437.39**

Figure 9-4. LTV of control group.

ists tends to go up. Customers cost $45 to acquire. The cost of serving customers tends to go down, the longer they are with the store. The store spends about $12 per customer per year on marketing programs. Loyal customers, who stay with the store for four years, are really valuable. They are worth more than $400 to the store.

Let's see the effect of the single promotion that is described above on the responders to the test. The long-range effect of the test on the respondents was to change three types of behavior. As Figure 9-5 illustrates, their retention rate has increased by 1 percent, their visits per month have gone up by a very small amount, and their average sale on a visit has increased by only $1. In the example, only 1,000 women responded to the test. So that we can compare the charts, we have assumed that the store went ahead and tested enough so that it had 20,000 respondents. The cost of the promotion was $19, including both the discount given to the respondents and the cost of mailing to the nonrespondents. Lifetime value in Year 1 has gone down slightly, due to

	Year 1	*Year 2*	*Year 3*	*Year 4*
Revenue				
Customers	20,000	13,200	9,372	7,123
Retention rate	66%	71%	76%	81%
Visits per month	0.55	0.65	0.75	0.85
Average sale	$66.00	$71.00	$81.00	$86.00
Annual revenue	$8,712,000	$7,310,160	$6,832,188	$6,248,050
Costs	60%	50%	48%	47%
Variable costs	$5,227,200	$3,655,080	$3,279,450	$2,936,583
Marketing costs $12	$240,000	$158,400	$112,464	$85,473
Promotion cost $19	$380,000			
Acquisition cost $45	$900,000			
Total costs	$6,747,200	$3,813,480	$3,391,914	$3,022,056
Profit	$1,964,800	$3,496,680	$3,440,274	$3,225,994
Discount rate 14%	1.00	1.14	1.30 1.48	
NPV profit	$1,964,800	$3,067,263	$2,646,364	$2,179,726
Cumulative NPV profit	$1,964,800	$5,032,063	$7,678,428	$9,858,153
Lifetime value	**$98.24**	**$251.60**	**$383.92**	**$492.91**

Figure 9-5. LTV of test group.

the cost of the promotion. But lifetime value in the fourth year has zoomed from $437 to $492.

How can we know that these things will happen? We can't. We can look for them, and test for them, and measure progress toward them. In time, we will become adept at being able to understand the short- and long-range effects of our marketing and relationship-building activities. These things we can learn only by setting up test and control groups.

Control Group Failure

I worked with a large financial services company that was persuaded by its direct agency to issue plastic "Preferred Member" cards to its customers who had used its services three times or more. The cards gave their holders check-cashing privileges and other benefits. There seemed to be a definite spike in sales to holders of the cards, so the company was happy with the results. A couple of years later, the marketing staff of the company was changed and the new managers asked the direct agency to show them evidence that the results from the Preferred Member cards were worth the money spent on them. The agency came to our company for help, since we were maintaining the database.

"We know that the cards are valuable, but how can we prove it?" the company asked.

"By comparing the performance of the cardholders with the performance of your control group that did not get the cards," I explained.

"What is a control group?"

"It is those people who used the service three times or more, but were not issued cards to measure the performance of those who got the cards."

"There is no such group. We gave the cards to everyone who deserved them."

"Then you are out of luck. You can't prove that the cards have done any good."

The agency lost the account.

Let that be a lesson to you. Using test and control groups can mean the difference between keeping your job and losing it. You *must* have a control group *every time* you do anything new that involves the expenditure of money.

Using Half-Life in Tests

One difficulty in testing is the length of time that it takes to learn the results of your test. If you sent out a promotion, it may take many weeks before all the responses come in. That is why half-life analysis is so useful in testing.

As soon as you launch any test, you should record every day how many responses have come in that day, the quantity sold, and the amount of money received. Let's say that you send out a catalog. If you don't have a definite cutoff date, the catalog may result in sales coming in over a period of many months. Assume that you get 2,000 orders from the catalog over a period of five months. If you have recorded your daily sales, you will find that there is one day on which the 1,000[th] response was received—exactly half of your total. That is your half-life day. Typically, the half-life day comes within the first 30 days after any promotion. On your next promotion, you will find that the half-life occurs on approximately the same day. Sears Canada, for example, mails out 13 different catalogs every year. It has discovered that its half-life day is Day 20. That is the day on which it has received half of the dollars that it will eventually receive on each catalog. All it has to do is to multiply the amount that it takes in by Day 20 by 2, and it knows the results of the catalog—several months early.

Figure 9-6 shows the daily response of a typical promotion. In the figure, the days since the first response are plotted across the bottom. The revenue received is on the left. It took 197 days before the full revenue of $133,986 from the promotion was received from all purchasers.

The details are shown in Figure 9-7. On the 35th day, in this example, you have taken in $67,000. That is just about half of what you will receive from the entire catalog, after waiting some 197 days.

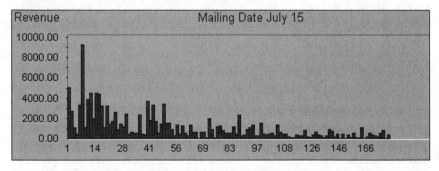

Figure 9-6. Daily response of a typical promotion.

	Days	Revenue
Total	197	$133,986.00
Half-life	35	$67,007.17
Third	15	$45,643.97
Quarter	12	$33,557.45

Figure 9-7. Details of the half-day analysis.

The beauty of half-life analysis is that you can conduct many more tests, and learn the results of your tests much faster. If you are doing tests—and you must, if you are going to be successful at database marketing—you must learn to do half-life analysis. Software available from the Database Marketing Institute enables you to do half-life analysis.

Outboard Motor Sales Test

Later in this book, we describe a nationwide launch of a new outboard motor. In this launch to the 250,000 selected for the first mailing, 20,000 were set aside as a control group. This group received no mailing, but tracked in their purchases. It was this group that permitted the marketers to learn the effectiveness of their entire program.

Once they began their rollout, the marketers, David Christensen and Stanton Lewin, did 32 mailings a year, setting aside 32 control groups to validate their results. They used the mailings to sell not only the new motors, but also parts and accessories. *The result:* They learned that parts sold 24 percent more to the test groups than to the controls.

They mailed 2 million pieces a year for the next three years, using the controls to validate their results. Some boat dealers experienced an 8 percent response to the mailings. The average response rate was 2.83 percent. It was a highly successful program, well researched and tested. They knew what they were doing, and really made database marketing history using tests and controls.

Measuring Sales

The examples in this chapter are easy ones. It is easy to measure sales made through a credit card, or to a bank, or to a utility. These sales are all posted to a marketing database, which can be used for the computations that follow.

Unfortunately, many manufacturers do not have any way of getting direct information on the sales of their products. A packaged goods company can measure coupons redeemed, but cannot effectively measure product sold to coupon redeemers versus nonresponders. How do we solve this problem?

Every marketer will have to come up with his own solution. One idea of the way this can be done is this: Measure monthly wholesale sales over a period of time to identify areas for which these sales can accurately be recorded (zip code, state, or region). Knowing average household annual consumption of your product, estimate the number of participating customer households by dividing annual wholesale shipments to the area by the annual household consumption. Once this base is known for both the test and control groups, run your test. After one, two, and three months, compute the sales per household in your test (promoted) and control (nonpromoted) areas.

Is this an accurate measure? Not as accurate as those already shown as examples. But it may be all that you've got. You must have some way of measuring your success.

Testing in Credit Card Sales to Existing Bank Customers

By now hundreds of banks have experience with credit card solicitation. They have learned which methods work and which do not work. To do comprehensive testing, they select two groups of existing bank customers: a test group and a control group. They must spend the money to prequalify each group as to age, income, credit history, etc. For the test to be valid, both groups must be identical. Then they can test various offers, packages, and methods to see which generates the most profitable cardholders.

Testing and evaluation of this program is quite complex and interesting. In the first place, the basic offering method can be tested: mail versus phone. Phone calls usually produce more sales, but cost much more to carry out. In each case, the cost of the entire promotion is measured against the number of people who sign up. The cost per new cardholder is calculated. These tests will tell which method is the most cost-effective. This, however, is only the beginning.

The real issue is not whether people take out a card; the issue is how much profit can be made from them as cardholders after they take out the card. This can be learned without the controls. Where the control group becomes important is to relate card ownership to the use of other bank products.

Does a card owner who uses a plastic card with the bank name on it several times a week tend to make greater use of other bank products as a result: checking accounts, money market funds, CDs, home equity loans, traveler's checks, mutual funds, etc.? Is the card ownership just the entrée to a whole new world of banking services for the customer? In such case, the money spent on acquiring the card membership needs to be judged not against the subsequent card activity alone, but also against the profits from the use of other products.

To determine the incremental sales that result from these additional uses of bank products, the subsequent history of the test group and the control group needs to be tracked over a period of time as the group members make additional purchases, make payments, pay annual fees, pay finance charges, take out loans, or fall into default. The control group should also be used to evaluate the success of the promotion by estimating the number and timing of the incremental accounts opened by the test group. Annette Champion, of Arthur D. Little, points out that we are borrowing from the future here. The test group members open accounts they would have opened anyway but at an earlier point in time. As these accounts are opened sooner, they are worth more.

The real test is lifetime value of the customer, not of the cardholder. Before the promotion, these were, after all, bank customers who already had their own lifetime value as owners of checking or savings accounts (or other bank products). One way of testing would be to divide both the test group and the control group into various customer profiles:

- Checking account customers

- Savings account customers

- Home equity customers

- Checking and savings customers

- Checking and home equity customers

- Etc.

Each would have his own lifetime value before and after the acquisition of a credit card. The change in the total lifetime value of the test group measured against the control group would provide an overall test of the value of the original marketing effort.

Long-Term Testing Difficulties

It all seems so simple when you describe testing as we have done in the previous few pages. Real life, however, is actually much more complicated. In the first place, the credit card promotion described here is not the only marketing activity at the bank by any means. During the average year, the bank is conducting promotions on a monthly basis for various products. Some of the same people who served in a test group for one promotion are in the control group for another, and in the test group for still a third promotion. How do you measure the long-term impact of any one promotion when people are constantly involved in many different promotions, all of which can affect their attitude toward the bank and lifetime value?

This is what makes database marketing and the Web so interesting, so complex, and so sophisticated compared with direct marketing or general advertising. The possibilities for creative thinking about the bank's relationship to its customers are rich with a wealth of detail that enables intelligent marketers to learn a great deal about their customers and about the best way to improve their overall relationships.

Several years ago, I took out a home equity loan with the Chevy Chase Bank in Maryland. The program was widely advertised; the rates were low. I used the loan to finance the building of a barn, a swimming pool, and an addition to my house.

Some time after I took out the loan, Chevy Chase sent me a preapproved invitation for a MasterCard at low interest rates. I have received dozens of others over the years, which I routinely toss in the trash. I responded to Chevy Chase because I had formed a favorable opinion of the bank from the home equity experience. I canceled my American Express card. American Express, by the way, did an excellent job of trying to keep me. It just couldn't accept the idea that anyone would voluntarily drop the card. I got three different telephone calls and more than four letters on the subject before it finally gave up.

A couple of years later, I noticed that my broker was handling Chevy Chase bonds. They were selling at about 40 percent of par, due to the national savings and loan problem. I asked the broker to buy some for me, because I had such good feelings about the bank. In a couple of years the bonds came up to 104 percent of par value, besides paying a 13 percent rate of interest. I became a loyal Chevy Chase customer.

The point of this personal story is to illustrate the way in which customer lifetime value builds up based on the way that the customer is treated by the institution in more than the specific situation under review. Chevy Chase, if it calculates lifetime value at all, should see me as a cardholder, home equity customer, and bondholder, each one of which contributes to overall bank profits.

In fact, Chevy Chase was not doing much of a job in profiling its customer base. A very persistent Chevy Chase telemarketer called me at dinnertime one night telling me that "as a longtime cardholder with an excellent record," I was being awarded two months' free life insurance, with no preconditions. After the two months, the policy would be charged to my credit card at the rate of $14.40 per month unless canceled by me. I asked how much the policy paid, and was told $2,000—a ridiculously small amount of life insurance. The worst part of the call was that Chevy Chase knew that I had $300,000 worth of insurance for which I was paying about $180 per month. How did it know? Because I had to write it on my credit application for the home equity loan. I left the phone angry with Chevy Chase for bothering me with a totally irrelevant offer. It saw me as a name on a list, not as the valuable customer that I thought I was. After a few months, I left Chevy Chase and have never gone back.

Most companies, like Chevy Chase, have data about their customers buried in their files somewhere. Digging those data out and putting them into the database to use in customer profiling and testing would be an inexpensive and profitable strategy before they ruin their customer base with worthless outbound telemarketing calls.

Keeping track of the long-term effects of any one promotion is almost impossible since there are many different promotions. How do we database marketers sort all this out?

The answer is a straightforward one: lifetime value. The lifetime value of every customer in your database should be calculated and maintained at all times. Every time money is expended on a customer: a promotion, a newsletter, a satisfaction survey, etc., the lifetime value effects should be calculated, and the revised lifetime value inserted in the customer record. The new values can be compared with lifetime values in the control group to determine long-term effects of any marketing activity. For more on this subject, see Chapter 13 on financial services.

Summary

To know if a marketing program is successful, you must test it properly. The steps are:

- Determine the objectives of the marketing program, and be sure that it will in the design phase result in a positive return on investment.
- Develop a controlled test design, including both test and control groups. Make sure that both groups are as exactly equal as possible, in every respect, except size.
- Determine the incremental profit rate that applies to your sales.
- Develop a method to measure sales. This may be easy, or may be the most difficult part of the whole effort.
- Carry out your marketing program to the test groups. Treat the control groups normally, except don't promote them.
- Measure the incremental sales by comparing sales in the test groups with those in the control groups.
- Calculate the direct costs of your program.
- Figure the short-term net profitability of your program, and determine the return on your investment.
- Figure the long-term net profitability of your program based on change in lifetime value of your customers.

Executive Quiz 8

Answers to quiz questions can be found in Appendix B.

1. Control groups are:
   a. For market research, not database marketing
   b. For promotions, not for long-term testing
   c. A waste of marketing dollars
   d. Not useful when sales go down
   e. None of the above

2. Nonresponders should act:
   a. The same way as the control group
   b. The same way as responders
   c. Better than the control group
   d. Better than the responders
   e. None of the above

3. The results of a given promotion can best be measured:
   a. For one month
   b. For three months
   c. For six months
   d. For twelve months
   e. For none of the above

4. For credit card promotions, qualification is needed for:
   a. All who respond
   b. All who respond plus a control group
   c. All who are promoted
   d. All who are promoted plus a control group
   e. The control group alone

5. Measurement of the lifetime value of bank credit card holders should cover:
   a. Credit card profits in the first year
   b. Credit card profits over more than one year
   c. Multiyear activity in all products
   d. Multiyear credit card activity plus one year of other products
   e. None of the above

6. When banks run multiple promotions, the results should be calculated based on:
   a. Response to each promotion
   b. Lifetime value updated for each promotion
   c. Response by test groups compared with lifetime value of control groups
   d. Return on investment from each promotion
   e. All of the above

7. The value of building a close customer relationship:
   a. Is worthwhile, regardless of the cost
   b. Helps profitability in ways that cannot be measured
   c. Must be done if competitors are doing it
   d. Can be measured by lifetime value analysis
   e. Is too complex to measure

8. Database marketing is harder to cost-justify than:
   a. Advertising
   b. Corporate planning
   c. Research and development
   d. Customer relations
   e. None of the above

9. What is the minimum number of customers required for a successful test if the expected response rate is 2.5 percent?
   a. 500
   b. 5,000
   c. 14,000
   d. 20,000
   e. 40,000

10. What will be the total sales from a catalog? The half-life day is 27. By that day 4,382 customers responded, buying $87,640.
    a. $87,640
    b. $438,200
    c. $262,920
    d. Cannot be known from available data
    e. None of the above

10

Finding Customers
through the Web

*The ordinary strategy for H&R Block would be to buy
magazine advertising—in Time, or US News &
World Report. However, the client and its agency (WJC
Chicago) both knew that with the budget available,
they'd never be able to interrupt enough people to cut
through the clutter.*

*Instead we used the Net. The banners were simple.
They read, "Play the H&R Block We'll Pay Your
Taxes Game"*

*About 60,000 people clicked on the banner. After click-
ing, they saw a registration page that explained that
in order to have their taxes paid next year (up to
$25,000), they had to answer a bunch of trivia ques-
tions about Block and taxes over the next ten weeks.*

*More than 50,000 people eagerly enrolled. Now, with
their permissions and their e-mail address, we went to
work. Twice a week for ten weeks we sent these 50,000
people an e-mail about the game and about Premium
Tax. We drove people to Block's web site to look up
answers to tax trivia questions and created a curricu-
lum that taught people about the benefits of H&R
Block and Premium Tax. Each e-mail averaged a 36
percent response rate. This is an astonishingly high
response rate for a direct response campaign—the
average in direct mail is closer to 2 percent.*

> *H&R Block saw a noticeable improvement in traffic to their site and, more important, saw traffic to all parts of their site. Because every e-mail we sent was different for each person, the notes were personal. They were opened because they contained a score—valuable information that made the message me-mail instead of e-mail.*
>
> SETH GODIN
> *Permission Marketing*

The Internet has grown so fast that virtually all large companies are trying to decide how to use it to reach their customers and prospects. There are more than a million web sites out there. If you create a web site, the odds of anyone finding it by chance are one in several million. For your web site to get noticed, you have to list yourself in the search engines such as Yahoo, AltaVista, Excite, and HotBot. You also need to explore banner ads.

A couple of thousand sites accept banner advertising. If you are interested in reaching prospects, where should you place your banner ad?

In traditional advertising, you use a media expert. This expert studies the demographics of your customers, figures out which media they pay attention to, and places ads based on careful targeting and cost. Media targeting has been a science for the past 30 years. Modern marketers might assume that they should use the same techniques for the web. But that would probably be a mistake.

Much of what we have learned about reaching prospects over the years does not apply to the web. Marketers who apply those time-honored principles to web advertising will lose their shirts and will fail.

The basic lesson that prior experience has taught us is that direct marketing, whether by direct mail, television, or print, is expensive. To reduce the costs, we must carefully target our message using the right lists or the right media. We try to apply that concept to the web. If we are going to sell sports outfits, the reasoning goes, we should pay a premium to advertise on a web site devoted to sports. This type of thinking is probably wrong. On the web, the waste cost is very low. It is better to cast your net very wide to reach audiences that you could not possibly address with traditional media.

Web advertising networks offer a single point of access to advertisers that want to reach millions of consumers quickly and easily. They acquire impressions given to them by their web site "affiliates" and sell the aggregated inventory. This process simplifies the acts of buying and selling for both the advertiser and the web publisher.

There are two objectives in web advertising. Image advertisers are trying to create an image in the mind of the viewer. Response advertisers, on the other hand, are trying to get the viewer to respond. Advertising on the web has focused on banner ads that can be placed on hundreds of sites. When a viewer clicks on a banner, she is usually transported to the advertiser's site where she sees their products and prices, and may place an order. Banner advertising is paid for by cost per thousand (CPM) impressions. An impression occurs when a web page that contains your banner appears on a viewer's screen. Figure 10-1 shows a banner for hotels. Clicking on that banner shifts you to the advertiser's web page, which, as you can see in Figure 10-2, offers a number of choices of cities that have those hotels. At this point, the Hotel Reservations Network has to do a good job of converting the response into a lead and the lead into a sale.

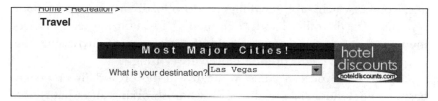

Figure 10-1. Banner ad for hotels.

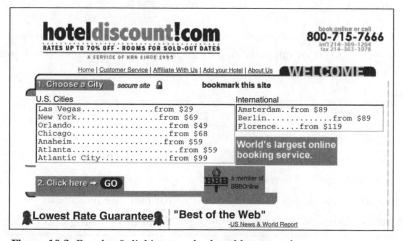

Figure 10-2. Result of clicking on the hotel banner ad.

How Web Advertising Differs

Web advertising differs from traditional media in a number of ways (see Figure 10-3). Traditional media must use surrogate measurements such as awareness, focus groups, coupons, and Neilson ratings, none of which measures actual consumer activities. The web, on the other hand, permits you to know who are looking at the page on which your banner is displayed, how long they are there, where they came from, and where they go afterward. There is a wealth of information that is not available in any other media.

Traditional advertising usually involves single messages. Thousands of dollars are spent on creating the perfect TV, magazine, or direct-mail ad. Most of these are single messages, since you cannot afford to send four letters to each household to measure which works best. Your tests have to be conducted on different households. On the web, you can change your message every hour every day and expose one customer to many different approaches. In addition, because of the limitations of the web, your creative copy must be relatively simple. Complex graphics and colors, which take too long to download, may result in poor response. On the other hand, "rich media" ads, utilizing high involvement and interactive formats, hold the promise of increasing the impact and overall effectiveness of web advertising.

On the web, you can adjust your advertising on a daily or weekly basis. You get immediate feedback on what is working and what is not. There are four steps that a customer goes through in making a purchase on the web:

- *Impression.* The customer clicks on a web site that has banners displayed. This is an impression. The advertiser pays from $5 to $40 per thousand impressions.

Traditional Media	Web Advertising
Surrogate measurements	Direct measurements
High cost of waste	Low cost of waste
Single messages	Multiple messages
Delayed feedback	Immediate feedback
Hard to adjust	Real time testing and tuning

Figure 10-3. Comparing traditional media and web advertising.

- *Response.* The person clicks on a banner in the web site, which transports the clicker to your web site. That is a response. You can measure the response rates and get a cost per response.

- *Lead.* The prospect views your offerings and fills out a form. This is a lead. You can figure both the percentage of responses that become leads and the cost per lead.

- *Sale.* The clicker buys the product by giving a credit card number and authorizing the purchase. This is a sale. You can figure the lead conversion rate and the cost per sale.

Advertisers are only responsible for the first two steps. They can get people to visit their sites, creating impressions. They can encourage people to click on your banner, creating a response. The last two steps are up to the marketers on each web site. Viewers can and do get lost at each step along the way.

So what's wrong with targeting—selecting the best possible sites for your banner ad, rather than just scattering your message any old place? As database marketers we *believe* in targeting. We use it all the time. Why not use it on the web? The reason is that the situation on the web is quite different.

Web advertising is growing at a furious pace. Pages can be created very rapidly. There is a glut of unsold ad space. Much of the space is really inexpensive. All of it can be measured and tracked.

There are three categories of web ad space:

- *Run of network (RON),* which is very cheap. It is not undesirable. It is not remnant inventory. There are very good bargains in RON. You pay $4 to $6 per thousand impressions.

- *Affinity group space* for categories such as sports, business, and travel. This space is more expensive than RON, but it can be a very good value. This space is not branded. You pay $10 to $20 per thousand impressions.

- *Branded space.* This is the most expensive and often has a very low response. You pay from $30 to $70 for branded space.

Figure 10-4 shows a comparison of the CPM for a variety of media.

A 1 percent response rate on the web is good. A good response in direct mail is 2 percent, but you have to spend a lot more for it. (See Figure 10-5.) Of course, a response in direct mail may well be a sale, but a response on the web is only a single step on the road to a sale. If you

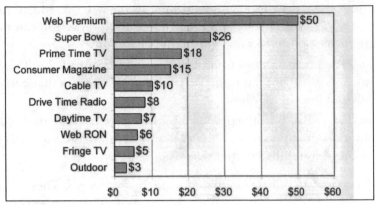

Figure 10-4. Comparison of costs (per 1000 impressions) of various media.

	Direct Mail	RON Web
Contacts	100,000	100,000
CPM	$400	$6
Cost	$40,000	$600
Response rate	2%	1%
Responses	2,000	1,000
Cost per response	$20	$0.60

Figure 10-5. Direct mail and web costs compared.

are going to pay a lot more for targeting, you have to be sure that the targeting is going to pay off. If you are paying $6 CPM for RON with a response rate of 1 percent you are paying $0.60 per response. If someone says that you should be on this really cool web site that costs $42, how much better would the $42 site have to be to give you responses at $0.60 each? If you look at the math, you will see that your $42 web site would have to give you a response rate of more than 7 percent to be better than RON. Few web sites give you that kind of response rate.

So if you should not target, how should you decide where to place your web advertising to make sure that you are reaching the right people? One of the experts in this subject is George Garrick, president of the Flycast Network, a leading web advertising firm. George has a very interesting answer to the question of targeting. He recommends testing, using RON. He calls it "zero-based media buying." Do no targeting at

Figure 10-6. Banner ad for a Casio digital camera.

all. Just throw ads out there and see where you get responses. Within a few days, at the most, you can figure out where your responses are coming from. You can group your responses by category (sports, business, entertainment) or by individual site. Or even better, you can create your own category—"people who respond to ads about my product." You cannot do that in any other media. He recommends to his clients that they begin with advertising on all Flycast sites (close to a thousand) for a week, and compare the response rates.

Casio provides a good example. It ran the banner ad, shown in Figure 10-6, as a RON ad for a digital camera. Figure 10-7 shows the response rates. What Figure 10-7 clearly shows is that the best category for Casio digital camera ads is travel. Sites aimed at women, games, and

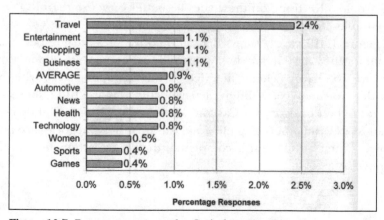

Figure 10-7. Response rates to the Casio banner ad.

	Response Rate	CPM	Response per 1000	Cost per Response
Run of network	0.009	$6	9	$0.66
Travel category	0.024	$15	24	$0.63

Figure 10-8. Comparison of cost per response with RON and travel sites for Casio.

sports are definitely not winners for this product. Would anyone have guessed this without this test? Not likely. Furthermore, this test can be conducted in a week. Responses are tabulated from all sites every day—every hour if you want. Rapidly knowing what works, you can immediately shift and place your digital camera ads on the right sites, dropping the less responsive ones. It is not possible to do that in any other media. It takes weeks to know what works using direct mail, and you may never really know using TV or print.

Response rate, however, is only a part of the story. You have to factor in the cost of the space. Would concentration on travel sites be a good idea for Casio? Figure 10-8 shows that at a cost of $15 per CMP, travel sites are just barely a better buy for Casio than RON. In subsequent weeks Casio should concentrate on travel sites, but only after testing whether the conversion rate of prospects who come from travel is equal to or not worse than those who come from RON.

Figure 10-9 shows a Microsoft CarPoint ad. Which would be the best site on which to advertise this Microsoft CarPoint web site? Would you guess automotive? Of course. But how about sports, shopping, and travel? Would advertising on these sites be better or worse than RON? We need to look at the CPM to know the answer.

Figure 10-10 clearly shows that automotive sites are the best placement for the CarPoint ad when we consider response rates alone. But to be sure, you have to check the prices of the competing sites. When you do this, you may get a different perspective. Figure 10-11 shows that even the best category for CarPoint, automotive, is only slightly better than RON as an advertising medium. All the other categories are much worse. When a RON test is completed, the software returns complete reports.

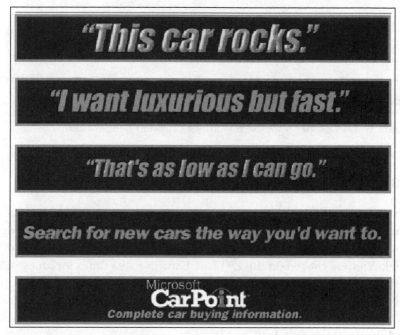

Figure 10-9. Banner ad for Microsoft CarPoint web site.

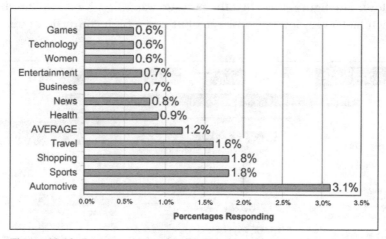

Figure 10-10. Response rates for CarPoint banner ad.

	Response Rate	*CPM*	*Response per 1000*	*Cost per Response*
Run of network	0.012	$ 6	12	$0.50
Automotive	0.031	$15	31	$0.48
Sports	0.012	$15	12	$1.25

Figure 10-11. Cost per response for various Carpoint banner sites.

Banners for E*Trade

The following figure is the top of a long report on a $13,000 test conducted for E*Trade over one week. A total of 94 sites were used for the test. In all, the advertiser paid for 2.1 million impressions during the week. Viewers clicked on the E*Trade banner 6,495 times for an overall response rate of three-tenths of 1 percent. These 6,495 clicks brought the viewers over to the E*Trade web site (Figure 10-12), where only 105 (1.62 percent) of them filled out a form to become E*Trade customers and thereby became a lead.

You can see from Figure 10-13 that the cost per lead varied from $3.68 to $542.02, with an average cost of $128.78. This one-week test enabled E*Trade to determine which sites were best for the subsequent rollout. The figure shows that the best site was IGive. Next was ShowBiz, which had a very low response rate, but had a high conversion rate.

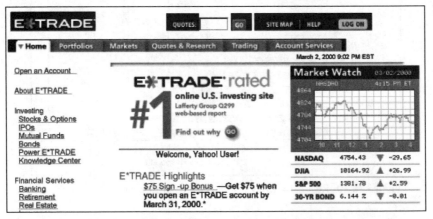

Figure 10-12. The E*Trade web site reached through clicking a banner.

Result of One Week's RON Test by Site
Top Eleven out of 780 Sites

Site	Impressions	Clicks	Rate	Leads	Lead Rate	Cost	Lead Cost
IGive	14,091	1,384	9.82%	23	1.66%	$85	$3.68
LotteryUSA	43,112	132	0.31%	12	9.09%	$259	$21.56
The Onion	126,732	263	0.21%	10	3.80%	$760	$76.04
The Huddle	62,722	49	0.08%	6	12.24%	$376	$62.72
123 Greetings	361,345	673	0.19%	4	0.59%	$2,168	$542.02
3D Files	56,600	57	0.10%	4	7.02%	$340	$84.90
Rogue Market	14,932	10	0.07%	3	30.00%	$90	$29.86
Netsurfer Digest	23,333	29	10.12%	3	10.34%	$140	$46.67
Nordic Music	28,397	34	0.12%	3	8.82%	$170	$56.79
ShowBiz	5,063	6	0.12%	3	50.00%	$30	$10.13
People-Talk	37,028	103	0.28%	3	2.91%	$222	$74.06
Total 780 sites	2,166,196	6,495	0.30%	105	1.62%	$12,997	$123.78

Figure 10-13. One week's E*Trade results arranged (from highest to lowest) by number of leads per site.

Who would have guessed that the two best sites would be IGive and ShowBiz? Probably nobody. This is the beauty of RON advertising. You are letting the customers—the market—decide which are your best media, instead of paying a high-priced media expert to make the decision for you. There is a whole new world out there on the web.

The next step is to take the raw data from the test, and arrange them by category to determine which categories are working the best for your particular product and offer. The E*Trade successful categories are shown in Figure 10-14.

After reviewing all the data, using software and intuition, it was possible to optimize E*Trade results into a few sites that had the lowest cost per lead, as shown in Figure 10-15. The majority of the successful sites were, as you could imagine, sites devoted to business and finance. A number of other successful E*Trade sites, however, would have been overlooked if RON had not been used first as a test. From the above, you can see that in subsequent weeks, E*Trade could spend about $5,000 per week on web advertising, obtaining about 95 successful conversions at an average cost of $51.61 per lead.

When to Run Your Ads

Once you have decided where to place your ads, you must decide when to run them. You have a choice of day of the week and hour of the day. Let's take a look at two different sets of response rates based on hours of the day.

Bank of America (B of A) ads peaked in the afternoon and evening (see Figure 10-16). They were below average in the morning. Does this mean that B of A should advertise only in the evening? Not necessarily. Perhaps the conversion rate from responses to leads was greater with people who called earlier in the day. These were, probably, people sitting at their desks in their offices. They might have been better possible customers. This can be easily measured. Or more important, perhaps the lifetime value of early-day responders was higher than that of evening responders. Now we are getting very sophisticated. But that is what database marketing, combined with web response advertising statistics, permits us to be.

If we look at CarPoint and Casio responses by hour of the day (see Figure 10-17), they were almost the opposite of the Bank of America responses. Their best responses came in the morning hours and tended

	Sites	Impressions	Clicks	Response Rate	Leads	Conversion	Cost	Cost per Lead
IGive	1	14,091	1,384	9.82%	23	1.66%	$85	$3.68
News and Information	2	98,626	203	0.21%	12	5.91%	$592	$49.31
Business and Finance	12	99,739	590	0.59%	11	1.86%	$598	$54.40
Automotive	7	19,610	43	0.22%	2	4.65%	$118	$58.83
Learning	2	24,105	77	0.32%	2	2.60%	$145	$72.32
Sports and Outdoors	5	74,706	128	0.17%	6	4.69%	$448	$74.71
Consumer Technology	15	270,169	502	0.19%	14	2.79%	$1,621	$115.79
Music	21	22,215	31	0.14%	1	3.23%	$133	$133.29
Entertainment and Movie	15	461,936	909	0.20%	20	2.20%	$2,772	$138.58
Search Directories	2	49,728	79	0.16%	2	2.53%	$298	$149.18
College	3	74,936	92	0.12%	1	1.09%	$450	$449.62
Shopping	51	484,580	882	0.18%	6	0.68%	$2,907	$484.58
Total	94	2,166,194	4,920	0.23%	105	2.13%	$12,997	$123.78

Figure 10-14. E*Trade banner results by cost per lead by category of site.

Site	Category	Impressions	Clicks	Response Rate	Leads	Conversion	Cost	Cost per Lead
MarketPlayer	Business and Finance	555	4	0.72%	1	25.00%	$3	$3.33
Igive	Charity	14,091	1,384	9.82%	23	1.66%	$85	$3.68
StockInvestor	Business and Finance	1,145	8	0.70%	1	12.50%	$7	$6.87
ShowBiz	Business and Finance	5,063	6	0.12%	3	50.00%	$30	$10.13
Regent Commerce	Business and Finance	2,037	37	1.82%	1	2.70%	$12	$12.22
CyberInvest	Business and Finance	2,442	13	0.53%	1	7.69%	$15	$14.65
Critical Path	Automotive	3,520	7	0.20%	1	14.29%	$21	$21.12
I-Escrow	Business and Finance	7,051	15	0.21%	2	13.33%	$42	$21.15
Lottery USA	News and Information	43,112	132	0.31%	12	9.09%	$259	$21.56
Rogue Market	Entertainment and Movie	14,932	10	0.07%	3	30.00%	$90	$29.86
ezines Database	Automotive	6,014	18	0.30%	1	5.56%	$36	$36.08
Netsurfer Digest	Consumer Technology	23,333	29	0.12%	3	10.34%	$140	$46.67
Nordic Music	Consumer Technology	28,397	34	0.12%	3	8.82%	$170	$56.79
Your New House	Learning	19,591	61	0.31%	2	3.28%	$118	$58.77
TheHuddle	Sports and Outdoors	62,722	49	0.08%	6	12.24%	$376	$62.72
People-Talk	Business and Finance	37,028	103	0.28%	3	2.91%	$222	$74.06
Total		817,123	3,108	0.38%	95	3.06%	$4,903	$51.61

Figure 10-15. E*Trade banner results arranged by cost per lead per site.

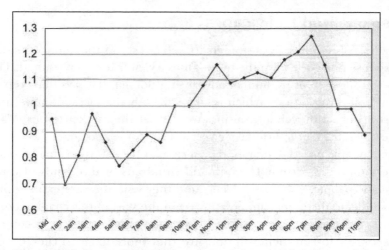

Figure 10-16. Bank of America response to banner ads by hour of the day.

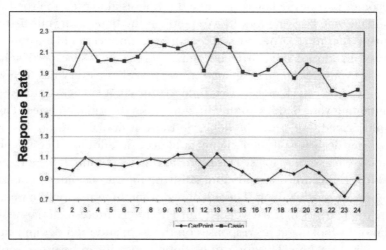

Figure 10-17. CarPoint and Casio response rate to banner ads by hour of the day.

to drop off in the afternoon and evening. Here is another area for rapid calculation and revision of our advertising mix. Similar graphs can be made of the response rates by days of the week. For some products there is a significant difference. The important thing to remember is that this type of detail has never before been available for any medium in the history of the world! We are entering a new age of database marketing combined with the web.

Personalized Landscapes

Analysis of response by customers to web ads shows that quite often the response rate goes down the more times a viewer has seen your ad. This flies in the face of traditional advertising dogma that says that "repetition builds responses." Which is correct? Only the market knows, and, fortunately, with web advertising, we can let the market tell us. Many sites keep track of individual viewers as they come and go. For example, some people use AOL or Yahoo on a regular basis. It is possible to know every time that Arthur Hughes, and hundreds of thousands of other specific people, visit a site. Every time they visit, they are exposed, for example, to the hotel banner featured in the start of this chapter. Some of them (perhaps 1 percent) will click on this banner to become a response. Most of them will not. Are they more likely to click on the banner the first time they see it or at some later time? The answer is (in most cases) the first time. Once they have seen it and passed it by, it becomes part of the landscape, like the houses alongside the road that you take when driving to work. You look at the houses on your first day driving that route. After a few days, you don't notice them any more.

So what do you do to avoid becoming part of the landscape? You have to vary your ad. You can change it every week, or every day, or every hour. Or you can change it every time Arthur Hughes clicks onto the site containing your banner, so that he never sees the same ad twice. This is sophisticated, but it can be done. Software is available to do this; web sites can do it for all their clients at almost no additional cost. This is database marketing, folks! This is one-to-one marketing. It is more profitable for the advertiser and more satisfying for the customers. The landscape is always changing. There is always something new on the web.

Even better is to learn what Arthur Hughes is interested in, by asking him or by looking at his responses on the web, and then design a landscape just for him. This too can be done. Since it can be done, sophisticated marketers will do it—and will profit from it.

Summary

- Direct marketing advertising always involves targeting because of its high cost. Web advertising can be based on zero-based media buying, which is essentially trial and error.
- With run of network (RON) ads, you can learn in four or five days which sites give you the best response.

- When viewers have a web page that includes your banner on their screen, that is an impression. You pay so much per thousand impressions.

- When they click on your banner, they go to your web site. That is called a response.

- On your web site, they may give you data about themselves, thereby becoming a lead.

- When leads buy your products, they become sales.

- Traditional advertising involves single messages: You cannot afford to send several different letters to every prospect. On the web, you can change your message every day or every hour, and at almost the same price.

- Don't assume that our conventional beliefs and practices hold true on the web. Start from scratch and let the market tell you what works and what does not work.

- Continually track, test, and tune your program based on the wealth of data that is now available.

- Vary your ads by week, day, or hour or by customer so as to avoid becoming part of the landscape

Executive Quiz 9

Answers to quiz questions can be found in Appendix B.

1. Using Figure 10-18, compute the ad cost, the cost per response, and the cost per sale for each of the four sites.

2. Which site gets the most viewers?
   a. Travel
   b. Sports
   c. Women
   d. News
   e. All the same

3. Which site gets the highest response?
   a. Travel
   b. Sports
   c. Women
   d. News
   e. All the same

	CPM	Impressions (000)	Responses	Sales
Travel	$12	45	22	4
Sports	$15	88	16	8
Women	$10	102	38	5
News	$20	76	42	7

Figure 10-18. Responses to a banner ad.

4. Which site has the lowest cost per response?
    a. Travel
    b. Sports
    c. Women
    d. News
    e. All the same

5. Which site got the most sales?
    a. Travel
    b. Sports
    c. Women
    d. News
    e. All the same

6. Which site has the lowest cost per sale?
    a. Travel
    b. Sports
    c. Women
    d. News
    e. All the same

7. If millions of web visitors see your identical web ad every day for 20 days, the response rate on the last 10 days will probably be:
    a. The same as the first 10 days
    b. Higher than the first 10 days
    c. Lower than the first 10 days
    d. Impossible to predict
    e. Impossible to measure

PART

3

Profiting by Experience

11

Retailing and Packaged Goods

For years, retailers have argued that having regularly advertised, deeply discounted prices brings price-oriented customers into their stores but that, over time, these customers convert to regular, profitable customers.

Research done by the Retail Strategy Center Inc. based in Greenville, South Carolina, shows that this widely held belief is a myth. A handful of these customers do convert into "good" regular customers, but the majority actually defect within twelve months of their first shopping visit. I have yet to find a retailer anywhere in the world whose investment in this type of shopper has yielded an attractive return on investment.

BRIAN WOOLF
Customer Specific Marketing

Retailing went through a series of shocks.

- Forced out of central cities by the flight to the suburbs, many central hub stores were closed.
- Stationed as "anchors" in large suburban malls, these stores saw many of their customers spending their time in the small specialty shops rather than in their departments. The specialty shops, collectively, offered more personal services and nonhomogeneous products than the department stores could afford.
- With "on sale" as a draw, the department stores found themselves trumped in this area by Wal-Marts and factory outlets that offered increasingly attractive merchandise at rock-bottom prices.

- The growth of the specialty catalog industry hit the large retailers especially hard. Affluent, fashion-conscious, busy, working women spent their few moments at home scanning high-fashion catalogs and ordering high-priced merchandise, rather than visiting department stores.

- To top it off, the Internet arrived, poised to steal away another group of affluent shoppers.

How to Compete?

Retailers at last fell back on the one group that was right under their nose all along, but that they were neglecting: their customers. Instead of concentrating on the products, and how to move them, they began to look at their customers and to figure out how to move them. They learned how to build loyalty and repeat sales by appealing to the hearts and minds of their customers.

Their solutions began to focus on a number of neglected areas:

- Creating interactive web sites, which recognized customers. A good example: See Figure 11-1, where Safeway welcomes me back.

- Increasing the number of people who held and used the store credit card, and getting customers who use Visa and MasterCard to regis-

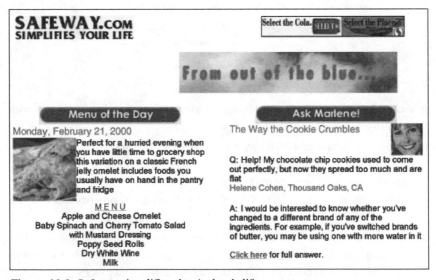

Figure 11-1. Safeway simplifies the Arthur's life.

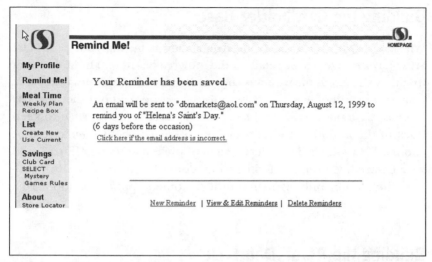

Figure 11-2. Safeway helps me remember Helena's birthday.

ter their cards with the store so that they could build a customer database. People who paid by check or cash were essentially lost to database marketing.

- Learning more about their customers through surveys and appended data, so that they could market better to them.

- Teaming up with external specialists to make targeted solo mailing offers to their customer base, drawing on their name and reputation to get the envelope opened and the sale made.

- Following up customer purchases with special personal services: thank-you letters and follow-up surveys and telephone calls; becoming specialists in customer service.

- Keeping track of birthdays, anniversaries, and other key personal events in their customers' lives and communicating one-on-one when those events occur, so that they could become a family friend, not just another store (see Figure 11-2).

- Understanding the geodemographics of their store trading areas so that they could do a better job of locating branches and bringing customers into their stores.

- Profiling their customers into profit groups and marketing differently to each group.

- Experimenting with cataloging as a way of reaching the busy working woman and luring her into the stores.

Building the Cardholder Base

Where does your business come from? Who is buying your products? Strangely enough, most retailers did not really know. The only thing that they could tell for sure was the percentage of their sales that came from store cardholders, as opposed to those who paid by other means.

Once customers used their store credit card, it was possible to keep track of them, find out what they bought, learn about their interests, and market to them. The effectiveness of these marketing efforts could be measured. Customer lifetime value could be calculated with precision. But all this could happen only if customers applied for and used a credit card.

Building the Retail Database

Any retailer that began to create a customer marketing database came up against a significant obstacle: the size of the file. To be useful, a marketing database had to have purchase history. However, the number of purchases made at a retailer's can cause a database to run into the billions of bytes.

For example, one department store had more than 10 million cardholders, who, over a two-year period, rang up more than 200 million transactions. The database was maintained in a central data warehouse on a large server network, which used it to send out the monthly bills. The marketing department wanted to profile these customers and target specific offerings to selected groups. For example, marketing wanted to find women who had purchased more than $X in three key departments over a six-month period. The MIS department made a heroic effort to satisfy the marketing request. It took two weeks and the full-time efforts of two people to produce the 60,000 names. The cost of the operation, as calculated by MIS, was about $16,000. There was no way that the promotion to the 60,000 (with all of its costs and uncertainties) would pay for the cost of selection. A rented list of names (at $80 per thousand) would have cost only $4,800.

This experience, and many like it, convinced marketing that they needed a marketing database, separate from the operational billing files. Marketing needed recency, frequency, and monetary (RFM) analysis and lifetime value put into each record. The operational MIS file could not do that for several reasons—the most important of which was that MIS only kept a few months' worth of data, whereas marketing wanted to go back two years.

To hold all the information needed in a marketing database for the store would consume about 40 gigabytes of disk. The disk was expensive. The store was at an impasse. As a solution, a plan was developed for the marketing database whereby:

- They would retain full purchase history for 90 days.

- Thereafter, purchases would be "rolled up" by department by month.

- Two years' worth of data would be stored on an inexpensive RAID disk.

- Data from prior years would be summarized and kept with customer records indefinitely.

This approach enabled the marketing department to carry out ad hoc counts, reports, and selects; create RFM analyses; determine life-time value; profile their customers; and have the results available on their PCs, linked to the server, in a few seconds. With the new system, the 60,000 women were selected in about 30 seconds, at a marginal cost of less than $10.

Determining Lifetime Value

Once you have a customer database constructed, you can learn won-derful things about your customers. Figure 11-3 shows what one super-market chain learned when it segmented its customers into five groups according to annual spending, based on the systems suggested in Brian

Segment	Customers	Visits per Week	Average Transaction	Annual $	Percent $	Retention
Gold	3,000	1.48	$33.07	$146,830.80	73.71%	96.00%
Silver	3,000	0.74	$17.56	$38,708.78	19.43%	90.00%
Bronze	3,000	0.43	$8.72	$11,111.63	5.58%	76.00%
Nickel	3,000	0.21	$3.15	$1,981.35	0.99%	56.00%
Occasional	3,000	0.14	$1.39	$562.95	0.28%	36.00%
Total	15,000	0.6	12.78	$199,195.50	100.00%	71%

Figure 11-3. Supermarket shoppers at one store broken into five segments.

Woolf's excellent book, *Customer Specific Marketing* (see Appendix A). This typical chain store had 15,000 customers. The top quintile brought in almost 74 percent of the sales, while the bottom two quintiles, together, produced a little over 1 percent. The annual retention rate varied from 96 percent in the top group to 36 percent in the bottom group. Let's use these data to compile a lifetime value table for two groups: the Gold customers at the top and the worthless occasional shoppers at the bottom.

As Figure 11-4 shows, the typical Gold customer arrived three years ago with a spending rate of $27 per visit. There were 4,525 of them then, who cost $181,000 to acquire. They made almost one visit per week. In the first year, 22 percent of them dropped out. By the third year, 3,000 were left. Their retention rate moved rapidly up from 78 percent to 96 percent in the three years. Their lifetime value today is $258.

	Year 1	Year 2	Year 3
Customers	4,525	3,530	3,000
Retention rate	78.00%	85.00%	96.00%
Visits per week	0.98	1.37	1.48
Average basket	$27.49	$31.62	$33.07
Total sales	$6,339,029	$7,950,583	$7,635,392
Cost percent	81.00%	79.00%	78.00%
Direct costs	$5,134,614	$6,280,960	$5,955,606
Labor + benefits 11%	$697,293	$874,564	$839,893
Card program $16, $8	$72,400	$28,236	$24,001
Acquisition cost $40	$181,000		
Advertising 2%	$126,781	$159,012	$152,708
Total costs	$6,212,087	$7,342,772	$6,972,208
Gross profit	$126,942	$607,811	$663,185
Discount rate	1	1.14	1.3
NPV profit	$126,942	$533,167	$510,142
Cumulative NPV profit	$126,942	$660,109	$1,170,251
Lifetime value	**$28.05**	**$145.88**	**$258.62**

Figure 11-4. LTV of Gold supermarket shoppers.

	Year 1	Year 2	Year 3
Customers	33,480	9,374	3,000
Retention rate	28.00%	32.00%	36.00%
Visits per week	0.1	0.13	0.14
Average basket	$1.31	$1.37	$1.39
Total sales	$228,066	$86,818	$29,272
Cost percent	81.00%	79.00%	78.00%
Direct costs	$184,733	$68,586	$22,832
Labor + benefits 11%	$25,087	$9,550	$3,220
Card program $16, $8	$535,680	$74,995	$23,998
Acquisition cost $40	$1,339,200		
Advertising 2%	$4,561	$1,736	$585
Total costs	$2,089,262	$154,868	$50,636
Gross profit	($1,861,196)	($68,050)	($21,364)
Discount rate	1	1.14	1.3
NPV profit	($1,861,196)	($59,693)	($16,434)
Cumulative NPV profit	($1,861,196)	($1,920,889)	($1,937,323)
Lifetime value	**($55.59)**	**($57.37)**	**($57.87)**

Figure 11-5. LTV of occasional supermarket shoppers.

Now let's look at the losers, the occasional shoppers at the bottom (see Figure 11-5). Because of their very low retention rate, there was a constant churn in the membership of this group. Out of a total of 33,480 customers who were acquired, only 3,000 were still around in the third year after acquisition. They visited only an average of five or six times a year, spending very little each time. Of course, they were given royal treatment with special express lanes for them whenever they showed up, while more profitable customers had to wait in long queues to get their heavy baskets rung up.

What were these people worth to the company? As you can see, their value was a minus $57. They actually cost the supermarket more in expenses than the profits made from the meager sales to these folks. They were being subsidized by the more loyal customers.

These were not necessarily worthless people. The chances are that they did the bulk of their shopping elsewhere, and just dropped into this supermarket occasionally to use the express lanes—and waste the company's time and money.

Now that you know about these people, what can you do about it? The answer, clearly, is to develop some simple policy that will nudge these losers into the profitable column. That is where customer-specific marketing comes in. Once you know who these people are, you should find a way to charge them more, and at the same time to reward the loyal customers.

Migrating the Silver Customers

A third group to look at are the Silver customers, those just below Gold. Research in Safeway, for example, shows that this group has the greatest potential for an improvement in lifetime value. The Gold customers are probably maxed out. They are loyal and are spending all their food money in this store. The Silver customers, on the other hand, are probably splitting their patronage among more than one store. This is something that we can change. Let's look at their lifetime value today, and then what we could do to modify it.

As Figure 11-6 shows, here we have a solid lifetime value of $32.30 based on about 38 trips per year, spending an average of $17.56. Let's do a little database marketing with this group. Let's really go all out on customer-specific marketing. We will use straddle pricing, with the average prices in the store a few percentage points higher than the competition, but the prices for cardholders a few percentage points lower than the competition. We will cut our advertising budget in half, using the resulting money to reward our Silver (and other loyal) customers with specials throughout the store. We will give free ice cream on frequent shoppers' birthdays, and reward them with occasional thank-you letters and certificates. Finally, we will admit heavy buyers into a special club that rewards them with points—points that they would lose if they shopped elsewhere. Figure 11-7 reflects the impact of all these changes on this Silver group.

Several things have happened to the Silver group as a result of these programs. In the first place, the retention rate has gone up from 90 percent to 92 percent. There are 3,106 of them instead of 3,000. Their visits per week have gone up from 0.74 to 1.08. Their spending per visit has also grown from $17.56 to $31.13. The lifetime value has grown from

	Year 1	Year 2	Year 3
Customers	4,412	3,530	3,000
Retention rate	80.00%	85.00%	90.00%
Visits per week	0.65	0.7	0.74
Average basket	$15.97	$16.70	$17.56
Total sales	$2,381,536	$2,145,573	$2,012,964
Cost percent	81.00%	79.00%	78.00%
Direct costs	$1,929,044	$1,695,003	$1,570,112
Labor+ benefits 11%	$261,969	$236,013	$221,426
Card program $16, $8	$70,592	$28,237	$24,001
Acquisition cost $40	$176,480		
Advertising 2%	$47,631	$42,911	$40,259
Total costs	$2,485,716	$2,002,164	$1,855,798
Gross profit	($104,180)	$143,409	$157,165
Discount rate	1	1.14	1.3
NPV profit	($104,180)	$125,797	$120,896
Cumulative NPV profit	($104,180)	$21,618	$142,514
Lifetime value	**($23.61)**	**$4.90**	**$32.30**

Figure 11-6. Lifetime value of supermarket Silver customers before migration programs.

$32 to $145. What does this improvement in LTV mean for the chain as a whole? Assume that the chain has 100,000 customers who are in the Silver group. The annual profit from this group has increased from $3.2 million to $14.5 million, an increase of more than $11 million. These are real profit increases, because LTV takes into account all costs, including the costs of getting the customers to change their behavior.

What did we have to do to create this $11 million increase in profits? We had to develop creative migration programs that cost us $13 per customer per year. We paid for much of these costs by cutting the advertising budget in half.

This is not a theoretical exercise. There are real-life examples throughout this book. This stuff works!

	Year 1	Year 2	Year 3
Customers	4,412	3,530	3,106
Retention rate	80.00%	88.00%	92.00%
Visits per week	0.86	0.96	1.08
Average basket	$22.24	$24.10	$31.13
Total sales	$4,388,055	$4,246,363	$5,430,182
Cost percent	81.00%	79.00%	78.00%
Direct costs	$3,554,325	$3,354,627	$4,235,542
Labor + benefits 11%	$482,686	$467,100	$597,320
Card program $16, $8	$70,592	$28,237	$24,848
Acquisition cost $40	$176,480		
Migration programs $13	$57,356	$45,885	$40,379
Advertising 1%	$43,881	$42,464	$54,302
Total costs	$4,385,319	$3,938,312	$4,952,391
Gross profit	$2,736	$308,051	$477,791
Discount rate	1	1.14	1.3
NPV profit	$2,736	$270,220	$367,532
Cumulative NPV profit	$2,736	$272,956	$640,488
Lifetime value	**$0.62**	**$61.87**	**$145.17**

Figure 11-7. LTV of Silver customers after migration programs.

Sears Canada Experience

Sears Roebuck terminated its big catalog in the United States several years ago, but the catalog was still going strong in Canada. It was the largest mail-order catalog in the country. Sears was also a big retailing presence in Canada, with 110 retail stores and 1,800 catalog agents. What's more, you could order any Sears Canada product directly off the web (see Figure 11-8). You couldn't do that in the states.

The Sears database had been maintained on a mainframe, using 35-year-old software. It took 120 people to do the manual file maintenance. The file was loaded with duplicates. The file was not on line. It could be accessed only through hard-copy reports that took a week to produce.

Figure 11-8. Sears Canada web site.

Fred Hagerman, list manager for catalog marketing, decided to make a business case for a new database system with modern software, and on-line acccss to do counts, reports, and selects. He showed that he could pay for the system by just finding and eliminating the estimated 10 percent duplicate names on the system. Saving the cost of 10 percent of the catalog mailings to an 11 million-name database amounted to a lot of money.

The data from the mainframe could be viewed by a client server through a simple spreadsheet. The new system permitted looking at circulation, media, performance analysis, growth and response rates, and tracking of promotions. The 11 million-name database was updated weekly in about two hours, producing all sorts of reports.

Building Active Customers

Before Fred arrived, active customers were defined as people who had shopped with Sears in the last 12 months. During the previous decade, the active file had been going down by 3 percent per year. Fred stopped the practice of dropping people who had not bought in 12 months. Each year, Sears was losing valuable data on people who hadn't purchased in a year. It was very difficult to maintain or build any kind of relationship, or any kind of long-term learning, with customers when you dumped their data after a year.

Six Capabilities

The new database system was able to do six new things:

- *Planning* was aimed at knowing how many customers Sears had and what they were doing. The marketers developed an RFM model, based on the customer's lifetime value, showing what he or she spent on catalog items. They created 189 RFM segments The segments tracked response rate, average order, and dollar per book across all 189 segments for every one of Sears' 13 catalogs. All the variable costs of each promotion, whether it was a catalog or direct-mail promotion, could be applied to each of the 189 segments to forecast segment profitability. This told Sears whether it would be profitable or not to mail to each segment. Sears could now understand the ramifications of what it was doing for each major promotion. It could accurately forecast what sales it was going to have at the end of the year.

- *Migration analysis.* This kind of analysis enabled Sears marketers to track customer migrations through all the 189 segments on a weekly basis. The marketers were able to learn the level at which the customers came in, how they were moving around in the file, and what their performance was. They were able to forecast an annual file growth projection on a weekly basis. They were able to know whether the customer base was growing or shrinking, and where they needed to worry and replan.

- *Tracking customers.* If a Sears customer had a lifetime value of $2,500 and had made a purchase in the past three months, the customer would be in a specific segment. If there was no purchase in the next three months, the customer would move to a lower segment. Using the new system, it was possible to do stimulation activities. The marketers could identify Sears customers who left and target them for reactivation programs. In addition to the RFM analysis, the marketers also developed a predictive model.

- *Early warning system.* With the new system, if business started off below the marketing plan, Sears could readjust and reallocate marketing expenses to deal with it. Customers were compared not just by RFM segment, but also by media. Do people perform better in a wish book, a sale book, or a spring and summer book? What kind of merchandise do they buy? Do they buy just men's clothing or women's or children's? Do they buy appliances through the catalog?

- *Payment methods.* With the new system, Sears could also look at segment payment methods: Sears credit card, third-party card, cash, and how performance differs among them. The company could also look at performance by catalog distribution method; there were eight different methods.

- *Half-life analysis.* By tracking sales in the past, Sears learned that the half-life of a catalog was 20 days after it was mailed. So Sears was able to track the entire success of a book by sales made during the first 20 days.

Results

What was the payoff for the investment in the Sears database?

- Customer activity and sales turned up, not down as they had for the previous decade.
- Every single medium but one, after the database kicked in, was up.
- The *Fall and Winter* catalog had a 10 percent increase in sales.
- The *Fall Values* catalog had a 7 percent increase.
- The *Super Sale* catalog sales were up 10 percent.
- The *Christmas Wish Book* sales increased by 26 percent.
- The *Winter Celebration* catalog dropped 2 percent, but space in the book dropped by 30 percent.
- The *Lowest Price* catalog sales were up 37 percent.
- The first reactivation book went out to people who did not receive the regular catalog. The breakeven response rate was 3.5 percent. The actual response rate was 4.5 percent. Sears reactivated 12,000 customers—and made a profit while doing it.

Later, Sears used the information developed in this database to make a major reorganization of the entire chain, combining catalog and retail in a single system. This major accomplishment is described in Chapter 14.

It is worth noting that at the time of this writing, Sears U.S. was not with it. Not only did it not have a catalog, but it did not have a web page where you could buy its products. The only toe in the water that Sears managed to put was an offer to sell appliances over the web.

This book will be around for several years. During this time, Sears U.S. will either get with it or die. A test of the company's success will be its web site. Click onto www.sears.com today and see if it has something more than an appliance page. If it doesn't, Sears U.S. may not be around much longer.

Supermarket Frequent Shopper Cards

Beginning just a few years ago, retailers began to issue proprietary cards to frequent shoppers. When these cards were presented at the checkout counter, point-of-sale equipment permitted the retailer to know what every household was buying and when. Retailers used these data to build databases to study their customers' shopping habits. They discovered, to their amazement, that the top 20 percent of their customers over the course of a year spent about 50 times the amount of their bottom 20%! Combining this knowledge with modern POS technology, it became possible for any retailer, according to Brian Woolf, president of the Retail Strategy Center, to "make one offer to a frequent, high spending customer, a completely different offer to a low spending customer, and yet a third offer to a new customer with moderate spending habits," *Customer Specific Marketing* (See Appendix A).

The Evil of Average Pricing

Trapped in mass marketing, retailers had always had to charge the same price to everyone. When they announced a sale, everyone got the sale price—both loyal customers and occasional transaction buyers. Using customer-specific marketing, retail stores could use their proprietary shopping cards to identify who was shopping. They could reward the best customers while they were in the store. The cards then became the basis of the store's customer database. With such a database set up, the stores could adopt two basic principles, as defined by Brian. The principles are:

■ Customers are not equal.

■ Behavior follows rewards.

To put these principles to work, retailers had to see that different customers received different offers. Occasional, unknown customers paid full price. Loyal, regular customers paid a lower price—on certain merchandise or on all merchandise. Furthermore, the loyalists were made aware that they were the favored ones. They were treated as Gold card customers—as long as their behavior warranted it. What retailers discovered is that they could modify customer behavior by the appropriate application of rewards.

Brian Woolf cites some interesting examples of customer-specific marketing:

- A retailer offered a free turkey to those customers who spent an average of at least $50 a week in the two months prior to Thanksgiving. The number of households spending over $50 per week increased 20 percent over the preceding year.

- A retailer told customers that 1 percent of their spending would be donated to the church of their choice. *Result:* Participating cardholders increased their annual spending by more than 5 percent.

- Senior citizens were given a 10 percent reduction at one chain if they purchased on Mondays. As a result, 67 percent of the seniors' shopping took place on Monday. That was five times the spending level of all other customers on Monday.

New Marketing Focus

"We are no longer trying to take customers away from our major competitor. Our focus is to make money on the customers who are already shopping with us," reported one retail chain executive who used the new system. These customer-specific marketers reduced their advertising costs because, through analysis of their databases, they learned the low profitability and low loyalty of the promiscuous shoppers who were attracted to their stores mainly by heavy advertising. The new customer-specific marketing had three approaches:

- Withdraw low-margin offers to unprofitable customers.
- Offer the best customers aggressive pricing and special benefits.
- Switch from item pricing to total pricing.

   This is accomplished by:

- Increased prices for customers with low profitability
- Decreased prices for high-margin customers

   How can this be done? One retailer's program illustrates the method. He:

- Took a quarter of the items featured in newspaper ads and aggressively priced them, but only for cardholders
- Converted 1,000 of the company's 3,000 temporary price reductions to cardholder-only specials

   The result was a jump of 6 percent in sales in some of his stores. Overall, his gross profits were 1 percent higher due to the new system.

How Customer-Specific Marketing Works

When a preferred customer presents her card at the checkout counter, she gets cardholder-priced items at a lower price than other shoppers. When she buys multiple units, she gets additional discounts not available to noncardholders. Many retailers adopted *straddle pricing*. This is a system in which regular shelf prices are higher than the competition, but cardholder prices for the same items are below those of the competition. In this way, the noncardholders subsidize the cardholders. As computer power was further enhanced, total customer profitability made it possible to keep track of annual purchases of cardholders. Stores could provide even better treatment for volume buyers than that extended to regular cardholders. In some cases, rather than have deep price reductions on advertised merchandise, upscale retailers offered heavy bonus points. This kept them from destroying the retailer's price image.

Sweepstakes Can Be Fun

Big Y, a supermarket in western Massachusetts, spiced up its Express Savings Club with a grand-prize sweepstakes of $1 million, plus numerous weekly prizes of $1,000 in cash and $50 gift certificates and state lottery tickets. A cardholder did not know whether she had won one of the fifteen $1,000 weekly cash prizes until she shopped the following week and her card was swiped. If the card carried a winning number, a red light started flashing in the ceiling and alarm bells sounded in the store. Everyone in the store stopped to see who the lucky winner was!

Noncash Benefits

Neiman-Marcus offered its best customers lunch with the store manager, along with two of the customer's friends, followed by a private fashion show. The penthouse at Caesar's Palace is available only to those who have at least a $1 million line of credit for gambling at the hotel. Paw Paw Shopping Center in Michigan sent customers, prior to their birthday, a gift certificate for a free decorated birthday cake. As a result, total cake sales increased tenfold in one year. Safeway offered free ice cream to cardholders for their birthday. Tracking showed an average of $10 increased sales when birthday certificates were redeemed.

At Lees Supermarket in Westport, Massachusetts, when the customer cards were swiped, the computer flashed information to the store clerk that he could use in conversation with the customer: It indicated how long she had been a customer, whether she was one of the best store customers, and how big a check she was authorized to cash without the manager's approval. Mark Dodge of Easy Access in Wisconsin set up a program to activate a store manager's beeper whenever any particularly good customer or group of customers used their card in the store. Albert Lees of Lees Supermarkets thought he knew the identity of his best customers until he set up his database. He was amazed to find that he didn't even recognize his top customer, who was spending over $10,000 per year in his store.

Customer Category Management

The cardholder database permitted retailers to group customers not by where they live, but by how much they spend per week. Research at the Retail Strategy Center showed that demographics were not particularly useful as a primary segmentation basis for retailers because there was little correlation to profitability. Instead, by classifying customers by spending, it was possible to determine the lifetime value of retail customers.

How else were these card-based customer data used? One retailer had a 40-foot aisle devoted to candy. Candy was profitable, but was that the best use of his space? Looking at his customer database, he found that his top customers (top 30 percent who provide 75 percent of the sales) did not buy much candy. What did they buy? Baby products. So he cut his candy counter to 20 feet, and added 20 feet to baby products. The reasoning? "We are concentrating on our *top customers,* not our *top merchandise.* It is more profitable that way."

Reasons for Failure

Not all attempts at customer-specific marketing have achieved success. There are a number of reasons for the failure. They include:

- *Timidity.* In some cases, top management was not committed and did not push the system sufficiently. If you have only 30 percent of your transactions recorded on your cards, there is no obvious profit gain from the system.

- *Puny rewards.* In some stores, the electronic discounts were not meaningful. If the savings are minuscule, the customers will leave their cards at home.

- *Overreliance on vendors.* In some cases, retailers tried to transfer all the costs of markdowns to the vendors. What happened was that the program featured mainly slow-moving items the vendors wanted to push, instead of those items the customers wanted to buy. These programs tend to fail.

- *Information starvation.* To reduce costs, some companies used their system as a shelf electronic discount without capturing customer purchases. Such practices lose the real value of customer-specific marketing, which lies in the information it can provide.

- *Failure to differentiate.* Where there was insufficient differentiation between the best and the worst customers, the systems did not reward profitable behavior sufficiently to improve the bottom line.

- *Customer-specific marketing was not the core strategy.* If customer-specific marketing did not become the core marketing strategy, the programs usually failed. When stores continue existing marketing practices, the new initiatives simply become another promotional program.

- *Internal political problems.* The bigger the chain, the greater the resistance to change. Unless top management is behind it, internal squabbles tend to kill customer specific marketing before its potential can be realized.

But Does It Pay Off?

What is the payoff from customer-specific marketing when it works?

- Daniel Lescoe, VP of sales and marketing at Big Y Foods in Springfield, Massachusetts, said, "Before we adopted this program, our market share in Western Massachusetts was $272,400,000 which represented about 25 percent of the market. Two years after adopting the system we moved into the number one position with sales of $364,662,474 and a market share of almost 29 percent. Every marketing program we develop has one mission: to promote our Express Savings Club. It is a religion for us, not just another promotion."

■ Roger Morgan, managing director of Morgan's Tuckerbag Supermarkets in Melbourne, Australia, reported on his first full year of customer-specific marketing: "In an industry that has seen average customer transaction values dropping, and customer visits increasing, our stores with this program in place radically went against this trend. We experienced increased customer transaction values with increased customer traffic as well. Some identical weeks experienced 40 percent sales increases over the previous year. Overall our annual increase over the previous year was in the 20 percent+ range."

Adding the Noncardholders to Your Database

Once you begin to experiment with building a retail marketing database, it will become obvious that there is a definite cash value for every name retained on the database. Profits (from a well-managed database strategy) will be a function of the number of customers (not necessarily credit card holders) on the database. How can you get at the anonymous majority who pay with cash, check, or nonhouse credit card?

One method, of course, is to provide applicants with a noncredit "check-cashing card" that speeds up the acceptance of checks. Supermarkets use such cards routinely. Department stores can do the same.

Jennifer MacLean reported how one retailer added thousands of customer names to its database in a short space of time. All cash and nonhouse credit card customers were asked to supply their telephone numbers as a part of the transaction. The numbers were keyed into the POS device.

Capturing the information on 304,427 transactions, the retailer discovered that 28 percent were repeat buyers. The unique telephone numbers were sent to a service bureau, where the numbers were looked up through an electronic reverse telephone directory system. The names and addresses of 129,623 customers were identified through this process.

The resulting file was checked against the house credit card file. It turned out that 36 percent of these customers were house credit card holders: Two-thirds were active, and one third were inactive. The remaining 82,869, of course, were new names that were added to the store's marketing database.

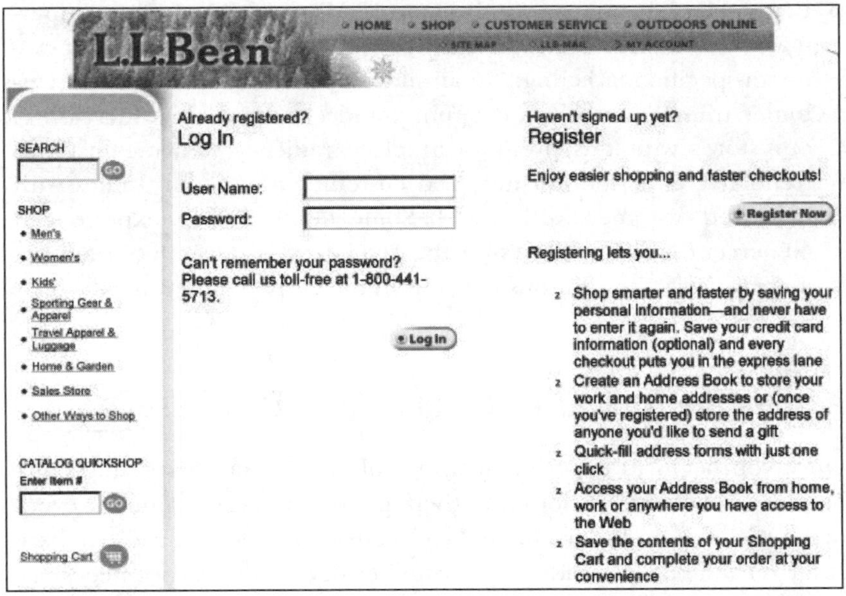

Figure 11-9. L.L. Bean registers prospective customers on the web.

The fact that many cardholders, previously thought inactive, were actually making purchases at the store came as a pleasant surprise, and added to the store's knowledge about its customer base.

Of course, today, one of the best ways to add names is to ask for them on the web. (See Figure 11-9.)

Nordstrom's Methods

Nordstrom's is legendary in the services it provides to its upscale clientele. The clerks are trained to send a personal thank-you letter to all customers who make significant purchases. In particular, the store take pains to acknowledge all orders that require personalization, a gift message, or other special service. The message is written in a narrative sequence in a conversational tone. The message provides an opportunity to reinforce Nordstrom's image and commitment to customer satisfaction. The company has a library of prewritten correspondence, which is used to respond to a wide variety of customer service requirements.

Profits from Promoters

What is your name worth? A retailer name carries an image that sends a message: Sears, JC Penney, Bloomingdale's, Nordstrom's, L.L. Bean, Lands' End. As you read each of these names, an image forms in your mind of the store, what it stands for, what a message from that store is likely to mean to you.

American Express spent years cultivating its name ("Membership has its privileges"). An envelope from American Express, or Bloomingdale's, is more likely to be opened than one from an unknown retailer. The name alone, in other words, is worth money. Some retailers have put their name to effective use by working with small promoters to make special offerings to their cardholders.

The way it works is this:

- The promoter comes to the retailer with a product and an idea. Let's say that it is a cellular phone, which fits into a woman's pocketbook.

- Together, they figure out the demographics and purchase behavior of the store customers most likely to respond to such a product.

- The retailer does an ad hoc search of the store's cardholder database to identify the likely prospects.

- The promoter prepares direct-mail materials describing the offer. A contract is signed with the retailer, indicating the percentage of sales going to the retailer and the percentage to the promoter.

- The promoter carries out the mailing using a list provided by the store, letterhead and envelopes from the store, and his own resources. The store pays nothing for the mailing. *Alternative:* The offer can be included in the store's monthly statement mailing. *Advantage:* It is less costly. *Disadvantage:* The response is much lower.

- Fulfillment is carried out by the store's fulfillment department. Payment is made to the store's accounting department. Once a month, the promoter is reimbursed for his share in the venture.

What are the advantages in such an arrangement?

- *Knowledge.* The retailer gets to experiment with direct marketing at very little cost. Valuable knowledge is learned about the customers, their responses, and their propensity to buy certain products.

- *Profits.* The profits from such an arrangement can be far greater than any similar retail venture. With virtually no investment, some retailers have made more total profits from such a system than from their entire retailing operation.

Is there a downside? Will customers feel "exploited" by having their names "used" in this way?

The answer involves the entire philosophy of marketing. In the first place, the retailer must scan each of these offers carefully to be sure that the products and the way that they are presented fully reflect the standards that customers have come to expect from the store. The promotion of trash in the name of the store will cheapen the store in many ways.

Second, the retailer must do a good job of targeting its mail to the right customers. Picking your targets is not only good economics; it is also a favor to the customer. If every letter from a department store is loaded with merchandise in which the customer has no interest, she will soon lose interest in the store, and in opening envelopes from the store.

Assuming that it is a quality product, well targeted to the right customers, retailers can only gain from such a system. If the customer is buying, she must be happy: She has made a profit from the transaction. Making customers aware of profitable opportunities that they take advantage of is doing them a favor.

Database Marketing, the Web, and Packaged Goods

Does database marketing or the web work for packaged goods? There is no clear-cut answer to this question. Many manufacturers have tried it. Some have succeeded. Most have failed. Does that mean that it can't be done, or does it mean that they didn't go about it correctly? That is the key question. Strategy is very important here. If you don't have a really good idea, and execute it well, you will lose your money trying to do database marketing or web branding with packaged goods.

There are several reasons why database projects promoting packaged goods seldom work out:

- *There is not enough margin to do database marketing.* The margin on packaged goods is pathetically thin. The last time I looked, Ivory soap was selling for $1.29 for four bars. There is no margin in such sales. In database marketing, you are trying to modify your customer's behavior in some way that will be profitable for you, and satisfying to the customer. To modify behavior, you have to provide some benefit for the customers who are on your database. There has to be some margin to pay for the communications—and for the benefit.

- *You can't find out what the customer is doing.* To do database marketing, there has to be a feedback loop. You have to have purchase history in the database. You have to know whether the specific people listed in the database are buying the product—and when, in what quantities, and in response to what promotions. You cannot do that with packaged goods. You can't afford to provide and redeem a coupon with every case of beer, over-the-counter medicine, or box of cereal. Most customers just won't bother to send in such coupons, even if you could afford to pay for them. Stores that have frequent buyer cards know exactly who is buying your product and when, but few of them will sell this information to manufacturers. Selling the data was the premise for the Reward America program started by Citicorp (and reported in Chapter 14). It failed. Since then, most retail stores are worried that privacy concerns would ruin their profitable frequent buyer programs if they began to sell the data to manufacturers.

- *Coupons have seriously eroded brand loyalty.* Billions of coupons are available from every conceivable source: Carol Wright, local coop programs, Sunday newspapers, in-store coupons, etc. Millions of people plan their shopping trips around the coupons they collect. Coupons can be placed in a Sunday newspaper for $6 per thousand. Coupons sent directly to targeted homes by mail cost a minimum of $300 per thousand. Your package, offer, and concept will have to be outstanding to permit your targeted offer to overcome this cost differential. Few companies know how to do it. Database marketing is almost impossible in these circumstances.

So What Can You Do?

You Can Pretend to Do Database Marketing. You can build a database of people who have responded to your promotions, and mail them offers from time to time. Does this work? Kraft General Foods has maintained a database of more than 20 million households for many years. Yet it is hard to see how the results can pay for the costs involved.

You Can Work with Retailers. Many retailers maintain customer databases that keep track of customer purchases in very great detail. From these databases, you can learn shopping habits, and you can learn the response to various promotions by different categories of consumers. The retailers won't let you correspond directly with these consumers, in most cases, but that doesn't matter. Direct communications are too expensive for packaged goods anyway.

You Can Build a Web Site. Several packaged goods retailers have built customer web sites. They put the web address on their packages and ads. Some of the web sites are quite creative, like the one shown in Figure 11-10. This was the web site for *I Can't Believe It's Not Butter*. It was designed strictly for young women.

The company collected my name. I received a coupon for 50 cents off on my favorite cooking spray. Can the company make money doing this? I doubt it. Can it influence more than a tiny fraction of its customers through such creative web sites? I doubt it. But on the other hand, such web sites are relatively inexpensive. You can build and maintain a very satisfactory web site for what a single annual direct promotion to 200,000 households would cost. Maybe the company will learn something worth knowing. I think that such a web site is a good idea. More manufacturers should look into setting one up. These web sites are part of building the brand. But will they do more for the brand than a full page in *Better Homes*? I doubt it.

Figure 11-10. I can't believe it's not butter web site.

You Can Set Up a Club. Kraft General Foods preserved and increased usage of Crystal Light among users on its 1 million-member club database, with a profitable return on investment for several years. Later the focus shifted to a web site. (See Figure 11-11.)

Figure 11-11. Crystal Light web site.

The Wacky Warehouse (club for children) increased Kool-Aid sales over several years to 83 percent of the powdered drink market and, at the same time, reversed the preference by youngsters for Pepsi and Coke over Kool-Aid.

Kraft General Foods pioneered user clubs for packaged goods. Clubs for gardening, sports, gourmet cooks, automobiles, children, computers, dieting, travel, and nature have been created using the web. The purpose of such clubs is to provide customers with something unusual, which does not involve price, but involves the use of the product. The idea is to build interest in the activity, not your product. The product, instead of being the central feature, is an assumed fact.

A case in point is the Buitoni web page shown in Figure 11-12. The idea is that "everyone uses Buitoni Italian products when serving a meal. But look at these great Italian recipes you can get. Look at Italy, the home of wonderful food." Digging deeper into this web site (Figure 11-13), we see Italy laid out for us.

Figure 11-12. Buitoni web site.

Join the Buitoni website on a journey discovering the beautiful and historic regions of Italy.

To find out more about these Italian regions, why not take a look at the Recipe Search section.

Figure 11-13. Buitoni takes you to Italy.

If your club is good enough and provides enough benefits for members, it can eventually become self-supporting through sales of services and merchandise (other than your immediate product) or paid ads in the club magazine.

The *Nintendo Power* newsletter built up a readership of 2 million customers eager to learn more about how to use the product. A 900 telephone number (paid for by the customer) was used by 10,000 kids a week. Up to 40,000 letters were received every month by readers, all of which were answered. Such a club created from newsletter readers, once established, is ideal for launching a new product. When Nintendo introduced *Game Boys*, it sold 5 million in the first year and 20 million cartridges in follow-up sales. The clubs are now reached through Nintendo's web site.

Can you copy Nintendo and build a club? It is a strategy that, if done well, will never go out of style. However, done poorly or half-heartedly, it will just drain your treasury.

You Can Set Up Affinity Groups. A little less demanding than a club is an identified affinity group to which you can mail a newsletter and invitations to purchase the product.

The average baby uses over $1,400 worth of disposable diapers per year. Kimberly Clark spent over $10 million to set up a database system for Huggies diapers; the system covers 75 percent of the expectant mothers in the United States. The names are obtained from doctors, hospitals, and childbirth trainers. During the time that they are pregnant, the expectant mothers receive personalized magazines and letters with ideas on baby care. When the baby is born, the mother gets a coded coupon for diapers. And when the coupon is redeemed, the information is fed into Kimberly Clark's database.

Every other manufacturer who provides consumable baby products has copied this idea and maintains a profitable baby product database. In this case, database marketing works.

You Can Use Referral Programs. There is a progression that most customers go through: awareness, trial, user, advocate, regular user. Once some people become hooked on your product, they want to tell their friends about it. They become advocates.

In most cases, there is little that advocates can do, except to tell a couple of friends at the office or a neighbor. Why not capitalize on this brief phase of infatuation? Before they become blasé regular users, give the advocates something positive that they can do to promote the success of this wonderful product—to spread to others the joy and satisfaction that they feel every time they use it.

This is where referral programs come in. If you can use your database to encourage advocates to spread the word in a positive way, you can boost your own sales, and make your customers happy.

The Perform program did this. Members were encouraged to recommend friends and neighbors who might want the product (pet food). When these friends and neighbors purchased, the recommender received a thank-you letter together with a $2 reduction on the next pet food bill. MCI did this with its Friends and Family Program. MCI, of course, is not a packaged good, but the concept still applies.

You can also boost sales and increase your database with on-pack referral programs, inviting people to send in names. You build a database of the recommender and the recommendee, with benefits accruing to the recommender when the recommendee takes some recorded action (proof of purchase, enrollment in a club, etc.).

Such a program can be quite inexpensive. On-pack offers have a delivery cost that is almost zero (compared with direct mail or advertising). The customer pays the postage. You pay only when you receive a response—this is the kind of payment that is really worthwhile because you are dealing with a customer, not a prospect.

Stash Tea built its database using on-pack offers. A small tea company in Portland, Oregon, founded by David Leger and Steve Lee in 1972, Stash sold its tea at first to health food stores and restaurants. Once the men began packing the tea into foil-sealed tea bags, they got the idea of putting a catalog offer on the back of the foil packet.

As many as 2,000 tea customers per month called the 800 number or wrote in for the catalog, which came out quarterly and sold a wide variety of products. It also gave historical information about tea, the name "Stash," the Stash Tea foster child, stores that carry the product, and letters from readers. This catalog lasted. It produced 35 percent of the company's net profits from only 10 percent of its sales.

Why has Stash Tea been successful when so many others have failed? Because it had an idea, a theme (exotic teas and tea lovers), and a sound economic program (an interesting catalog), plus excellent execution of the idea. The catalog goes only to people who *ask for it*. Since Stash Tea is sold only in upscale restaurants and specialty stores, the customers are, in general, more affluent, and in a position to buy the products in the catalog. It is niche marketing at its best.

Determining Member Benefits

Any free-market transaction produces a profit for both parties. What is the profit that customers will receive for being in your database? Is this profit enough to make them want to be in the database, and want to fill out your survey forms and respond to your letters and telephone calls? This profit must be sufficient to encourage the customer to be loyal.

Profits for customers do not necessarily have to be cash. Profits can be an interesting web site, a magazine, a membership in a club, access to a technical hot line, a coloring book—anything that people cannot easily get elsewhere and that will be perceived as a benefit. If you cannot come up with an adequate profit level for the customers, stop right there and drop or revise your project. The database will fail if the customers do not benefit from being in it.

Recapitulation

If you feel that I am warning you to go slowly and carefully before you rush into database marketing for packaged goods, you have gotten the message. A really creative idea can build a packaged goods database. Stash Tea did it. Could Lipton? Kool Aid did it. Could Buitoni?

My feeling is that, with the exception of baby products, it is tough to surmount the economics of packaged goods. The database, in almost all cases, will make only a modest incremental increase in sales. Will that increment be sufficient to provide enough benefits to the members of the database that they will want to be members of whatever affinity group you establish, and will develop a loyalty to your product and company? Will the modest increment be sufficient not only to pay the benefits to the customer, but also to pay all the expenses of the database? Will the fact that you will never really know in detail whether your efforts are paying off ruin your chances for approval by management—and reduce your self-respect?

Summary

- Retailing is tough. Database marketing and the web today, however, offer a new solution to the retailing problem.
- The first step is usually to boost the number and percentage of customers who use the store's credit card or are registered on the web. This forms the basis for the database.

■ Retail database files can be very large. The solution to the size problem can be found in keeping detailed data for a short time only, rolling up older data by department, and using modern marketing software that provides access to customer files to do ad hoc counts and selects.

■ Retailers can combine with external promoters to market directly to retail customers. The result can be very profitable for the retailers.

■ Database marketing for packaged goods is particularly difficult because margins and loyalty have been seriously eroded by billions of coupons issued yearly. Many companies that have entered this field have failed to build a satisfactory long-term database system.

■ Coupons in a newspaper cost $6 per thousand. Any type of direct mail costs a minimum of $300 per thousand. You have to prove that direct mail is better, or give up the project.

Executive Quiz 10

Answers to quiz questions can be found in Appendix B.

1. All but one of the following is commonly used to build retail customer loyalty:

   a. Special personal services

   b. Solo mailings

   c. Incentives for store card members

   d. Fast checkout for card members

   e. Rewards for customers on their birthdays

2. Migration programs aimed at moving customers to higher LTV levels can affect which of the following?

   a. Visits per week

   b. Average basket size

   c. The retention rate

   d. All of the above

   e. None of the above

3. Sears Canada used how many RFM segments for its customer database?

   a. 5

   b. 60

   c. 125

   d. 189

   e. None of the above

4. Why do migration programs focus on Silver rather than Gold customers?

   a. Gold customers tend to be maxed out.

   b. Silver customers have more income.

   c. Occasional shoppers are often profitable.

   d. All of the above.

   e. None of the above.

5. Programs for birthday and anniversary reminders and gift suggestions:

   a. Seldom affect customer behavior

   b. Are very expensive to set up

   c. Are always more trouble than they are worth

   d. Require data that are difficult to obtain

   e. Can be tracked using lifetime value

6. For occasional shoppers:

   a. The acquisition cost is usually higher than the advertising cost

   b. The lifetime value is always positive

   c. Direct costs tend to go up each year

   d. The retention rate is usually quite high

   e. None of the above

7. What was the half-life day for Sears Canada's catalogs?

    a. 15

    b. 20

    c. 25

    d. 30

    e. 35

8. Straddle pricing is when:

    a. Prices vary from day to day

    b. Cardholders subsidize noncardholders

    c. Competitors' posted prices are higher

    d. Occasional shoppers can use express lanes

    e. None of the above

12

Building Retention and Loyalty in Business Customers

It's a familiar saying that business would be great if we didn't have to deal with customers. But have you ever stopped to consider that your business might be more profitable without customers—without some of them, at least? ... Cooper and Kaplan reported the astonishing case of a heating wire company which analyzed its customer profitability and discovered that the famous 20–80 rule, which would suggest that 80 percent of profits came from 20 percent of customers, had to be revised:

"A 20–225 rule was actually operating: 20 percent of the customers were generating 225 percent of profits. The middle 70 percent of customers were hovering around the break-even point, and 10 percent of customers were losing 125 percent of profits"

Even more amazing: it was the largest customers who were producing the biggest losses.

Lynette Ryals
Cranfield University, UK

There are many products and services where database marketing has limited value. In business-to-business marketing, however, relationship-building activities *always* pay off. Why is the business-to-business area so productive? There are several reasons:

- The sales amounts are usually large. Sales are large enough that there is a significant margin available for relationship-building activities.

- The data on customer purchases are almost always available since so much of the business is on open accounts. Getting the names of the decision makers, influencers, and ultimate users is often a challenge, however.

- The number of customers is usually quite small. In many cases we are dealing with 50,000 customers or fewer. We can concentrate on these companies and build a complete database of contact history, purchases, and preferences, and use these data to support our relationship-building activities.

- Business customers have problems of their own to solve, including channel conflicts, inventory maintenance, and customer acquisition and retention. The supplier is often in a position to help customers solve their problems.

Professor Paul Wang divides business customers into four basic categories, as shown in Figure 12-1. The two axes in this figure represent price and service. Some business customers pay a high price and get little service. On the other end, some pay very low prices but get the best service. Let's see why that is.

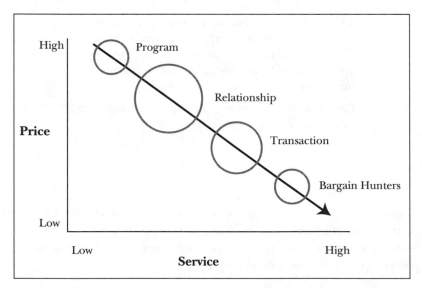

Figure 12-1. Types of business customers.

Bargain hunters are customers who have tremendous market power. Wal-Mart is an example. Here is a customer that demands—and gets— the absolutely lowest prices in the market. Wal-Mart is in a position to make massive purchases at rock-bottom prices. At the same time, it can demand—and get—a very high level of service from its suppliers. Wal-Mart often makes its suppliers provide daily shelf restocking. Some goods are placed on Wal-Mart shelves on consignment so Wal-Mart has little investment. In some cases, the suppliers must clean up the sales areas each day. Few other retailers can get such services from their suppliers.

For bargain hunters, the supplier has to meet specified requirements in order to sell massive amounts at very low prices. There are many such bargain hunters around. Anyone who sells to Home Depot or Staples knows that it is like holding a tiger by its tail.

Program buyers are at the other end of the scale. Small purchasers of office supplies, for example, do not have the time or the economic incentive to shop around for the best deal. They don't have the market power that comes from volume purchases. Typically, they will buy from a nearby source one month and shift to another source the next month, without any really well-thought-out plan. Many governments, including the federal government, are program buyers. They issue purchasing manuals to their employees which restrict how, what, where, and when purchases can be made. These program buyers have the worst of both worlds. They pay the highest prices and get the lowest level of service. The famous Defense Department purchase of $130 toilet seats is a well-known example. Their purchases are either so small or so specialized that few suppliers find it profitable to do much to attract them. Relationship building may not work here.

Transaction buyers, on the other hand, represent a major segment of any market. These customers try to engage in comparison shopping for every transaction. They read the ads, make phone calls, get comparative bids. For them, the past has no meaning. They have absolutely no loyalty. Never mind what the supplier did for you in the past; the question is, what is your price today? They will shift suppliers of any product for a few pennies' difference in price.

Transaction buyers usually get little service. Service is not important to them. Price is everything. There is not much point in trying to win their loyalty since they have none to win. Database marketing will not work here—only discounting. They are seldom profitable customers, even though they may buy a lot of product and represent an important segment of any market. The best thing that could happen to these transaction buyers would be for them to shift over to buying from your competition. Give them the competition's catalogs and phone numbers and hope they take the hint. Paul Wang suggests that the only way to make money with transaction buyers is to negotiate annual volume-purchase agreements. The buyers get a good deal on price, and you get the volume without having to spend valuable marketing and customer service dollars.

Relationship buyers are the customers for whom database marketing was invented. They are looking for a dependable supplier:

■ Someone who cares about their needs and who looks out for them

■ Someone who remembers what they bought in the past and gives them special services as a reward

■ Someone who takes an interest in their business and treats them as individuals

Relationship buyers know that they could save a few dollars by shopping around. But they also recognize that if they do switch suppliers, they would lose something that they value very highly: the relationship that they have built up with a dependable supplier that recognizes them and takes good care of them. Many of them also realize that there is an emotional and monetary cost to shopping around for every purchase. They want to concentrate on their business success, not on their purchasing prowess.

By classifying your customers into these four segments, you can focus your marketing efforts on the one segment that is really profitable: relationship buyers. Your database is used to record the purchases of these buyers, and to give them personal recognition and special services. You recognize your Gold customers. You communicate with them. You partner with them.

Classifying Customers by Segment

How can you classify customers by these four segments? Part of it is easy. You already know who the bargain hunters are. No one who deals with Wal-Mart or Sears or other giant retailers has to be told who they are. Program buyers can almost be ignored. They make small purchases on an occasional basis. They pay full price and seldom respond to sales offers. They, too, are easy to classify.

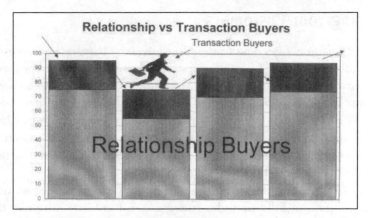

Figure 12-2. Transaction buyers shifting from supplier to supplier.

Your big problem lies in distinguishing transaction buyers from relationship buyers. Here's how one retailer does it. New customers are given a survey form. One question asks:

> How important are the following in making your decision about where to buy this product? Rank from 1—most important—to 5—least important:
> a) Price
> b) Service
> c) Reputation of manufacturer
> d) Recommendation of a friend
> e) Company policy
> f) Previous experience
> g) Customer service

Those who code "price" as most important are probably transaction buyers. The others may well be relationship buyers. This can be tested later in other ways.

Your management may insist that most of your customers are transaction buyers. Your staff will point out that when you are on sale, you get more sales. When you are not, the sales decrease. Figure 12-2, however, shows what may be happening. Each of the four companies, A, B, C, and D, has a stable base of relationship buyers that stay with it. There is a floating group of transaction buyers that jumps from company to company, taking advantage of the sales. They never pay full price for anything. No one makes much money from them. Each company assumes that all of its customers are price sensitive, when, in reality, few of their loyal customers are price sensitive at all.

Training Your Customers

How do customers become transaction buyers? They are not necessarily born that way. They become transaction buyers through exposure to their environment and their management. As suppliers, we may feel that we have to take the world as we find it, but that is not necessarily true. We can take a group of customers who are quite prepared to develop a relationship with us and *ruin* them by converting them into transaction buyers. How do we do this? By talking price to them all the time, instead of talking relationship. Look at how we do it:

You attract customers by offering discounts. Once you have acquired the customer, you hold periodic sales and send out literature extolling your low prices. What a mistake! You are training your customers to think of your product or service as a commodity whose value can be measured only by price. Once you have implanted this idea in their minds, they will learn to shop around. Soon they will find someone who sells something cheaper. Of course, if you are truly an everyday low-price dealer like Staples, the focus on price is a valid tactic. But most business-to-business suppliers do not want to be in that league.

What should you do for relationship buyers?

- Describe what your products do, how various businesses are using them, how they are made, and new developments in your field.

- Divide your customers into groups, based on their SIC code—surveyors, architects, builders, contractors—and send them different messages.

- Create an advisory panel for each group, putting key executives from among your Gold customers in each group on the panel.

- Create a newsletter for each group, with the advisory panel on the masthead.

- Sponsor contests in trade associations for the most creative use of your products.

- Learn the birthday of key people in your customers' companies and send them a card.

- Write thank-you letters periodically for their purchases—not combined with a pitch for more sales—but just a genuine thank you.

Integrated Account Management

At a business-to-business conference, I was asked, "How big a customer base do you have to have so that you can profit from database marketing?" It was an interesting question. The answer, it seems to me, is to divide customers into three categories, as shown in Figure 12-3.

The top group (the Gold customers), in most business-to-business situations, is visited directly by the sales force. The salespeople know these customers by sight and name. You can build a database of these customers, but it may not help the sales force much. If you only have 300 customers, and all of them are large enough to justify a sales visit, you don't need a database.

Relationship marketing really works with the middle group. These are profitable customers whose sales do not justify a sales visit. Here, you can organize effective teams to reach these customers by a combination of techniques using the database.

Hunter Business Direct developed a method for doing this, described in Mark Peck's book *Integrated Account Management.* (See Appendix A, Maria Meyers Association, 1997.) The idea, *integrated account management* (IAM), developed first by Hunter for Amoco and Shell, was outlined in my book *The Complete Database Marketer* (pp. 461–471). IAM works this way: The existing sales force is replaced by region-

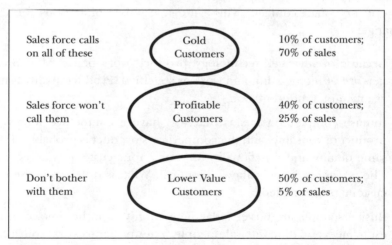

Figure 12-3. Typical business-to-business customer grouping.

al marketing teams, each headed by a regional marketing chief (RMC) who talks to customers on the phone or by e-mail. The RMC schedules the visits of the field reps. The field reps no longer sell. Instead, they become business consultants who help the customers to solve their business problems. They help them with their own sales, customer support, accounting, hiring and training of employees, etc. The RMC works from a database that includes all contacts with each customer. Typically the RMC negotiates an annual contract with each customer with prices based on volume. All sales are taken by phone, or by e-mail, or from a web site, under the control of the RMC.

Under integrated account management, customer service is empowered to solve problems. When a customer calls with a problem, the customer service rep (CSR) must stay with the case until it is solved. Cases are not handed over to someone else. The field reps not only *don't* sell. They don't get bogged down in solving product delivery problems either.

Integrated account management is usually highly efficient compared with more traditional methods of dealing with business-to-business customers. Customers like it better and respond well to the new setup. Part of the reason for its success is the change in the business climate which developed in the 1990s. In earlier days, surveys showed that business customers often welcomed sales visits. By the 1990s the pace of business picked up to such an extent that most business customers preferred phone or e-mail contacts. There are a number of reasons for this change:

- Because of advanced technology, products work better. Most products are of high quality, and work as specified. Product quality is not as much of a differentiator.

- Intense competition means that you have a competitor for every product in your line, and the competitor's product is probably of the same quality and functionality as yours. Your customers know this. The prices are usually almost identical. What is different is the way customers are treated.

- Businesspeople are busier today. They don't have the time or interest to meet and dine with salespeople. They prefer to work from a catalog, placing orders using the Internet, e-mail, fax, or phone. We are living in a new world.

Business-to-Business Lifetime Value

Lifetime value tables for business-to-business customers are easy to develop and are highly useful for evaluating strategy. Let's develop the lifetime value of customers of an artificial construct: the Weldon Scientific Company, which sells high-tech equipment to factories and laboratories.

The table in Figure 12-4 shows Weldon's LTV. This table is similar to those explained in Chapter 3, with some exceptions. Weldon has about 20,000 business customers, including 1,800 independent distributors. The average customer placed an average of 1.8 orders in the year of acquisition, with an average order value of $2,980. Weldon retained 70

	Year 1	Year 2	Year 3
Customers	20,000	12,000	7,800
Retention rate	60.00%	65.00%	70.00%
Orders per year	1.8	2.6	3.6
Average order size	$2,980	$5,589	$9,016
Total revenue	$107,280,000	$174,376,800	$255,696,480
Direct cost %	70.00%	65.00%	63.00%
Direct costs	$75,096,000	$113,344,920	$161,088,782
Acquisition cost $630	$12,600,000	$0	$0
Total costs	$87,696,000	$113,344,920	$161,088,782
Gross profit	$19,584,000	$61,031,880	$94,607,698
Discount rate	1.18	1.36	1.49
Net present value profit	$16,596,610	$44,876,382	$63,495,099
Cumulative NPV profit	$16,596,610	$61,472,993	$124,968,092
Customer lifetime value	$830	$3,074	$6,248

Figure 12-4. LTV of Weldon Scientific Company.

percent of its first-year customers into the next year. As customers became more loyal, they placed more orders per year, of increasing size, and the retention rate of the remaining customers also increased.

The acquisition cost was $630 per customer. The cost of servicing customers came down substantially after the first year. Most interesting in this table is the discount rate, which is developed in a separate table, shown in Figure 12-5.

The formula for the discount rate is:

$$\text{Discount rate} = [1 + (\text{interest rate} \times \text{risk factor})]^{\text{year}+\text{AR}/360}$$

In the first year, Weldon is trying hard to acquire new customers. They accept some risky accounts and provide extended payment terms. In subsequent years, as their client base becomes more stable, the risk factor declines significantly. Customers pay their accounts more rapidly.

Relationship Building Initiatives

Let's suppose that Weldon has decided to experiment with database marketing. It will take the following steps:

- Build a web site with distributor and direct customer access by means of a PIN. The site will include all of its products, with the prices shown based on the customer's volume situation. Distributors and direct customers can place orders directly on the web site, or by phone, e-mail or fax, as they prefer. Distributors' customers can use the web site, with shipment directly from the distributors. All of this is controlled by the PIN.

- Set up an integrated account management team that contacts all medium-sized and large customers at least six times per year, learn-

	Year 1	Year 2	Year 3
Year	0	1	2
Risk factor	4.0	2.1	1.5
Interest rate	13.00%	13.00%	13.00%
A/R days	140	100	90
Discount rate	1.18	1.36	1.49

Figure 12-5. Computation of the discount rate.

ing the names of the decision makers, influencers, and actual users of Weldon's products. Annual sales agreements are negotiated with volume discounts. There is a special team to work with the 1,800 independent distributors that handle the Weldon line. The other teams work with end-user accounts. IAM is expensive to set up at first, but once in operation, it should be less expensive than previous methods of reaching customers.

- Create an advisory council for each of its six major customer groups, complete with a newsletter that is published on the web and with prizes given at professional trade shows for the best use of Weldon's products.

- Design a series of communications to each identified Weldon contact in customer firms. Each new customer receives a welcome letter with a survey form and thank-you letters for large orders. During the year, other communications are developed describing industry developments and new products of interest to the particular customer, based on the survey results. If the survey is not completed, a phone call is made to get the survey information. Weldon averages a 92 percent response rate to its surveys, although only 24 percent come in by mail or fax in response to the first welcome letter.

What the Web Site Does

The web site could make the largest change in the way that Weldon does business. Before the web site, orders arrived in four ways: phone, mail, fax, and e-mail. Because of the detailed nature of Weldon's products, the order processing is complicated, requiring skilled people who look up each product in the catalog to verify the part number, price, shipping method, and regional specifications. The web site could create a revolution. Customers will have their own PINs, which will trigger software that determines the correct price for each item, the shipping method, the distributor, if any, and the regional specifications. With some exceptions for custom items, all products could be ordered from the web site with the click of a mouse. If the customer enters a part number by typing, the software could verify the entry, and refuse incorrect part numbers.

In time, all distributors will develop their own web sites. When a customer wants to order a Weldon product, he will click on that product on the distributor's web site display, and will be shifted immediately to the

Weldon web site where the order is processed. The codes transferred in the link inform Weldon that this is a distributor's customer with a unique PIN. Arrangements with the distributor dictate whether the order will be filled out of the distributor's warehouse, or directly by Weldon, with the distributor getting a commission. If the order is to be filled by the distributor, the Weldon web site will transmit the order electronically to the distributor. What is the advantage to Weldon and the distributor having the Weldon link? The customer may want some Weldon item that the distributor does not have in stock or on display. Weldon can show the customer everything in the line, with the distributor making a commission no matter where the product is actually shipped from. Also, by browsing the wider and up-to-the-minute Weldon product display, the customer may order additional items, supplies, refills, etc., with credit going to the distributor. It is a win-win situation for both. In some cases, distributors may become "virtual distributors" with no inventory at all, but simply a highly productive web site listing the products of many manufacturers in a given field.

The result, in terms of order-processing time, can be amazing. Whereas phone orders typically require an average of 28 hours, and mail, fax, and e-mail require 42 hours from receipt of the phone call until the completed order arrives in Weldon factories in Taiwan or Singapore, the web orders can arrive in the factory in an average of 1.6 minutes (see Figure 12-6). This mirrors the experience of both Panduit, described later in this book, where order-processing time was cut to 1.5 minutes, and Intel, which saved 75,000 faxes to Taiwan per month after its web site became active in July 1998.

The savings cost from the web site is larger than the time saved would indicate. Because orders are processed so much faster, and without

	*Order Processing Time**	*Cost per Order*
Phone	28 hr	$27.00
Fax, e-mail, mail	42 hr	$18.00
Web site	1.6 min	$1.62

*From order receipt until paperwork arrives at factory

Figure 12-6. Order-processing times and costs of various ordering systems.

human intervention, personnel are saved in the order-processing department. In addition, by cutting more than a day from each order-processing time, customers get their products faster, which gives Weldon an edge over its competitors. Finally, by getting bills out one day earlier, Weldon's cash flow is improved by a measurable amount. In all, use of the web site ordering system can cut costs by 3 percent per order. The problem is that in the beginning, only about 10 percent of Weldon's customers would use the web site to place their orders. To change this, Weldon could give a discount of one-half of 1 percent for all orders placed on the web site. By the second year, the percentage of customers using the web site could grow to 60 percent, and by the third year it could be close to 90 percent. The cost savings might well look like that in Figure 12-7.

	Year 1	Year 2	Year 3
Old costs	70.00%	65.00%	63.00%
% using web site	10.00%	60.00%	90.00%
Net saving per order 2.5%	0.25%	1.50%	2.25%
New costs	69.75%	63.50%	60.75%

Figure 12-7. Cost reduction from the use of a web site for orders.

Let's assume that the cost of the first three initiatives is as shown in Figure 12-8. The relationship-building communications to customers, based on their preferences as shown on the survey, have an average annual cost per person of $40 each. The average customer has about 2.4 people whom Weldon needs to contact, so the average cost per company of the relationship-building program is about $96. For each customer that recommends a new customer who becomes a Weldon customer, Weldon provides a reward worth $200.

	Year 1	Annual Incremental Cost
Web site	$1,600,000	$300,000
IAM	$600,000	($100,000)
Advisory councils	$200,000	$150,000
Total	$2,400,000	$350,000

Figure 12-8. Cost of relationship-building initiatives.

The result of the initiatives is a major change in customer lifetime value, as shown in Figure 12-9. The effect of these new initiatives is to increase the average customer lifetime value in the third year from about $4,422 to $7,216. What does this really mean for Weldon? Assuming that its acquisition program continues to replace the lost customers and that Weldon has a steady customer base of 20,000 customers, the program has increased Weldon's profits by $55 million (see Figure 12-10).

As you can see from Figure 12-10, the first year is costly. Introducing these changes reduces Weldon profits by $1 million. But these figures show that if Weldon were to institute the relationship building programs described here, its profits in the third year would increase by over $55 million. Business-to-business relationship building works—and can be shown to work by careful and controlled tests. Where do these fig-

	Year 1	Year 2	Year 3
Referral rate	4.00%	6.00%	8.00%
Referred customers	0	800	828
Retained customers	20,000	13,000	9,660
Retention rate	65.00%	70.00%	75.00%
Total customers	20,000	13,800	10,488
Orders per year	1.9	3.4	4.8
Average order size	$3,078	$6,170	$11,005
Total revenue	$116,964,000	$289,496,400	$554,018,112
Direct cost %	69.75%	63.50%	60.75%
Direct costs	$81,582,390	$183,830,214	$336,566,003
Acquisition cost $630	$12,600,000	$0	$0
New initiatives	$2,400,000	$350,000	$350,000
Relationship building $96	$1,920,000	$1,324,800	$1,006,848
Referral icentives $200	$0	$160,000	$165,600
Total costs	$98,502,390	$185,665,014	$338,088,451
Gross profit	$18,461,610	$103,831,386	$215,929,661
Discount rate	1.18	1.36	1.49
Net present value profit	$15,645,432	$76,346,607	$144,919,236
Cumulative NPV profit	$15,645,432	$91,992,040	$236,911,275
Customer lifetime value	$782	$4,600	$11,846

Figure 12-9. LTV of Weldon customers after new initiatives are in place.

	Year 1	Year 2	Year 3
New LTV	$817	$3,516	$7,216
Old LTV	$867	$2,553	$4,422
Difference	($50)	$963	$2,794
With 20,000 customers	($1,000,000)	$19,260,000	$55,880,000

Figure 12-10. Effect of new initiatives on Weldon profits.

ures come from? How do we know that we can increase the orders in the third year from 3.6 to 4.8 and the average order size from $9,106 to $11,005? By careful testing using control groups, as described earlier.

Of course, Weldon would probably not apply this program to its entire customer base. Weldon, like all other companies, has some highly profitable customers and some highly unprofitable customers. The relationship-building program will probably work best with the middle group. The top group—Weldon's Gold customers—are probably maxed out. They are loyal customers. Many companies have found that they cannot profitably cross-sell or up-sell their best customers. In the same way, Weldon probably cannot have this kind of success with its unprofitable customers. Building a relationship with losers is not a recipe for success. The most profitable group for Weldon's program is the one just below the top—consisting of those who are profitable, but probably dividing their spending for Weldon-type products among a number of different suppliers.

Once Weldon has been able to determine its average customer lifetime value, it can compute the value for various segments. The results are often interesting. In Figure 12-11, you look at Weldon sales, you will see that the big money is clearly in light manufacturing, with $213 million in annual sales. But if you look at lifetime value, the 44 heavy manufacturing customers account for almost $1 million a piece. Clearly, any retention strategy should start with heavy manufacturers. You are going to get much more bang for a marketing buck. Next would be metal production, which is low in overall sales, but clearly high in average customer lifetime value.

Figure 12-11 represents the ultimate users of Weldon products. Most of the 15,442 light manufacturing firms and laboratories are served through Weldon's 1,800 independent distributors. That does not mean that Weldon should not cultivate them; it just should not try to sell directly to them. By keeping its distribution channel on its database,

Weldon Instruments Corporation

	Customers	Average Sales	Total Sales	Sales Ranking	Lifetime Value	LTV Ranking
Metal production	254	$339,736	$86,292,944	4	$145,067	2
Light manufacturing	15,442	$13,851	$213,887,142	1	$5,914	4
Heavy manufacturing	44	$2,314,189	$101,824,316	3	$988,146	1
High technology	612	$299,007	$182,992,284	2	$127,676	3
Others	3,613	$2,176	$7,861,888	5	$929	5
Total	19,965	$29,695	$592,858,574		$12,679	

Figure 12-11. Weldon customers divided by type of industry.

	Number of Customers	Lifetime Value	Firm Value Total	Percent LTV
Platinum	3,967	$50,410	$199,976,470	79.0%
Gold	4,004	$9,603	$38,450,412	15.2%
Silver	3,881	$2,903	$11,266,543	4.5%
Bronze	4,210	$1,108	$4,664,680	1.8%
Lead	3,903	($309)	($1,206,027)	–0.5%
Total	19,965	$12,679	$253,152,078	100.00%

Figure 12-12. Weldon customers organized by lifetime value.

Weldon can direct its efforts at driving customers to visit or call their authorized distributor.

Finally, let's look at the distribution of Weldon customers by total lifetime value. In Figure 12-12, we have divided Weldon customers into five, approximately equal groups based on lifetime value. The top group, the Platinum, has an average lifetime value of $50,410 and represents about 79 percent of the total customer lifetime value. The bottom group of 3,903 customers is made up of true losers, being responsible for a net lifetime value of minus $309. What can we do with this chart? It probably should be combined with the previous chart to determine the direction of Weldon's retention efforts. Why spend money trying to retain customers with a negative lifetime value? Even if they are in a favored group, such as heavy manufacturing or metal production, if they persistently result in a loss of value to Weldon, the retention effort should be reconsidered. Figure 12-12 reflects the situation in many companies that is illustrated in the quote that began this chapter.

Business-to-Business on the Internet

To build relationships with their customers, in the 1980s, companies adopted the toll-free customer service line. Millions of Americans called companies to ask questions. To support their customer service reps, companies built operational databases that gave the reps vital information about the company's products, technical specifications, delivery status, etc. Soon all the customer service reps had a computer in front of them. As the calls came in, they manipulated the keys to bring the needed information on their screen, which they would read to the callers.

When the marketers caught on to what was happening, they added to this system to provide the reps with access to the marketing database so the reps could see who the customers were and what they had bought. Caller ID was added to bring the customer's database record onto the screen before the call was answered

Customer service, however, is expensive. At a cost of $3 to $8 per call, with thousands of calls per day, companies have seen a significant drain on the bottom line. Customer lifetime value analysis must be used to determine whether the helpfulness and relationship building is worth the cost. In some cases, companies found that it was not paying its way. Most banks that have done profitability analysis have discovered that about half of their customers are unprofitable. A good part of the lack of profits can be traced to the expense of customer service. Federal Express provided a shining example of customer support by having customer reps who could field questions on the exact status of every package shipped at any time. A couple of years later, UPS set up a similar system. But these shining examples came at a significant cost. If all the customers called to learn the status of their shipments, all shipments would cost at least $3 more than they do.

Letting Them Come behind the Counter

When people looked at e-commerce on the Internet, they complained that the value of the products sold directly on the web was still a small fraction of the value of products sold through other channels. They pointed out that few companies, including Amazon.com, were making profits from sales to consumers. This shortsighted criticism ignored the fact that the web was already a highly profitable medium for reducing the costs of customer service. The Internet was replacing the customer service rep. Instead of paying for a toll-free call, plus the cost of a customer service rep who was reading off a computer screen, companies are learning that their customers can look at that same screen directly on the Internet and get the answers themselves. What's more, customers like it better. As we already noted, when Sears Canada put its big book on the Internet, it found that 97 percent of the customers buying products on the web had the paper catalog in front of them. At the bottom of each page in the catalog is an 800 number. Customers preferred to click their orders on the web to calling a live operator. What is the saving to Sears Canada? About $4 per order. Banks were discovering the saving from the Internet. Transactions on the phone cost banks a dollar or more. Those on the web cost about a penny each.

The big savings, however, come from inviting customers to come into our companies to read the same screens that our employees read. All companies have somewhere a sign on the wall that says "Authorized Personnel Only." That sign means, "customer stay out." But with the web, we can change all that. We give customers direct access to our most private areas. We "let them come behind the counter." Customers become part of our company family. This is real relationship marketing.

A good example: Picture the situation of a company meeting planner setting up a two-day seminar for about 50 customers. The planner was looking for a suitable hotel near Fort Lauderdale that had the facilities she wanted at a cost that was within her budget. Let's see what could be done by clicking on the Marriott.com web site, shown in Figure 12-13.

The web site asks meeting planners to specify the number of guests and the features and amenities (golf, swimming, beach, skiing, etc.) that they want nearby. The screen showed the planner that seven Marriott hotels matched the specifications exactly. Clicking on the Fort Lauderdale Marriott North Hotel, the planner saw the available meeting rooms and specifications (Figure 12-14). Another click brings up a picture of the hotel, and another a map of how to get there (Figure 12-15).

This is great marketing. The Marriott web site was created in 1997. It provided information on 1,500 hotels whose annual revenue exceeded $10 billion. Think back to how you would have planned a meeting

Figure 12-13. Finding meeting space at Marriott.

Meeting Planner Information

Meeting Room	Dimensions (L × W × 11)	Area (ft²)	Capacity (m²)	Theater	Schoolroom	Conference	U Shape	Reception	Banquet
Grand Cypress Ballroom	66 × 77 × 12	5082	472	700	300			800	500
Salon A	22 × 33 × 12	726	67	75	45	40	35	110	60
Salon B	22 × 33 × 12	726	67	75	45	40	35	110	60
Salon C	22 × 33 × 12	726	67	75	45	40	35	110	60
Salon D	44 × 66 × 12	2904	269	300	180			450	200
Birch	25 × 18 × 10	450	41	50	30	25	20	70	40
Broward	25 × 18 × 10	450	41	50	30	25	20	70	40
Stranahan	25 × 18 × 10	450	41	50	30	25	20	70	40
Sam Jones	22 × 32 × 10	704	65	95	40	35	30	105	70
Flagler	26 × 33 × 10	858	79	115	50	45	40	130	70
Hamilton	26 × 33 × 10	858	79	115	50	45	40	130	70

Figure 12-14. Meeting planner information on a specific hotel.

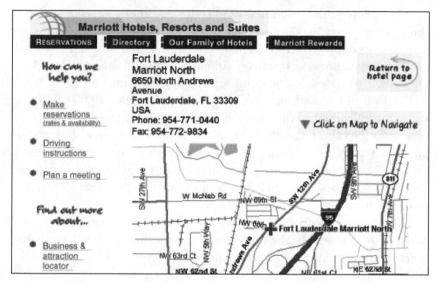

Figure 12-15. Where the hotel is located.

before all this was available. You had to call Marriott, or other hotel chains, on the phone. A customer service rep, looking at information on her computer screen, would attempt to describe to you what she saw. She would offer to send you an expensive packet of information on hotels in the Fort Lauderdale area that would arrive a few days later. In the meantime you would probably have booked a hotel somewhere else. Your call would have cost Marriott at least $10, plus the cost of the fulfillment.

At the time I wrote this book, Marriott's meeting planner web site was way ahead of the other hotel chains. Since then, I am sure that many of them have worked very hard to catch up. But this type of web site is not just for hotels. Every business-to-business company in America (or the world, for that matter) can profit by opening up its internal company data and making them available to customers on the web. There are three reasons:

- The web site will probably pay for itself in the saving of toll-free calls and operator time.
- It may increase sales to new prospects (although that is not a sure thing).
- It provides a way to recognize and build relationships with customers that will improve loyalty and retention.

Who is doing this? Customers used Dell Computer's web site to check their order status 50,000 times per week. The same calls to Dell's customer service reps cost Dell $200,000 per week. Dell also saved several million dollars per year by encouraging 200,000 customers per week to make their troubleshooting inquiries through the web.

But Dell did something else. It created more than 20,000 Premier Pages for individual companies. Each page displayed standard machine configurations and prices that were negotiated in advance with the company management. A secure page linked to the Premier Page with a password provided account information for senior purchasing managers of the company so that they could track their company's acquisition of computers.

Hundreds of companies are *saving money* and *building customer relationships* on the web. In the long run, these two functions will probably be more important than the total amount of direct sales to new people.

Virtual Distributors

One of the biggest shifts in business-to-business marketing due to the web will be felt by distributors. Typically, distributors service retail stores and contractors. They stock building materials, electrical parts, electronic components, etc. They usually stock items from a dozen or more suppliers so that their customers can always find what they want, and will have the opportunity to do comparison shopping without visiting another distributor. This means that distributors have to stock millions of dollars' worth of items, many of which move slowly or not at all. They have to have large warehouses, inventory control, fork lift trucks, and other warehouse equipment. Their margins are usually very low.

Hold that picture in your mind while you think about what Amazon.com has done with its business partner program. It had 30,000 web sites as partners. The Database Marketing Institute was one of those partners. Our web site featured about 25 books that we thought were great reading for people in our industry. At first we kept a stock of these books in our warehouse. It was a nuisance. We had to order the books from the publishers in bulk, paying for the shipping. We had to take the orders, process the credit cards, and wrap and ship each book ordered. We made very little money from this business. Then we discovered Amazon. We became an Amazon.com business partner. Our web master linked on each book in the Amazon.com bookstore that we wanted to feature on our web site www.dbmarketing.com. A visitor to our web site sees the covers of these books in living color with a few lines of text about why we recommend the books. When a visitor clicks on the picture of the book, he is transported electronically to Amazon.com, where he orders the book. Amazon takes the money and fulfills the order. It sends us about $1 per book in a quarterly check. We have no inventory, no cards to process, no wrapping and packing, and no employees. It is wonderful.

IBM developed software to facilitate this system. To secure point-and-click buying, IBM created World Distributor, a marketing and sales tool for wholesalers and distributors—some of whom previously were uninvolved with the Internet. The software helped them to extend their reach to new customers the world over. The merchandise offered by World Distributor customers included many in the wholesale distribution sector, covering industrial and commercial supply, dental, optical, electrical, security, and safety products as well as industrial and specialty gases, food, computer peripherals, and outdoor power equipment products.

What will systems like this do for distributors in the future? It is plain that many of them will soon become virtual distributors. The requirements are these:

- Manufacturers need to set up an extranet with a special page for each of their customers (the distributors). These pages permit instant electronic processing of orders with shipment either to the distributors or to their customers.

- Manufacturers have to be set up to ship less than skid-load amounts to destinations specified by their customers, the distributors.

- Distributors need to create catalogs of all the items that they sell. At the bottom of each page, they need to include their web site address, in addition to their toll-free number.

- When retailers or contractors place an electronic order using the distributor's catalog, they will log onto the distributor's web site using their PIN assigned by the distributor. They will view an extranet page just for them, similar to the Dell Premier Pages. This page will enable them to place their orders with a single click of a mouse. They don't have to enter their name, address, credit card number, or anything of that nature: just the numbers and quantities of items ordered and the desired delivery date.

- The distributor's web site will be linked to the customer marketing database and to the distributor's inventory and ordering system. As each order comes in, the web site will automatically process it and determine whether the item is in stock at the warehouse or must come direct from the manufacturer.

- If the item is to come from the warehouse, it can be shipped the same day.

- If it is to come from a manufacturer, the software will enter the order electronically with the manufacturer within a few seconds, accessing the distributor's extranet page on the manufacturer's web site.

- The manufacturer must ship the item the same day to the distributor or to the designated customer. The software bills the distributor for the shipment the same day, as soon as the shipment is completed.

Once a system like this is set up and functioning, it will become clear to all that keeping most items in the distributor's warehouse is a waste of time and money. We have moved to being a just-in-time business society. If distributors can ship the same day, why can't manufacturers do the same thing? The list of products that distributors need to keep in their warehouse will be limited to "walk-in" trade. Distributors will come closer and closer to the ideal of being "virtual distributors" with no warehouse, no inventory, no employees, and profitable margins.

In the past, distributors have been limited to selling only a few products, because they could not afford to stock all the products of all the manufacturers. They had to keep costs down. The risk, of course, is that their customers would shop around if they did not find what they wanted. In the shopping process, the customers could be lost.

With the new system, it will cost virtually nothing to add a new manufacturer and all of the manufacturer's products. Like Amazon.com, which has 2.5 million book titles, all distributors should be able to handle all cleaning products, electronic components, music scores, etc., that exist in the country—or the world—in their specific field. The economics will push each distributor to list more manufacturers and products rather than less. Once one paper products distributor, for example, has built itself up to Amazon.com proportions, with all the paper product manufacturers that there are and all the products that exist, the distributor should be able to capture a huge market share. There will be room for only two or three such paper product distributors, rather than thousands as there are today.

These virtual distributors will work very hard to create a Premier Page for every retailer and contractor in their field, offering them substantial discounts for volume orders placed over the web. Web orders should cost a small fraction of the cost of regular fax or paper or phone orders, which should give the distributor the margin necessary for the volume discounts.

This is where we are going. The web will reshape business-to-business marketing more than any other business sector.

Summary

- Business customers can be divided into bargain hunters, program buyers, transaction buyers, and relationship buyers. There is profit in all types, but relationship buyers respond better to database marketing than do other types.

- Once you have identified your relationship buyers, you can increase their loyalty and sales by a number of techniques, including:

  Special communications

  A web page with PINs for each customer

  Advisory panels

  Newsletters

  Professional contests

  Thank-you letters

- Set up test and control groups to prove that what you are doing is paying off.

- Shift from the sales-force full-court-press model to an integrated account model, with the field reps becoming business consultants, and orders taken by phone, fax, e-mail, or the web site.

- Use measurement of the lifetime value of your customers to determine the value of a strategy before you have spent serious money on it.

- The formula for the discount rate in business to business is:

$$\text{Discount rate} = [1 + (\text{interest rate} \times \text{risk factor})]^{\text{year}+\text{AR}/360}$$

- Web sites can reduce processing time, improve accuracy, save processing costs, and improve cash flow. On the other hand, they are expensive to set up, and require regular maintenance. Their effect on costs should be estimated in advance.

■ The old-fashioned method of looking at sales by industry has been replaced by looking at lifetime value by industry. It helps to focus your attention on the most important companies.

■ Customers can also be ranked by lifetime value, with retention activities focused on the more valuable customers

■ Businesses now serve their customers over toll-free lines, with agents reading company data off a computer screen. The web will permit customers to access the data directly, saving the cost of the agent and the telephone call.

■ Distributors will soon become virtual distributors with no warehouses. Their web sites will enable them to list all the products from all the manufacturers in their field. The web pressures will result in their being only two or three distributors in every field in the future.

Executive Quiz 11

Answers to quiz questions can be found in Appendix B.

1. Professor Wang's four basic business types include all but one of the following:

   a. Bargain hunters

   b. Reference buyers

   c. Program buyers

   d. Transaction buyers

   e. Relationship buyers

2. Which of the following gets the least service and pays the highest price?

   a. Bargain hunters

   b. Reference buyers

   c. Program buyers

   d. Transaction buyers

   e. Relationship buyers

3. The risk rate is 1.6. The interest rate is 8 percent. The average payment period is 80 days. What is the discount rate in the third year?

   a. 5.38

   b. 1.95

   c. 3.21

   d. 1.22

   e. None of the above

4. The chapter shows that compared with e-mail, web site ordering can reduce order-processing time by a factor of:

   a. 2 to 1

   b. 8 to 1

   c. 16 to 1

   d. 64 to 1

   e. None of the above

5. Customers receive more communications with IAM than with traditional methods. The extra cost of this method is about:

   a. 10 percent

   b. 20 percent

   c. 30 percent

   d. 40 percent

   e. None of the above

6. What is a valid reason for a company to work to retain a customer with a negative lifetime value? The customer is a:

   a. Reference account

   b. Relationship buyer

   c. Transaction buyer

   d. Gold customer

   e. None of the above

7. A successful "virtual distributor" does not need:

   a. A web site

   b. A warehouse

   c. Customers

   d. A marketing program

   e. Industry knowledge

8. In integrated account management, the field sales reps:

   a. Solve delivery problems

   b. Sell services, not products

   c. Are independent agents

   d. Solve customers' problems

   e. Sell products, not services

9. A business-to-business control group:

   a. Is not needed in most cases

   b. Receives more promotions than the average

   c. Is used to measure performance of a test group

   d. Should contain mostly relationship buyers

   e. None of the above

10. Which group should receive the most cross-sales promotions?

    a. Unprofitable customers

    b. Transaction buyers

    c. Advisory council members

    d. Those with the highest lifetime value

    e. Profitable customers in the second LTV quintile

11. In the future, what will happen to business-to-business distributors?

    a. They will become virtual distributors.

    b. They will list every manufacturer in their field.

    c. They will list every product in their field.

    d. They will have small or nonexistent warehouses.

    e. All of the above.

13

Financial Services

Over the past three years, research has taught us several lessons: Nearly half of our customers are unprofitable; almost 20 percent are very unprofitable. Balances are only loosely correlated with profitability. Demographics are even more poorly correlated with profitability. As a result, every day, over half the new accounts sold will never be profitable. Every day our staff work very hard to retain customers who destroy customer value. ... We have also learned that it is hard, if not impossible, to profitably cross sell our most profitable customers. Most sales to them cannibalize profitable usage. Sales efforts to these good customers should be restricted to retention-aiding devices.

RANDALL GROSSMAN
SVP Fleet Bank

Financial services offer one of the most profitable applications for database marketing. This is so because financial institutions:

- Usually have a lot of useful information about their customers' demographics and purchase history
- Can accurately determine the profitability of each customer
- Are usually important to their customers' lives
- Have many opportunities to interact with their customers during the average month

Despite these advantages, banks and other financial institutions have been slow in taking advantage of their database marketing opportunities. The history of database marketing in this field explains why.

American Express pioneered in this field. In 1978 John Stevenson was the first direct marketing professional to manage the American Express Card Division. As vice president, he was in charge of the consolidation of direct marketing for AMEX and responsible for the application of new systems and advanced technology. He managed a multimedia communications program, which included more than 1 million pieces of direct mail per day.

John was one of the earliest inventors of the concept of database marketing in 1978, through his innovations at American Express. At that time AMEX had one of the few huge computer operations available to build a marketing database. John had the dream and the resources. He was given sufficient latitude by AMEX management to mobilize outside advertising agencies, service bureaus, and AMEX internal staff talents in statistics, marketing research, operations, and systems. The successful concept he created at that time has spread throughout the world.

Banks were slower than AMEX to use this technique. They had more obstacles to overcome. To build a marketing database, most banks had to start by attempting to consolidate all their customers' accounts into a single marketing customer information file (MCIF), so that they could understand each household's financial situation. This was not easy. Most banks had their mortgage loans on one computer, checking accounts on another, and credit cards on a third. The records were created by different people in different formats, based on accounts, not on customers. It took most banks several years to realize the importance of an MCIF and to muster the resources to create one. This all came at a time of great turmoil in the banking industry, in the 1990s, during which almost half of all U.S. banks were acquired and consolidated with other banks—thus further complicating the MCIF creation problem.

Once the MCIFs were created, however, there was no great rush among banks to do any relationship marketing. Why was this so? Mainly because banks were then, and still are today, organized along product lines. There were separate vice presidents for credit cards, retail banking, home mortgages, automobile loans, trust accounts, etc. Each VP was expected to improve sales and profits in his department. The manager of credit cards was not compensated for the number of credit card customers who signed up for a checking account or an auto loan. Nor did the other VPs care much about credit card operations. People do what is in their own economic self-interest.

I was approached at a recent conference by an assistant vice president of a bank who was in charge of selling insurance. He asked me what he could do to sell more insurance to his customers and to improve the retention rate of those whom he already had. He explained that he had been sending letters to existing insurance customers trying to build a relationship with them, but it was not paying off.

"The best way to sell insurance to bank customers," I told him, "is to examine the MCIF to determine which customers are most likely to buy insurance, and market to them. If they don't have insurance with you now, but they already have another account with the bank, they should be responsive. For those who now have insurance with you, the best way to retain them is to sell them another noninsurance bank product. Once they have two or more bank products, their retention rate for insurance should be higher."

"Oh, I couldn't do that. They won't let me have access to the names of other bank customers."

This is the problem.

Many banks today have gotten religion. They understand that customers look at their bank as a single institution, not as a bunch of unrelated products. They understand that to improve sales and retention, they have to become a single institution, looking at customers and households, instead of individual product owners. Banks have discovered that there is a clear relationship between the number of bank products owned by a customer and the customer's retention rate. It looks something like the graph in Figure 13-1.

Why is this so? Because if you only have a credit card at a bank, you obviously have your checking account somewhere else. You don't think of this card issuer as your bank. If you get an offer for a cheaper card, you might well take it. But if you have your checking account and savings account at a bank, plus the credit card, you will most likely tend to think of the credit card as a part of your total banking experience. You may know the branch personnel. Won't they wonder why you dropped their card?

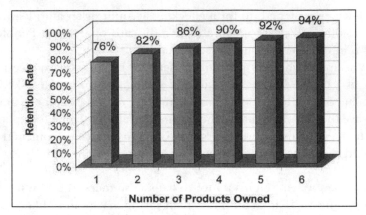

Figure 13-1. Increasing retention rate based on number of bank products owned.

Unintended Consequences

I had breakfast one day at the National Center for Database Marketing with a marketing officer from a medium-sized bank. The bank's management had come to realize how important it was to customer loyalty to have multiproduct customers. The management offered a substantial bonus to all senior branch personnel in those branches that had a high percentage of 5+ customers—meaning customers who were using five or more of the bank's products. The policy was working: Every branch was focused on this objective, but the results were far from what was intended. Many branches were turning down new accounts: they ruined the branch's 5+ percentage!

Many banks, however, have found a way to organize themselves to take advantage of their MCIF files and create profitable relationships with their customers. The key to their success is the analysis of profitability. There are three steps:

- Develop an accurate and credible system for determining the profitability of each customer, on a periodic basis, preferably at least monthly, using day-to-day inputs on interest rates and costs.
- Develop segmentation schemes that divide customers into useful and actionable segments based on profitability.
- Develop and implement tactics, based on these segments, which are used to modify the behavior of employees and customers to increase sales, improve retention, lower costs, and improve profits.

Profitability Calculation

Profitability calculation is the heart of the system. It is complex, but it is computed automatically by bank software for every product for every customer every month. To understand it, one must understand a few banking terms. It is worth taking the time, because profitability determination is the foundation for a number of very profitable and advanced database marketing segmentation and behavior modification techniques. One of the experts in the use of profitability analysis in banking is Robert James, who was group manager at the Centura Bank. Bob, a graduate of the Database Marketing Institute, had 24 years of banking experience. Here is how he listed the concepts vital to understanding profitability:

- *Cost of funds.* Banks obtain money from depositors and loan it out to borrowers. They make money on the difference in what they pay depositors and what they earn from borrowers. The *cost of funds* is the amount of interest expense paid for the funds used.
- *Funding credit.* The amount earned by the bank on the deposits employed.
- *Margin.* The difference between the interest earned and the interest expense.
- *Loan loss provision.* All loans have risk, and some loans never get repaid. The *loan loss provision* is a pool of dollars reserved by banks to cover expected loan losses.
- *Capital allocation.* Capital is the equity of the company—the difference between assets and liabilities. *Capital allocation* is the amount of capital set aside for each product to cover unexpected losses and is based on the overall risk profile of the product.
- *Capital charge.* The capital allocated multiplied by the bank's desired rate of return on the capital assigned to the product.
- *Overhead.* The fixed and variable expenses associated with the product. These include origination expense, transaction expense, maintenance, and personnel expense. The cost of a customer visiting a branch to cash a check may amount to $1.65 per visit. This is part of overhead.
- *FDIC expense.* The cost of providing deposit insurance through the Federal Deposit Insurance Corporation.

These are banking terms. But the concepts underlying profitability apply to any industry where detailed costs are available, such as insurance, and many service industries.

Using these terms, let's compute the monthly profitability for a typical customer product—an automobile loan. This four-year loan originated two years ago for $15,500 at a rate of 8.5 percent. At this point, the average outstanding balance is $9,806.66. The net profitability of this loan, last month, was $13.74. Table 13-1 shows how that profitability was calculated. The table says that for this product for this customer this last month, the bank made a profit of $13.74 after all costs related to the product were deducted from the revenue.

Table 13-1

Automobile Loan

Average balance	$9,806.66
Capital allocated	$ 367.75
Interest income	$ 69.46
Less cost of funds	$ 46.50
Margin	$ 22.96
Fees	$ 0.00
Gross profit	$ **22.96**
Less:	
Capital charge	$ 4.88
Loan loss provision	$ 3.27
Overhead	$ 1.07
Total costs	$ **9.22**
Net product value	$ **13.74**

For comparison, look at Table 13-2, which shows the profitability calculation for a checking account. In this case, the bank lost $3.49 on this account last month. The gross monthly profit of $11.74 from the average balance of $1,184 was overwhelmed by the high overhead costs of $15.17. The overhead includes the fact that this customer visited the branch several times last month to make deposits or cash checks. At

$1.65 expense per visit, his branch visits wiped out the profitability of this particular product. By comparing these two calculations, you will note that the capital allocation for a checking account is significantly less than for a loan. This is because, for a bank, loans are more risky than checking accounts.

Table 13-2

Non-Interest-Bearing Checking Account

Average balance	$1,184.84
Capital allocated	$ 2.96
Funding credit	$ −5.24
Fees (service charge)	$ 6.50
Gross profit	$ 11.74
Less:	
Capital charge	$ 0.04
DIC expense	$ 0.03
Overhead	$ 15.17
Total costs	$ 15.24
Net product value	$ −3.49

The same process is repeated each month for every product owned by every customer with the bank. Once the process is completed, a customer's household profitability is computed by summing the net product values for all products owned by the household. For example, see Figure 13-2. This customer's total monthly profit to the bank is $101.51.

Creating Profitability Segments

After computing every customer's monthly profitability, you group the customers into customer profitability segments. Figure 13-3 is an actual example of the way one bank grouped its customers into profitability segments. As you can see, the bank created five groups. This can be graphed as a (by now) familiar chart, shown in Figure 13-4.

	Average Balance	Profit
Automobile loan	$9,806.66	$13.74
Checking account	$1,184.84	($3.49)
Certificate of deposit	$15,000.00	$27.05
Credit card	$2,917.66	$8.11
Home equity loan	$20,420.90	$56.10
Total profit		**$101.51**

Figure 13-2. Monthly profitability calculation.

Segment	Households	% Households	Total Profit	% Profits
5	20,126	5	$11,180,791	79.67
4	46,706	11	$3,483,724	24.82
3	118,273	28	$2,221,018	15.83
2	119,804	28	$212,669	1.52
1	118,394	28	−$3,063,817	−21.83
Total	423,303	100	$14,034,385	100

Figure 13-3. Bank customers segmented by profitability.

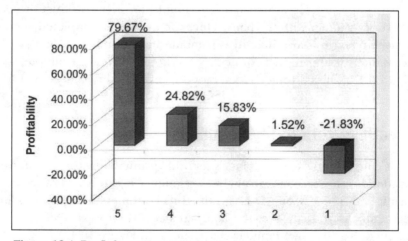

Figure 13-4. Profit by customer segment.

To obtain the graph in Figure 13-4, every customer in the bank was classified as a 5, 4, 3, 2, or 1, where 5 represents the most profitable customers and 1 represents the least. What this graph shows is that the top group, representing only 5 percent of the bank's customers, was responsible for almost 80 percent of the bank's total profit. The bottom group, consisting of 28 percent of the bank's customers, was responsible for a loss of almost 22 percent of the bank's profit. This is amazing and insightful information. Until the creation of MCIFs and monthly profitability analysis, no bank in America had this kind of information. Most banks still lack it today.

Once a bank has done this calculation, the profitability segment designation is stored in each customer's database file every month. A personal profile of each bank customer is made available to all customer contact personnel at each point of contact with the customer, including teller lines, service desks, and branch managers' offices. The profile can include:

- Addresses and phones numbers
- Birth dates and social security numbers
- Home ownership with date at present address
- Occupation and employer
- Other financial institutions where the person banks
- The bank officer assigned and the branch
- Whether the customer has filed a financial statement
- All accounts with their current balances, line amounts, and amount owed
- The profitability segment to which the customer belongs
- Suggested next best product for the customer

Turning Knowledge into Action

Statistical analysts at the bank use these data to build models to predict the lifetime value of each customer, which products a customer is next most likely to need, and which behavior change will improve the customer's profitability. These solutions are shown on the customer's database record screen. Customer contact personnel then utilize the knowledge to improve cross-sell and up-sell opportunities, to make better decisions regarding pricing and fee waivers, and to suggest alternative channels for certain types of transactions.

Each of the five profitability segments has different customer behavior goals:

■ For 5s—the Gold customers—and 4s, the goal is to retain them, acquire more like them, and expand their purchase of bank products. Since the profit segment 5s and 4s represent only 16 percent of the customer households, but up to 105 percent of the monthly profit, the bank will want to allocate substantial human and marketing resources toward retaining these customers. And since human resources are limited, particularly those resources devoted to sales, the bank should attempt to direct the acquisition activities of its calling officers to prospects who have the potential to be profit segment 5s or 4s. In general, you cannot market profitably to the 5s because they are maxed out. All their money is in your bank. Your goal is retention.

■ For 3s the goal is simply to get them to expand their use of products.

■ For 1s and 2s the goal is to reprice their unprofitable products such as loans or certificates of deposit as they mature or are renewed. Concerted efforts are used to migrate these customers' routine transactions to less expensive alternative channels of delivery, such as ATMs, call centers, or internet banking.

Gold Customer Programs

Once you know who the Gold customers are, what can you do to be sure you retain them? Banks are using such tactics as:

■ Identifying and assigning personal bankers to them

■ Making sure that they get the best service, including:

Priority problem resolution

Priority telephone response

Discretionary pricing initiatives

■ Providing special communications strategies, including:

Outbound calls from their personal banker

Special mailings and product offers

Annual thank-you mailings

Reward programs

One bank has the profitability segment built into the software that controls its customer service call director. Gold customers' calls are identified before they are answered and are picked up on the first ring. Unprofitable customers may have to wait for five or six rings before anyone answers.

Analysis of Behavior by Profitability Segment

Beyond identifying profitability segments is analysis to determine why some customers are so profitable or so unprofitable. For example, one bank divided its entire customer base into 50 segments, from most profitable to least, each representing 2 percent of all customers, and ranked them by the number of bank products that they were using. We have already established that the more products a customer uses, the higher is the retention rate. But how does the profitability vary by product usage?

What the bank learned from this analysis was that both the best and the worst customers used a lot of bank products (see Figure 13-5). The average customers used only a few. This suggests that while high product use leads to high retention, it does not necessarily lead to high profits.

A similar analysis was done of the same bank customers ranked by the number of times that they visited bank branches. This also showed that both the best and the worst visited bank branches a lot. The average customer banked by mail or at an ATM. Any policy designed to discourage expensive branch visits would seriously threaten the bank's very best customers, who bring in 80 percent of the bank's profits.

Computing Lifetime Value and Potential Lifetime Profitability

It is not enough to know the current profitability of a customer. You need to be able to predict the future by making accurate forecasts of each customer's potential lifetime profitability. To forecast the future,

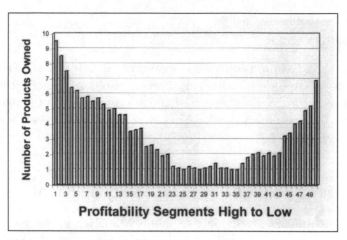

Figure 13-5. Product use by profitability segment.

you determine for each customer the likelihood of your being able to sell him or her additional profitable products, and the expected net revenue from usage of those products minus the promotional expense involved in the sale of the products. This forecast is added to current profitability to create a reasonably reliable lifetime profitability forecast that can drive bank marketing strategy and tactics.

Fleet developed a bankwide MCIF originally maintained with an external vendor. Once it was up and running, the bank took its first measure of customer value by simply adding up all nonmortgage deposit and loan balances for each customer. This was a beginning. Next it created the software necessary to determine the net income after deduction of the cost of capital (NIACC) for all retail customers. For a typical customer, it looked something like Figure 13-6. This is a slightly different method of profitability calculation from that shown earlier. It arrives at the same basic number, however. In this annual calculation for a typical customer, her net profitability is $63, due principally to the fact that she invested in mutual funds. Without this investment, she would have represented a loss of $166 to the bank.

As a second step, Fleet extended this system to its commercial customers. It used industry benchmark costs for computing profitability. Then, when these processes were working properly, the bank created an in-house data warehouse, which enabled the bank to keep all these data current, and to use actual Fleet activity-based costs, rather than industry benchmark numbers. The system looked something like Figure 13-7.

	Check and Savings	Home Equity	Credit Card	Mutual Funds	Total
Revenue					
Net interest	$210	$248	–$280	$0	$178
Fees	$18	$18	$396	$1,500	$1,932
Total revenue	$228	$266	$116	$1,500	$2,110
Expenses					
Amort. sales costs	$20	$120	$67	$75	$282
Account maintenance	$30	$75	$40	$900	$1,045
Transaction cost	$193	$21	$0	$30	$244
Allocated overhead	$0	$0	$0	$0	$0
Total expenses	$243	$216	$107	$1,005	$1,571
Loss provision	$0	$23	$160	$0	$183
Net income	–$15	$27	–$151	$495	$356
Taxes	–$6	$11	–$60	$198	$143
NI after taxes	–$9	$16	–$91	$297	$213
Cost of capital	$1	$49	$32	$68	$150
NIACC	–$10	–$33	–$123	$229	$63

Annual revenue and costs for typical bank customer having these products

Figure 13-6. Alternative method of profitability calculation.

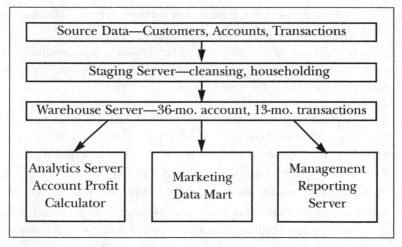

Figure 13-7. Fleet customer data management system.

At their PC workstations, power users, including both marketing and business analysts, accessed the data on each customer, did analytical work and modeling, and developed marketing initiatives. The analysis server, for example, provided for statistical analysis, neural networks, ad hoc query and analysis, and geodemographic analysis. The data mart provided summarized, preformatted data for promotion design, tracking, and analysis, and enabled the users to do point-and-click, drill down analysis. The management reporting server provided on-demand parameterized reports.

Preliminary Lessons Learned

The new system enabled Fleet bank management, for the first time, to really understand its customer profitability and to do something about it. As Randall Grossman, senior vice president and director of Customer Data Management and Analysis at Fleet Financial Group explained, the data showed that:

- Half of all customers were unprofitable
- Twenty percent were very unprofitable
- The balances that people maintained were only loosely correlated with profitability
- Demographics were even more poorly correlated with profitability
- Half of the new accounts being currently sold would never be profitable
- The bank staff was working hard every day to retain customers who would destroy customer value

Even though half of all customers were considered unprofitable, the marketing staff realized that they could not simply walk away from half of their customer base. Further analysis showed that:

- It was almost impossible profitably to cross-sell the most profitable customers. Most of these sales cannibalized existing profitable products. For these Gold customers, it was determined that marketing should focus on retention, not cross- or up-selling.
- Some customer profits and losses were temporary, not permanent.
- Some low-profit customers had great potential, sometimes because their assets were elsewhere, and they were, in fact, Gold customers at another bank.

- Some unprofitable customers could be nudged into profitability if they were offered the right products at the right prices.
- There are, however, many customers for whom there is very little potential for profit.

What to Do with the Information?

Faced with these sobering facts, Grossman's marketing staff decided to figure out ways to use the database that they had created to turn the situation around. The key to their strategy was to develop three measures of customer value:

- Lifetime profitability
- Potential profitability
- Potential customer value

Lifetime Profitability

Lifetime profitability is the net present value of the expected future stream of net income after the cost of capital, discounted at the corporate hurdle rate. It is calculated based on the current products that the customer is now using, including planned repricing. As calculated by the bank, customer profitability differs from organizational or product profitability for several reasons:

- Many customers' business with the bank cuts across business lines, whereas organizational profitability is computed by adding up the profits from each line of business.
- Some costs in the Fleet system, such as overhead, were not allocated to each customer, since the methods for doing this involved arbitrary decisions that Fleet managers thought might distort the real profitability of the customer to the bank.
- For those costs that are allocated to the customer, the allocation had, of necessity, to use standard cost factors (such as the cost of a branch visit, telephone call, or product sale) for which it was not cost-effective to determine accurately based on each specific event.
- Customer profitability does not "roll up." If two customers share the same account, the bank gives full credit to both (which one is the decision maker?). For this reason, you cannot add up each cus-

tomer's profitability to get total bank profitability. Organizationally, of course, the account is only counted once, not twice, so product profitability does add up to a bank total.

Given these qualifications, lifetime customer profitability was calculated for each bank customer and stored in the customer's database record each month. Customers were then ranked and segmented. It was possible to pick out the Gold customers, those just below Gold, the average customers, and the unprofitable customers. Each customer's profitability status was flagged in each customer record so that marketers and branch personnel could recognize the customer's value to the bank, and develop appropriate strategies and tactics.

Potential Profitability

Potential profitability carried the Fleet analysis one step further. A typical customer had a limited number of bank products. There were usually many other bank products that the customer could be using. The probability of a given customer purchasing an additional product was determined using CHAID analysis. For example, if a customer owned a home with a mortgage of $\$W$, had a checking account with an average balance of $\$X$, had a savings account with an average balance of $\$Y$, had a monthly credit card usage rate of $\$Z$, was 44 years old, and had two children in college, CHAID was used to predict the likelihood of the customer purchasing:

	Probability
An auto loan	12%
A home equity loan	16%
A personal loan	12%
Mutual funds	21%
A certificate of deposit	3%

CHAID was also used to predict the average balance that the customer would maintain on each of the possible additional products. Logistic regressions were then used to determine the expected NIACC that the bank will realize from the possible sale of each of these products to the customer. In each case, an estimate was made of the promotional expense involved in getting the customer to purchase the product. Next, the potential profitability was calculated for each product as:

Probability of purchase × expected NIACC from usage
− promotional expense

The profitability calculation software then added up each of the products for this customer with a positive NIACC to get the potential profit.

Potential customer value was then determined for each customer by adding together the lifetime profitability (with current products) and the potential profitability (from possible new products). This value was stored in every customer's database record and used to select the most likely candidates for promotion for each product in direct-mail promotions. It was also used to suggest the next best product when branch personnel were talking to the customer or when customer service had the customer on the line.

Mobilizing Branch Personnel

Knowing potential customer value and keeping it in a database would be useless unless the data could be put to work by customer contact personnel. The central marketing staff, for example, could use the data:

- For retention programs and preferred customer efforts
- For product design analysis and decisions
- For channel reconfiguration and service introductions
- For product pricing

In addition to the central marketing staff, Fleet wanted to mobilize its branch personnel to use the new customer data (see Figure 13-8). Grossman, like Bob James, is a graduate of the Database Marketing Institute. His marketing staff had 12 Ph.D.s who used the data to help them dream up and implement creative ideas to increase profits. On the other hand, Fleet had 1,200 branches, many of which had more than one officer who was interested and skilled at identifying targets for bank programs, and determining the appropriate tactics for each particular case.

Here is where branch empowerment became important. Too many marketing staffs assume that they know what is best. They use statistical programs on computers to determine what should be done. Since there are only a few central marketing people, but there are a million customers, the recommendations of the marketing people, while useful in general, may miss the mark in most particular cases. Branch personnel, on the other hand, who know their customers, and see them once a week or more often, can identify those customers who are obvious candidates for particular products. They can devise creative ways of sug-

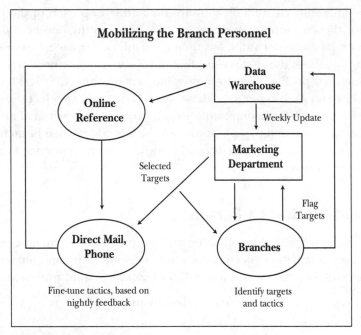

Figure 13-8. How branch personnel participate in the marketing process at Fleet.

gesting these products to their customers. By mobilizing the imagina-
tions and entrepreneurial skills of these branch officers, Fleet was able
to put its calculations of potential customer value to work in changing
customer behavior and improving bank profit.

Customer Retention Tactics

Knowing who is profitable and who is not is important. But eventually
you have to come down to tactics: How do you persuade customers to
do what you want them to do? How do you keep customers from defecting? Credit card managers have to deal with defections on a daily basis.
They call it "churn." A high percentage of the American public receive
competing credit card offers every week. Some of them accept the
offers and drop cards that their banks had spent more than $80 to get
them to accept. How can you get customers to keep their cards?

As already explained, the best method is to sell them another product. The more products bank customers have from a particular bank,
the less likely they are to drop any particular product. But, ultimately,
we will have to do something directly for the credit card customers who
are likely to drop their cards.

There is, by now, a fairly straightforward method of churn reduction, which combines lifetime value and probability modeling to achieve satisfactory results. Here is the way it works.

Let's consider a typical bank that has 369,502 credit card customers, with an annual churn rate of about 18 percent. If it costs the bank $80 to acquire a credit card customer, the annual loss of the acquisition costs due to churn is about $5,320,829—a tidy sum. Something has to be done. Most banks with a large number of credit card holders allocate an annual retention budget to be spent on projects aimed at getting these defectors to change their minds. Let's suppose that the bank management has set up a retention budget of $700,000. The management wants to make the best use of this fund. If it allocates the fund equally to all cardholders, it will amount to $1.89 per cardholder per year. It is not going to change many minds for $1.89 each. Either the budget must be increased, or it must be allocated in a much more intelligent way than spending it equally on all cardholders.

The intelligent way to begin is to build a statistical model of all cardholders to determine which customers are most likely to drop their cards. Such a model can be based on experience over the last several years. From these years, we know who dropped the card. The model can include such factors as:

- Average amount charged per year
- Average unpaid balance each month
- Number of other bank products owned
- Number of other cards owned
- Income of the cardholder
- Number of years with the bank and with the card
- Balances maintained on other product accounts

A regression model or a neural network can be run, using these and other factors, to develop a score for all cardholders. The score indicates who is most likely to drop the card in the near future. A score of 95 indicates that the cardholder is 95 percent likely to drop the card in the next six months. A very low score predicts that this customer will probably keep the card. Figure 13-9 shows what the model could predict.

To be sure that our retention budget does the most good, we should ignore those loyal customers who are unlikely to drop their card. In this illustration, we are going to concentrate on all customers who have a score of 60 percent or better. There are 276,560 of these customers. We

A	B	C	D	E
	Total	Actual	Percent	Cumulative
Score	Base	Attrition	Attrition	Base
95	3,315	1,619	48.84	3,315
90	15,014	3,974	26.47	18,329
85	26,378	4,858	18.42	44,707
80	39,923	7,139	17.88	84,630
75	32,874	5,226	15.90	117,504
70	33,926	6,182	18.22	151,430
65	53,536	6,992	13.06	204,966
60	71,594	9,274	12.95	276,560
55	34,870	2,709	7.77	311,430
50	18,733	907	4.84	330,163
45	12,844	412	3.21	343,007
40	9,833	513	5.22	352,840
35	7,400	223	3.02	360,240
30	6,411	205	3.20	366,651
25	2,355	74	3.16	369,006
20	464	0	0.00	369,470
15	32	0	0.00	369,502
Totals	369,502	56,672	11.28	369,502

Figure 13-9. Selection of credit card customers ranked by likelihood to churn.

have safely cut 92,942 customers from our retention program—which gives us more money to spend on the more likely droppers.

Next, we want to consider lifetime value. We can compute the lifetime value of cardholders based on methods developed throughout this book. Figure 13-10 shows the lifetime value of a group of customers who are using the bank's credit cards. This segment of customers had an annual profitability of $241. It cost $80 to acquire them. Their retention rate was about 85 percent. The bank spent about $8 each year in retention programs. In the third year, the lifetime value of the customers in this segment was about $451. If you compare this lifetime value chart

	Year 1	Year 2	Year 3
Card members	13,433	11,418	10,048
Retention rate	85.00%	88.00%	92.00%
Annual profitability	$241	$248	$255
Total revenue	$3,237,353	$2,831,676	$2,562,210
Acquisition cost $80	$1,074,640	$0	$0
Marketing costs $8	$107,464	$91,344	$80,383
Total costs	$1,182,104	$91,344	$80,383
Profit	$2,055,249	$2,740,332	$2,481,827
Discount rate	1.00	1.20	1.44
Net present value profit	$2,055,249	$2,283,610	$1,723,491
Cumulative NPV profit	$2,055,249	$4,338,859	$6,062,350
Lifetime value	$153.00	$323.00	$451.30

Figure 13-10. Lifetime value of bank customers based on profitability.

with those in Chapter 3, you will notice that the costs are computed differently. That is because bank profitability includes all costs except acquisition and marketing costs. As you can see, the retention rate of loyal customers goes up, and their profitability goes up as well. The actual computation of lifetime value for bank customers is more complicated than this chart appears to show because of the fact that most bank customers tend to have more than one bank product. Their retention rate and lifetime value tend, therefore, to be higher than those who have only one product.

This type of lifetime value is computed for all credit card customers. They are ranked in lifetime value groups for the purpose of allocating the credit card retention budget. Figure 13-11 shows the rankings.

As you look at Figure 13-11, you can see that some customers are more valuable than others. What is the point of working to retain customers with a lifetime value of minus $74? Once you know their lifetime value, you can spend your retention budget on those who have the highest lifetime value. In this case, the bank decided to make a major effort to retain those 55,323 likely droppers who have a lifetime value of $450 or more. What can you do to retain these people? You can, of course, sell them additional products. That is the first step. A second step would be to provide some inducements.

Lifetime Value of 276,560 Cardholders Most Likely to Churn				
A Average Lifetime Value	B Number of Members	C Cumulative Members	D Cumulative % Members	E Total Lifetime Value
$637.24	17,723	17,723	6.41	$11,293,800
$550.00	11,334	29,057	10.51	$5,628,700
$500.00	12,833	41,890	15.15	$6,416,500
$450.00	13,433	55,323	20.00	$6,044,850
$400.00	15,534	70,857	25.62	$6,213,600
$350.00	18,556	89,413	32.33	$6,494,600
$300.00	20,356	109,769	39.69	$6,106,800
$250.00	25,543	135,312	48.93	$6,385,750
$200.00	31,456	166,768	60.30	$6,291,200
$150.00	35,993	202,761	73.32	$5,398,950
$100.00	41,789	244,550	88.43	$4,178,900
$50.00	26,578	271,128	98.04	$1,328,900
$0.00	5,432	276,560	100.00	$0

Figure 13-11. Credit card customers arranged by lifetime value.

There are many possibilities. Here are seven typical inducements:

- Increase the credit line
- Upgrade the card to Gold status
- Provide free PC banking
- Reduce the interest rate
- Reduce the annual fee
- Waive the annual fee
- Provide air miles for every dollar spent

Each inducement has a cost to the bank. Each inducement also is more or less effective in reducing attrition. The average attrition rate is 18 percent per year. The chart in Figure 13-12 shows how a budget of about $700,000 can be spent most efficiently in reducing churn among the 55,323 people most likely to drop the card who have an average lifetime value of $450 or more.

Credit Card Retention Budget Calculation Chart

Inducements	C Members Selected (Max. 20,000/line)	D $ Budgeted (Col. C * Col. E)	E $ per Member	F Attrition Reduction %	G Estimated Attrition (18% of Col. C)	H Estimated Reduction (Col. G * Col. F)	I Average Lifetime Value	J Total LTV Gain (Col. H * Col. I)	K $ Gained per $ Spent (Col. J/Col. D)
Increased credit line	20,000	$157,600	$7.88	14.000	3,600	504	$531	$267,624	$1.70
Upgrade to Gold	2,000	$25,040	$12.52	21.00	360	76	$531	$40,144	$1.60
Free PC banking	20,000	$70,000	$3.50	6.50	3,600	234	$531	$124,254	$1.78
Reduce interest rate	7,323	$204,971	$27.99	49.00	1,318	646	$531	$342,967	$1.67
Reduce annual fee	2,000	$70,000	$35.00	60.00	360	216	$531	$114,696	$1.64
Waive annual fee	2,000	$80,000	$40.00	69.00	360	248	$531	$131,900	$1.65
Provide air miles	2,000	$90,000	$45.00	72.00	360	259	$531	$137,635	$1.53
Total	55,323	$697,611			9,958	2,183	$531	$1,159,220	$1.66

Figure 13-12. Calculation of the ideal allocation of a credit card holder retention budget.

What Figure 13-12 shows is that since the average lifetime value of these 55,323 customers is $531, we can save that amount by preventing the attrition of some of these cardholders. We know that 18 percent of them are going to leave us if we do nothing about it. By using these inducements, we can persuade 2,183 cardholders to stay. Their lifetime value is $1,159,220. We have spent $697,611 to keep these cardholders, a return of $1.66 for every $1 spent.

Keep in mind that we are making the assumption here that management has limited us to a budget of $700,000, and further required that we not include more than 20,000 customers in any one inducement, with a minimum of 2,000 in each inducement as a test of its effectiveness. The mathematics of this chart is tricky since we want to stay within the budget, provide some inducement for all 55,323 cardholders, stay within management's arbitrary limitations, and maximize the lifetime value gain. You may enjoy working with this chart in the software that is available to readers of this book. The free software is at www.dbmarketing.com.

Summary

- Most banks today have found a way to create a marketing customer information file for each customer, which enables the bank to view the customer's entire portfolio at one time. Some banks have gone beyond this to calculate the profitability of each customer each month. They can segment customers by profitability. Others have gone even further by calculating future profitability to compute a potential customer value.

- Only a few financial institutions have achieved the level of customer knowledge and resulting behavior modification programs outlined in this chapter. Profitability calculation is hard work, with a lot of time, effort, and imagination going into the creation of the appropriate algorithms. Somewhat easier is grouping the bank's customers into a manageable number (such as five) of profitability segments based on these monthly ratings.

- The final step is the most important. It includes using the knowledge created to develop appropriate strategies and tactics for improving profitability and customer service. This includes tactics to modify the behavior of employees, customers, and prospects. The entire system drives the bank's resource allocation, expansion plans, relationship- and retention-building programs, and even their telephone call answering systems. Those banks that have such systems in place have taken a giant step forward that will take their competitors years of very hard work to equal.

Executive Quiz 12

Answers to quiz questions can be found in Appendix B.

1. Financial services marketing has one advantage over other database marketing in that all but one of the following are true:

   a. Customers identify with their banks.

   b. More customer data are available.

   c. Many bank customers are unprofitable.

   d. Banking data are usually located on one central computer.

   e. Banks can compute profitability.

2. Creating an MCIF file involves:

   a. Changing the bank accounting system

   b. Merging customer accounts

   c. Setting up a separate marketing database

   d. Putting all bank product accounts on one computer

   e. None of the above

3. Customer profitability:

   a. Adds up to the same total as product profitability

   b. Is easy to calculate

   c. Should not include overhead

   d. Is often below zero

   e. Is a product of general ledger accounting

4. In most banks the employee reward structure and organization is based on:

   a. Service to the customer

   b. Meeting the needs of a household

   c. Marketing individual products

   d. Improving penetration ratios

   e. Transfer of data across department lines

5. Which is the best way to improve retention of credit card customers?

    a. Build a relationship.

    b. Sell them another bank product.

    c. Waive the annual fee.

    d. Assign a personal banker.

    e. Issue a Gold card.

6. The bank's 5 percent most profitable customers:

    a. Account for 10 percent of the bank's profits

    b. Are ideal targets for up-selling

    c. Have low retention rates

    d. Typically exhibit high churn

    e. None of the above

7. Who visits bank branches the most? (Choose the most correct answer.)

    a. The best customers

    b. The worst customers

    c. Both the best and the worst

    d. Cannot be measured

    e. The medium-value customer

Match the following with the correct definition:

8. Interest paid for funds used	**a.** Overhead
9. Fixed and variable expenses associated with a product	**b.** Funding credit
	c. NIACC
10. Interest earned less interest expense	**d.** Capital charge
11. Amount earned on deposits employed	**e.** Cost of funds
12. Pool of dollars to cover losses	**f.** Capital allocation
13. Capital multiplied by the banks desired rate of return	**g.** Loan loss provision
	h. Margin
14. Equity set aside for product losses	
15. Net income less cost of capital	

14

Why Databases Fail

A group of faculty members were having dinner at one of the database marketing conferences when conversation turned to promising database marketing projects that had failed. One woman described Citicorp's Reward America, probably the largest such project ever tried. Another brought up the Quaker Direct project, which was widely publicized beforehand, but withdrawn after the first mass mailing.

"Does anyone remember the Barbie Pink Stamps Club?" one of us asked. "That club was set up to build a database of the names and ages of Barbie owners, their parents, their buying habits, and the other children in the household. It was a long-term project, but they canceled it after only three years."

"My favorite was the Society to End Dull Meals Forever," someone exclaimed. "McCormick, the spice people, built a database of more than 200,000 cooks who were going to receive regular mailings of coupons and product samples. I called them to get on the list, but they told me that it was dropped because of mailing costs. It's a shame, because it was a great idea."

"There are more canceled projects than you realize," said one veteran. "Somebody should write a book about why database projects fail. All the books and articles you read are about success, success, success, but really, there are a lot of flops too. You often learn more by studying the mistakes than you do by reading about the triumphs."

I recently received my copy of *Great Shakes,* the Burger King Kids Club magazine. I joined the Kids Club (as an interested marketer) a few years ago. It was still going strong. At first Burger King Corporation mailed out a personalized membership card and letter, stickers, and a poster featuring Kids Club characters. A four-page color newspaper with games, puzzles, and movie reviews was published five times a year and distributed free of charge in the restaurants.

Later, the Kids Club was expanded to include a quarterly magazine that sold advertising to national advertisers. The magazine was published in three separate editions: *Small Fries* for 0–5-year-olds, *Great Shakes* for 6–8-year-olds, and *Have It Your Way* for ages 9–10. The circulation grew to over 4 million, and was growing at the rate of 100,000 per month. When the Internet came along, the Kids Club expanded to the web.

What has been the result of the Burger King Kids Club? When the program was launched, children's meals accounted for about 1 percent of total sales. Three years later, the sales had grown by a very significant percentage. Most of this growth can be attributed to the Kids Club. Unfortunately, the coupons in the magazines are not personalized; therefore Burger King Corporation does not know which of its members are using them. However, since the coupons appear only in the magazine, Burger King does know that they are being used by club members.

The Burger King Kids Club has almost everything that successful database marketing requires:

- A practical idea with a realistic goal: Sell more kids meals by reaching the kids directly.
- A concept based on lifetime customer value which permits calculations of growth due to the database.
- A farsighted management that continued the funding for several years to get the benefit of experience and the accumulated acceptance by the members. A willingness to experiment and innovate.

The coupons are not personalized, and so Burger King Corporation does not know who is reading the magazine and using the coupons. It only knows that sales are going up. That, however, is plenty: It's wonderful. It's a great success story. And now, they have a web site (www. burgerking.com/kidsclub).

But not every great idea results in a long-term profitable experience. In many cases, what sounds good ends up by being discontinued because it isn't paying off. Is it the concept or the execution that stumbles?

The *Morris Report,* a monthly magazine for cat owners, produced by Nine Lives cat food, received thousands of letters from cat owners. Hailed as a clever and effective way of reaching the vast number of households that own a cat, the project was expected to be much more efficient than mass marketing. Unfortunately, this magazine was canceled.

The fact is that many database marketing projects fail. It is not all win-win. Some projects are lose-lose. The purpose of this chapter is to explore in some detail why databases fail, and what can be done by marketers to assure themselves that they do not start something that will bomb in a few months, or years.

Database marketing, properly conceived and executed, can bring your company customer loyalty, repeat sales, reduced costs, cross-sales, improved identification of prospects, and a continuing boost to your bottom line. But if you go about it in the wrong way, it will not bring you any of these things—and it could be a costly failure.

The Nine Mistakes

In this chapter, we are going to discuss nine fundamental mistakes, any one of which can serve to doom your database project.

Mistake 1: Lack of Marketing Strategy

Database marketing has at last caught on. There isn't a corporation that isn't discussing it. Many have positions devoted to it. All over America, marketers are collecting names of people who have bought their products. "When we get enough," they say, "we will have a marketing database!" But what they seldom think through is what they are going to do with the names once they have them. How can they turn a list of names into profits? That is a tough question to answer.

A marketing plan using a database aims at building a relationship with each customer: making the customer feel recognized and special. You become an old friend. You give your customers things that they want: recognition, information, and service, and they give you what you want: loyalty and repeat sales.

But how are you going to do that? To go from a list of names and addresses to building a relationship is a giant leap. Somewhere in your plan there must be a practical program for using the names which accomplishes a definite objective. You will need:

- Some benefit that the customer will gain by being on the database
- A control group that does not get special attention so you can measure whether your relationship building really pays off
- A series of practical steps that modify customer and company behavior to reach the goal
- An achievable numeric goal that can be translated into profits
- A segmentation system that separates profitable customers from unprofitable customers and treats them differently
- A long-range (three-year) plan with a budget that lasts long enough so that it is possible to show results

The list of possible steps might contain:

- Membership cards with points and credits
- Newsletters with coupons
- Surveys and responses
- A personalized web site
- Recognition and special services

Many, many database projects have been undertaken without spelling out the goals, having the budget, or having worked out what the practical steps should be.

Constructors and Creators

Two general types of people are interested in database marketing: constructors and creators.

- A *constructor* is someone who is interested in building a database: collecting and cleaning the names, designing the computer access, planning instant retrieval and segmentation.
- A *creator* is someone who figures out how to make money with the database by designing practical relationship- and sales-building programs.
- You need both kinds to have a successful database. The creators are the hardest to find. Without them, you are doomed to failure.

A major national corporation collected the names of 7 million of its customers as a result of a number of promotional activities with baby food, pet food, and adult food products. Marketing executives decided that this pool of names constituted an important corporate asset. The money was found to merge/purge these names and to put them into a common format. NCOA was applied to update the addresses. A database was created.

The only problem was that no one knew what to do with the names once they were ready. None of the brand managers had any promotions planned which could use the names. There was no newsletter or other vehicle in the works. As a result, the 7 million names hung on a tape rack for three years, while the names got stale. No one was willing to admit it, but every penny spent on this database was totally wasted.

Before any database project is undertaken, therefore, or any money is spent to put a database together, you need to have drafted a document that states:

- The goal of the database project—a numeric achievable goal
- The method whereby the database will achieve that goal
- The time frame necessary to achieve the goal
- The budget required getting from here to there

Then, of course, you need to sell your plan to whoever approves multi-year budgets.

Mistake 2: Focus on Price Instead of Service

What do you offer a customer to build a relationship? A discount is the last thing you should consider. Before neighborhood stores went out of business in the 1970s, people kept coming back to them because they liked the owner, they liked the employees, and they liked the friendly atmosphere at the store. The store was convenient. The owner recognized you and did favors for you. You would not think of asking the owner to cut the price. The relationship was built on trust and service.

That is not true today. Mass marketing stores are based on price, not on relationships. Databases are built on relationships. Once you begin talking discount, it sends the wrong message.

A discount is what everyone else offers. Discounts do not build loyalty or relationships. They make people forget about quality, service, and loyalty, and think about the price.

If all you can think of to do with your database is to use it as a channel for offering discounts, your database will fail. Why? Because a database costs money. There are a lot cheaper ways of providing discounts, particularly coupons. Once you begin to play the discount game, any competitor with a deeper discount can rob you of your customers.

The Quaker Oats Company launched a major national database program built on that idea. Quaker Oats began a major database marketing effort called Quaker Direct. After a test mailing, with a budget of $18 million, Quaker Direct sent co-op mailings of coupons to 20 million households carefully selected from Computerized Marketing Technology's compiled database Select and Save. Unlike free standing insert (FSI) coupons, the Quaker coupons were bar-coded with a Quaker household number so that data could be collected on the response of each of the 20 million households.

The central idea in the promotion, according to Dan Strunk, the director of the Quaker program, was to gain knowledge of the market, and to begin a dialog with a select group of confirmed Quaker users, thereby building brand loyalty.

Although the program cost approximately four times as much as the cost of sending the same coupons in a Sunday newspaper, and twice as much as the cost of Donnelley's Carol Wright's co-op program, Quaker Direct reasoned that because of the correct targeting, the redemption rates would be much higher than would be obtained with those other programs. The net effect, therefore, would be a reduction in overall costs by "mailing smarter." Another means of reducing the cost of the promotion was enlisting national advertisers who paid to share the mailing with Quaker.

Quaker hoped to achieve a real "one-to-one bonding" with the consumers of its brands, through the dialog created by the receiving and redemption of coupons. After the first mailing, however, the entire project was canceled, and the director was terminated. Quaker did not comment on the reasons.

Quaker Oats is a household word in America, with an excellent reputation with the public. Why did its database project fail?

First, coupons do not build a relationship. People love Quaker because of the wonderful wholesome food that Quaker is famous for, not because Quaker discounts its products. People won't love Quaker more because they got a coupon in the mail giving them 50 cents off. The entire basis for the Quaker program was mistaken.

Second, the customer did not get as many co-op advertisers as it had hoped to get, and so the program was more expensive than it had assumed. Quaker was smart to stop it before more money was wasted.

Contrast the Quaker fiasco with what Kraft General Foods did with the Crystal Light program. Beginning in the late 1980s, John Kuendig, director of direct marketing, created the Crystal Light Lightstyle Club. Crystal Light is a low-calorie artificially sweetened drink powder, selling for less than $3 per box. Heavy users buy 10 or more boxes during the summer.

There were about a million members in the club at any given time. These were medium-to-heavy users of the product. The goal was to preserve this group and increase their usage.

Members received a package that contained a club newsletter on diet and fitness, discount coupons for General Foods products, a cover letter, and a catalog. The catalog was part of the club image, because it offered watches, mugs, jogging suits, and other gear that bore the Crystal Light emblem. Catalog items could be purchased with cash plus proof-of-purchase seals from Crystal Light boxes.

Each year, market research was used to measure the effectiveness of the program in building and maintaining sales of the product.

How did this program differ from the ill-fated Quaker Direct? It was built upon three key concepts, all of which were missing from Quaker:

- A theme (fitness, exercise, weight loss, diet)
- A club (with a logo, clothing, and website (www.kraftfoods.com/crystallight).
- Exclusivity (a very focused, narrow group of consumers interested in the club and the theme)

Of course, Crystal Light used discount coupons, but the program was not *based* on the coupons. They were not the main idea. They were a sweetener, which supported the program and facilitated the dialog. I would venture to say that if Kraft simply mailed out coupons alone, the program would have quickly died.

When mailing programs are built on discount coupons as the core, instead of building a relationship focused on the product or the manufacturer's established name and reputation, they are doomed to failure.

So what's wrong with discounts?

- A discount, of course, erodes your margin.
- A discount tells customers that your product is overpriced. They know that you are making a profit at the discounted price. So you must be ripping them off if you charge the regular price.

- A discount makes people think about how much they are paying instead of how much they are getting. You want them to think about the value of the product and the service, and the relationship you have created, not about the price.

- Any competitor can match your discount. No one can match the relationship you have built up with your customers.

Solid relationships built through database marketing are immune to discounts. Your customers prefer you because you are an old friend who recognizes them, who provides personal services, and who delivers a well-known quality product. You would be insulted if a friend gave you money for doing him a favor. Your database and your web site should aim at that same kind of friendship.

Mistake 3: Getting the Economics Wrong

What could you do with a clean list of all the households in America that buy Ivory soap? Mail letters to them to sell them more soap or some similar product? Wrong! What you could do is to lose a lot of money. Recently, Ivory soap was selling for four bars for $1.29. The margin is so pathetically thin that there is no way you could communicate with these households by mail, fax, e-mail, or phone and have the incremental profit pay even for the cost of the communication. The economics just aren't there. That is true of most packaged goods. Who wants to get letters from the people that make our paper clips? Life is just too short to spend it corresponding with the makers of all the products and services that we use every day. There are plenty of situations in which database marketing just isn't going to work. We have to get the economics right.

On the other hand, if you sell automobiles, rental cars, insurance, power tools, vacation cruises, software, or computers, your customer list could be turned into a valuable database.

Big-ticket items, repeat-sales items, cross-brand possibilities—these are the lifeblood of marketing databases. Too many companies rush into building a database without thinking about the economics. Say to yourself: "How am I going to make money with these names?" Your answer must be simple and practical—something that you can explain to your mother so she can understand it.

A major packaged goods company compiled a list of 6 million names of its customers. Executives of the company were repeatedly asked how they were going to use the names to build relationships and sales. Their answer was a simple one: "The boss wants a database." They continued to spend efforts maintaining the names. No one has yet been able to figure out how they can use these names to make money.

Citicorp, one of the nation's largest banks, became a major entrant into the database marketing field for retailers in the middle 1980s. Citicorp's idea, called Reward America, was to help grocery chains build up a valued customer database, with each customer having a family membership card. When the family came to shop, they would bring their card and present it for scanning while their shopping cart contents were rung up. As a result, the computers in each cash register would have a record of all the purchases made by that family: the date, the time of day, the SKU, the quantity, the price.

The idea caught on fast. Several chains were signed up, and the software was installed. Every night, the cash registers were electronically polled. The data on the day's transactions were fed over the telephone lines to each chain's central computer. From there, on a weekly basis, Citicorp retrieved each member household's purchasing data for storage on its mainframe in Connecticut.

With detailed information on the shopping habits of millions of Americans, Citicorp figured it would be able to realize a profit from the sale of these household data to manufacturers: who was using Camay, Pampers, Kraft General Foods products, Quaker products.

It was a great idea. The stores would use the data to learn more about their customers: where they lived, when they shopped, what they bought. They could use the data to pursue members who stopped buying, and to reward loyal member customers with daily specials and premiums.

Many different types of discount arrangements were made by the different chains that installed the system. For example, in some systems, members using their cards to purchase goods that were "on special" would receive $2 for buying eight cans of this juice, or $1 for buying three boxes of that cereal. The system would keep track of purchases, so the products did not have to be bought on the same visit. Each month, members could receive a mailing including a purchase summary and a certificate for the amount they had earned so far. In other systems, the reward would be instant—with a discount for special items with each visit, and no retention of credits.

Citicorp made retailers a deal that they couldn't refuse: free. Citicorp planned to make its money on the other end, by selling the purchase data to manufacturers. It hoped to build a database of 40 million households.

Most of the dozen chains that signed up for the system did so because the program was free and offered a way to learn about frequent shopper programs. Unfortunately for Citicorp, many things went wrong.

What did go wrong?

1. *Rewards must be instant.* The concept of rewarding customers three months down the road for purchases just didn't go over. If you are going to give grocery shoppers money, they want it now, which explains the success of the instant discounts and electronic coupon programs—such as those run by Catalina marketing. Catalina is the company that makes the systems in supermarkets that generate coupons during the checkout process. If you bought one brand of yogurt, the Catalina coupon generated might offer you a discount on a rival brand.

2. *The data problems were immense.* Citicorp's central computer choked on the data. The bank didn't realize how huge the volume of grocery chain purchase data could be. It did not have adequate software in place. After the program was canceled, Citicorp had thousands of tapes stored in its computer center, unprocessed and gathering dust. What can anyone do with the information that on August 3 at 3:40 p.m. Arthur Hughes bought 6 pounds of potatoes? Nothing profitable! Add to that tens of millions of other transactions that take place every day in American supermarkets and you will soon bring any computer to its knees.

3. *Few companies wanted the names.* Manufacturers did not jump at the chance to buy the names of their customers, as Citicorp expected they would. The fact is that names and addresses of purchasers of packaged goods are almost worthless. What can you do with data about someone who has bought frozen spinach? Spam? Clorox? Cool Whip? Think about it. You can't make any money with these names.

4. *Costs exceeded revenues.* The program cost too much to support. The bank spent $200 million and generated about $20 million in revenue. After three years, it canceled the program and fired the 174 employees who worked on the program, leaving many retail chains with no way to maintain a system that they had been promoting to their customers.

Looking at the broad picture, what lessons can we draw from the Citicorp experience?

■ *Test first.* Before you do something big in the database field, you should test, test, test. Citicorp, a very large and successful bank, approached this project the same way it successfully approached credit cards and other projects: Pour in money; get a national foothold before the competitors know what is going on. This strategy may have paid off in credit card acquisitions, but it certainly did not work in retailing. If Citicorp had been prepared to start on a small scale with one or two chains, experimenting and learning (with just a few employees on the project), it could have gotten the bugs out of the concept at a modest cost—such as $10 million. Then it would have been ready for a successful national rollout in two or three years.

- *Compute the costs.* Don't underestimate the data processing aspects of database marketing. When you compute the data on one household's grocery purchases in a year, you may be talking 6,000 or more items purchased by a family of four. Multiply that by 40 million households and you have 240 billion transactions in one year alone. Without really efficient software, the costs and time consumed will bring even the most powerful data center to serious grief and high costs.

- *Work out lifetime value.* Put yourself in the customer's shoes. Successful database marketing is relationship building: one-on-one with the customer. Some marketers might be thinking "How can we make money selling data about these rubes?"—instead of saying, "Why would anyone want to join a frequent shopper club?" You have to start with the basics. Profits should be created by having built a relationship with the customer that is satisfying to all concerned.

- *Know your market.* The economics were wrong for the product manufacturers. Few packaged goods manufacturers today know what to do with a database of their own customers. Most of them have millions of names stored in their data centers from previous promotions. They haven't yet figured out how to turn these names into relationships, loyalty, repeat sales, cross-sales, and profits. If that is the case, why would they go out and pay money for more customer names?

If there were a demand for the names because the manufacturers had a way of making money from them, the profits would have solved all the other problems. But, alas, the demand was not there.

A satisfactory economic solution to database marketing won't come looking for you. You have to find it. And if you can't, maybe it isn't there!

Mistake 4: Making the Project
Too Big and Taking Too Long

How long should you take to build a marketing database and web site?
One year, tops. Many unsuccessful databases are the result of a long-
range plan—and very little action. Why should you move fast?

■ Technology is racing ahead. If you take too long to plan, your database and web site will become obsolete.

■ Your marketing database will teach you a lot about your customers
  and how to market to them. It will build your bottom line. None of
  this will happen during the planning phase—only after you have gotten started.

■ You need funding and top-level support for a marketing database. If
  you wait too long, the funding will dry up, and the top-level support-
  er will transfer to a new job. Good-bye database.

■ By waiting you will be losing money. A successful database earns
  money. Without it, those customers will keep slipping away.

■ Your competition is probably experimenting with their database and
  web site right now. It takes several years to build relationships and get
  the database system working correctly. You are losing out in a competitive race if you wait to get started too long.

A major bank had a long-range plan for building a marketing database on its mainframe in three years. A large committee made up of
staff from all parts of the bank met every two weeks to plan the system.
At the end of three years of meetings, the committee decided to shift to
a five year plan, since the bank had just bought two other banking systems and needed time to absorb the new branches. This bank was not
doing any database marketing.

How many other companies are making this same mistake right now?
Hundreds.

Mistake 5: Failure to Track Results

At a database conference one gets a picture of success stories. We marketers are all ad men at heart. We warm to the superlative. It comes nat-
urally to us. But when we get back to the office, we know, deep down,
that we are always operating on the brink of disaster.

Computers are marvelous. They make it possible to communicate with millions of customers in very personal ways. But there is another side to the computers. They make it possible to botch relationships with millions of customers though very simple mistakes that don't get caught on the way out, but seem so obvious after the communications hit the fan.

Rather than give you a book filled only with success stories and exhortations to go out and build relationships (which generally this book does), I would like to provide a little balance, by warning those who don't know that database marketing is not all easy riding. Things can go wrong—sometimes seriously wrong.

Forewarned is forearmed. Read and heed. If you look for these things, you can avoid them.

What Can Go Wrong with Source Codes?

Most new database marketers don't think about details like source codes. They plan great campaigns that produce wonderful responses, but fail to get accountable results. Many very good campaigns have been designed and run, but could not be tracked at all because the planners neglected to construct a useful source code tracking system.

The list of failures is endless and universal.

1. *Failure to get an organized system in the beginning.* Most companies that have participated in direct marketing for several years have failed to set up a well-thought-through source code system. They begin, for example, with one set of marketing campaigns (such as a direct-mail program using many lists, offers, segments, and packages). Then they undertake an entirely new program (such as a web site data capture campaign) that is really incompatible with the first system. In the course of trying to patch several different systems together, they run out of numbers or letters.

2. *Failure to design the mailing piece to include a space for the source code or ID number.* Quite often the mailing piece is designed by someone other than the database marketer who is planning the overall campaign. This creative designer works out an eye-catching promotional piece, or letter, complete with a response device. There have been many cases in which the designer did not know about the mail code and so did not leave space for it. At the last minute, the mail shop has to cram it in somewhere on the printed piece, usually where it does not exactly fit and can be lopped off when the customer tears off the coupon to mail it in.

3. *Failure to capture the source code in the data entry process.* It happens more often than you realize. A well-designed campaign includes source codes printed on the tape and the response device. Someone forgets to tell the fulfillment house to capture the source code in addition to capturing the name, address, and order information. Thousands of orders are fulfilled before anyone notices that none of them contain a source code. Tracking is lost, and it is too expensive to rekey all the responses over again to learn the source codes.

Solutions

- Set up a foolproof, universal, long-range source code system.
- Put the source code definitions *in the database* as well as in a note-book.
- Have the database manager check the design of the mailing pieces and the keypunching format (used by fulfillment houses) rather than leaving these matters to production people.

Reaching the Wrong People

The marketing staff of a major pharmaceutical firm tried their first DRTV program. There had been opposition from management which pointed out that the company had never experimented with DRTV before, and that, in all likelihood, no one would respond. Despite this contention, the marketing staff placed attractive TV ads that invited viewers to call an 800 number to order a welcome kit. The kit provided the names of several nearby physicians and a coupon for the office visit. The promotion was for a vanity product that cost customers about $600 per year.

The campaign was very successful. The first year more than a million people called the 800 number and were shipped welcome kits. The pharmaceutical company management was thrilled. But in analyzing the results, the company's database provider was dismayed. Out of the 1 million welcome kits shipped, fewer than 2,000 people redeemed the coupons. They weren't visiting the doctors. Why not?

To find out why not, the database provider appended Prizm codes to the database. They discovered that the majority of the responders were poor people who lived in rural communities. These people could not afford the $600 per year for a vanity product, so they did not bother to visit a doctor. The campaign was a bust. Why were the wrong people responding? In further research, the database provider found out that the ad agency had purchased daytime television spots, because they were cheaper. The problem was that most of the people who could afford the product would be working people who normally do not watch daytime TV.

So what was wrong? The marketers did not follow through. They didn't check to see where their ads were placed or who was responding. There was a total disconnect between the marketers and the ad agency.

At the Database Marketing Institute, Paul Wang and I send first-class personalized letters to about 35,000 database marketers several times a year inviting them to attend our two-day seminars. These letters contain, in addition to the name and address, personal references, such as "This is a personal invitation to you, Bob, to attend. ..." There are usually three such references. You have to check your mailing carefully before it goes out to be sure it is correct. One spring, we did not check properly. We sent out 20,000 letters, all addressed properly to Bill, Harry, Nancy, and Edward, but in the body of the letters they all said "This is a personal invitation to you, Mary, to attend. ..." Twenty thousand letters all said "Mary." When the letters hit the fan, I got 412 phone calls, faxes, e-mails, and letters protesting. Some people said, "I would never go to a database marketing seminar that advertises itself in such a sloppy way." Others said, "My secret is out. How did you find out about me and Mary?" Paul and I thought that this letter would destroy the Institute. We decided to send out a first-class apology to all 20,000 recipients, first taking out the 169 people whose name actually was Mary. We apologized to these professional marketers for sending them such a stupid communication. It worked. We received many letters back thanking us for the apology, saying that they had never received an apology for a direct-mail communication mistake before. Attendance was the same as at previous seminars. We learned that you can ruin your reputation with thousands of prospects or customers by a simple mistake.

Mistake 6: Building Models instead of Relationships

Some marketers look on a customer database as an opportunity for multiple regressions: model building to determine which of the demographic, lifestyle, and psychographic variables that can be appended to a household are the key determinants of response and purchasing behavior.

This school of marketers overlays the database with quantities of external data: assumed income, age, home value, presence of children, educational level, psychological profile, media interests, etc. Since this work is expensive and time consuming, these marketers often work with a statistically representative sample (such as 10 percent) of the file, and assume their conclusions hold for the entire file.

The goal of their work is a set of simple statements: "People who buy our product have qualities B, C, and D. We can, therefore, write our copy to emphasize these qualities, and seek in our prospecting programs to find others who have these same qualities."

There is value in this work. It can help write copy. It can help in selecting mailing lists. But it is not database marketing. A few years ago one of these modelers accepted a large contract from a liquor firm to model the firm's customer base. His conclusion was that most bourbon drinkers were white males over 50 years of age—hardly an earth-shaking discovery!

Perhaps this mistake comes about through failure to understand the difference between market research and database marketing. What is database marketing supposed to do? Let's put it in a few simple sentences: Database marketing aims at building a profitable individual relationship with each customer. The relationship should make the customer feel that she is recognized and that she receives personal service and attention; as a result, she will develop a loyalty to your company which will result in continued sales. The relationship is based on a dialog—an exchange of information—not on implied characteristics.

Modeling rests on the assumption that purchase behavior can be deduced from demographic and psychographic data. Sometimes this is true. But in many cases it either is not possible or—like the bourbon case—is obvious and hardly worth the money and effort.

The fact of the matter is that what people decide to do in the market varies from day to day based on their own subjective values, the products they have already acquired, their family needs, and their hopes and fears.

Helena and I used to go out to a restaurant once a week. We loved it: exploring a different section of the city each time and trying out different exotic foods from different countries.

Then we found that we were getting too fat. We cut out the restaurants altogether. We only go out now when we have company visiting us.

The point: Helena and I are the same people, with the same income, home value, presence of children (none), educational level, and age as before, but our behavior is entirely different. Can our behavior (restaurant-goers or stay-at-homers) be deduced from any demographic factors? Obviously not.

I used to rent two videos every week. We love watching movies. Then Helena's job became much more demanding. She got home after 9 p.m. on most nights. We cut out the movies.

Everyone reading this chapter has had a similar experience: We sometimes change our spending habits without a corresponding change in externally measurable demographics. For this reason, it is safe to say that your market activities cannot be predicted with any precision based on static demographic data. But these are *the only data available to modelers which can be applied to lists of customers or prospects.*

What can help in predicting customer behavior or that of prospects is *previous behavior* when combined with demographics:

- If I buy a music CD, I am much more likely to buy another music CD right away than someone who has not bought a CD in the last year.

- If I have purchased mutual funds and have an income of over $100,000, I am a better prospect for buying $20,000 more mutual funds than another mutual fund buyer with an income of under $25,000.

Modeling can help in deciding whom to promote out of the universe of people that you could conceivably make an offer to. Using modeling, you can reduce the cost of your mailing and still maintain your sales. Modeling can also help to predict who is most likely to drop your cellular phone service or your credit card. Such models are usually based largely on behavior.

Us versus Them

Excessive reliance on modeling based on demographics will divert the database marketer from his main objective: building an individual relationship with each customer. Rather than spending money on appending external data (which may be inaccurate), it is better to use the same money to survey your customers and ask them why they bought your product, what they would like to see in the way of new products and services, what their plans are for next year. Once you know these things, you can really build a relationship, and your bottom line.

The conduct of modeling and market research tends to perpetuate the "us versus them" psychology of marketing: looking at customers as a mass of data, instead of a group of individuals with loyalties, desires, and personalities. It gets marketers thinking: "How can I move this product?" instead of: "How can I make these people love our company?" Moving products seldom builds lifetime value. Winning the hearts and minds of customers does.

Mistake 7: Failure to Link Your Database to the Web

A few years ago you could build relationships with your customers using database marketing without a web site. This is no longer possible. The Internet has become an indispensable tool for customer relationship management. Not every customer is on the Internet, of course. There will always be some who just don't get it. That group is getting to be very tiny. Today, any savvy customer will want to look you up on the web to see what you have to offer, and how you compare with the competition.

I worked with a successful company that built up a loyal base of 1.5 million customers who generated $65 million in sales. The customers were recruited by direct mail. They were retained by 220 live customer service agents. Business was good, but the good days were numbered. The company had failed to create a web site.

The first sign of trouble came from the company's partners. These partners were banks who provided the names of prospects, and providers of services to the company's customers. These included companies providing insurance, travel-related products, health products, etc. The service providers wanted the company to link to web sites so customers could buy more products. The banks wanted to be sure that their customers were getting the best possible service offerings. Both banks and service partners threatened to leave unless the company got onto the web.

Worse, the company's competitors were already there. Two years before, the company's four principal rivals had built their own web sites. One had even had a highly profitable IPO by spinning off their web site. The handwriting was on the wall. The company was scrambling to catch up.

Building a web site and providing wonderful services both directly and through partners is not enough, however. Once it began to build its web site, the company realized that its value proposition that worked quite well with direct mail, was inadequate on the web. It ran into what

I call the "Wal-Mart Effect," or "How're you going to keep them down on the farm, after they've seen Paree?" Most of its customers were lower-middle-class people. They didn't get that much direct mail, so when they got an offer from the company, they opened it, and many of them bought it. The Wal-Mart Effect tends to destroy that one-to-one relationship.

When Wal-Mart comes to a rural community, many small businesses are wiped out. They can't match the Wal-Mart prices or variety of products. The web is like Wal-Mart. Once customers have learned what is available on the web, they may realize that what they bought by a direct mail offer is inferior to what they can get elsewhere at a lower cost. You have to rethink your offer, or you will lose your customers.

Once you have studied the competition, and recrafted your offer to make it competitive, you can't rest there. You have to link your database to the web. Loyal customers expect that your relationship with them will continue on the web as well as in direct mail and on the phone. When I click on American Airlines (*www.aa.com*) they recognize me by name. They know that I am a Platinum member with more than a million miles and they say so on the web site when I click in. The web site provides the same relationship that American has with me in direct mail and on the telephone. Few companies have yet been able to achieve that continuity of relationship. You may have friends at the local branch, and warm greetings by direct mail, but on the web, you are just another stranger clicking in. This is a good way to lose customers.

What do you have to do? Link your database to the web. Feed the database with the results of web visits, as well as the results of direct marketing and customer service calls. After all, the old corner grocer did that instinctively. He remembered who you were, and what you wanted, and what you bought. You have to do the same in your customer relationships if you want to be successful.

Actually, we have been talking about one-to-one marketing for years, but most of us have not really been doing it. With the web, it is actually possible. By linking our database to the web, we can create a different web experience for every single customer, based on her preferences, demographics, and previous purchases. If we know that she buys presents for other people, we can suggest gifts, and ask her to list birthdays of her relatives and friends.

So if you have not yet linked your database to the web, your database will ultimately fail, and so will you.

Mistake 8: Failure to Change Organization and Compensation

Everyone says that companies should organize themselves around customers: to become customer-centric. Database marketing is often called *customer relationship management* (CRM) as a result. But if you look around, you see that little has really changed. Brand or product managers are still in charge. What is the evidence that customer-centric marketing is profitable?

- Eighty percent (or some very large percentage) of every company's revenue or profits comes from the top 20 percent of the customers.

- The bottom 20 percent of customers is usually unprofitable. In some companies the losses from this bottom group are very substantial.

- Long-term customers have higher retention rates, higher spending rates, and higher referral rates, and are less expensive to serve than new customers.

- Marketing dollars spent on up-selling, cross-selling, or retention-building programs that are focused on existing customers produce more revenue than the same dollars spent on new-customer acquisition.

- A small percentage increase in the retention rate will produce a very significant increase in company profits.

- The more different products or categories that a customer buys from a firm the more likely that the customer will become loyal, long-term, and profitable.

These beliefs underlie customer relationship management: the idea that marketing activities should be focused on increasing customer lifetime value. To achieve an increase in LTV, the company has to recognize customer segments, and develop customer segment managers who develop customer-focused programs based on these beliefs. Yet most corporations are not organized in this way. Their compensation systems work to frustrate customer relationship-building activities. Look at the typical bank organization:

In Chapter 13 we learned that in a typical bank there are vice presidents for each major product: credit cards, home equity loans, retail (checking and savings accounts), insurance, etc. The credit card manager receives no bonus or special recognition if some of his credit card customers sign up for a checking account. The retail vice president gets no special reward if some of her customers apply for a credit card. Yet any analysis of bank customers will show that the more bank products the average customer has, the higher that customer's loyalty to and profits for the bank. The organization and compensation system does not reflect the theory of customer relationship management.

What does it take to change an organization to begin to focus on the customer?

- Gathering and organizing information. Group all household purchases on one record so that you can understand what customers are doing and what they want.
- Determining customer profitability and lifetime value.
- Grouping customers into profitability quintiles.
- Developing different strategies for each quintile: service strategies, marketing strategies, reward strategies, migration strategies, and management strategies.
- Looking at these strategies to determine whether the present organization and compensation system permits you to carry them out.
- Changing your organization and compensation system to assure that you become customer-centric.

Banks that have built a marketing customer information file (MCIF) have proved to themselves that customer retention is a function of the number of products owned. The graph in Figure 14-1 presents the results from a large bank. This graph proves the point: The best thing

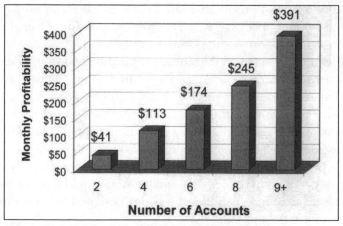

Figure 14-1. Bank profitability by number of products.

that the VP for one bank product can do to improve retention of his customers is to sell his customers additional products from some other department of the bank. But few banks are set up to do that. The VPs compete with one another. The compensation system has to be changed, or the organization will never truly focus on the customer.

How Sears Canada Became Customer-Focused

In Chapter 11, we learned how Sears Canada used its database to target its customers. Sears Canada was the largest general retailer in Canada, with sales of more than $5 billion. It had more than 110 full-line retail stores, 8 whole home furniture stores, 8 outlet clearance stores, 79 dealer stores, and 2,000 catalog agents. Its big book catalog reached 5 million households in Canada every year. Two-thirds of all sales in both catalog and retail were done on the Sears credit card.

In the database described in Chapter 11, Sears Canada gained a new insight into its customer base by putting data from catalog and retail sales, for the first time, on the same household record. It was an eye-opener.

At the time the database was built, there was an senior vice president (SVP) for retail stores and an SVP for catalog operations. These two channels competed with each other openly. Their rivalry went back a long way in Canada. In early Canadian retailing history, the Sears Canada pioneers were the catalogers. They built a strong base in rural Canada. Once this base was established, Sears would open retail stores, based on the growth of the catalog. To the company it was profitable. But to the catalogers, it created a sense of cannibalization. The catalog merchants who had previously owned these markets saw sales attrition due to the stores. They saw it as channel competition. Over the years, the competition became quite heated.

The competition was reflected in where the catalog operation was located in the typical Sears retail store. In Canada, as well as in the United States, Sears stores put the catalog office way back in the store, where you have to walk through the whole store to get there. It was viewed as an overhead to the selling operation, taking up valuable space that should be used for merchandise. The catalog desk was put as far as possible from the entrance to the store to generate store traffic. Customers coming in to pick up a catalog item would have to walk past aisle after aisle of merchandise. It was not designed for customer convenience—just the opposite, in fact.

Once the database was built, Sears was able to measure the performance of catalog customers versus retail customers. The data were very revealing. Sears found that the average catalog customer spent $492 per year. The average retail customer spent $1,102 per year.

What about customers who were shopping both channels? These customers bought more than the average in both channels. When Bruce Clarkson, general manager of relationship marketing, looked at these cross-shoppers, he found that the average cross-shopping customer spent $584 on catalog items *and* $1,299 in retail stores. Leaving these cross-shoppers out of the total figures, the customers who only shopped one channel spent $409 on catalog items or spent $994 in retail stores. Cross-shoppers were spending $1,883 per year with Sears, compared with half that or less spent by single-channel shoppers.

The facts were staggering. The marketing staff provided their findings to top management. Management could clearly see that the way the business was being managed was inconsistent with customer behavior. The leadership said things like, "I knew it, but we did not have the numbers to prove it!" "We have to do something to encourage cross-channel shopping."

Once top management saw what was happening, Sears began to make major changes. No longer were catalog and retail each under a competing SVP. Instead, Sears Canada shifted to have three major divisions:

- Executive vice president (EVP) for marketing
- EVP for sales and service
- EVP for merchandising

Each EVP works across all channels: retail, catalog, and several others, including the credit cards, long distance services, gift registries, etc. Marketing does branding, advertising, TV, preprint, catalog production, in-store marketing, design to establish the look and feel of the store, arrangement of the store, customer relationship marketing, and e-commerce. Sales and service delivers service excellence through all the channels.

One of the first fruits of the reorganization was the change in the location of the catalog desk in the retail stores. Stores began to look contemporary: bright, functional, and convenient. The catalog desks were put at the most used entrance of each store. Throughout the retail store, Sears created outposts where it put copies of the catalog. At each outpost, there were telephones for immediate access to the call centers. The catalog was positioned as an extension to the retail store. Selected catalog pages were displayed throughout the store, so if you were in the footwear division, you would find catalog pages laminated in the footwear department. If you couldn't find the size or style you wanted, you could pick up a phone and order it. It was not promoted as being a catalog order. It was just another way of shopping at Sears.

To promote telephone shopping, Sears developed 48-hour national service on most orders. No matter where you were in Canada, Sears could arrange delivery for you at a convenient location near your home within 48 hours. Plus, it didn't charge for shipping or handling. With 2,000 locations throughout Canada, goods could be shipped free to nearby locations. The whole idea was to increase the number of cross-shoppers, whom Sears recognized as being its most valuable customers.

What was the result of this? Before Sears provided the catalog and telephone service in the store, clerks would say, if they did not have what the customer wanted, "Gosh, I am sorry. Maybe they have it at so and so down the mall." With the new system, Sears in its first year with the new system saved sales that were equivalent to adding another mid-sized store to its 110 store chain with no bricks and mortar—essentially at almost no cost. That virtual store became the largest single store in the Sears Canada chain.

To extend the customer-centric idea, Sears included a teleshopping icon in its flyers and preprint programs. You could call to obtain by phone any product that was available in the stores. It looks like retail, but it acts like direct. The customers do not know that they are ordering from a catalog. They think that they are calling a retail store with the teleshopping number. Sears customers were capitalizing on the convenience of the system. People called the number and then picked up their products at the retail store. In teleshopping, Sears had double-digit growth in its first 15 months. The incremental sales from teleshopping were equivalent to putting out a new catalog and sending it to 5 million households. The cost, however, was virtually nil. This is what came about through reorganization to integrate catalog and retail.

But the database and the reorganization did not stop at integrating catalogs with retail. Marketing moved toward the goals of retention, acquisition, and purchase stimulation. Clarkson developed customer attrition models. His first effort was to find out why people were not shopping through the catalog any more. What he discovered was that the strongest predictive variable for not shopping the catalog was exposure to bad service: merchandise that was out of stock or that was not satisfactory. He proved that money spent on improved service would increase customer retention. The performance of the EVP for sales and service is now measured based on a customer loyalty index.

To focus attention on customers, Clarkson developed 14 active customer segments and two lapsed customer segments:

- One segment was the *Super Spenders*. This group had the highest retail transaction dollars, the highest total revenue overall, and the highest revenue in five out of twelve merchandise categories. Their credit limit was very high. They were nuts about using the Sears card. In terms of demographics, they owned, not rented, their homes. They tended to live in affluent suburbs. These Super Spenders were only 2 percent of the customer base.

- At the bottom were the *Occasional Store Shoppers*. They were the highest in terms of returns and the highest in payment to the credit balance. They paid off their account every month. They were the lowest in terms of overall revenue and the lowest in catalog purchases. But there was a paradox: The Occasional Store Shoppers were demographically identical to the Super Spenders. They lived in the same subdivisions. Twenty-eight percent of them lapsed each year. Since they used the Sears card, it meant that Sears had constantly to do acquisition programs to keep their card holder membership up. Occasional Store Shoppers accounted for 17 percent of the customer base. They absorbed a tremendous amount of expense.

Sears's experience shows how a company can become truly customer-centric. But it took a massive reorganization to do it. How many other companies are willing to make the changes in organization and compensation needed to achieve customer relationship management?

Mistake 9: Lack of a Forceful Leader

Too many databases fail through the lack of a strong leader to head the project. Leadership is vital: There is so much to be coordinated, both within the company and with the outside suppliers, that is required to make a database possible. Successful databases usually have outside telemarketers, a service bureau, a creative agency, a fulfillment house; inside they need the coordination of marketing, market research, sales, billing, customer service, and MIS. Pulling the team together requires a forceful leader. The committee system will never work here. Decisions are needed on a daily basis to keep the database going, responsive, dynamic—to keep building customer relationships and making sales.

If you are planning a database in your company, be sure that you have found a strong leader, and that he or she has been delegated the responsibilities and authority to make it work. Without this, your database will never get off the ground.

A Failure of Leadership

As of today, one of the biggest failures in database marketing continues to be American automobile companies. They have all the prerequisites necessary to do an excellent job, and yet they have failed. What are these prerequisites?

- A product with a large enough margin to finance database activities—and a clearly delineated lifetime value that can be modified by relationship-building activities.
- An easy way to keep track of the identities of their customers: registrations and dealer service calls.
- A product that has a well-known cyclical purchase pattern that can be predicted with some precision.
- A product in which the average customer is intensely interested: Cars speak for the customer's lifestyle, income, age, family composition. People *identify* with their cars. They would like to *identify* with the manufacturers.

Yet in spite of all these advantages, in general, American automobile companies have not succeeded in building solid, lasting relationships with their customers. Why not?

I recently met with the marketers responsible for creating the customer database for one of the big three companies. They have a database of 25 million names of owners of their products. They are working on the problem. From what I could see of their activities, I believe that they will fail. Why can't they succeed?

All the marketers that I talked to from this company were *constructors*. They were awed by the huge size of the database. They were exploring technical solutions to storage of and access to the names. Should they use UNIX based workstations? How much data should they keep? How can they do ad hocs with such a large file?

Successful databases cannot be built by constructors. You must have a *creator* leading the pack—someone who has a vision, a drive, and a practical idea of how to build a profitable customer relationship. This person is thinking every day, "What can the customers gain from being on our database? What can we give them that will solidify their identification with our company? How can we build loyalty? How can we include dealers in the relationship loop?"

A friend of mine has owned automobiles made by the same company for the last eight years. In all that time, he has received only one letter from the company. It was a federally mandated recall to repair the engine emission.

Here was a wonderful opportunity. The company had to write to him by law. The money for the communication had to be spent. The company could have used the opportunity to consult with him, to build a relationship and start a dialog. It could have included an owner survey, an announcement of new models, an invitation to take a test drive. What did it do? Nothing. Why?

The recall probably came from the legal department. The company is too large and too bureaucratic to consider the idea of letting marketing participate in the recall effort. Database marketing, in this company at least, is considered to be a technical problem involving computers, disks, workstations, and sophisticated software. Relationship building, if there is ever to be any, has been relegated to some committee that is holding monthly meetings. It is a failure of leadership.

What would I do if I were in charge of sales at the automobile company? I would tell the database director to forget about the 25 million and concentrate on the 1 million current customers. I would tell him to find an external direct response agency with great ideas on how to build customer loyalty and repeat sales. I would tell him to contract out the database to an external service bureau, and to stop playing around with computer hardware and concentrate on marketing. I would tell him to make a specific quantifiable increase in the lifetime value of those 1 million customers within the next three years, which would translate into a big boost in the bottom line. But, of course, I am not in charge, and whoever is in charge does not understand database marketing.

How to Do Things Right

What should you do to avoid these mistakes? There are a few simple steps that you can take to be sure that you go about building your database properly:

- *Put yourself in your customer's shoes.* Don't think of what you want to sell, think of what you, as a customer, would want from your company. It may not be primarily a product at all—it may be recognition, attention, information, helpfulness, service, or friendship. If you can deliver on these things, the sales will follow. A database may be the best way to provide these things.

- *Build a database team.* Successful databases have a strong, creative, imaginative leader who has pulled together a team composed of marketing, sales, the service bureau, the creative agency, MIS, customer service, outside telemarketers, brand managers, fulfillment, and billing.

- *Think small and think fast.* Start your database with a small elite group of customers. Start soon. Make every action a test. Conduct your test, and evaluate your results. Build bigger as you accumulate experience.

- *Keep your eye on the bottom line.* Database marketing is supposed to *make money.* Plan your economics. Calculate lifetime value. If you can't quite see how what you're doing will be profitable, then *don't do it!* Rack your brains and find a way to turn your customer relationship into a profitable customer relationship.

Summary

- You can easily go wrong in database marketing. There are nine deadly mistakes enumerated in this chapter:

  Lack of marketing strategy

  Focus on price instead of service

  Getting the economics wrong

  Making the project too big and taking too long

  Failure to track results

  Building models instead of relationships

  Failure to link your database to the web

  Failure to change organization and compensation

  Lack of a forceful leader

- To be successful you need to:

Put yourself in your customer's shoes

Build a database team

Think small and think fast

Keep your eye on the bottom line

Executive Quiz 13

Answers to quiz questions can be found in Appendix B.

1. The Sears Canada reorganization was undertaken primarily because:

   a. Catalog shoppers had a higher lifetime value than retail store shoppers

   b. RFM analysis showed that 14 percent of Sears buyers contributed 50 percent of the revenue

   c. Cross-shoppers spent more than single-channel shoppers

   d. Sears executives believed that customer-centric marketing was a good idea

   e. It permitted organized teleshopping

2. Quaker Direct failed mainly because:

   a. Coupons do not build loyalty

   b. Database marketing does not work with packaged goods

   c. The budget for the project was too small

   d. Direct mail is not a good medium for relationship building

   e. None of the above

3. Reward America failed for the following reason(s):

   a. The computers choked on the data.

   b. The marketers failed to test first on a small scale.

   c. Manufacturers did not want to purchase the names.

   d. The reward system was faulty.

   e. All of the above.

4. How long should it take to build a functioning marketing database?

   a. No general rule: depends on the size of the customer database.

   b. Less than one year in all cases.

   c. More than one year in most cases.

   d. Financial services require more time; retailing requires less.

   e. None of the above.

5. Why may a data warehouse be bad for successful database marketing?

   a. Warehouses are never run by marketing.

   b. Warehouses are designed by accountants and MIS professionals.

   c. Warehouses tend to be very large, cumbersome projects.

   d. Warehouses have much data that are not needed for marketing.

   e. All of the above.

6. Which of the following is an ideal use for modeling of a customer database?

   a. Determining customer preferences

   b. Determining those most likely to drop the service

   c. Determining customer lifetime value

   d. Creating RFM cells

   e. Building a relationship with customers

7. Which of the following is true?

   a. Most large companies outsource their marketing databases.

   b. Customer data are too sensitive to entrust to an outsider.

   c. Outside construction is too expensive.

   d. In-house construction can be done much faster.

   e. Marketers can easily master the programming skills needed to build a database.

8. Which statement is *not* true?

   a. After a year, many companies lose track of what old source codes mean.

   b. Fulfillment houses sometimes forget to capture source codes.

   c. Creating a good system for source codes is difficult.

   d. The American Source Code Institute provides useful standards.

   e. Most marketers fail to think seriously about source codes.

9. Which of the following is *not* true of most American automobile manufacturers' marketing database operations?

   a. A product with a large enough margin to finance database activities

   b. A clearly delineated lifetime value that can be modified by relationship building activities

   c. An easy way to keep track of the identities of their customers

   d. A profitable database marketing program that builds customer loyalty

   e. A product in which the average customer is intensely interested

10. Which of the following is required to develop a customer-centric organization?

   a. Group all household purchases on one database system.

   b. Determine customer profitability and lifetime value.

   c. Group customers into profitability quintiles.

   d. Develop different strategies for each quintile: service strategies, marketing strategies, reward strategies, migration strategies, and management strategies.

   e. All of the above.

15

Database Types
That Succeed

*The U.S. version of the Air Miles loyalty program came
crashing to earth a year later, although the more successful Canadian and British programs continued
uninterrupted. The U.S. program had 40 corporate
sponsors and 2.2 million members, less than half of
whom actively collected Air Miles. The Canadian program had 56 corporate sponsors and about four million consumers signed up.*

*The differences: in the U.S. program, consumers had
to clip out proofs-of-purchase and mail them in to
receive credit. In Canada, a mag stripe, UPC code,
and embossing on the Air Miles membership card
allow members' purchases to be tracked the same way
credit card purchases are tracked. "In Canada, we created a card that makes collecting easy," said Joanna
Fuke, Loyalty Management Group Canada's director
of consumer marketing. "In the U.S. they took a packaged goods strategy and had a clip-and-snip program.
... That probably made it a little tougher for consumers to play the game, and depressed the activation
rate."*

STEPHEN P. LLOYD
Canadian Direct Marketing News

By now, you are aware that database marketing and the web are zooming ahead in some areas and failing in others. It is not all win-win. Some marketers have lost their jobs by betting on database marketing or the web in areas where they did not work.

Before you risk your career, let's see if there are some rules that will guide us to success, and steer us away from failure, in this new marketing mode. To begin with, you must pick the product situation where database marketing is likely to work.

Picking the Right Product Situation

There are really two separate (but related) forms of database marketing:

- *Relationship building* with current customers
- *Marketing to prospects* selected by developing profiles of the most profitable customers

This second activity is much easier to succeed in than the first. Marketing to prospects, when done right, always involves a test. Before a rollout of 1 million, you do a 20,000 test, study the results to determine the factors leading to response, and mail smarter on the rollout. If you follow the rules, you can't fail. There is no problem in this area.

Relationship-building database marketing or web site construction is the area where most mistakes are made. Why? Because you are supposed to treat customers differently from unknown prospects. You must recognize them and remember what they have bought and what they have told you. It is much harder to see the immediate results when dealing with customers. You can count the number of customers that you have acquired. How do you count the number that you have not lost through attrition? It takes months or years before relationship building begins to pay off. By the time you discover that it doesn't pay off, millions of dollars may have been wasted. That's why this chapter is so important.

Relationship Marketing

The principle that underlies relationship marketing is the same as that of any free-market transaction: Both parties make a profit. Why would I want to have a relationship with the makers of my shirts, shoes, or soap?

I really don't. I don't care enough about these products to want to waste time corresponding with their manufacturers. But, at heart, the main reason that I don't want to be on their databases is that I can't visualize any particular benefit to me in the relationship.

If the shirt manufacturer could come up with something really personally interesting, I might listen. If the manufacturer offered to sell me a high-quality shirt that said "Hughes" on the pockets, or AMH on the cuffs, I might listen. But life is too short to spend it corresponding with the makers of the 1,000 or more different products that I use in any given month.

As I look around my office, I see that I am using Dixon pencils, a Swingline stapler, a Texas Instruments calculator, a Westclox clock, a Radio Shack diskette case holding 3M diskettes, a Scan desk, and a Rubbermaid wastepaper basket. I don't want to hear from any of these companies. I can't imagine what they could say to me that would be worth the time it would take me to open the envelope and read, or to answer their telephone call. Not all customer relationships can result in a mutual profit. Most of them, in fact, probably cannot.

On the other hand, I am typing on a computer from Gateway and using a Hewlett Packard printer. I certainly hope that they have me on their databases and correspond with me about upgrades and accessories. I can see how I could profit from a relationship with them.

When American Airlines writes to me, I pay attention. I earned several free trips to Chile and England on American, and I am working on more. I can see the profit to me in the relationship. When Microsoft or Intuit sends me notices of upgrades, because I am on their databases, I will read them, and probably buy the upgrades.

I bought a Honda Odyssey. I love it. I am about ready for a new one. If I were to get a letter from Honda about the new models, you can bet that I would read it, and would probably go for a test drive if one were offered. But, of course, Honda does not have a database. There is no possibility of it writing to me because it doesn't write to anybody. I would love to have a relationship with Honda, but it doesn't want to have a relationship with me.

Relationship marketing is like courtship and marriage. In the beginning, there is often unfamiliarity or indifference. There are plenty of courtships that begin when an unlikely boy forces his attentions on an indifferent girl; the girl discovers some good features in the boy that she had not noticed before. They fall in love, get married, and live happily ever after. Most successful databases begin like that.

But not all marriages or web site relationships are successful. For a marketing relationship or a marriage to last, both parties have to want the relationship and want it to last. They have to see some value in staying together. Both parties have to make a profit from the exchange of communications, services, or products.

Database marketing that is designed to maintain a relationship works wonderfully in some areas and does not work at all in others. Let's look at the lists in Figures 15-1 and 15-2 and see how they illustrate our general principles.

I published these lists in the first edition of this book. I thought then that some marketers with products on the "won't work" list would write me or call me up telling me of a very successful case where a profitable relationship was built with one of these "won't work" products. I heard from thousands of readers since then, but no one has challenged the list. An imaginative marketer can easily prove me wrong. My purpose in the two lists is simply to alert you to the problems, and encourage you to think especially carefully, if you have a "won't work" product, how you are going to make money with your database.

Underlying these two lists is a general principle:

> Relationship marketing works when the provider can supply sufficient benefits to the customer to make it worth the customer's while to modify his or her behavior. At the same time, the average customer has to be in a position to modify his or her behavior in ways which benefit the provider, and which exceed the provider's costs in creating and maintaining the relationship.

To explain this in my case, I will be willing to play my part in a relationship with a supplier of products and services if I can see some benefit to me which is greater than the work I have to do or the money I have to pay: filling out survey forms, answering the telephone, buying products, etc. As a customer, I have to make a profit from the relationship, or I won't play.

Suppliers, on the other hand, have to be able to increase the lifetime value of their customers by means of the relationship-building activity. Let's take a specific case: my Swingline stapler.

I have had this stapler on my desk for more than 10 years. It is a heavy, solidly built, excellent product that is still working as well as when I bought it at an office supply store. It probably cost about $25. Swingline, as far as I know, does not have a database, and if it does, I am not on it. I don't need another stapler. I need staples occasionally, which I buy from the office supply store. Would I buy them direct from

Products	Services
Automobiles	Auto service
Baby products	Banks and financial services
Books, records, video	Business to business
Business to business	Communications
Children's food products	Credit cards
Computers	Diet and health centers
Department stores	Doctors and dentists
Diet food products	Entertainment
Drug stores	Home maintenance services
Florists	Hospitals and physicians
Fuels and utilities	Insurance
Gasoline and car care	Lawyers
Gardening supplies	Medical care and glasses
Heating and air conditioning	Membership and non-profits
Lumber and hardware	Restaurants
Magazines	Sporting events
Pharmaceuticals	Supermarkets
Sewing and knitting supplies	TV and radio
	Travel and related services

Figure 15-1. Relationship marketing possibilities.

Products	Services
Apparel and upkeep	Contractors
Appliances and electronics	Electricians
Building supplies	Home remodeling and additions
Carpets	Locksmiths
Food (exceptions)	Movers
Furniture and home furnishings	Painters
Glass and mirrors	Paving
Linen and draperies	Pest control
Office supplies and equipment	Real estate
Packaged goods (exceptions)	Roofers
Toys and sporting goods	Towing
Water treatment	Wallpaper

Figure 15-2. Difficult relationship marketing situations.

Swingline if it wrote to me? Perhaps. But I buy them once a year and spend less than $5. Swingline's profit on the sale would not justify the cost of the database or the communication costs.

The person that should be on the Swingline database is the owner of the office supply store. He, more than I, is responsible for this piece of equipment on my desk. I bought the best thing that he had. If he had featured some other brand at the time, I would have bought that.

The conclusion: Thousands of products find their way into consumers' hands, for which the manufacturer should not create a consumer marketing database because the consumers cannot profit by being on the database. Since that is so, neither can the manufacturer profit by maintaining it. The same thing applies to a web site. Why would I want to check out the Swingline web site? What would be in it for me?

Alternative Database Uses

On the other hand, there are circumstances in which the customer database or web site for such mundane objects as a high-quality stapler might be profitable after all.

If Swingline has a broad line of office products grouped in a catalog, it might send me the catalog, since my ownership of an expensive stapler probably indicates that I have an active business, which might need office supplies.

If Swingline does not have such a catalog, but it has captured the names and addresses of the owners of its top-of-the line staplers, it could rent these names and addresses to someone who needed a list of likely office supply prospects.

In the absence of such alternative uses, there are many products like my stapler for which a relationship-building consumer database will probably never have any economic value to either party.

Further Criteria for Success

Just being on the "might work" list does not guarantee that web sites and customer databases will be profitable. There are other criteria. Databases and web sites for relationship-building purposes are more likely to be profitable if some or all of the following are true:

■ *The provider has a well-thought-through marketing program.* Such programs are hard to think up. There must be a creative marketing
director who has designed a program that will return real benefits to
the customer in exchange for which the customer will furnish real
benefits to the provider: loyalty and repeat business resulting in
increasing long-term value.

■ *There must be a payment system for the product or service that makes it easy to
get names, addresses, and purchase behavior.* This is true in utilities, transportation, communications, banks and financial services, insurance,
magazines, credit and gasoline cards, etc. The providers of these products and services have to have the name and address of the customer
to provide the service in the first place. Many of them mail monthly
statements. This type of activity leads very easily into the building and
maintenance of a customer database. Unfortunately, with most products, purchase behavior is much more difficult to capture.

This is the central idea behind POS membership programs, in which
customers at a supermarket, hardware chain, office supply store, or
department store use their membership card when making purchases.
The membership database record in the store then begins to accumulate records of all their purchases.

This is a great idea in theory. In practice, though, few people have
been able to find a sufficiently profitable use for the data to pay the
cost of capturing and storing them. We are talking about billions of
transactions made by the American public every week. Just retaining
those data is a multimillion dollar enterprise. What are the profitable
payoffs that will come from using the data?

"Aha! Arthur Hughes has just spent $3.59 for a box of staples for the
Swingline stapler he bought five years ago." Think about it: Who can
make any money from that piece of information? I can't think of anyone, and neither can you. If I had just bought a pair of skis, a recre-
ational vehicle, a baby crib, or a saddle for a horse, I can think of
many profitable uses for the data. But these items are needles in the
POS haystack. There are less expensive ways of capturing them than
vacuuming up all the data in all the transactions in America every
night and storing those data in computers.

■ *The product or service involves periodic repeat purchases plus name capture
at point of sale.* This is true for automobiles, automobile servicing,
medical care, pharmaceuticals, diet and health centers, and home
services (such as heating and air conditioning, plumbing, lawn care).

- *There is a definite affinity group from which a database can be constructed.* This applies to parents of new babies; sports enthusiasts; nonprofits; buyers of gardening, knitting, sewing, music, and supplies; etc.

- *The provider can construct a frequency reward system with significant benefits for both parties.* This applies, of course, to the travel industry, to department stores, to supermarkets, and to the entertainment industry.

Why the "Won't Work" List Exists

What is wrong with the products and services on the second list that makes them unlikely candidates for relationship-building database marketing? A couple of factors apply to most of these products and services:

1. *The product is a commodity with a markup that is too narrow to finance relationship-building activity.*

2. *The purchase is made seldom and unpredictably.* Furniture is a good example. A family pays $2,000 for dining room furniture. It may last 5 years, 10 years, 20 years. Furniture is usually purchased from a dealer that displays the products of many different manufacturers in one location. Can a relationship be developed by the manufacturer of one specific brand of furniture and the customer that will assure that that brand of furniture is considered when the next major purchase takes place? It seems like a long shot to me.

The furniture manufacturer's database should be a business-to-business one that the company uses to market to furniture dealers. On the other hand, furniture retailers (not manufacturers) can use a consumer prospect database to good advantage (see below).

In the case of lumber and hardware, there exists the handyman who spends his life puttering and fixing up his house or boat or car. If the retailer can locate such people and build a database of them, a profitable relationship can ensue. Can the *manufacturer* of these products profit from building a relationship? In some cases, yes. Black and Decker and Skilcraft, both of which have a wide line of power tools, could build a relationship by using surveys combined with catalogs, a web site, or a newsletter on carpentry. There are always new tools coming out which handymen want to learn about. A few years ago, one company made a good business of selling nuts, bolts, and screws by direct mail to handymen. From what I could tell, no attempt was made to build this into a database. Could Armstrong develop a relationship with customers who bought floor covering once which would lead to them buying floor covering a second time? Who knows? It seems unlikely to me.

To illustrate why the second list is something to worry about, let's see whether companies like Hoover or Hotpoint could profit from building a customer database and doing relationship marketing with their customers. They could get the customer's name from a registration form inside the shipping container, and could initiate a direct-mail program, selling replacement bags and attachments, leading to an announcement of new models when they become available. Would such a database be successful? The analysis that follows applies to any household appliance, such as a dishwasher, washer, dryer, refrigerator, lawn mower, room air conditioner, television, or computer.

One characteristic of such appliances is that they are seldom purchased every year. Some appliances last for 20 years or more. Most of them do not wear out rapidly. Customers buy new ones most often when they move, remodel, or purchase a second home. To begin our analysis, we have to estimate the annual repurchase rate. We start with some statistics that can be gleaned from an appliance registration database. We want to know what percentage of customers repurchase after one year, two years, three years, etc. We also want to know what percentage of the customers repurchase the same brand versus another brand. The chart in Figure 15-3 uses the formula developed at the end of Chapter 3. This formula determines the annual purchase rate for an appliance that is purchased infrequently over a number of years. The formula is:

$$RR = (RPR)^{(1/Y)}$$
$$RR = (0.35)^{(1/4)}$$
$$RR = 76.9\%$$

In this example, we are assuming that 35 percent of the people buy an appliance every four years, and they buy the same brand when they do. Figure 15-3 uses this formula for a large group of customers of a particular appliance. The chart in the figure estimates that 5 percent buy an appliance every year, 10 percent every two years, etc. The last column averages people who buy appliances after five or more years. This boils down to 40 percent buying the appliance every eight years.

Those who buy every year tend to be more loyal to the brand than those who purchase less often. The formula is used to develop the annual retention rate for each group of customers. The last line develops the

Years between Purchases of Vacuum Cleaners					
	Year 1	*Year 2*	*Year 3*	*Year 4*	*Year 5+*	*Average Years 3.6*
Customers	5.00%	10.00%	20.00%	25.00%	40.00%	100.00%
Same brand	80.00%	60.00%	50.00%	40.00%	30.00%	52.00%
Annual rate	80.00%	77.46%	79.37%	79.53%	86.03%	80.48%
Weighted	4.00%	7.75%	15.87%	19.88%	34.41%	16.38%

Figure 15-3. Vacuum cleaner purchase frequency.

weighted average of purchases by all customers. The final number, 16.38 percent, is annual sales to be expected from all customers each year. Using these numbers, let's create a lifetime value chart for our vacuum manufacturer.

As Figure 15-4 shows, we are tracking 400,000 customers who bought a vacuum cleaner for $200. Their annual retention rate is about 80 percent. About 20 percent buy parts or service. Those customers who are still loyal to the brand buy higher-priced models. It costs $4 each to create the database. Thereafter, each customer costs $1 per year to maintain the names.

Now let's do a little customer relationship marketing. We will create a web site with information on spare parts and new models with a dealer lookup. We will concentrate on relationship building, friendship, and communication. We will encourage the direct sale of filter bags, motor belts, and attachments. Figure 15-5 shows what happens to retention rates with these customer relationship management programs in place.

In the first place, our activity will accomplish two things: We will increase the number of customers who repurchase the same brand when they buy. We will also increase the frequency of repurchase. By keeping track of customers and notifying them of new models and new features, we will increase the number of those who buy a new vacuum in the third and fourth years. Figure 15-6 clearly shows the impact of these improvements on lifetime value.

As the figure shows, we have made many important improvements in sales and retention through our customer relationship management programs:

■ The retention rate has gone up from 70 percent to 85 percent in the first year.

	Year 1	Year 2	Year 3	Year 4	Year 5	Year 6
Customers	400,000	280,000	197,990	145,880	107,963	88,289
Retention rate	70.00%	70.71%	73.68%	74.01%	81.78%	74.04%
Purchase price	$200	$205	$210	$220	$225	$230
Weight	100.00%	3.50%	7.07%	14.74%	18.50%	32.71%
Purchases	$80,000,000	$2,009,000	$2,940,000	$4,729,360	$4,494,481	$6,642,354
Parts and service	$100	$105	$110	$115	$120	$125
Buying	20%	18%	16%	14%	12%	10%
Parts and service	$8,000,000	$5,292,000	$3,484,622	$2,348,671	$1,554,673	$1,103,610
Revenue	$88,000,000	$7,301,000	$6,424,622	$7,078,031	$6,049,154	$7,745,963
Costs	80.00%	75.00%	74.00%	73.00%	72.00%	71.00%
Direct costs	$70,400,000	$5,475,750	$4,754,220	$5,166,963	$4,355,391	$5,499,634
Database $4/$1	$1,600,000	$400,000	$400,000	$400,000	$400,000	$400,000
Total costs	$72,000,000	$5,875,750	$5,154,220	$5,566,963	$4,755,391	$5,899,634
Profit	$16,000,000	$1,425,250	$1,270,402	$1,511,068	$1 29 3,763	$1,846,329
Discount rate	1	1.2	1.3	1.6	1.8	2.1
NPV profit	$16,000,000	$1,228,664	$944,115	$968,078	$714,534	$879,061
Cumulative NPV profit	$16,000,000	$17,228,664	$18,172,779	$19,140,857	$19,855,391	$20,734,452
Lifetime value	$40	$43	$45	$48	$50	$52

Figure 15-4. Lifetime value of vacuum cleaner customers.

- The average repurchase price of new models has gone up (people are buying higher-priced models).
- We have persuaded a higher percentage of people to buy parts and service.
- We have sold them more parts and service when they buy.
- Annual revenue has gone up significantly each year.

Years between Purchases of Vacuum Cleaners						
Year	*1*	*2*	*3*	*4*	*8*	*Average*
Customers	5.00%	10.00%	25.00%	30.00%	30.00%	100.00%
Same brand	85.00%	60.00%	50.00%	40.00%	30.00%	53.00%
Annual rate	85.00%	77.46%	79.37%	79.53%	86.03%	81.48%
Weighted	4.25%	7.75%	19,84%	23.86%	25.81%	16.30%

Figure 15-5. Improved retention rates of vacuum customers with retention programs.

	Year 1	Year 2	Year 3	Year 4	Year 5	Year 6
Customers	400,000	340,000	263,363	209,031	166,236	143,010
Retention rate	85.00%	77.46%	79.37%	79.53%	86.03%	81.48%
Purchase price	$200	$210	$220	$230	$240	$250
Weight	100.00%	4.25%	7.75%	19.84%	23.86%	25.81%
Purchases	$80,000,000	$3,034,500	$4,488,000	$9,539,722	$9,518,614	$9,227,154
Parts and service	$105	$110	$115	$120	$130	$140
Buying	25%	23%	21%	19%	17%	15%
Parts and service	$10,500,000	$8,602,000	$6,360,213	$4,765,912	$3,673,825	$3,003,210
Revenue	$90,500,000	$11,636,500	$10,848,213	$14,305,635	$13,192,439	$12,230,364
Costs	80.00%	75.00%	74.00%	73.00%	72.00%	71.00%
Direct costs	$72,400,000	$8,727,375	$8,027,678	$10,443,113	$9,498,556	$8,683,558
Database $4/$1	$1,600,000	$400,000	$400,000	$400,000	$400,000	$400,000
CPM programs $2	$800,000	$800,000	$800,000	$800,000	$800,000	$800,000
Web site	$800,000	$800,000	$800,000	$800,000	$800,000	$800,000
Total costs	$75,600,000	$10,727,375	$10,027,678	$12,443,113	$11,498,556	$10,683,558
Profit	$14,900,000	$909,125	$820,535	$1,862,521	$1,693,883	$156,806
Discount rate	1	1.2	1.3	1.6	1.8	2.1
NPV profit	$14,900,000	$783,728	$609,792	$1,193,239	$935,516	$736,454
Cum NPV profit	$14,900,000	$15,683,728	$16,293,520	$17,486,759	$18,422,275	$19,158,729
Lifetime value	$37	$39	$41	$44	$46	$48

Figure 15-6. LTV of vacuum cleaner customers with retention programs in place.

On the other hand, these very real improvements have come at a cost. We have spent an average of $2 per customer per year on relationship-building programs. This is rock-bottom minimum. We have set up a web site at an annual cost of $800,000. These two programs cost us $1.6 million per year. As a result, lifetime value has gone down. Look at the final score card, in Figure 15-7.

You can see that we are getting deeper and deeper into a hole. There is no way that I can see that database marketing can work with rarely purchased appliances or packaged goods. I would love to say that it works, but it just doesn't. The connection is too indirect. The benefits to the customer are too small. People are just not interested enough to correspond with their vacuum cleaner or dishwasher manufacturer all

	Year 1	Year 2	Year 3	Year 4	Year 5	Year 6
Old LTV	$40.00	$43.07	$45.43	$47.85	$49.64	$51.84
New LTV	$37.25	$39.21	$04.73	$43.72	$46.06	$47.90
Difference	($2.75)	($3.86)	($4.70)	($4.14)	($3.58)	($3.94)
Times 400,000	($1,100,000)	($1,544,935)	($1,879,259)	($1,654,098)	($1,433,116)	($1,575,723)

Figure 15-7. Results of investment in vacuum cleaner customer retention program.

the time. If the appliance works OK, most people are not willing to go the expense and trouble of buying a new one on the basis of direct-mail messages. They will buy a new one when the old one breaks down or when they move, but not when they get a nice, folksy letter. Too bad.

The database that the vacuum cleaner company should be counting on is the retail store database. The retail stores are the ones that tell their customers, "You know, there are a lot of good ones out there, but nothing beats a Hoover." That sentence alone can make or break the company's future. How do you get the dealer to say that? Database marketing can work with dealers. Let's not get too optimistic about what it can accomplish with consumers.

I think that you can see that there are no definite, firm lines that can be drawn. For any product that you select, it is possible to visualize how a profitable relationship building database *might* be constructed. Whether it *can* be constructed depends on the economics of the product and the creativity of the marketers involved.

Summary

- Using database marketing to find new prospects is relatively easy. Building a profitable long-term relationship with existing customers is often rather difficult.

- In some product situations, relationship marketing may not be possible at all. A list of the easy and difficult products is helpful as a starting point, but keep in mind that the list is probably full of holes.

- To be successful, relationship building requires a well-thought-through marketing program; an easy way to get names, addresses, and purchase behavior; and repeat purchases with name capture at the point of sale, an affinity group, and some sort of system that benefits both parties.

- Even the best database program can be defeated by mistakes in execution, which occur all too often.

- Seldom-purchased appliances may not be profitable candidates for database marketing, although a web site would not be inappropriate. It is possible to use lifetime value analysis to determine whether database marketing would work before serious money is expended on building a database.

Executive Quiz 14

Answers to quiz questions can be found in Appendix B.

1. The U.S. air miles program was inferior to the Canadian program because:

    a. It required proof of purchase clipping and mailing

    b. There was a mag stripe and UPC code on the Canadian card that the Americans didn't have

    c. The U.S. program was a packaged goods strategy

    d. All of the above

    e. None of the above

2. Why are more mistakes made in relationship building than in profiling and prospecting?

    a. In relationship building, results take longer to show up.

    b. Tests are seldom possible in relationship building.

    c. Neural networks are of no use in relationship building.

    d. In large prospect mailings, mistakes are seldom made.

    e. All of the above.

3. Successful relationship marketing requires that:

    a. The buyer make a profit from being on the database

    b. The seller make a profit from the database

    c. There is communication between the seller and the buyer

    d. All of the above

    e. None of the above

4. Which of the following is an unlikely area for successful relationship marketing?

    a. Sewing and knitting

    b. Prescription drugs

    c. Apparel manufacturing

    d. Gasoline

    e. Insurance

5. Who should probably not be kept on the marketing database of a medical thermometer manufacturer?

    a. Consumers

    b. Physicians

    c. Nurses

    d. Medical supply companies

    e. All of the above

6. Which is not on the list of requirements for a profitable relationship database?

    a. A valid marketing program

    b. Benefits to the consumers on the list

    c. An easy way to get names and addresses

    d. All retail transactions stored in the database

    e. An affinity group from which the database can be built

7. To make a successful relationship-building program, it is best if:

    a. The markup is rather small

    b. The product is highly competitive in price

    c. The product is identical to the competition

    d. The date of a future purchase is predictable

    e. All of the above

8. Successful database activity usually affects all but one of the following:

    a. Discount rate

    b. Retention rate

    c. Annual sales rate

    d. Referral rate

    e. Lifetime value

16

Choosing Business Partners

*Partnership produces a long array of benefits in the
management of change. ... State Farm refers to its
agents as marketing partners, and that's more than
just a pretty phrase. Neither agent nor company can
survive without the other; for either to prosper, both
must meet their separate responsibilities with energy
and skill. ... By structuring partnerships with the
right value-sharing incentives, the company has managed to thrive for more than seventy years, creating the
largest network of independent business locations in
North America—half again as many as McDonald's
or 7-11.*

FREDERICK REICHHELD
The Loyalty Effect

Why Outsource?

If you have been to one of the National Center for Database Marketing's
conferences, you will notice that most of the success stories involve outsourcing to external partners. While anyone can do some form of database marketing, those who are most successful seek outside help. What
functions can you outsource?

- Strategy development
- Designing and building a database
- Customer service and communications
- Telesales
- Building a web site

- Maintaining a database and a web site
- Fulfillment

Why would you want to outsource functions to external partners? There are a number of important reasons:

- *Experience.* Many companies have designed, built, and maintained databases for other companies in the past. If you get them to help you, you will get the benefit of their experience—the mistakes they have made in the past which they will try not to repeat, and the new ideas that others have thought up which you may pick up from them.
- *Expertise.* Some companies have achieved unique knowledge of particular fields, such as financial services, pharmaceutical direct to consumer, business to business, loyalty programs, direct response TV, or web advertising, that you simply could not replicate in-house in a short time.
- *Speed.* If you are going to set up a database, a web site, or a teleservices operation inside your company, it will take a lot longer to do it internally than if you go to an outside experienced provider. Internally, you will have to hire skilled people and train them. This takes time and money. Outsourced functions can usually get started in half the time.
- *Economy.* If you compare the cost of doing these functions inside with doing them at an outside source, you will find that in many cases you can save money. To do database marketing, there is a lot of software to be purchased, and people to be trained to use it. This is expensive.
- *Entrepreneurship.* Building inside usually involves full-time people. They may not all work for the marketing department. Typically, your MIS department may want to build the web site or maintain the database. When you need something done now, and not a month from now, your MIS director may say, "I have two programmers out sick, and a four-month backlog of regular work. You will just have to wait." And she is probably right. But if you tell your external service bureau partner to undertake a new project, she is likely to say, "Great! When do I start?" Why the difference? For the service bureau, this is money. She is maintaining four other databases right now. She can divert other people or take on additional contract programmers to meet your needs. That is not so easy inside. It is easy to throw your weight around with a contract service bureau. It is not as easy to do that inside your company.

To outsource a function, you have to find someone to do business with, and that is where you need a request for proposals, or an RFP. In this chapter, we will give you some suggestions on how to write such a document. First, however, you might want to consider outsourcing the RFP function as well.

Outsourcing the RFP Function

There are consultants who write RFPs for other companies. Using such consultants can save you many weeks of one-time-only learning—learning that you will not need to use again. Using the skills and resources of someone who has done the same function two or three times for other companies can save you time and money. Rather than provide a list of such experts in this book, which could rapidly become obsolete, I suggest that you consult the web site of the Database Marketing Institute, www.dbmarketing.com. The Institute maintains a register of reputable consultants who can help you through the processes described in this chapter.

Creating an RFP Committee

Any significant RFP will require some sort of internal committee to prepare it and to select the winners. Typically, a committee will consist of people from marketing, MIS, sales, customer service, contracting, and, if available, your direct agency. Marketing should chair the committee to keep it focused on the marketing goals.

Qualifying the Participants

Your first job is to decide whom to send the RFP to. You can solve this problem by calling people you know in the industry and asking them. Attend meetings sponsored by the National Center for Database Marketing, where you can meet with a dozen companies over a couple of days. Consult the Database Marketing Institute's web site, www.dbmarketing.com, to learn the names of several firms. It is important to prequalify the participants so as not to waste your time and that of unqualified firms. You might consider sending out a one-page e-mail or letter survey form that would ask some key questions to determine if the recipient companies have the skills and the interest in your project. For those who respond positively, you might follow up with a confidentiality agreement, getting this signed before you send out the RFP.

Don't send out too many RFPs. Six is plenty. What is wrong with sending out 10 or 15 or more? Two things: You will be wasting the time of scores of people in answering your RFP. And you will be wasting possibly weeks of time of your committee members, who will have to review thick responses from far too many companies. Trim the project down to size before you send anything out. Do your homework in advance, not afterward.

Writing the Scope of Work

The first step in an RFP is a definition of the work to be done. A well-developed scope of work will guide your thinking and actions, and help your prospective partners understand what is required. There are several parts to a scope of work.

- *Background.* You need to describe your company, its products, and its customers. Start a few years back, and tell how you got to where you are today. Explain whether you are in a growth phase or a mature phase. Talk about how products are sold. Is there a channel of distributors and retailers? Are there independent or company-owned dealers or agents? How are you organized to sell? Describe the marketing staff and the sales staff. If there is a database already, describe it. How big is it? What data are in it? How is it updated and maintained? Who uses it, and what for? What is the culture of your company, and where is it going?

- *The problem.* You would not be writing this RFP today if there were not some problem to be solved. How did the problem come about? Is it caused by external competition? By a change in the market? What steps have already been made to solve this problem, and why did they not work out?

- *The solution.* Describe how you think that the problem can be solved by using external resources. What do you think that outsiders can do to help? Explain what changes in the database, or the web site, or customer service, or inside sales, or sales force automation, you think would lead to a satisfactory solution to the problem. Give your ideal answer.

- *The goal.* You need a one-paragraph statement of the goal of your database marketing program. *Examples:*
  Reducing attrition by 5 percent within the next year
  Increasing customer lifetime value by 10 percent in the next year
  Increasing the customer base by 20 percent per year for the next three years
  This goal should give a meaning and purpose to your entire scope of work.

- *Your strategy.* To support your goal, the scope of work must spell out an overall strategy, outlining how you are going to get from here to there. The specific project for which you are seeking assistance may be as mundane as "producing thank-you letters" or "responding to DRTV ads." The strategy indicates how this particular activity is aimed at achieving the specified goal. Without this strategy statement, your outsource partners may not see the real purpose in what they are doing. You may miss your objective because the implementers don't have the full picture. There is a second reason why this strategy statement is important. By putting it in writing, you may realize that what you are asking the outsourcers to do cannot achieve the goals you have set. You may have to change the scope of work before you issue the RFP.

- *The customers.* Provide a description of your customers. What are they like? What problems have they had in working with your company? What do they want from your company that they are not getting? Why are the defectors leaving? What would you like to do in the way of communications with customers that would be better than what you are doing right now?

- *The size of the work.* How big a solution are you looking for right now? Most companies make the mistake of thinking too big. They look for some huge comprehensive solution that will take several years to implement, and could pose great funding difficulties. You are much better off coming up with a master design that begins with only one small step for mankind. Database marketing is best accomplished by a series of small successes, rather than massive reorganizations. Lay out a series of small improvements that you think that an outside firm can undertake within a few months, which will demonstrate to your management that real progress is being made. In the course of implementing these small improvements, you will undoubtedly see new projects that should be carried out. These could be amendments to the original contract.

- *Break the job down into phases.* If the project is very large, it is better to break it down into phases. You can scope out Phase 1 in great detail, and list what will happen in Phases 2 and 3 in less detail, since you can get separate bids on them later. The winner of Phase 1 will probably get Phases 2 and 3 as well, but that is off in the future. If the winner of Phase 1 does not work out, you can bid out the other phases. It gives you much more flexibility than bidding the whole thing out at once. Once you get started on database projects, you will be learning a lot, and changing your strategy and direction based on what you learn. So the phase idea may make very good business sense.

- *Quantitative measures.* You have to give your prospective partners some idea of the numbers they are dealing with. If you are thinking of a call center, estimate the number of calls per day, per week, per year. If it is a database, tell how many records are in the database now and how many will be added each month. Provide a sample of the data, on a diskette, which you provide to all the bidders so they can get a feel of what you are talking about.

- *Organizational location.* Who is going to use the data? Describe the divisions of your company, and what they will do with the data. If possible, provide a flowchart that explains where the data come from, who works on the data, and where the data go. Explain the mission of each group: "Inquiries go to the telemarketers, who qualify them and set up appointments for the sales force. They enter data into the database, which is used by the fulfillment staff to send out brochures. The data generate an automatic e-mail or fax that thanks the inquirer for the call and reminds him of the appointment."

- *The timing.* When do you plan to begin the project, and when do you expect to see the first results? Lay out a time line that covers the first year of the project, so that the bidders will see what resources they have to commit, and when.

- *The pricing scheme.* This is a most difficult requirement. You will be getting bids from several possible partners. You want to be able to compare apples to apples. It would be helpful, therefore, for you to give them some sort of numerical measurements to price out. You might ask the bidders how they prefer to submit the prices: Answer your questions, submit their own price section, or fill in a spreadsheet or table. To be sure that the prices are comparable, each bidder should submit one table that shows the total amounts to be spent in Year 1 and in Year 2. That will help you to understand what each is suggesting.

Examples of individual price comparisons might be:

Database updating, based on the number of records involved

Web site creation and maintenance

Fulfillment costs per piece

Modeling costs per hour

- *The budget.* You probably should not announce your budget in the RFP, but you have to have agreement from management about the amount of money that is budgeted for this project before you send anything out. If there is no budget, do not send out the RFP. The size of the budget will affect the scope of work. You simply cannot create a practical RFP without a budget. If asked by the bidders, it is helpful to tell them a range. "We expect to spend between $300,000 and $500,000 on this project during this next year." If you say that, you will eliminate bids in the $1+ million range, which are far beyond your budget. It will also encourage some bidders to think of creative ways to end up in the low end of your range.

- *A competition is a good idea.* If the project involves cleaning your records and providing access using the bidder's system, you might create a file of 25,000 of your customers (complete with all the messiness and duplications that currently exist), and give the same file to each of the bidders, asking them to show you what they can do with your actual data. A competition like this can really separate the sheep from the goats.

- *Evaluation criteria.* Tell the prospective partners how you will go about evaluating their responses, including any weighting that you want to include: "innovation 40 percent, experience 30 percent, price 30 percent," etc. Tell them how long you will take to review their RFPs and when you expect to announce a winner.

- *A confidentiality requirement.* If your scope of work is any good, it will contain proprietary information about your company. Before the bidders are allowed to see it, they should have signed a confidentiality agreement. Your RFP simply refers to this agreement.

Rules of the RFP

- *Due date.* Specify exactly when the responses are due, including date and time of day. Be sure to allow at least 30 days from the date you send out the RFP.

- *Questions.* Announce when you send out the RFP whether questions will be permitted (you should), and how bidders can ask the questions and of whom, and whether the questions may be asked in writing or at a meeting or by phone. Unless your project is very large (and we do not recommend large projects—see below), you should entertain telephone or e-mail questions, with a cutoff date. By that date, you should send out an e-mail letter to all the bidders with a summary of the questions and the answers. It is important that you be fair to everyone, and that you appear to be fair. You will want to do business with these people in the future.

- *Digital submission.* In the old days, responses to RFPs arrived at the last minute by FedEx, with 10 or more copies. That was before the days of the Internet. Today, companies accept proposals by e-mail or through a web response device. We are getting very digital these days. The advantage in a digital submission is that you can easily put several proposals on a spreadsheet to compare them. We are database marketers. Let's be up to date. You may want to have the responses in two separate reports: the work proposal and the pricing. Sometimes it is useful to decide on the proposal without being influenced by the prices.

- *Where to send.* If you do insist on hard-copy proposals (which is very old fashioned), tell the bidders where to send the proposal, providing a FedEx-compatible address (not a post office box), since many of the proposals will come in at the very last minute.

- *Extensions.* Provide in the rules of the road whether extensions of time will be permitted and how to go about getting an extension. You may not think that this is important, but it almost always comes up, so think it through in advance.

- *Bidders list.* Decide whether you will release a list of the bidders to the bidders. I think that it is a good idea and could help in the bidding process. I would issue the list early enough so that all bidders can know what they are up against before they bid. It will help you to get relevant and comparable offers.

Your Partners

If you are going to accomplish the objectives spelled out in the scope of work, you will need your contractors to become your partners. Too many inexperienced marketers look on their outside help as "vendors." They tell them as little as possible about the overall project, saying, in effect, "Don't ask too many questions. Just do what I tell you, and shut up."

You won't get their hearts and minds involved in your database project if you treat them as vendors. Without their hearts and minds, you may miss some vital ideas about improving your customer relationships. In turn, this may make your project less effective than it could be, or could even get you into real trouble. To wit, two examples:

- *Partner example.* A partner maintained the database for a Fortune 500 company that was doing DRTV. The program got 1 million responses in the first six months, for which the partner did the fulfillment. It was great business and highly profitable. There was only one problem. The people answering the ads were the wrong people. They were not buying the product. No one at the company asked the partner about this. The partner's dilemma: Should we tell them about it? The partner decided that they had to. Some of the company's marketing staff were thankful for the information. But others thought that the partner had exceeded the contract, which was to do the fulfillment and shut up. What do you think?

- *Vendor example.* Another company asked its vendor to select a group of preferred customers, who were to receive special recognition and benefits. The vendor was not asked to set up a control group. The vendor was not told what was to be done with the preferred customers, but it thought the absence of a control group was bad database practice. On the other hand, pointing this out might anger the direct agency that had set up the program—and that considered the partner a mere vendor. The vendor decided to keep quiet. Later the direct agency was fired when the absence of a control group was shown to undermine the validity of the results. What should the vendor have done?

Your objective in the RFP, therefore, is to find a partner that feels as involved in the success of your database marketing or web site project as you do. How can you do that? The psychology of management tells us that your effectiveness as a manager is determined by the extent that you allow your employees to influence you. If you listen to what your employees say, and use your influence to carry out the good suggestions that they make, then they will feel that they are an important part of the company. They will put their hearts and minds into the work. You will be successful as a supervisor. The same principles apply to outsourcing functions. Treat these companies as partners, and you will reap significant benefits.

Key Questions

How can you find out if the people bidding on your job have the imagination, drive, resources, skills, and chemistry necessary to become your partners? There is a simple answer: Treat them as professionals. Ask them these questions:

- *Company history.* Who are they? What have they done in the past. What is their company philosophy? Ask them to provide references.
- *Their solution to the problem.* Have them describe, in their own words, how they propose to go about carrying out the scope of work.
- *The training involved.* Most database or Internet projects involve training for company employees in the new system. The response should describe this training and provide the pricing for it.
- *Who owns the software?* Since proprietary software is usually involved, the response should indicate what that software is and who owns it. The proposal should spell out how the updates to the software will be provided and who is supporting the software.
- *Innovative ideas.* Ask them to describe some innovative ideas that they have for your project or that they have introduced in working with other clients.
- *Biographies of the leaders.* Have them tell you about one or two of the key people whom you will be working with and what their background is. There is a caution here. If you have a big project, the partner will have to hire additional workers. Few firms have enough employees sitting around doing nothing, waiting to see if they win a contract with you. Don't insist, therefore, that you know, in advance, all the people who will be working on your job. If they are able to tell you, it will probably be a lie anyway.
- *References.* You absolutely must have a list of names and telephone numbers from companies that have used your prospective partner's services in the past. Call these people up and ask them what it is like working with this partner.
- *Executive summary.* Tell them to write a one-page summary listing the key benefits of the system they propose.
- *Project costs.* They should use the scheme that you have laid out for the project. However, by all means, if they request it, permit them to give you their pricing in addition on some other basis that they feel more comfortable with.

What Not to Do

RFPs can become very deadly bores for everyone involved. In 20 years of direct marketing, I have seen some really horrible examples. Here is what to avoid:

- *Too many questions.* Many RFPs are designed by a committee. When you get 20 people together, they are apt to throw in anything that they can think of. The questions can go on for 10 pages or more. To get good responses to an RFP, keep the questions to a minimum: one page or less.

- *Too many pages.* Many RFPs are up to 100 pages in length. They include all sorts of legal restrictions such as antidiscrimination, environmental protection, etc. A good solution to this problem is to have your legal team draft a separate document containing all the legal restrictions that they want. Ask the bidders to sign this document. Then put a clause in the RFP referring to the fact that the document is signed, and covers the work to be done under this RFP.

- *Covering too much in one document.* As I already pointed out, successful database marketing consists of a number of small successes, which lead up to a great overall success. If you make the project too big and comprehensive at the beginning, you may have trouble getting the money for it, or finding one external supplier that can do everything that is required. You should break the work down into phases.

- *Not enough time to fill it out.* Many RFPs require that the responses come in within two weeks. That is not enough time. For a good RFP you should allow 30 days. You will then have solid, well-thought-through responses. Some companies just don't bid on documents where the time frame is too short. They may be your best partners.

- *Boring.* Database marketing should be fun for the marketer and for the customer. We are going to use the data in our database to delight the customer with unexpected recognition and relationships. Our employees will be happy with the system because they will feel the goodwill coming to them from the delighted customers. Your RFP should reflect the joy and enthusiasm that comes from successful customer relationship management. If your document is boring and puts people to sleep, your partners may get the wrong idea about your company or your project. If your RFP is boring, rewrite it before it goes anywhere.

- *No money*. Some companies make the mistake of issuing an RFP before there is any approved budget within the company for the activities to be covered under the RFP. This is a terrible waste of time for your company and for the many partners that you get to bid on your project. Some marketers think, apparently, that the RFP process will jump-start their marketing program. The winning partner will be so impressive that management will cough up the money. This seldom happens. Why not? Because RFPs that have no budget soon get out of control. The committee members put anything into it that they can dream up. Since there is no budget, there is little reason for leaving anything out. The final monstrosity looks exciting to outside partners, but it is all a sham. It will hurt the reputation of your company in the database marketing community, and make it more difficult later to get good partners to pay attention to you.

- *Scam RFP*. Sometimes a company has decided to build its database inside with MIS. To be sure that the project is well designed and cost-effective, it issues an RFP, getting outside prospective partners to bid, hoping that they can come up with some innovative ideas. The marketing staff have no intention of awarding the project to anyone outside, since it is already "wired" for MIS. This is a fraud and a deception. If you are a self-respecting database marketer, you should have nothing to do with such a deceitful scheme.

- *Gullibility*. The RFP process can generate lies, mistruths, and exaggerations. Take everything you are told with a pound or two of salt. Question the references closely and get to the bottom of any claim. If it sounds too good to be true, it probably is.

Evaluating the Results

If you have drafted a long, boring RFP with too many questions and legal paragraphs, now is when you will pay for it. You will have to review six or eight thick and boring responses. Every member of your committee will have to read through hundreds of pages of boring responses., You will have to use a spreadsheet to compare the results. This may take you a couple of weeks if your documents are too voluminous. Finally, you get your committee together and pick out the finalists.

Try to stick to your schedule. Most companies fail to do this. They get the responses in by October 15, announcing that they will make a decision by November 1. In fact, the evaluation process is much more complicated than they thought. There is no decision until late in January. By this time, they have missed the schedule for the early spring launch. The winner will have to race to get going, skipping several important steps. The project will be in trouble from the start.

Meeting with the Finalists

The last step is a half-day session with each of the finalists. Before these sessions, your committee should agree on a simple list of evaluation criteria, based on what they have seen in the RFP responses. Don't pay the expenses of the bidders who come to your meeting. Let them get there on their own. The atmosphere should be cheerful, not formal. After all, these may be your partners for years to come. See how you relate to them. See how interesting and innovative they are. Let them do any kind of presentation they want. Have a nice long question-and-answer session after their presentation.

Before the meeting, let everyone know how much time is available for the meeting. The time should be the same for all the bidders. Let them know what you want them to do at the meeting (one hour for presentation, one hour for questions). Let them know what is available for them to use, such as a PC projector, or monitor, or outside telephone line.

When the last presentation is over, have your committee meeting right away. If possible, have the interviews in the first part of the week and the committee meeting in the last part of the same week when everything is fresh in everyone's mind. Make a decision. Announce it. Get started.

The Contract

When you have selected a partner, that is not the end of the process—it is the beginning. You need to draw up a contract that incorporates all the concepts of the winning partner's proposal. That may take some time. It is a good idea to begin work immediately based on a purchase order from your company, so valuable time is not lost while the lawyers fight over detailed provisions. Time is of the essence. You are not building relationships with your customers while you haggle over contract wording.

The Transition Team

To hit the ground running, you need a single point of contact in both companies. It should be someone who has authority to make decisions and to get answers. One of the first problems will be to get MIS to provide the essential data: the customer database and the definitions of the fields. Sometimes that takes *months*! Knowing that you will have this problem, you should begin to plan for the transition long before you have finally selected a partner. MIS may drag its feet because it wanted the project in the first place, and is unwilling to help the partner. You may have to go to a higher level to get this problem resolved.

In the early weeks, you will be inundated with detailed questions:

"What is the format for the product codes?"

"How can you tell which region a customer is in?"

"The format for the customer data changed last year. Where is the format for the old data?"

These questions have never come up before. You don't know the answers, *and nobody else does either*! Your business partner will have to get these answers, or the project will never get off the ground. Be prepared for the questions, and figure out a way to get rapid answers.

Summary

- Successful database marketing and web development make use of external business partners that do a variety of outsourced functions, such as construction and maintenance of the database or web page, customer service, and fulfillment. These companies should be partners, not vendors.

- Outsourcing contributes experience, speed, economy, and entrepreneurship.

- The scope of work of the RFP should contain a definition of the problem, goals, strategy, quantitative measures, timing, and pricing.

- You should have a budget for the RFP, and send the RFP out to no more than four recipients, whom you narrow to two or three after the review.

- Don't make the RFP too long, ask too many questions, or make it too comprehensive.

- Give people enough time to fill out the response. Don't make the RFP boring. Make sure that you have enough money to pay for it.

- When you have narrowed your search to two or three firms, have them come in for a presentation, pick one, and move ahead rapidly.

Executive Quiz 15

Answers to quiz questions can be found in Appendix B.

1. Which function(s) should you consider for outsourcing?
   a. Strategy development
   b. Fulfillment
   c. Web page maintenance
   d. Customer service
   e. All of the above

2. In which of the following cases should you not use an RFP?
   a. When your budget is small
   b. When MIS will build the database
   c. When your project is clearly defined
   d. When you need to save money
   e. When you need to move fast

3. Your company is very large. What is the maximum number of companies you should send an RFP to?
   a. 20
   b. 15
   c. 12
   d. 9
   e. 6

4. The budget for your database project is very large. What is your best course of action?
   a. Do the project in-house.
   b. Find a very large external supplier.
   c. Allow a couple of years for the RFP process.
   d. Break the project down into smaller pieces.
   e. None of the above.

5. Which of the following is least likely to be true of an outsourced database marketing project compared with in-house?

   a. Costs more

   b. Built more rapidly

   c. More flexible

   d. More entrepreneurial

   e. None of the above

6. If the budget for your database project has not yet been determined, what should you do with the RFP?

   a. Send it out, since the bidders may solve the funding problem.

   b. Get quotes anyway, and construct the budget from them.

   c. Postpone the RFP until you have an approved budget.

   d. Build the project in-house.

   e. None of the above.

7. What is the best way for RFP bidders to understand your data?

   a. Give them a copy of your MIS manual.

   b. Invite them to visit your data center.

   c. Send them a diskette with real data.

   d. Give them web access to your database.

   e. All of the above.

8. Why do most successful companies outsource their database projects?

   a. Cheaper

   b. Faster

   c. Enables you to profit from others' mistakes

   d. More entrepreneurial

   e. All of the above

17

Database Marketing and the Internal Struggle for Power

In a market economy at any given time, an enormous amount of ignorance stands in the way of the complete coordination of the actions and decisions of the many market participants. Innumerable opportunities for mutually beneficial exchange ... are likely to exist unperceived. Each of these opportunities also offers an opportunity for entrepreneurial profit. Each of the potential parties to each of these unexploited exchange opportunities is, as a result of the imperfection of knowledge, losing some possible benefit through the absence of coordination represented by this situation.

ISRAEL KIRZNER
Competition and Entrepreneurship (Chicago 1973), p. 217

Losing Your Champion

In our business, you have to have a champion at the top, or there will be no database marketing program. In most industries, database marketing is not the main marketing vehicle. It is something new and additional to whatever was already in place. Often it is viewed with suspicion or fear by other units in the same company. These rival units often include sales, advertising, dealers, agents, and top management. If you look good, you might make them look bad. You might steal their customers, or commissions, or bonuses, or budgets. It is dog eat dog in the corporate world.

To illustrate these principles, here is the story of a couple of guys who developed a highly successful database marketing program, only to have

397

it killed in its fourth year by a new executive who had other ideas. It is a fable of modern corporate life.

Start-Up

A few years ago, David Christensen was director of marketing for the Outboard Marine Corporation (OMC), manufacturer of the Johnson and Evinrude outboard motors. OMC had a 50 percent brand penetration in a very stable industry that had about 4,000 independent dealers nationwide. There were only two big domestic manufacturers, OMC and Mercury. Yamaha led the growing foreign competition.

David realized that database marketing was ideal for his industry. There was a finite, identifiable market of about 10 million U.S. households that owned an outboard-powered boat. OMC had a database of 2 million customers who had filled out warranty cards. In 1992 OMC decided to launch a new series of products to meet the Yamaha intrusion into the U.S. market. David called on Stanton Lewin to help him. Stanton was director of client services at LKHS, a direct response advertising agency in Chicago specializing in database marketing. Together, they were to make database marketing history.

They decided to build a database of boat owners, and use that database to drive customers to dealers. They were looking for those customers most likely to buy a new outboard in the near future. They decided to focus on saltwater boaters, because salt water was very corrosive to outboard motors. It destroyed most of them in three or four years. The new motor that OMC was launching was highly superior to any other motor in the market at that time. It was built with many stainless-steel parts, which were impervious to the corrosive effect of salt water.

The Florida Test

They began with a major test in Florida, which had a very large number of saltwater outboarders—750,000 boats were registered in the state. Their goal was to create a Florida boaters' database that would identify exactly those boaters who needed a new motor in the near future. Secondly, they wanted to do research to determine the right message and the right offer.

The database was built by combining the 750,000 registered boats in Florida with the 2 million-name OMC customer database. The data included the size, type, age, and propulsion system of the boat. From the data, they were able to pinpoint 250,000 Florida households that owned a boat that was at least three years old, was used in salt water, and was the right size for the type of outboards that they were selling. They divided the group into OMC customers and prospects.

Next step: To create an offer. David and Stanton tested seven different messages each in seven creative executions. The message positions were:

- Reliability
- Durability
- Technology
- Warranty
- Corrosion resistance
- Made in America
- Price

They tested the messages in focus groups in three cities in Florida. The winning message was technology. The new engine had more stainless steel and hence would last longer in salt water. Their slogan was: "Their warranty is written on paper. Ours is written on stainless steel." After several tests, their stroke of genius was a free gallon of oil for anyone who would bring the coupon to a dealer to check out the new motor. Outboarders use a lot of oil.

To get the program launched, they had to get the support of dealers throughout the state. If the field sales force were not on-line, such a program would not happen. They visited dealers from one end of Florida to the other to sell the idea. The dealers had to understand the program and stock plenty of oil, which was paid for by OMC. The dealer message was reinforced with trade advertising to communicate the battle cry and rally the members. Before the campaign began, they launched a dealer communications package both to remind the dealers of their commitment to stock up on oil and to reiterate the dealers' role in the program.

The direct-mail pieces, along with the fulfillment to TV and print respondents, contained local dealer names. When people called in, they were asked five questions, including when they planned to purchase. Hot leads were sent daily to the dealers, many of whom followed up by phone. The media were highly integrated. Even though the marketers used consumer ads, direct mail, television, in-store materials, and fulfillment, all media had the same look and feel.

As a part of the 250,000 selected for the mailing, 20,000 were set aside as a control group. The members of this group received no mailing, but were tracked in their purchases. The control group permitted OMC to learn the effectiveness of the entire program.

The results were dramatic. Over a 16-week period:

- The company stunned the competition with its most dynamic product launch ever.
- The efforts of David and Stanton directly increased OMC's market share for this segment by 17 points.
- For every dollar spent on the program, the company increased gross incremental profits by $1.21.

The National Rollout

Throughout the Florida test, David and Stanton kept the CFO of OMC fully informed of their efforts. It was the OMC accountants who confirmed the fact that every $1 produced $1.21. With this type of proof, they had no trouble in getting the budget necessary for a national rollout. In the second year, their marketing budget was increased by 400 percent to multimillion dollar size. They used this to create a mega-database.

Their new national database was the largest database of registered boaters in the United States. It combined 46 different sources of legacy data:

- Thirty-nine state registrations
- Two million customers
- Subscribers to publications
- Show attendees
- Demographic data from Polk

The database included 30 key element fields in all 7 million records, including:

- Type of water craft and year
- Type of propulsion and year
- Recency and frequency responder data
- Type of boating application
- Age, income, education
- Spending indexes

The database became a shared corporate resource. They did 32 mailings a year, setting aside 32 control groups to validate their results. They used it not only to sell the new motors, but also to sell parts and accessories. *The result:* They sold 24 percent more parts to the test groups than to the controls. They sent videos to dealers to educate them on the program.

Eight hundred dealers nationwide participated in the program. This group comprised the largest boat dealers in the United States. OMC mailed 2 million pieces a year for the next three years. Some dealers experienced an 8 percent response to the mailings. The average response rate was 2.83 percent. In subsequent years, the saltwater program was broadened to bass boats, freshwater fishing, and performance outboards. It was a highly successful program, well researched and tested. David and Stanton knew what they were doing, and really made database marketing history. Then it all came to an end.

They lost their champion. When the original VP for marketing left, his replacement supported their efforts, once he understood what they were doing. Two years later, he was replaced with a new man, who was totally hostile to database marketing. One of his first questions was, "What idiot came up with the oil thing?" The database project was abandoned. OMC went back to traditional marketing, such as advertising in the swimsuit edition of *Sports Illustrated,* advertising in enthusiast publications, and sponsoring fishing tournaments. David and Stanton went on to other projects in other companies.

This is the story of corporate America. You lose your champion, you lose your program.

The Budget Battle

Inside every company, contests are always being waged between different individuals and units seeking larger budgets, more personnel, larger programs, and more power. There is only so much money to go around at any given time, and each unit believes that it needs more to accomplish its vital functions.

For many years, marketing—particularly database marketing—had a real struggle to get any funding at all. Sales and advertising were usually much more successful in their efforts. Sales could point to the revenue it generated. The results of advertising can be seen by all in the company when they look at magazines, newspapers, and television or the web. Database marketers, on the other hand, operate out of the limelight on obscure programs that many people don't understand.

The money for any new program—like a web site or a marketing database—has to be taken out of someone else's budget. Those who stand to lose seldom take a cut lying down. Only when the CEO gets religion and decides to make the customer the focus of the company marketing strategy will database marketing and e-commerce get a chance to show what they can do. When that happens, the marketers have to produce something useful fast, or they will be swept aside. The attention span of top management for any new program seldom exceeds 12 months.

Database marketing is faced with a catch 22 problem: Database marketing cannot prove itself unless it receives:

- Enough funding over a three-year period to permit the building of the database or functioning web site
- The launching of a group of relationship-building programs
- The setting up of a functioning web site
- The establishment of control groups
- The measurement of lifetime value change during those three years to prove the long-run effect

No one is going to allocate sufficient funding for all these steps unless the marketers can first prove that it works. What is the answer?

There are really two ways that database marketers can get the resources they need to begin their work: by educating top management and by demonstrating results through successful experiments. Successful experiments are described throughout this book. Let's concentrate here on educating management.

Educating Management

It is a commonplace of economics that the most successful production techniques are usually the most roundabout. For primitive man to be successful at hunting, he first had to build a bow and arrow—which usually involved much experimentation with different types of wood and different materials for the cord. To an outsider, such a primitive man did not look as if he were engaged in hunting, but he really was going about it in a very intelligent and roundabout way. Database marketing is also very roundabout.

To be successful at building customer loyalty and repeat sales, we must first build a marketing database that involves much experimentation with lists, software, data cleaning and correction, construction of reports, and customer profiles. We must build a customer web site. None of this looks to outsiders as if it were connected with the generation of customer loyalty or repeat sales—but it really is an intelligent way of beginning the process.

Early man probably had a wife and children who were demanding that he bring home some food; and asking him why, instead of attempting to catch an animal for supper, he was experimenting with pieces of wood and cord. Database marketers have the same type of disbelievers looking over their shoulders, wondering what all this data processing and web site creation activity has to do with the generation of profitable sales.

Because database marketing is so roundabout, marketers have to conduct a major educational campaign within the company. Such campaigns are really directed at influencing top management, even though they begin by educating people at lower levels.

Management involvement is necessary, because management has to understand the process before it will be willing to commit the funds necessary to make the marketing a reality. How do you educate management?

1. You can send top-management executives to conferences on database management and e-commerce.

2. You can send marketing executives to training courses and seminars on database marketing and e-commerce, getting them certified in these new professions so that they can help in the sales and execution process.

3. You can sign up a direct response consultant or agency with database experience to advise you and brief top management.

4. You can form an in-house team—a web site and database marketing planning committee that meets regularly to lay out the groundwork for a comprehensive relationship-building system, providing regular progress reports to top management.

All of these methods are useful, and in most cases, all of them should be attempted.

Database Conferences

It is amazing how much progress is made at national database conferences. I have been to almost 100 such meetings in the last 15 years. I learned a great deal from each one. The speakers are usually executives from direct response agencies, service bureaus, or marketing departments of companies. Many of the exhibits enable you to get a good idea of what is available. There is no better way to learn the state of the art. The conferences not only educate, but also bring marketers into direct contact with service providers. The National Center for Database Marketing devotes considerable effort to networking: getting people together. I had a very interesting experience at one of the center's conferences in Orlando.

In the opening session, the conference chairman, Skip Andrew, asked all 700 attendees to stand up, introduce themselves, and shake hands with the person behind them. I did so, meeting a woman from Michigan, an account executive from a small direct response agency. She had come to the conference seeking help in building a database for one of her clients, a large pharmaceutical firm. I had come to the conference to speak, and to find account executives just like this delightful woman. In the 60 seconds that Skip Andrew gave us to talk, we found out about each other and arranged to meet for breakfast the next day.

At the "all you can eat" buffet breakfast the next day, she and I spent two hours together. I ate 6 scrambled eggs, 14 sausages, French toast, and mounds of rolls. I also persuaded her to come to visit us in Reston to meet our staff and discuss the pharmaceutical database. A month later, we had a signed contract and were happily creating a fascinating marketing database, which is described elsewhere in this book. I have had other equally rewarding conferences, but this was the one at which I gained the most weight.

This conference, which is held twice a year, is probably the best single event for finding out about the science and practice of database marketing and e-commerce. If you can get your senior executives to go to such an event, you are halfway on your journey to introduce database marketing to your company.

Seminars

Most professions have training programs, leading to certification as a financial planner, association executive, direct marketer, or travel agent. The closest we have come in our industry is the two-day seminar run by the Database Marketing Institute. You can learn about these seminars at www.dbmarketing.com.

Enlisting Outside Help in Your Struggle

The hardest part of database marketing is developing an intelligent and productive strategy that uses the database. Building a database is comparatively easy. Making money with one is the real trick.

The famous economist Joseph Schumpeter drew an important distinction between inventions and innovations. Inventions, he pointed out, are really not worth very much unless someone has invested some capital in their development. Once money has been invested in them, inventions become innovations; they change the course of human events. Leonardo da Vinci invented the airplane and a great many other things, which were, essentially, ahead of their time; but nothing much came of them. They came long before the Industrial Revolution. Capitalists were not available to take advantage of them.

Today many companies are resting on their past laurels, and simply won't go out on a limb for some new marketing idea. There are others, however, that are still struggling to get to the top, that are looking for ideas that they can turn into successful innovations. Converting database marketing or e-commerce from an invention to an innovation requires these two ingredients: a profit-making idea and a company with the capital resources and the entrepreneurial spirit to take advantage of the idea. Where do such ideas come from?

Ideas, of course, can come from anywhere. Many people have the ability to think up a better way to do the job that fate has assigned to them. With any luck you, the reader, will hit on a winning concept that will enable your company both to make its customers happy and to build the bottom line with database marketing.

There are powerful reasons for believing that the best place to look for profit-making database ideas that can lead to successful innovations is on the payroll of direct response agencies and consultants. These reasons are:

- Direct response agencies and consultants have usually helped several companies to build successful—or unsuccessful—databases already. Either way, they have learned something valuable, which you don't know, and which can help to make your company's road to profitable database marketing a little easier.

- Such agencies and consultants must live by their wits. By losing an account, they may lose their jobs. The entrepreneurial spirit is strong. In large corporations, on the other hand, marketing employees are just that: employees who can count on a paycheck whether they win or lose. The entrepreneurial spirit is weak or nonexistent. Large corporations tend to stifle innovators and reward people who go along.

- Outsiders, like agency executives and consultants, can often go right to the top with an idea. Top corporate managers often listen to ideas from a consultant or executive from a database marketing agency.

For these reasons, you should have the assistance of an experienced and creative outside database marketing strategy agency in building your program and selling it to the top. After spending several years watching one of these creative database marketing and internet development companies from the outside (M\S Database Marketing—www.msdbm. com), I decided to join it as VP for Strategic Planning. I discovered in Bob McKim and Evelyn Schlaphoff two people who are highly successful in applying the concepts in this book.

Forming an In-House Team

Database marketing is different from any other marketing program. It requires building a lasting relationship with your customers. They will come to see your company as a friend who listens to them, asks their opinions, and reacts to what they say. How can you deliver on that concept?

The only way is to get a large number of internal groups actively involved in the relationship building:

- Customer service and technical support
- Your web designer
- Sales and dealer support
- Advertising
- Corporate communications
- Fulfillment and delivery
- Accounts receivable
- MIS
- Marketing research
- Your outside direct response agency and database service bureau
- Your outside telemarketers at your 800 number
- Your outside data entry and fulfillment house
- Representatives of your branches, dealers, or independent agents

Few companies have all these groups, but all companies have some of them. Your job, as a marketer, is to pull all these units together as a working team, which coordinates policies and activities relating to the customer. For example:

- If you classify customers into Blue, Gold, and Platinum, how are you going to assure that the appropriate groups within your organization work to treat these different levels differently, recognizing the privileges of the Gold and Platinum customers?
- If you promise 24-hour turnaround, how are you going to assure that this happens?
- If you ask people to bring one of your promotional letters in to your branches, how are you going to assure that the branch personnel react properly to the letter, and *let you know that they have received it, noting the customer's ID number*?
- If you have a customer with a 10-year buying history and a lifetime value of $2,000, how are you going to assure that accounts receivable takes that into consideration when the customer falls 60 days behind in payments because she is traveling in Europe?

Looking at the above, you can see that you, as a marketer, must become the leader of a relationship-building team that completely restructures the communications between your customers and your internal units.

Getting these in-house, and outside, people lined up in support of the plan is a major job, but one that is worthwhile, since they will be a source of your strength. If and when you form such a team, they will see the value of what you are doing. They will appreciate the importance of customer lifetime value and the part that they can play in making it grow. Once they have gotten religion, they will be your key allies in selling your program to top management, and getting the multiyear funding that you require.

Knowledge of the Market

How can you learn what is in your customers' minds or what your competition is doing? Economists who assume that all knowledge of the market is shared by the participants just don't understand the market. The fundamental problem that all marketers face is ignorance: lack of knowledge of what is out there, of what customers want, of how to let them know what we have to offer. Every piece of knowledge about the market, about how to price our products, about what the customer is thinking, is valuable and can be converted, by alert marketers, into profit opportunities.

The difference between those who are successful marketers and those who fail can largely be attributed to the ability of the former to gain knowledge about the attitudes and plans of existing and possible customers, and to put that knowledge to work in a productive way. Successful marketers are alert to opportunities; but they also have developed ways of making the opportunities turn up—by increasing their knowledge of the market.

Building a successful marketing database fed by a web site is one of those ways. Just as a CFO can look at a balance sheet and an income statement and determine a profitable direction for company activity, so an alert marketer can look at the information stored in a customer database and detect profitable marketing opportunities. Such knowledge, in the hands of a skillful marketer, is market power. It is also internal power in the struggle for success within the corporate hierarchy.

The data in a customer database are still rarely understood. Database marketing is now being taught in some business schools and in many marketing courses. Analyses of sales figures are well known and widely studied. Income and expense reports, inventory, stock prices, and balance sheets—these are all common management tools. They give the CFO his power and influence. He uses them to control the destinies of most units of the company.

Customer data, on the other hand, constitute an entirely new breed of information, which many on the corporate ladder do not yet understand. Certainly, what customers are saying and thinking about current products and services, and their desire for changes, can be, in the right hands, one of the most powerful marketing tools imaginable. Let's take an example from real life.

Knowledge of How to Bring in New Business

What inducements are needed to get existing customers to persuade a neighbor to become a customer as well? Of those new customers brought in by such a program, how long will they remain customers—what is their lifetime value? From the answers to these two questions, how much can the company afford to spend on such a program?

These are detailed questions. The answers are far from universal. Success depends a great deal on the specific product, the offer, the method of selection of the customers, and the timing. If the marketer is alert to opportunities, and able to experiment and test, the database can provide very useful answers to these questions. These answers, in the right hands, represent real market power. Larry Hawks of Marketing Communications, Inc., provided an interesting example:

> A major propane gas distribution firm with over 500 district offices nationwide, had a customer base of over 500,000 households and businesses, located mainly in rural areas.
>
> Several years ago, a marketing executive launched a referral program to generate new customers. The referral package offered either a $15 credit on the customer's next statement, or a flannel-lined jacket as the premium. Existing customers were asked to supply three referral names, which were then followed up with personal sales calls by the district office. District managers loved the program because the conversion rate to customers was quite successful.
>
> The letters to customers inviting their participation were highly personalized, bearing the digitized signature of the local district manager. The envelopes containing the responses went directly to the local office, instead of to the headquarters that sent out the letters. The marketer believed that making the program appear to be a very local affair would improve the participation rate, and hence the overall success.
>
> In the first year of operation, the program signed up 3,000 new customers who generated over $3 million of revenue. One year later, more than 80 percent were still buying gas at the same rate. The total cost of the program in terms of mailings and premiums was less than $350,000.

What does the knowledge of how to go about creating such a program mean to the propane gas company? Market power. What does the ability to use that knowledge to generate $3 million in increased revenue give to the marketer who possesses it: internal power—the same type of power possessed by a CFO whose authority comes largely from his ability to analyze the company income statement.

Is the propane gas company spending too much or too little to acquire new customers? How much should it spend? Lifetime value calculation will answer the question.

Uses for Market Knowledge

A marketer who has built a marketing database, *and who knows how to use it,* as in the case of the propane gas marketer, thus has very powerful knowledge in his possession. He can use it to win customers away from oil and electric heating in the marketplace. *He can also use it to justify his marketing budget within the organization.* Here, for the first time, is a chance to stand up to the CFO and argue for a higher allocation for marketing *in terms that the CFO can understand.* This is powerful. It is more than the advertising chief can do—yet, because of tradition, advertising budgets are always many times larger than direct-marketing budgets.

In time, this type of market knowledge will make its mark within most companies. The logic and precision of this type of calculation are unassailable. But to get to a position where he has that knowledge, the marketer must first get the resources to build his database, and learn how to use it. Many steps are necessary before arriving at the position of power within the corporation that most database marketers will attain in the future.

Steps to Knowledge

To gain market knowledge, leading to market power, the database marketer must:

- Build a customer marketing database, complete with purchase history and demographics.
- Develop an active marketing program that uses the database both to gain new customers and to retain and increase sales to existing customers
- Build a web site that involves the customers in the activities of the company
- Use the database and the web site to analyze his marketing activities with precision and predictive capability so that he becomes the master of his marketplace.
- And finally, use the knowledge gained within his company to obtain sufficient resources for the database marketing program so that it becomes the most powerful marketing force in the organization.

Obstacles to Database Realization

These are exciting ideas. They are powerful ideas. But realization of the potential of database marketing is not going to be easy for anyone. Here are some of the obstacles:

- Brand managers and the ad agencies that they work with are not going to roll over and play dead when a marketing database comes along. Every dollar for a database or the web site is one less dollar for the advertising budget. It will be tough.

- The CFO, and the MIS department that reports to him, are used to being the information resource for the company. A customer database or a web site, the CFO will begin to realize, will, in time, represent an independent source of knowledge and power. This independence will rival the power that the CFO has gained through cash-flow reports and balance sheets. (Some CFOs have caught on to this and are requiring such information as customer visitation frequency and the retention rate in the monthly reporting system throughout the company.)

Power within a corporation tends to be a zero-sum game. For everyone who gains internal influence, the dominance of other groups tends to be lessened. Few leaders will take the loss of power lying down. To the extent that consumer databases and web sites confer authority and influence on the marketing staff, there will be a counterreaction from other parts of the corporation that feel their position threatened by these new techniques. In many cases, there has been, and will continue to be, active opposition to database marketing and the Internet as they pose a threat to established centers of internal power. Ultimately, top management will have to intervene, or potentially potent sources of sales and profits will be sabotaged by internal bickering.

How does this opposition manifest itself? Let's look at a couple of examples of real situations in major companies.

The product design department of a growing company began to pack registration cards inside every unit that the company manufactured. The cards were quite detailed in the information they requested of the registrant. The idea was to figure out who was using the product and what the users were doing with it. That way, the product design department could anticipate market trends and come up with features that were most in demand.

The project was a great success. Thousands of cards were received and poured over by designers, who soon learned a great many things that they hadn't known before. For example, they learned that large numbers of people went out and bought—from external vendors—hardware, which they plugged into the product to make it more useful. In effect, this highly successful product was carrying a dozen other companies, like parasites, on its back, whose existence depended on inadequate product design! Gradually they redesigned the product to incorporate these features so that the profits from these extras came to the company, not to the outsiders. The existence of the built-in features also provided a very useful selling point, which contributed to the growth of overall sales.

So many cards were received that the product design team couldn't handle them all. After reviewing them, they shipped them in cardboard boxes to the company librarian. This enterprising woman knew a professor at a local university whose specialty was public opinion surveys. She persuaded him to take the cardboard boxes off her hands. A local data entry firm keypunched the cards into tapes, which were sent to the professor at the university computer department.

Within a few months, the professor was able to furnish the librarian with printed reports that summarized the findings from the cards. The company library soon became a haven for internal researchers who wanted to learn more about the uses of their rapidly expanding product. There were several problems, however. The computer printouts were very bulky and hard to read, particularly the copies. Even though the professor presented the information in a dozen different cross-tabs, it always happened that the exact relationship sought by the researchers was not on any of the cross-tabs. There was a demand for additional reports. The professor and the university programming staff soon grew months behind in their ability to keep the librarian satisfied.

The librarian drew up an RFP, which was sent to three service bureaus, one of which was selected to take over the growing database. The change in the library was dramatic. Reports were now printed on easy-to-read laser copies. There were 56 different cross-tabs for each of the new models, which came out four times a year. There was so much information that the librarian became an essential resource in all company meetings involving the product or public reaction to it. Her growing status increased the power and prestige of both her job, to which two assistants were soon added, and that of her supervisor, who was given a substantial raise and a new title. In effect, without realizing it, they had created a powerful consumer database.

It wasn't long before the marketing department learned of this valuable resource. After studying the reports, the marketing staff tried to get tapes from the system to do test mailings. They were firmly rebuffed; being told, "Our customers are not going to be bombarded with junk mail. If we did that, the flow of customer cards would soon cease." The marketing department's pleas fell on deaf ears within the company, because for the next six years, the company had more orders for products than it could handle. Marketing was almost irrelevant, and database marketing was never attempted.

After a few years, intense competition in the industry brought this company its first loss after years of growth. New management determined that this would be "the year of the customer." The marketing department was told to begin active marketing operations. The marketing staff began to rent outside lists of names from magazine subscribers and others. The one source they could not tap was the company's customer base, which by this time included more than a million names. These million people had each purchased a by-now obsolete model. Marketing wanted to get these customers to "trade up." Selling to satisfied customers is the easiest sell in the world, but the company did not attempt it. Why? The database manager was protecting his fiefdom. As he saw it, if he gave up his database to the marketers, his monopoly of information would be at an end—and so would his power and position within the company. He successfully fought any use of the customer base for marketing, alluding to a "sacred understanding with the customers that we will not use their names."

Needless to say, this company, which had one of the finest and most comprehensive consumer databases in the world, did not do any database marketing. Internal opposition effectively killed this possible marketing route.

Later, a competitor developed a web site that permitted customers to create their own personal products. The competitor, Dell Computer, became a major player almost overnight, stealing market share from everyone in the industry. The effort to compete with Dell in its web site was sabotaged within the company we have been studying because of opposition from the division that managed the independent dealers. "They will drop us if we sell direct." So another opportunity was passed up until it became too late to catch up.

Is this attitude unique? Not at all. It is quite common. The General Electric Answer Center received 3 million calls a year from customers from whom it usually obtained the name, address, and telephone number, and an interest in a specific GE product. Were these names placed into a marketing database? Not at all. They were destroyed 90 days after the telephone calls were made. Customer service, you see, considered itself as a higher calling than mere sales. Customers do not want to be bombarded with sales literature just because they called to inquire about a GE product—that is the rationale for not turning these names over to the marketing department.

Conflicts between marketing and market research or customer service are not rare at all. Market research, in particular, is often staffed by statisticians whose interest is to discover "truth" rather than to increase sales. They see themselves as researchers, not marketers, and resent the implication that they have a responsibility for the bottom line. They feel that the results of customer surveys should not be put into the database. Real database marketers, on the other hand, want to write to all the customers who have filled out surveys and thank them for their help, starting a profitable dialog with them.

Sales organizations also oppose database marketing. Database marketers want to get their hands on the customer names to put them into the database. Once this happens, the next step, as sales sees it, is direct marketing to the customers, cutting the sales staff out of their commissions. Database marketers find that the names of customers in many companies are denied to them.

The fact is that information is power in corporate America. Those who have gotten their hands on information seldom like to give it up to others—else, where is their source of power?

> The XYZ Company maintained ongoing records of the monthly service use by its 1 million customers. Augmented by credit data compiled during the customer's application process, the database represented a tremendously valuable resource for marketing, market research, financial analysis, customer service, product design, technical support, and dealer relations. In the early days, no one knew how to get information out of the database. An enterprising researcher, whom we will call Phil, imported the software package FOCUS that enabled him to extract data and produce useful reports. His services were soon in great demand on all sides. His boss soon told Phil to drop all other work so that he could become an information resource to the entire company.

> Demand for reports led Phil to a much-deserved promotion, and to the hiring of a full-time assistant. Two years later Phil hired another assistant. Despite the staff increase, the team consistently maintained a six-month backlog of requests for reports and data.

> Realizing it was time that the company entered the database marketing world, top management approved an RFP for an outside service bureau. The choice was eventually narrowed down to two firms. The first one would collect the data on its server and then transfer the data regularly to the company's server, where the data could be used by Phil and his staff to service data requests much more rapidly than they had in the past. The second contender would also collect the data on its server, but would provide direct access by telephone linkup to PCs from all the departments that needed information, thus largely doing away with the need for Phil and his staff.

> The decision-making process was an agonizing one for the company. Phil maintained that giving users direct access to the data would be a disaster: Inexperienced users would not know how to interpret their results correctly, leading to erroneous conclusions, disputes over data, and mistaken marketing decisions. Users argued that their programs were hampered by the inability to get information. They had no faith that Phil's famous six-month backlog would be reduced by the new system, as it represented a cushion for Phil at budget time to assure him of continued support for his operation.

What can we conclude from this?

- Knowledge derived from a consumer database or web site confers significant market power on the company that possesses it and uses it appropriately.
- Failure to use the knowledge confers no power at all.
- The ability to capture and use the knowledge also confers internal power in the quest for advancement inside the company.

- Companies that allow this knowledge to be centralized to a limited group—for their own advancement—are weakening their market power and are denying themselves the benefits that come from proper use of a consumer database.
- Every company should:

  Assure that all relevant sections have access to the data

  Build a strategy for their use

Winning over Top Management

You want to build a marketing database. You need to convince top management. Here is a strategy that will work:

- Determine lifetime customer value using the present system.
- Create a picture of lifetime value with the database and the customer web site.
- Show the effect on the bottom line.

A Final Example

Let's conclude the chapter with a final example of the way database marketing and the Internet can be linked to build profits. A health information company produced a monthly wellness newsletter, suggesting the use of vitamins, hormones, enzymes, and various herbs designed to deal with arthritis, aging, prostate problems, etc. The newsletter provided valuable information on these subjects. After a year's worth of these monthly reminders, most people did not renew their subscriptions. Their renewal rate was 19 percent. As a separate business, the company sold bottles of pills containing the remedies recommended in the newsletter. When the Internet arrived, the company added two web sites: one for the newsletter and one for the vitamin pills. There were three vice presidents in charge of the three businesses: newsletter, drug sales, and Internet. They were highly competitive, but overall, the business was profitable.

The main problems occurred in the newsletter. Several million pieces of direct mail went out each year to generate the 300,000 subscriptions (see Figure 17-1). The cost per acquired subscriber was $40. The subscription price was a nominal $70 per year, but everyone was given a discount to $40. On that basis, the newsletter never was prof-

	Year 1	Year 2	Year 3
Subscribers	300,000	57,000	22,800
Retention rate	19.00%	40.00%	45.00%
Price paid	$40.00	$40.00	$40.00
Subscription revenue	$12,00 000	$2,280,000	$912,000
Costs			
Cost percentage	25.00%	20.00%	19.00%
Direct costs	$3,000,000	$456,000	$173,280
Acquisition cost $40	$12,000,000	$ —	$ —
Renewal costs $6	$ —	$342,000	$136,800
Total Costs	$15,000,000	$798,000	$310,080
Profit	($3,000,000)	$1,482,000	$601,920
Discount rate	1	1.2	1.44
NPV profit	($3,000,000)	$1,235,000	$418,000
Cumulative NVP profit	($3,000,000)	($1,765,000)	($1,347,000)
Lifetime value	($10.00)	($5.88)	($4.49)

Figure 17-1. Newsletter subscriber lifetime value.

	Year 1	Year 2	Year 3
Subscribers	300,000	57,000	17,100
Retention rate	19.00%	30.00%	45.00%
% of order vitamins	19%	35%	45%
Vitamin customers	57,000	19,950	7,695
Average vitamin order size	$72.00	$73.00	$81.00
Orders per year	2.5	2.8	3.9
Vitamin spending	$10,260,000	$4,077,780	$2,430,851
Costs			
Cost percentage	37.00%	34.00%	32.00%
Direct costs	$3,796,200	$1,386,445	$777,872
Total costs	$3,796,200	$1,386,445	$777,872
Profit	$6,463,800	$2,691,335	$1,652,978
Discount rate	1	1.2	1.44
NPV profit	$6,463,800	$2,242,779	$1,147,902
Cumulative NVP profit	$6,463,800	$8,706,579	$9,854,481
Lifetime value	$21.55	$29.02	$32.85

Figure 17-2. Vitamin customer lifetime value.

	Year 1	Year 2	Year 3
Customers	20,000	6,000	2,100
Retention rate	30.00%	35.00%	45.00%
% of order subscriptions	12.00%	18.00%	21.00%
Subscription sales	$96,000	$43,200	$17,640
% of order vitamins	70%	80%	90%
Average vitamin order size	$72.00	$73.00	$81.00
Orders per year	2.5	2.7	3.6
Total revenue	$2,616,000	$989,280	$568,764
Costs			
Cost percentage	37.00%	34.00%	32.00%
Direct costs	$967,920	$336,355	$182,004
Total costs	$967,920	$336,355	$182,004
Profit	$1,648,080	$652,925	$386,760
Discount rate	1	1.2	1.44
NPV profit	$1,648,080	$544,104	$268,583
Cumulative NVP profit	$1,648,080	$2,192,184	$2,460,767
Lifetime value	$82.40	$109.61	$123.04

Figure 17-3. Web site customer lifetime value.

	Customers	Year 1	Year 2	Year 3
Newsletter LTV	300,000	($10.00)	($5.88)	($4.49)
Newsletter profits		($3,000,000)	($1,765,000)	($1,347,000)
Vitamin LTV	57,000	$4.26	$26.46	$49.84
Vitamin profits		$242,606	$1,508,503	$2,840,982
Web LTV	20,000	$82.40	$109.61	$123.04
Web profits		$1,648,080	$2,192,184	$2,460,767
Total profits		($1,109,314)	$1,935,687	$3,954,749

Figure 17-4. Combined annual profit of all three divisions.

itable by itself. It was worthwhile only in combination with the vitamin business.

The pressure was always on the newsletter staff. "Why are your acquisition costs so high? Why do you have such a miserable renewal rate?" They tried everything they could think of, but the situation never got any better. On the other hand, the vitamin business was very healthy (see Figure 17-2). It depended on the newsletter for sales, so the acquisition cost was zero. Was this a great business, or what?

Meanwhile the web site began to become profitable (see Figure 17-3). The web served mainly as a distribution vehicle for the vitamins. The site published the previous month's articles from the newsletter and had the vast archives of past newsletter articles available. The web site's sales were only a fraction of the total vitamin sales, but they were growing steadily.

In total, the three vice presidents produced an overall profit, as shown in Figure 17-4.

A marketing expert was called in to look into the newsletter situation. He created the lifetime value tables shown in Figures 17-1 to 17-3. For the first time, people began to see what was really happening. He made some recommendations:

- Combine all three businesses under one leader.
- Concentrate on the customers, not on the product lines.
- Build a database that includes information about the customers' preferences, age, lifestyle, and interests.
- Use RFM to sell new products to existing customers.
- Personalize the web by issuing each customer a PIN, printed in the label for the newsletter. When the customer enters this PIN, the web page will say, "Welcome back, Susan. Click here to find out how to slash your risk of breast cancer by up to 80 percent. ... Jane Goodwell successfully got off heart drugs. Click here to find out how she did it."
- Feature the web throughout the newsletter. After each article, say, for example, "To find out more about estrogen therapy, visit *www.xxxxhealth.com* and click on estrogen."
- Eliminate the subscription fees for the newsletter. The newsletter is a loser. Vitamins and the web are winners. Instead of a charge, have the subscribers fill out a questionnaire about their health, lifestyle, and interests. Use that information to create a personalized newsletter and web page. Have the newsletter subscription be a negative option decision. *Result:* Greatly increased renewal rates.

	Year 1	Year 2	Year 3
Subscribers	300,000	210,000	157,500
Retention rate	70.00%	75.00%	80.00%
% of order vitamins	33%	40%	50%
Vitamin customers	99,000	84,000	78,750
Average vitamin order size	$74.00	$75.00	$82.00
Orders per year	2.6	2.9	4.2
Vitamin spending	$19,047,600	$18,270,000	$27,121,500
Costs			
Cost percentage	40.00%	37.00%	35.00%
Direct costs	$7,619,040	$6,759,900	$9,492,525
Customer acquisition $40	$12,000,000		
Total costs	$19,619,040	$6,759,900	$9,492,525
Profit	($571,440)	$11,510,100	$17,628,975
Discount rate	1	1.2	1.44
NPV profit	($571,440)	$9,591,750	$12,242,344
Cumulative NVP profit	($571,440)	$9,020,310	$21,262,654
Lifetime value	($1.90)	$30.07	$70.88
With 300,000 customers	($571,440)	$9,020,310	$21,262,654
Previous profit	($1,109,314)	$1,935,687	$3,954,749
Increase	$537,874	$7,084,623	$17,307,905

Figure 17-5. Combined customer lifetime value.

The effect of these changes on LTV is presented in Figure 17-5. Can intelligent use of the web and database marketing produce results like these? Only you can find this out. You have the tools. Do the analysis, and see what you can accomplish.

Good luck.

Summary

- Database marketing has a struggle to obtain funding. Programs take many years to show real results. The money must come from some other unit's budget. Programs can be funded only by persuading top management to fund them.

■ Methods include sending top management to database conferences, enlisting the help of a direct response agency, and forming an in-house database marketing planning committee.

■ Direct response agencies are essential because they usually have broad experiences building databases for others, they have the entrepreneurial spirit, and they can gain access to your top management more easily than you can. In addition, they have large creative staffs that can really flesh out an idea.

■ An in-house team is essential for database marketing. A dozen different disciplines are needed to craft a relationship-building program with customers. It is hard to get such a team together, but it is worth it because such a team is a source of strength for the marketing staff.

■ In-house coordination is needed to assure that preferred customers get preferred treatment, that turnaround time is given as promised, and that customer contacts are reported to the database.

■ Most company executives know how to compute customer lifetime value and relate it to the bottom line, as they can sales figures and corporate balance sheets. Marketers have to get on top of this discipline if they want to succeed.

■ Both experience in database marketing and precise calculation of lifetime value can be powerful tools in getting database marketing budgets approved.

■ There are many obstacles: Brand managers and ad agencies will fight any cut in their budgets. MIS will fight to keep marketers from getting their own independent sources of information.

■ Information about the company's customers can provide market power. Too often, however, this information is locked away inside market research, customer service, or some other unit where it cannot be used to build market share. Companies that allow this to happen are throwing away money.

■ By combining database marketing and the web, it is possible to change from a product focus to a customer focus. The result can be a major increase in the bottom line.

Executive Quiz 16

Answers to quiz questions can be found in Appendix B.

1. Database marketing usually has difficulty getting adequate initial funding because:

    a. It is hard to do cost-benefit analysis for relationship building

    b. Rivals seek to keep budgeted funds for their own programs

    c. Advertising is usually more productive of sales

    d. Database marketing is an unproven technique

    e. Many databases fail

2. Which method is suggested for educating management on database marketing?

    a. Making them read this book

    b. Sending them to conferences

    c. Getting help from an outside consultant

    d. Building an in-house team

    e. All of the above

3. The conferences of the National Center for Database Marketing provide:

    a. A way for vendors and companies to meet each other

    b. High-level briefing on marketing techniques

    c. Exhibits from practitioners

    d. All of the above

    e. None of the above

4. Which of the following was not suggested as a member of the in-house database marketing team?

    a. CFO

    b. MIS

    c. Database service bureau

    d. Customer service

    e. Sales

5. Database and web marketing today are:

   a. Taught in many advanced business schools

   b. Taught in many marketing departments

   c. Taught by the Database Marketing Institute

   d. Learned on the job

   e. All of the above

6. Which of the following is unlikely as an opponent of database marketing within a corporation?

   a. Market research

   b. MIS

   c. Sales

   d. Advertising

   e. None of the above

7. Why are market research and database marketing often opposed to each other?

   a. Market research has different goals.

   b. Database marketing cannot use models.

   c. Database budgets usually come from market research.

   d. MIS sides with database, not with research.

   e. Customer service wants market research as one of its functions.

8. Companies that relegate customer data exclusively to research or customer service staffs:

   a. Are protecting their customers from junk mail

   b. Are feeding internal corporate power struggles

   c. Are gaining major marketplace power

   d. Are helping to build a corporate asset

   e. None of the above

A Farewell to the Reader

Congratulations on getting this far. You are a glutton for punishment! As we say farewell to each other, let's review the things that (I hope) you have learned:

- Database marketing and customized web sites do not always work. They are generally quite useful in marketing to prospects, where they usually permit reduction in marketing costs and improvement in response and profits. They are most difficult to carry out successfully in marketing to existing customers. In the right situations they will create loyalty, reduce attrition, and build your bottom line. There are some product and service situations, however, in which a database or personalized web site may not be economically justified.

- The biggest difficulty in making database marketing or e-commerce work is the development of an effective and profitable marketing strategy. Too much attention is focused on hardware and software, and not enough on marketing.

- The way to estimate the possibilities of proposed database marketing and Internet strategies, and to evaluate the effectiveness of existing ones, is to create test and control groups and calculate the lifetime value of both groups. Lifetime value is the *net present value of future profits to be received from the average customer.*

- In free-market transactions, both the buyer and the seller *always* make a profit. The way to increase your sales, therefore, is to find a way for the buyer to make a profit. In today's market situation, what the buyer sees as a profit may not necessarily be a low price. It may be recognition, helpfulness, service, information, convenience, and an opportunity to identify with a friendly and reliable organization: your company. A customized web site with an extranet and a database program may be the ideal way to provide those things at the least cost.

Conclusion

Let us end with the ideas we set forth in the Introduction: Database marketing and personalized web sites are not just a way to increase profits by reducing costs and selling more products and services, although that is, and must be, one of their results. They are tools that provide management with customer information. That information is used in various ways to increase customer retention and increase customer acquisition rates—the essence of business strategy. The web site and the database provide both the raw information you need and a measurement device essential for the evaluation of strategy.

Looked at from the customers' point of view, database marketing and customized web sites are ways of making customers happy; of providing them recognition, service, friendship, and information for which, in return, they will reward you with loyalty, reduction in attrition, and increased sales. Genuine customer satisfaction is the goal and hallmark of satisfactory customized web sites combined with database marketing. If you are doing things right, your customers will be *glad* that you have a web site and a database and that you have included them. They will appreciate the things that you do for them. If you can develop and carry out strategies that bring this situation about, you are a master marketer. You will keep your customers for life, and you will be happy in your work. You will have made the world a better place to live in.

A

How to Keep Up with Database Marketing and Commerce on the Web

To keep up with the many new innovations and developments in this field, you will have to read, to talk to people, and to attend conferences. During the last 10 years, hundreds of readers have called me up to talk about their web site or database marketing experiences. I have used much of the knowledge gained from these talks in the present book. As a reader, you should feel free to contact me if you think that the call would be useful for both of us. Send me an e-mail at dbmarkets@aol.com, or call me at M\S Database Marketing at 703-525-9637, or visit the Institute's web site at www.dbmarketing.com, or M\S Database Marketing web site at www.msdbm.com.

Magazines and Newsletters

Magazines and newsletters that you should subscribe to are:

Bank Technology News, Faulkner & Gray, 11 Penn Plaza, 17th Floor, New York, NY 10001, www.electronicbanker.com.

Call Center Solutions, One Technology Plaza, Norwalk, CT 06854, 203-295-2000, www.ccsmag.com.

Canadian Direct Marketing News, 1200 Markham Road, Scarborough, Ontario M1H 3C3, 416-439-4083, lloydmedia@compuserve.com.

Card Marketing, Faulkner & Gray, 11 Penn Plaza, 17th Floor, New York, NY 10001, http://cardmarketing.faulknergray.com.

Card Technology, Faulkner & Gray, 11 Penn Plaza, 17th Floor, New York, NY 10001, http://cardtech.faulknergray.com.

CRM Journal, 1200 Markham Road, Scarborough, Ontario M1H 3C3, 416-439-4083, lloydmedia@compuserve.com.

Direct, Intertec Publishing, 11 River Bend Drive South, Stamford, CT 06907, 203-358-9900, www.intertec.com.

DM News, Mill Hollow Corporation, 19 West 21st Street, New York, NY 10010, 212-741-2095, fax 212-633-9367, www.dmnews.com.

DM Review, Faulkner & Gray, 11 Penn Plaza, 17th Floor, New York, NY 10001, www.dmreview.com.

Financial Services Marketing, Thomson Information Services, One State Street Plaza, New York, NY 10004, 800-221-1809, sraeel@tfn.com.

FutureBanker, Thomson Information Services, One State Street Plaza, New York, NY 10004, 800-221-1809 sraeel@tfn.com.

Imarketing News, Mill Hollow Corporation, 19 West 21st Street, New York, NY 10010 212-741-2095, fax 212-633-9367, www.dmnews.com.

Inter@active Week, 100 Quentin Roosevelt Boulevard, Suite 400, Garden City, NY 11530, 516-229-3700, www.interactive-week.com.

Internet Telephony, Technology Marketing Corporation, One Technology Plaza, Norwalk, CT 06854, 203-295-2000, www.itmag.com.

Sales & Field Force Automation, 29160 Heathercliff Road, Suite 200, Malibu, CA 90265, www.sffaonline.com.

Target Marketing, 401 North Broad Street, Philadelphia, PA 19108, 215-238-5300, www.targetonline.com.

Teleprofessional, 501 Sycamore Street, Suite 120, Waterloo, IA 50703, 319-235-4473, www.teleprofessional.com.

US Banker, Faulkner & Gray, 11 Penn Plaza, 17th Floor, New York, NY 10001, www.electronicbanker.com.

Books about Database Marketing and the Web

All of the following books are reviewed and can be ordered at www.dbmarketing.com:

Gates, Bill, *Business @ the Speed of Thought,* Warner Books, 1999, 470 pp. Filled with very good ideas and case studies. You need this book.

Godin, Seth, *Permission Marketing*, Simon & Schuster, New York, 1999, 255 pp. An excellent short study of the concepts espoused in the book you are reading now.

Hatch, Denny, and Don Jackson, *2239 Tested Secrets for Direct Marketing Success*, NTC Business Books, 1997, 358 pp. The title says it all. Thousands of nuggets of profitable ideas.

Hughes, Arthur M., *The Complete Database Marketer*, 2nd ed., McGraw-Hill, New York, 2000, 610 pp. This is, of course, the best book on the subject around.

Peppers, Don, and Martha Rogers, *The One to One Future*, Doubleday, New York, 1993, 441 pp. Every one has read it. It has become a buzz-word in our industry.

Reichheld, Frederick, *The Loyalty Effect*, Harvard Business School Press, Cambridge, MA, 1996, 322 pp. A tremendously stimulating book full of good ideas.

Siebel, Thomas, *Cyber Rules*, Doubleday, New York, 1999. An excellent book.

Seybold, Patricia, *Customers.com*, Random House, New York, 1998, 360 pp. An excellent introduction to customer relationship marketing on the web.

Silverstein, Barry, *Business-to-Business Internet Marketing*, Maximum Press, 1999, 398 pp. The best treatment of this subject to date.

Woolf, Brian, *Customer Specific Marketing*, Teal Books, 1996, 249 pp. The best book on retail customer card marketing ever written.

Conventions and Seminars

The following three events are probably the best two or three days you could possibly spend on learning about database marketing. The seminars include small groups of marketers from (mostly) household-word companies. There is lots of interaction and networking. The conferences are held every six months in Chicago, Orlando, and other cities. The conferences are attended by over 1,200 people each time, with more than 100 speakers. You will hear about new things, and meet all sorts of people in our business:

Database Marketing Seminar Two-day seminars featuring Paul Wang, Arthur Hughes, and Mark Peck, run by the Database Marketing

Institute, 4141 North Henderson Road, Suite 1219, Arlington, VA, 22203, 703-908-9309. Registration at www.dbmarketing.com.

National Center for Database Marketing Conference & Exhibition   11 River Bend Drive South, Stamford, CT 06907-0232, 800-927-5007.

Direct Marketing to Business   National Conference, 11 River Bend Drive South, Stamford, CT 06907, 800-927-5007.

There are also other valuable database marketing conferences that are called from time to time by such institutions as Canadian Direct Marketing News (see above) and Target Marketing (also above).

Technical Assistance

The first edition of this book, which appeared in 1994, was the basis for a series of 7 two-day seminars at York University in Toronto from 1993 to 1995. It was also the basis for more than 30 two-day seminars by the Database Marketing Institute held in Washington and San Francisco beginning in April 1994. More than 2,000 marketers have been through these seminars. Many of them have contributed their ideas and case studies, a number of which appear in this book. There has been a general clamor from these participants for technical assistance on the mathematics of lifetime value, RFM, tests and controls, etc. Therefore, the Institute has made available free software on its web site, www.dbmarketing.com. At that location, you will find many of the spreadsheet tables and formulas that are used in this book, plus RFM for Windows, a software package that has been used by scores of Institute alumni in their work. By clicking on www.dbmarketing.com, you can obtain:

- Books on database marketing and the web
- More than 80 published articles on database marketing and the Internet
- Software with spreadsheet tables and formulas
- RFM for Windows
- Information on sources
- Registration information about seminars and other events
- Networking information to reach other database and Internet marketers

B

Answers to Executive Quizzes

Chapter 2
1. c, 2. a, 3. c, 4. a, 5. a, 6. e, 7. a, 8. d, 9. d, 10. c

Chapter 3
1. See Figure B-1.
2. b, 3. c, 4. e, 5. b, 6. b, 7. d, 8. c, 9. e, 10. c

Chapter 4
1. e, 2. c, 3. c, 4. c, 5. d, 6. b, 7. c, 8. e

Chapter 5
1. c, 2. b, 3. c, 4. d, 5. c, 6. b, 7. e, 8. a, 9. e, 10. c

Chapter 6
1. e, 2. b, 3. a, 4. c, 5. c, 6. e, 7. e, 8. d

Chapter 7
1. b, 2. a, 3. a, 4. b, 5. d, 6. a, 7. c, 8. b

Chapter 8
1. c, 2. c, 3. d, 4. b, 5. c, 6. a, 7. e, 8. b

Chapter 9
1. e, 2. c, 3. d, 4. d, 5. c, 6. e, 7. d, 8. e, 9. d, 10. e

Chapter 10
1. See Figure B-2.
2. c, 3. d, 4. a, 5. b, 6. a, 7. c

Chapter 11
1. d, 2. d, 3. d, 4. d, 5. e, 6. a, 7. b, 8. e

Chapter 12
1. b, 2. c, 3. c, 4. e—the factor is about 1050 to 1, 5. e, 6. a, 7. b, 8. d, 9. c, 10. e, 11. e

Chapter 13
1. d, 2. c, 3. d, 4. c, 5. b, 6. e, 7. c, 8. e, 9. a, 10. h, 11. b, 12. g, 13. d, 14. f, 15. c

Chapter 14
1. c, 2. a, 3. e, 4. b, 5. e, 6. b, 7. a, 8. d, 9. d, 10. e

Chapter 15
1. d, 2. a, 3. d, 4. c, 5. d, 6. e, 7. d, 8. a

Chapter 16
1. e, 2. b, 3. e, 4. d, 5. a, 6. c, 7. c, 8. e

Chapter 17
1. b, 2. e, 3. d, 4. a, 5. e, 6. e, 7. a, 8. b

	Year 1	Year 2	
Customers			
Referral rate	8.00%	9.00%	
Referred customers	0	1,359	a
Retention rate	50.00%	60.00%	
Retained customers	0	8,494	b
Total customers	16,988	9,853	
Spending rate	$200.00,	$220.00	
Total customer revenue	$3,397,600	$2,167,669	c
Expenses			
Variable cost percentage	60.00%	55.00%	
Variable costs	$2,038,560	$1,192,218	d
Acquisition cost $40	$679,520	na	
New strategy $15	$254,820	$147,796	e
Referral incentive $20	0	$27,181	f
Total costs	$2,972,900	$1,367,194	
Profits			
Gross profit	$424,700	$800,475	
Discount rate	1.00	1.20	
NPV profit	$424,700	$667,062	g
Cumulative NPV profit	$424,700	$1,091,762	h
Lifetime value	25.00	$64.27	i

Figure B-1. LTV chart.

	CPM	Impressions (000)	Ad Cost	Responses	Cost per Responses	Sales	Cost per Sale
Travel	$12	45	$540	22	$24.55	4	$135
Sports	$15	88	$1,320	16	$82.50	8	$165
Women	$10	102	$1,020	38	$26.84	5	$204
News	$20	76	$1,520	42	$36.19	7	$217

Figure B-2.

C

Glossary

Acquisition. Most companies are set up to acquire new customers, rather than to retain existing ones. Acquisition programs are seldom profitable, but must be continued to balance the constant loss of customers.

Affinity Group Space. Web sites grouped in categories such as finance, travel, or shopping.

Affinity Groups. Customer or product groups. Customer groups might include parents of new babies, sports enthusiasts, or people who like to travel. Product groups might include categories such as financial service products, women's clothing, or automotive.

AutoCAD. Computer-aided design programs used by surveyors and others.

Average Pricing. A system in which all customers in a retail store pay the same price, regardless of the volume of their purchases.

Banner Ads. Small advertisements inserted on web sites. A viewer who clicks on a banner is transported to the web site of the advertiser paying fo the banner. There the viewer can register and purchase products. Banner advertising is becoming one of the most successful of reaching new customers. The ads can be very scientifically calculated.

Brand Loyalty. Loyalty to a brand, such as Hertz or Amazon.com, is valuable both to the advertiser and to the customer. The advertiser spends a lot of money to build up a brand image in the minds of millions of people. This helps to acquire and retain customers. The customers benefit because they enjoy shopping for well-known name products.

Branded Space. Web space that has a brand name, such as Yahoo.com or AOL.com.

Breakeven. An RFM cell breaks even on a test or a rollout if the net profit from sales to the cell exactly equal the cost of mailing to or telephoning to the cell. The formula for the breakeven rate is BE = (cost per piece) / (net profit from the average sale).

Call-Me Button. A button on a web site that, when clicked, will initiate a text chat or a live phone call between the customer and an agent at the web site. Call-me buttons are becoming more and more popular as more people use the web.

Caller ID. A feature of telephone systems whereby the receiver of the call knows the number of the party before picking up the phone. Used by commercial customer services to get the customer's database record on the screen before the call is taken. It is very helpful and friendly for the customer.

Cardholders. People who own and use plastic cards issued by a retail store. Use of these cards permits the retailer to know who the shoppers are and what they are buying. A powerful marketing tool.

Cookie. A small file stored on your computer by a web site that permits the web site to recognize you when you return, so they can say "Welcome back Arthur!"

Deciles. A method of dividing customers into 10 groups based on their spending or response. Very common in marketing research. Too numerous for RFM.

Direct Marketing. Any marketing system in which the customer is expected to respond directly to the advertiser (rather than going to a store). Direct marketing can use advertising, mail, phone, or the Internet.

Discount Rate. In lifetime value calculation, it is necessary to determine the net present value of future revenue or profits. The discount rate is divided into future dollar amounts to calculate the net present value. The formula for the discount rate is $D = (1 + i)^n$ where i = the rate of interest including risk, and n = the number of years you have to wait to receive the money.

Discounts. If database marketing is done properly, it is not necessary to give discounts to customers, since they value the relationship with their supplier more than the discount. Discounts reduce the perceived value of the product and the relationship, and erode margin. If you have to give something, give points or premium, not discounts.

E-Mail. Fast becoming the most popular method of communication between customers and suppliers, electronic mail is rapidly replacing fax and regular postal mail. Companies are being flooded with e-mail from customers, which they must answer rapidly. E-mail response is becoming a new business.

Employee Loyalty. Frederich Reichheld in *The Loyalty Effect* pointed out that the best way to assure customer loyalty is to have loyal employees, since many customers build relationships with the sales and customer service personnel.

Entrepreneurship. To be successful in marketing, it is useful to outsource as much as you can to specialists who are entrepreneurs. Entrepreneurs have the freedom to be creative and the financial incentive to be successful. The opposite of an entrepreneur is an employee working for a regular salary that does not go up much even if the employee does a very good job.

Extranet. A system whereby your best customers are given their own private page on your web site which they reach through a password (PIN) or cookie. There they see messages, products, services, and prices just for them. Extranets build customer loyalty.

File Fatigue. Sending too many unwelcome messages to your customers produces file fatigue, whereby they cease to read or be interested in your communications.

Frequency. The number of times that a customer has made a purchase from you, such as orders per month, phone calls per month, checks and deposits per month, or items per month. A part of RFM analysis, frequent buyers respond better than infrequent buyers.

Frequency Programs. Programs designed to increase the frequency of purchase by customers by rewarding them in some way. Frequency programs often work quite well.

Frequent Shopper Cards. Supermarkets issue these cards to give customers special benefits when they shop using the cards. The cards enable the supermarket to know who is buying what and when, and to reward desired shopping behavior. These cards are scanned at POS terminals when the shopper goes through the checkout lines.

Fulfillment. The process of sending goods or literature to a prospect or customer. Fast fulfillment is essential to successful database marketing.

Geodemographics. Customers can be grouped by geodemographics such as zip code, age, income, presence of children, type of home, etc. In some cases, geodemographics are very useful in segmenting prospects and customers. In many cases, they don't work at all.

Gift Certificates. A highbrow name for a coupon. In Gold customer programs, customers are rewarded with gift certificates that they can exchange for products and services.

Gold Customers. A very small percentage of all customers are always responsible for a very large percentage of revenue and profits. This top group consists of the Gold customers. Special programs are developed to reward and retail these valuable customers. In some cases, it is not possible to market to them, because they are already giving you their entire purchases in your category. You give them superservices.

Half-Life. When you send out an offer or catalog, it may take months until the last sale has been registered from the offer. On one day, half of the dollars or 4 responses will have come in. This is your half-life day. Once you know what that day is, you multiply your sales up through that day by 2 and you will know the eventual success of the offer. Half-life permits rapid tests.

Impression. A measure of web advertising. Every time a viewer clicks on a web site that includes your banner ad, that counts as an impression. You pay the web site $X per thousand impressions (CPM).

Integrated Account Management (IAM). A system developed by Hunter Business Direct in which a central telemarketer supervises a customer account team including customer service and a field sales force.

Internet. A modern system that links computers all over the world, including e-mail and access to web sites. The Internet has a lookup system so that you can find and view any web site if you know its name (URL).

Lead. In business to business, a prospect that has expressed interest in your product and has supplied his name and address is considered a lead.

Lifestyle. Each consumer has a unique lifestyle, which may resemble that of millions of others. A wealthy senior citizen may have a very different lifestyle from a young unmarried hospital nurse. Each may be interested in buying different products and services. Once you understand these consumers' lifestyles, you can market differently to them.

Lifetime Value. The net present value of the profit to be realized on the average new customer during a given number of years. Lifetime value is used to measure the success of various marketing strategies, including retention, referrals, acquisition, reactivation, etc.

Losers. Customers who cost you more in expenses than they deliver in profits. Every company has losers, but few companies have figured out what to do about them.

Loyalty. Customer loyalty is usually measured by the retention, renewal, or repurchase rate. Loyalty can be increased or decreased by things that you do for customers. Loyalty is easier to achieve if you recruit loyal customers to begin with. Loyalty is seldom increased by discounts.

Loyalty Programs. Programs designed to increase customer loyalty. The term also applies to points programs, whereby customers earn credits for purchases.

Marginal Utility. The extra value you get by acquiring one more unit of a product or service. Typically, marginal utility decreases with each additional unit acquired.

Market Rate of Interest. The interest rate paid for waiting to receive future sums of money.

Market Research. A scientific method of determining what products and services people want and are willing to pay for. Uses surveys, focus groups, and modeling. Differs from database marketing, which is designed to build relationships with customers.

Mass Marketing. A highly successful method of reaching millions of people to tell them about available products and services. Uses TV, radio, print ads, and the Internet. It will never be replaced by direct or database marketing. It works best for packaged goods and services that are sold through channels, rather than directly.

MCIF (Marketing Customer Information File). A system used by banks to view all the bank services used by a household. MCIF is an essential first step for banks wishing to do database marketing.

Migration. Customers can be encouraged to migrate from standard to deluxe products, from a few products to many products, from small balances to large balances. Customer migration is a valid marketing technique.

Minimum Test Cell Size. What is the least number of people who can be included in a test for the results to be valid? There is a formula that is used for test cells within a larger test: Minimum test cell size = 4 / (breakeven rate).

MIS (Management Information Services). A shorthand way of naming the central data processing staff of a company.

Modeling. Market research uses models to predict customer behavior based on past behavior plus demographics. Models use CHAID or multiple regressions. They usually require the appending of demographic data, and are costly to run. In some cases they can accurately predict churn or identify those customer segments most likely to purchase a product.

Monetary Analysis. Part of RFM analysis. Monetary analysis involves categorizing all customers by the total amount that they have purchased (per month, year, etc.) and sorting all customers by that amount. The resulting file is divided into quintiles. The top quintile (highest spenders) usually responds better than lower quintiles.

One-to-One Marketing. A marketing system in which each customer gets marketing messages specifically tailored for her, based on information about her preferences and purchases contained in her database record.

Premiums. What you give customers in lieu of discounts. Premiums are better than discounts because they do not appear to reduce your price point or margin. They build loyalty, whereas discounts do not.

President's Club. Many companies create President's Clubs or advisory panels for their best customers. It is a way of recognizing and rewarding your best customers. It helps to keep them for a lifetime.

Profiles. A method of understanding customers by segmenting them into groups with similar lifestyles and purchasing habits. A retail store may identify profiles as Gold, regular, or occasional shoppers.

Profitability. Banks have developed a system using their MCIF where the profitability of each household is measured every month. Customers are segmented into profitability groups. The profitability of a household adds all revenue received during the month, and subtracts all costs and interest paid.

Program Buyers. Types of business-to-business buyers for whom their purchasing manual or buying schedule is more important than price or marketing messages. Many government agencies are program buyers.

Quintiles. A method of dividing customers into five equal groups based on spending or response. Quintiles are more useful for RFM than deciles, which are used in marketing research.

Recency. The most powerful single factor affecting customer repurchase. The customer most likely to buy from you again is the customer who bought from you most recently. A basic factor in RFM analysis.

Reference Accounts. Business accounts that may not be profitable in themselves, but in a lot of other business because the account is prestigious or well known.

Referral Programs. Programs designed to foster referrals by rewarding those who refer people who become customers. Can be more cost-effective than almost any other database marketing program.

Referrals. Referred customers have a higher retention rate than the average newly acquired customers. For that reason, it is vital that you keep track of both referred people and those who refer them, maintaining the information in your database.

Regression Analysis. A statistical method used in modeling. Using regression analysis, you assign a weight to various variable factors in accordance with their ability to predict a known outcome, such as a purchase or a response.

Rewards. Something that you give customers besides the product or service to thank them for their patronage. Rewards can be premiums or points or status symbols. An important database marketing tool.

RFM (Recency, Frequency, and Monetary Analysis). A very old and very powerful method of coding existing customers. Used to predict response, average order size, and other factors. The most powerful predictive system available in database marketing.

RFP (Request for Proposals). The first step in outsourcing to database partners.

Risk-Revenue Matrix. A simple matrix where the likelihood of churn is on one axis and lifetime value or revenue is on the other. The matrix is used to focus attention on those customers who have the highest lifetime value and the highest likelihood of leaving. You save your retention program dollars by concentrating on these rather than on all customers.

Rollout. After a successful test in direct marketing, you expose a much larger group to your offer. This is called a rollout.

RON (Run of Network). An Internet advertising term. Advertisers who place a RON ad simultaneously on a large number of sites get instant feedback about which sites are giving them the best response. RON is the cheapest form of Internet advertising—and may be the best.

Segment. A group of customers that you have identified as having similar purchase patterns.

Source Codes. Codes of letters or numbers used to identify a particular offer on a particular date. The codes are stored in the customer's database record so you have a promotion history.

Spending Rate. The amount that a customer spends with you in a month or a year.

Straddle Pricing. A retail pricing method in which prices for occasional shoppers are set higher than the competition's prices, whereas prices for regular customers are set lower than those of the competition.

Strategy Development. Database marketing is only successful if it is accompanied by a winning marketing strategy. No one system works universally. Strategies are always being upset by the market competition.

Surrogate Measurements. In marketing, the success of an offer is often measured indirectly by awareness, focus groups, Neilson ratings, etc. These are surrogate measurements. It is not necessary to use surrogate measurements in direct marketing and Internet marketing, where success is measured directly by responses and sales.

Targeting. The system in which a specific group of prospects is selected for marketing, based on assumptions about their interest in the product or ability to purchase.

Teaser Rates. Introductory, very low credit card interest rates that are then raised to normal high levels after the introductory period of a few months has passed.

Telesales. Selling conducted by salespersons who talk on the telephone to prospects and customers. In business to business, telesales is preferred by many customers over sales force visits. In consumer situations, outbound telesales is often resented. Inbound telesales (where customers call a toll-free number) is preferred.

Test Groups. Groups of customers, selected by an Nth, who are made an offer so that the marketer can test the validity of the offer. If the response is good, the marketer will go to a rollout.

Touches. Customer contacts through personal visit, phone, letter, e-mail, or fax. Customers like to hear from their suppliers. Touches should be planned in advance.

Trade Deficit (Surplus). The difference between what we sell to foreigners and what they buy from us in a year. A high trade deficit is not necessarily bad for U.S. consumers or businesses.

Transaction Buyers. Customers who are only interested in price, not quality or service. They have no loyalty and will leave you for a better offer at any time. It is hard to make money from transaction buyers.

Virtual Distributors. Unlike regular distributors, who have warehouses and who stock a limited number of products, virtual distributors have a web site and may have no warehouse at all. They arrange shipment to customers directly from the manufacturers.

Web Advertising. Banner ads on web sites have become a universally successful method of reaching new customers. A good response rate to a web ad is usually less than 1 percent. Web advertising is paid for by CPM, cost per thousand impressions.

Web Site. Every company in the world will soon have its own web site on the Internet, advertising its products and services. An increasing percentage of business, particularly business-to-business commerce, will take place through web sites. Best customers are given personal pages on company web sites.

World Wide Web (www). Another name for the Internet. Company web sites names (URLs) usually begin with www, for example, www.dbmarketing.com.

Index

Acquisition cost, lifetime value and, 62-63
Advertising on web to find new customers *(see* Finding customers through the web)
Average pricing, overcoming problem of, 262-263

Balance, need for, 15-16
Banks *(see* Financial services)
Banners, 238-240
Bargain hunters, business customers as, 283
Books about database marketing and the web, 426-427
Breakeven, calculating, 115-116
Budgets, power struggles over, 401-402
Business customers, 281-306
  classifying by segment, 284-285
  e-commerce on Internet and, 297-302
  integrated account management and, 287-288
  lifetime value of, 289-290
  relationship building initiatives for, 290-291
  training, 286
  virtual distribution and, 302-305
  web sites for, 291-297
Business partners, 381-395
  contracts and, 393
  key questions for, 390
  outsourcing and, 381-383
  transition teams and, 394
Business-to-business files, RFM for, 121-123

Champion, loss of, 397-401
Cluster coding, 192-199
Communication with customers, 137-159
  amount of, 152-153
  customer contact strategy for, 152
  extranets for, 141-143
  increased revenue and, 154-156
  increasing sales and, 147-150
  retention and, 143-147
  risk-revenue matrix and, 151-152
  role of, 139-141
  targeted, to boost retention, 150-151
Compensation systems, 354-355
Competition in retailing, 250-251
Contracts with business partners, 393
Control groups, 211-213
  failure of, 219
  setting up, 211-213
  substitutes for, 213-219

Conventions for keeping up with innovations and developments, 427-428
Costs, acquisition, lifetime value and, 62-63
Customer acquisition, 176-177
  reasons for spending for, 18-19
Customer category management in retailing, 265
Customer loyalty, 162-180
  acquiring customers and, 176-177
  dropping losers and, 167-170
  employee loyalty and, 179
  interviewing defectors and, 177-178
  points to bolster, 170-176
  treating loyal customers better and, 166-167
  value for maintaining, 179
Customer needs, fulfillment by database marketing, 45-46
Customer profiles, 183-206
  classification by product affinity and, 185-189
  cluster coding and, 192-199
  demographic, 189-192
  for financial services customers, 203-205
  need for, 184
  reasons for lack of use of, 205
  for retail customers, 199-203
Customer profitability *(see* Profitability)
Customer relationship management (CRM), 354
Customer retention:
  by banks, tactics for, 326-331
  communication for, 143-147
  increasing efforts for, 75
  profitability of, 18
  targeted communications to boost, 150-151
  (see also Retention rate)
Customers:
  business *(see* Business customers)
  coding by monetary amount, 111-113
  coding by recency, 106-109
  coding for frequency, 109-111
  collecting information about, 46-49
  defecting, interviewing, 177-178
  factors motivating, 37-40
  factors valued by, 26
  gold *(see* Gold customers)
  silver, improving lifetime value of, 256-257
  viewing as assets, 71-72
Customer segments, 23-24
Customer-specific marketing, 263-267
  customer category management for, 265
  failure of, reasons for, 265-266
  noncash benefits for, 264-265

Customer-specific marketing (*continued*)
overcoming average pricing and, 262-263
process of, 264
successful, payoff of, 266-267
sweepstakes for, 264
Customer wants, 12-13

Database conferences to educate management
about database marketing, 403-404
Database failure, reasons for, 335-363
building models instead of relationships as,
349-352
economic errors as, 342-345
failure to change organization and compensation as, 354-359
failure to link database to web as, 352-353
failure to track results as, 346-349
focus on price instead of service as, 339-342
lack of forceful leader as, 359-362
lack of marketing strategy as, 337-339
making project too large and taking too long
as, 346
Database marketing:
emergence as industry, 27
for packaged goods, 270-276
Databases:
successful (*see* Successful databases)
unsuccessful, 26-27
Demographics, customer profiling by, 189-192
Discount rate:
including payment delays in, 80-81
lifetime value and, 63-64
Discounts, problems with, 20-21
Disloyal customers, eliminating, 4-5
Distributors, virtual, 302-305

Economics as reason for failure of database,
342-345
Employee loyalty, importance of, 179
Extranets for customer communications, 141-143

Financial services, 309-333
analysis of behavior by profitability segment
and, 319
branch empowerment and, 325-331
creating profitability segments and, 316-317
gold customer programs for, 318-319
lifetime profitability and, 319-324
potential lifetime profitability and, 319-322,
324-325
predicting lifetime value and, 317-318
profiling customers and prospects for, 203-205
profitability calculation and, 313-316
Finding customers through the web, 229-245
banners for, 238-240
personalized landscapes for, 244
timing of ads for, 240, 243
web versus traditional advertising and, 232-236

Frequency (*see* RFM approach)
Frequent shopper cards, 262

Gift-buying database, 9-10
Gold customers, 89
bank programs for, 318-319
customers just below, 89-90
Gross profits, lifetime value and, 63

Half-life in tests, 220-221

Industrial Revolution, 30-31
Information:
about customers, collecting, 46-49
providing to customers, 43-44
Integrated account management (IAM), 287-
288
Internal power struggles, 397-420
educating management and, 402-407
knowledge of how to bring in new business
and, 408-409
loss of champion and, 397-401
market knowledge and (*see* Market knowledge)
obstacles to database marketing and, 410-415
over budgets, 401-402
winning over top management and, 415
Internet:
e-commerce with business customers and,
297-302
(*see also* Web)

Leadership, strong, need for, 359-362
Lifetime profitability, computing, for banks, 319-
322
Lifetime value, 57-79
acquisition cost and, 62-63
of business customers, 289-290
computation period for, 72
computing, for banks, 319-322
definition of, 58
determination in retailing, 253-256
discount rate and, 63-64, 80-81
gross profits and, 63
increasing retention efforts and, 75
keeping management informed about, 77
net present value profits and, 64-65
predicting, for banks, 317-318
product and, 74
reasons for former lack of use of, 58-59
referral rate and, 66-68
retention rate and, 60-61, 68-69, 79-80
selling marketing programs to management
and, 76-77
of silver customers, improving, 256-257
for single customer, 73
spending rate and, 61-62, 69

Lifetime value (*continued*)
   steps in calculating, 75-76
   strategies for increasing, 74-75
   strategy development and, 65-66
   table of, 59-60
   usefulness of, 73
   variable costs and, 62, 69-70
   viewing customers as assets and, 71-72
Losers:
   dealing with, 90-92
   dropping, 167-170
Loyal customers:
   attracting, 23
   focusing on, 19-20
   providing institution to be loyal to and, 44-45
   (*see* also Customer loyalty)
Loyal employees, importance of, 179

Magazines for keeping up with innovations and
   developments, 425-426
Management:
   educating about database marketing, 402-407
   keeping informed about lifetime value, 77
   resistance to testing, 210
   selling database and web site to, 25
   selling marketing programs to, 76-77
   top, winning over, 415
Marketing:
   in American market, 32
   central role played by, 31
   mass, growth of, 32-34
Marketing objectives, testing and, 210-211
Marketing strategy:
   choosing, 92
   designing, 93-94
   lack of, as reason for failure of database, 337-
     339
   new approaches to (*see* New marketing strate-
     gies)
   steps in developing, 92-93
Market knowledge, 407-408
   steps to, 410
   uses of, 409-410
Mass marketing:
   future of, 49-50
   growth of, 32-34
   reasons for change in process of, 42-43
Modeling:
   relationship building versus, 349-352
   RFM compared with, 123-124
Monetary amount (*see* RFM approach)
Motivation of customers, 37-40

Net present value profits, lifetime value and, 64-
   65
New marketing strategies, 94-101
   effect of, 99-101

Newsletters for keeping up with innovations and
   developments, 425-426
Noncash benefits in retailing, 264-265

One-to-one marketing, 183-184
Organizational structure, 354-359
Outsourcing, 381-383
   of RFP function, 383

Packaged goods, database marketing and the
   web for, 270-276
Partnering with Amazon.com, 8
Partners [*see* Business partners; Requests for
   proposals (RFPs)]
Personal contact, aided y web, 20
Personalization, of ads, 244
Point programs, 170-176
Power struggles, internal (*see* Internal power
   struggles)
Prices:
   average, overcoming problem of, 262-263
   focus on, as reason for failure of database,
     339-342
   transaction versus relationship buyers and, 13,
     21
   uniformity of, 41
Product affinity, customer classification by, 185-
   189
Products:
   consumable, RFM with, 119-121
   continuity, measuring recency with, 128
   lifetime value and, 74
   uniformity of, 41
Profitability:
   of bank customers, calculation of, 313-316
   lifetime, of bank customers, 319-322, 323-324
   measurement of, by RFM, 130-131
   measuring, 86-89
   potential, of bank customers, 324-325
Profitability segments for banks, 316-317
   analysis of customer behavior by, 319
Program buyers, business customers as, 283
Promoters, 269-270
Promotions, testing, 114-118
Property transfer database, 5-7
Prospect database, 4

Qualifying RFP participants, 383-384

Recency (*see* RFM approach)
Referral rate, lifetime value and, 66-68
Relationship building:
   with business customers, 290-291
   importance of, 349-352
Relationship buyers, 13, 21
   business customers as, 283-284
Relationship effects, dropping unprofitable cus-
   tomers and, 168-170
Relationship marketing, 367-371

Requests for proposals (RFPs):
evaluating results of, 392-393
meeting with finalists and, 393
outsourcing RFP function and, 383
qualifying participants and, 383-384
RFP committee and, 384
rules of, 387-388
things to avoid with, 391-392
writing scope of work for, 384-387
Retail customers, profiling, 199-203
Retailing, 249-278
adding noncardholders to database and, 267-
268
average pricing and, 262-263
benefits of database membership and, 277
building retain database in, 252-253
building store cardholder base in, 252
competition in, 250-251
customer-specific marketing in (see Customer-
specific marketing)
database for, 258-261
determining lifetime value and, 253-256
migrating silver customers and, 256-257
packaged goods and, 270-276
promoters in, 169-170
supermarket frequent shopper cards and, 262
Retention rate:
for infrequent purchasers, computing, 79-80
lifetime value and, 60-61, 68-69
RFM approach, 118-119
for business-to-business files, 121-123
coding by monetary amount and, 111-113
coding by recency and, 106-109
coding for frequency and, 109-111
with consumable products, 119-121
with continuity products, 128
measurement approaches for, 132
measuring frequency and, 128-130
measuring profitability and, 130-131
modeling compared with, 123-124
quintiles for, 127-128
rollout rate predictions and, 131-132
sorting process for, 118-119
test cell size for, 126-127
uses of, 125
when not to use, 124-125
Rollouts, predicted response rate for, 131-132

Sales, communication to increase, 147-150
Sales testing, 221-224
in credit card sales to existing bank customers, 222-224
Scope of work for RFP, 384-387
Segmenting customers, 23-24
business customers and, 284-285
Seminars:
to educate management about database marketing, 404

Seminars (continued)
for keeping up with innovations and developments, 427-428
Silver customers, improving lifetime value of,
256-257
Source codes, problems with, 347-348
Spending rate, lifetime value and, 61-62, 69
Store credit cards, building cardholder base for,
252
Straddle pricing, 264
Strategy, 15
development of, lifetime value and, 65-66
Successful databases, 366-378
alternative database uses and, 371
picking product situation and, 367
products and services that won't work and,
373-378
relationship marketing and, 367-371
Supermarkets, frequent shopper cards in,
262
Sweepstakes, 264

Targeted communications, to boost retention,
150-151
Technical assistance, 428
Testing, 209-226
control groups for (see Control groups)
half-life in, 220-221
long-term difficulties with, 224-225
management's resistance to, 210
marketing objectives and, 210-211
need for, 209-210
of sales (see Sales testing)
setting up test groups for, 211-213
Time, importance to customers, 41-42
Timing of advertisements on web, 240, 243
Tracking results, importance of, 346-349
Transaction buyers, 13, 21
business customers as, 283-284
training business customers to become, 286
Transition teams with business partners, 394

U.S. market, 32
success of, reasons for, 35-37
of today, 34-35
Value:
lifetime (see Lifetime value)
to retain customers, 179
Variable costs, lifetime value and, 62, 69-70
Voice-over-IP (VoIP), 7-8
Web:
business customers and, 291-297
failure to link database to, 352-353
finding customers through (see Finding customers through the web)
keeping up with database marketing and commerce on, 425-428
packaged goods marketing using, 270-276

About the Author

Arthur Middleton Hughes is one of the acknowledged pioneers of database marketing. His experience includes twenty-two years spent designing and building marketing databases for such companies as Compaq, Western Union, Nestle, US West, and CIBA. Hughes is now Vice President for Strategic Planning of M\S Database Marketing (www.msdbm.com) in Los Angeles where he has helped to develop database and Internet marketing strategies for such companies as E*TRADE, ebay, BMW, Air New Zealand, Disney Interactive, Isuzu, and Hewlett Packard. Along with frequent articles in leading industry publications, he wrote *The Complete Database Marketer* (first and second editions) and is a popular speaker at marketing and economics conferences throughout the world. Arthur lives with his wife, Helena, in Arlington, Virginia.